# The Uses
## of a Liberal Education
### and Other Talks to Students

# The Uses of a Liberal Education

### and Other Talks to Students

## Brand Blanshard

### Edited by Eugene Freeman

1973
Open Court Publishing Company
LaSalle, Illinois

*The Uses of a Liberal Education and Other Talks to Students*

*First Edition*

Library of Congress Catalog Card Number: 73-76196
ISBN Number: 0-87548-122-1

# Contents

v

## III.   Homilies

# *Preface*

The essays in this book are, for the most part, not essays but speeches. They were given to student audiences in many places and at widely different times. If they have the disadvantages of such a collection—lack of continuity, lack of system, lack of the thoroughness, detail, and precision appropriate to a monograph—I hope they also have some of its advantages. When one talks instead of writing, one must try to be immediately intelligible, for there will be no second chance. One must deal with essentials since the time is short, but these must not be bare essentials in the sense of bare bones; the bones must be fleshed and brought alive by every means one can lay one's desperate hands on—example, quotation, the omission of subtle qualifications, a style of heightened emphasis and, not least, laughter. There are no doubt those who think such expedients on the part of a philosopher an unseemly surrender of scholarly dignity. But scholarly dignity can become discourtesy when it forgets that the purpose of a speech is to communicate as simply and vividly as possible.

I have grouped the talks under three heads: Ends, Corollaries, and Homilies. The first group deals with the goals or purposes of education. The second sets out some implications that follow from the acceptance of these ends. The third consists of lay sermons, frankly presented as such, though without the theological trappings that usually accompany and in some minds give authority to sermons.

These homilies reflect some of the starry-eyed excitement with which I approached my own college education long ago. Students of the present are more blasé, and less willing to be preached at; some of them are cynical about the whole educational process and inclined to regard the baccalaureate type of homiletics as hypocrisy. And if enthusiasm about American education is hypocrisy, I admit to being a monumental whited sepulchre. I am not only enthusiastic about it, but endlessly grateful to it. As a poverty-stricken youngster who would not have had a chance in most other lands, I was exhilarated by the openings it gave me, and I look back at its offer of a helping hand as the most fortunate thing that ever happened to me. Nor do I regard the current wave of student disenchantment with education as more than a passing mood. I offer my homilies to those who have ears for them, and do so the more cheerfully because no one is forced to listen.

Philosophers should not be dogmatic, and the tone of these addresses is perhaps more confident than the evidence offered would warrant. That is partly because they are based on a philosophy which has been developed elsewhere but can hardly be set out convincingly in the course of a brief address. This philosophy has been developed in three books of mine, *The Nature of Thought, Reason and Goodness,* and *Reason and Analysis.* It may be of help to some readers if, instead of asking them to piece this philosophy together from scattered fragments, I state it now in its essentials so far as it bears on education. Readers not interested in theory had better turn to the talks at once.

I conceive of human nature as composed of a number of drives directed towards various ends. These ends are at work implicitly from the beginning in the lives of both the individual and the race. I have made no attempt to enumerate them exhaustively, and I doubt if it could be done, since human nature is still evolving; but in my book on *The Nature of Thought* I have traced the growth of that one among them which is most important for education, namely the cognitive impulse. Thought is that activity of mind which aims directly at truth. It is not confined to man; it begins far down in the evolutionary scale with the first identification of anything as this rather than that. It is therefore present in every perception of an object. The perception of an apple or a motorcar is not an affair of sensation only, for a mere sensation cannot be mistaken, while the perception of an apple or a motorcar can. This element of perception, the interpretation or inference which is in principle capable of error, is the element of thought. It construes what is given in sensation as belonging to some kind of whole, and in this sort of construction thought is engaged from first to last.

For the goal of thought is understanding. And what is it to understand? It is always to place something in a whole that renders it intelligible. The wholes or systems that we construct in our efforts to understand make use of very different relations. Sometimes these relations are causal, as they usually are in natural science. A disease, for example, is always explained or understood in terms of causal laws which connect certain symptoms with their causes. The understanding of human artifacts is usually in terms of another kind of structure, a structure of means and ends, as when one explains the "exhaust" of a car as a pipe designed to conduct away the gases produced by combustion in the motor. In logic and mathematics the system constructed is different again. If one asks why an angle inscribed in a semicircle with the diameter as a base must be a right angle, the explanation would be a demonstration of this statement as necessitated by other propositions of geometry.

Now in a book on philosophy I should feel bound to raise the question which of these ways of understanding is the most satisfactory, and I have argued that in a purely intellectual point of view it is the last or logical type that stands first, since if one has reached it, one has so complete an answer to the question Why? that it cannot intelligibly be raised again. The explanation of the world in such terms I accept as the ideal of the philosopher, as it was for Spinoza, and in a somewhat different sense for Hegel and Bradley. Being a rationalist, I am inclined to think that the world is a system in which every fact and event is connected necessarily with every other. I admit that this is not the conscious assumption of the scientist. The scientist would agree, I think, that every event is connected with every other *causally;* the law of gravitation, for example, seems to connect all physical particles with all others; but he would not maintain that causal connections are also necessary, in the sense of logically necessary. I am inclined to think they are, and therefore that the system of causal relations is also a system of intelligible relations, that the universe is an intelligible whole. It is the business of the philosopher to approximate his thought to this system as closely as he can.

The aim of education on its intellectual side is to facilitate understanding in all its forms. This conception is sharply distinguished from two other and current conceptions. One is that the aim of education is knowledge or information. But one may know an immense range of facts without understanding any of them; and if one is master of the laws or relations that govern them, most of them may be dispensed with. What is essential to the medical man is the grasp of the laws governing health and disease, not the multitudinous details about his patients, John, James, and Henry. What is important to the economist is the laws governing production, distribution, and exchange. Particular cases are obviously needed in acquiring such understanding, but the inquiry does not terminate upon them. The man of learning without understanding is a guaranteed bore.

The other common misconception is that education is professional or vocational training. That such training is necessary is clear enough; no one wants unqualified surgeons, engineers, or lawyers. But technological proficiency, however necessary, is not the same as enlightenment of mind, and it is such enlightenment that a liberal education seeks to give. Here my theory parts company with educational pragmatism.

It is here too that I part company with the permissivists in education. The subjects pursued in universities are far from equal in importance, and my theory proposes a test of such importance. That test is the degree to which a given subject enables us to understand the world we live in. I have no doubt that volcanology and conchology are subjects of intense interest to specialists, but I do not think they are as important as physics or the principles of biology, because they illuminate a smaller area of the world of knowledge. And to allow students not only to elect subjects as they please but to reshape the curriculum to their own adolescent ends is a betrayal of educational responsibility. If they know enough to make fundamental decisions of this kind, they already have the kind of insight that an education is designed to give, and why should they struggle further?

I am not wholly without sympathy with the so-called "revolt of youth." There is much deadwood in our faculties, much neglect of the art of teaching, much expensive specialization which produces little of value, theoretical or practical, and in our large universities a too frequent reduction of the student to a punched card in a computer file. These are legitimate grievances. But they should be dealt with one by one, while the fabric of our education is respectfully preserved; it is fatuous to tear this down and try to reconstruct it from the ground. No one is wise enough to do that properly, not even undergraduates; for it is the product of many generations of experimentation with the means of education, and of reflection about its ends. I certainly did not know, at the age of eighteen, what subjects were of most worth, and I should not like to take an oath about it now. I can only believe that age, reflection, and experience bring some advance over the judgments of eighteen. I have heard a student question this belief as itself one of the dogmas that are being imposed on the young. Some students need saving from themselves.

Any theory of education should be natural, in the sense of being based on human nature and the ends that human nature appoints; the education of a man is not the same as the training of a parrot, a seal, or a chimpanzee, because human nature has capacities and yearnings denied to other living things. What these yearnings are can be determined only by an inside view of human nature, only by looking into our own minds when we are trying to know, for example, and by bringing to light what would really satisfy us. Aristotle attempted to do that, and I should like to think my theory an Aristotelian one. Professor Dewey attempted to do it, and reached a view of the aim of intelligence that is different from mine, though most of his thought on education I can gratefully accept. On the other hand, such a view as Professor Skinner's, which rejects any appeal to conscious ends and regards education as the physical conditioning of physical behavior, the same in principle for a man as for a pigeon, seems to me distorted and distorting, because based on a radical misconception of what sort of being man is.

My own conception of education turns on the results of an early voyage of self-discovery, directed to bringing to light the end I was half-consciously pursuing in the endeavor to know. I had no reason to doubt that the end at work in my own quest was the same in me and in others, or that in making my own end clear I was catching a glimpse of the natural and immanent end of the race on the cognitive side. I seemed to see this end gradually emerging into greater definition in the course of evolution, and I was fortified by such philosophical evolutionists as Hobhouse, whose works on mind and morals in evolution gave happy documentation to my theory.

The theory was supported further by the continuity I seemed to find in individual understanding as it passed successively from common sense to science, and from science to speculative philosophy. These three levels seemed to me stages in the realization of an immanent ideal which was the same throughout, and which directed the advance. Science is refined common sense, and philosophy is an extension of science at both ends of the scientific spectrum. As C. D. Broad has pointed out, philosophy has two very different functions, in both of which it is continuous with science. Critical philosophy is scientific reflection exercising itself upon the meanings and assumptions with which science begins; speculative philosophy is an extension of science at the other end; it is an attempt to synthesize the conclusions of the various sciences into a coherent view of the world. There are no sharp boundaries either between the three levels or between the scattered provinces of knowledge. The career of reason is one unbroken movement of analysis and synthesis controlled by one increasingly conscious end.

If understanding is the end, what about the training of reason as a means to the end? Is there not some common pattern of the working of intelligence at all levels, some framework of its procedure that can be singled out and made the paradigm of our thinking? Some people say there is, and find it in the abstract forms of mathematics and formal logic. That these disciplines do give valuable models of clearness and rigor, I agree. But it is easy to overestimate their value. The thinking done in politics, the law, and even in natural science is not thinking of this abstract kind; it is immersed and dyed in its particular subject matter. For every argument that goes amiss through a formal fallacy, there are four or five that go wrong from psychological causes—prejudice, indolence, lack of interest, habits of looseness in thought and speech. The mind trained to deal with the exactitudes of formal logic is not always proficient among the richer and vaguer concepts of actual life; Napoleon soon had to dismiss Laplace for trying to introduce into his administration "the spirit of the infinitesimals." If one would learn to think well, the best way is to think with a determined regard for truth in one's own field, whatever it may be. Every course in the curriculum should be a course in thinking, in the sense that it should give the student discipline in the sifting of evidence, the drawing of conclusions, and the checking of those conclusions against the facts.

I have not attempted here or elsewhere to work out how my view of the intellectual end should be applied in organizing a curriculum, still less in administering a college. The practical problems that face American education, with its courageous and unprecedented attempts at mass education, are too vast to be dealt with in passing. One suggestion as to method, however, I can make with some confidence, since it grows out of forty years of working with classes ranging in size from four to seven hundred. The best results have been gained with small groups of four to six, meeting for two or three hours, and conducted in Socratic fashion. In such a group a student learns from the criticism of his peers what is effective pleading and what is not; the instructor can pursue an argument, if need be, all the way back to first principles, and correct or encourage a student while the argument is still warm; and both instructor and students share the excitement of a common pursuit, forgetting for a time the differences in age and status. Such teaching is as near an approximation to Mark Hopkins on one end of a log and a student on the other as the college can provide.

I have been dealing with the end of education on its intellectual side; what about its appreciative side, its introduction to the experience of values and to discrimination among them? Here again I have something to say about theory, though little about practice.

Knowledge seems to me to have a very different status among the values of life from that of the other values, such as beauty, comfort, and love. Knowledge is at once fulfillment and revelation—fulfillment of the desire to know and revelation of a world outside. The other values lack this revelatory character. The beauty that we find in music, for example, is not a beauty that exists out there apart from our hearing the music, as two planets and two others would still make four apart from our knowing the fact; the beauty of the music lies solely in the fulfillment and satisfaction realized in the experience of it. Whether the value of music comes into being at all depends on the presence of a sensibility for it. And for a person without the sensibility, music is not music at all, but merely noise, and perhaps disagreeable noise; "all music," says Evelyn Waugh, "is positively painful to me."

A word must now be said about my theory of intrinsic value. In the addresses that follow, I make much at various points of the distinction between means and ends. In our gadget-ridden culture, the distinction is important, for much of the trouble in our hurried and harried lives arises from neglecting that distinction. One who writes about education should keep it before him constantly. Colleges, classes, grades, budgets, laboratories, gymnasiums, the millions or billions of money that we lavish on education, are all extrinsic goods, valuable only as they lead on to goods that are wholly different—intrinsic goods, experiences that are good in themselves. And the goodness of these experiences lies solely, I have said, in their realization of the impulses or drives of human nature. We can take a further step of analysis by pointing out that in this realization there are always two components: on the one hand, the fulfillment of the impulse, and, on the other, the feeling of pleasure or satisfaction that accompanies such fulfillment. What gives an experience intrinsic value, I have argued, is always the joint presence of these two.

Many of the subjects pursued in college, mathematics for instance, appeal to the intellect almost exclusively. And all studies in any field, even those in music and painting, should bring the student's intelligence into play, for analysis is required for the full appreciation of any art. But it is only courses in the humanities that take appreciation, as distinct from knowledge, as a prime goal. Courses in poetry, fiction, drama, music, and the histories of architecture, sculpture, and painting (as opposed to the study of their respective crafts), are designed to increase and refine the sensibility to values.

There have been recent critics, of whom F. L. Lucas was a distinguished one, who held that taste is a matter of ultimate, unarguable preference, and that the attempt to lay down objective standards for it can only be arbitrary and dogmatic. I do not agree; and the analysis I have suggested of intrinsic value would, if true, provide an escape from the prevalent aesthetic anarchy. The devotee of rock and roll is inclined to argue: "If I enjoy Bob Dylan more than I do Bach or Brahms or Beethoven, surely that is all the justification I need for preferring him to these others"; and some teachers of English in high school and college are inclined to give the students their head and encourage them to write their reports not on books that have won critical suffrage, but on the latest libidinous best seller. If pleasure were the only component of value, these persons would have a case. They have no case if value depends on fulfillment as well. Those who, enjoying rock and roll, have gone on to the musicians we have named seem to have found a much richer fulfillment in the more sophisticated art; and those who have entered imaginatively into the classics of poetry and fiction feel that they would have been fenced in tragically if they had had to live within the confines of the day's best sellers. Great art is great not only because it "speaks to our condition," but because it fills and stretches the mind; we have the sense, after exposure to it, of being larger persons.

So there *is* a better and a worse among intrinsic goods, and it is the business of the college to make students aware of the difference. It is an uphill business because the college gets small cooperation from the media of news and entertainment to which the students are constantly exposed. Magazines, television screens, and the Hollywood and Broadway stages jumble together masterpieces and trash, genuine heroes and iron-jawed brutes, genuine heroines and shapely nitwits, vulgarity and distinction, until the sense of better and worse becomes thoroughly blurred. We are threatened with a blight of standardlessness, and it is no wonder that students complain of alienation and the meaninglessness of life. I have returned again and again in the addresses that follow to the fallacy of democracy among values, the supposition that one man's vote in this realm is as good as another's, and that there is something snobbish in a determined choice of the better and eschewing of the worse. If this is snobbishness, the duty of snobbishness is one of my more emphatic preachments.

In sum, my philosophy of education is one of fulfilment on the sides of both knowledge and value, and in widest commonalty spread. That is the end of education, as it is of life. It may be thought that this is less than consistent with another theme that runs throughout these addresses, the theme that the end is reasonableness. There is no real inconsistency here. To me the good life and the reasonable life are synonymous terms. Reason or intellectual insight is for me the ultimate court of appeal in questions of taste and morals as well as in questions of truth. The judgment that intense happiness is intrinsically better than intense pain seems as truly a self-evident rational insight as a judgment of mathematics. The judgment that I ought to make the world as much better as I can seems to me also a rational insight, one indeed on which the whole of ethics is founded. The weighing of my competing goods against each other, the weighing of my own goods against those of others, the ultimate decision as to what is right between conflicting claims of any kind, all rest with reason. Thus for me the reasonable life is not only one in which the mind follows with its understanding the structure of the world; it is also one in which rational insight selects the goods one is to pursue and governs both will and feeling in the pursuit of them. I have argued that the best product of education is the rational temper. It is an attitude in which self-respect is identified with the living of a rational life. The use of reason, to be sure, is a means, not an end, but rationality, the habitual appeal to reason in belief and practice, is so intimate a condition of the good life that means and end are practically one.

With convictions like these about education, I am only too likely to repeat myself when I talk about it, and I fear I have done so frequently in these addresses. In running over them, I have caught and eliminated some bad cases of iteration, but I have not felt bound to cut out the repetition of a point if it was important to the argument and was restated or illustrated in a fresh way.

Though the papers are in the main speeches given to college audiences, there are three exceptions. Number 8 was one of a collection of essays by various authors, entitled *Our Emergent*

*Civilization* and published by *Harper's* in 1947. Number 11 was an article that appeared in *The Monist* for January, 1968. Number 16 was a toast given at a dinner of the British Academy in London in 1953. Many of the papers have had a fugitive life in college publications, and where permission to reprint was necessary, acknowledgment is made on a separate page.

I am especially indebted to Professor Eugene Freeman, who not only urged me to collect these papers in a book, but offered to edit them for me and to oversee their publication by the Open Court Publishing Company, where he is the editor of the Philosophy Division.

BRAND BLANSHARD

# Acknowledgments

Most of these addresses have had that limited kind of publication which consists in appearance in an occasional college pamphlet or alumni bulletin.

No. 1, "The Test of a University," which was given at Rice University at the inauguration of President Spitzer, is reprinted from *Rice University Studies, Vol. XLIX, Supplement 2*, entitled *Man, Science, Learning and Education*, by permission of the university.

No. 2, "The Uses of a Liberal Education," given as a convocation address at Wheaton College, Norton, Massachusetts, is reprinted by permission of the Wheaton College Alumnae Association.

No. 3, "Education as Philosophy," No. 20, "Art," No. 21, "Courage," and No. 22, "Books," are reprinted from the *Swarthmore College Bulletin* by permission of the college.

No. 4, "In Defense of the Humanities," an address delivered as part of the inauguration of President Bly, is reprinted by permission of Thiel College, Greenville, Pennsylvania.

No. 5, "What Is Education For?" is reprinted from *Education in a Free Society*, Pitcairn-Crabbe Lecture Series 2, Pittsburgh, Pennsylvania, by permission of the University of Pittsburgh Press.

No. 6, "Education and Values," given as a Cooper Lecture at Swarthmore, is reprinted from *The Goals of Higher Education*, edited by Willis D. Weatherford, Cambridge, Massachusetts, 1960, by permission of the Harvard University Press.

No. 7, "What Should We Get from College?" was a Dana Lecture at Carleton College, Northfield, Minnesota, and is reprinted by permission of the college.

No. 8, "Can Men Be Reasonable?" appeared in *Our Emergent Civilization*, edited by Ruth Nanda Anshen, copyright 1947 by Harper & Row Publishers, Inc., and is reprinted by permission of the publishers.

No. 9, "Quantity and Quality in American Education," appeared in *The Student Seeks an Answer*, Colby College Press, 1960, and is reprinted with the permission of that Press.

No. 10, "The Specialist and the Humanist," was given as a graduate school convocation address at Brown in 1963 and is reprinted from *Brown University Papers No. XL* with the university's permission.

No. 11, "Some Current Issues in Education," appeared in *The Monist* for January, 1968, and is reprinted with the permission of the editor.

No. 12, "Limited Minds and Unlimited Knowledge," given at the inauguration of President Martha Lucas at Sweet Briar College, is reprinted by permission of the college.

No. 13, "Sanity in Thought and Art," is reprinted from the *Riecker Memorial Lecture Series No. 8*, 1962, Tucson, by permission of the Arizona University Press.

No. 14, "The Idea of the Gentleman," appeared in the *Oberlin Alumni Magazine* for May 1957, and is reprinted with the editor's permission.

No. 15, "Some Fringe Benefits of Education," a commencement address of 1954 at Chatham College, Pittsburgh, is now printed with the approval of the college.

No. 16, "The British Scholar," is also now printed for the first time.

No. 17, "Conformity," was a convocation address at Simpson College, Indianola, Iowa, in 1961, and is reprinted from an alumni bulletin by permission of the college.

## Acknowledgments

No. 18, "Serenity," a Fox-Howe lecture at Buck Hill Falls, Pennsylvania, has been revised and reprinted with permission from a pamphlet issued by the Fox-Howe Association.

No. 19, "Machines," was given as a Beckman Lecture at Wells College in 1966, and in a somewhat different form as a Nielson Lecture in 1967 at Smith College. It is here reprinted with permission from the Smith College pamphlet entitled "The Life of the Spirit in a Machine Age."

No. 23, "Admiration," a baccalaureate address at Mt. Holyoke College, is now printed for the first time.

For all these permissions to give my words a wider hearing I am very grateful. Though my acknowledgments are offered chiefly to those institutions that have put an address into print, my thanks go also to the many other colleges and audiences that have given these talks a patient hearing.

# I

## *Ends*

# 1
## *The Test of a University*

The most searching question that can be asked about a university is, What sort of person does it produce? Of course, there are other things besides persons of quality that we may justly demand of it. It must pay due regard to the practical needs of society and of its students. When statesmen remind us that we are short of foresters, nurses, or medical men, our universities must try to act accordingly. Students who propose to spend four years and some thousands of their fathers' savings in a university expect, not unreasonably, that it will contribute to their success in the economic battle, that whether their lot in life is building bridges or pulling teeth or teaching a language, the university training should give them some claim to the title of experts. But range and expertness of product are not the crucial tests. The question of overriding importance for any university is, What sort of man walks out of its doors?

That is the question we usually ask when we turn an appraising eye on educational systems other than our own. We look at the French system with its rigorous lycée training, its standardized courses, its national competitive examinations—a system very different from our own—and we wonder what to say of it. There would seem to be no way of judging it except by appraising its product. That may be a complex business, I admit. The French university graduate exhibits greater precision in his scholarship than our own, greater readiness and skill in expression, greater adroitness in intellectual fence. French critics also charge him, however, with a somewhat parochial insularity from anything non-French, a fierce individualism that produces for three Frenchmen four opinions and excludes political compromise, and an odd combination of intense loyalty to France with an invincible reluctance to pay his taxes. The German gymnasium and university are both notably different from our own; the break between them is sharper, and it throws the advanced student more ruthlessly back on his own resources. Is the system better than ours or not? The decision again must rest on the product. The German graduate is probably more rigorously disciplined and highly specialized than ours, and perhaps intellectually more sophisticated. But two world wars have made plain that there was something amiss about him. The people who were supposed by themselves and others to be the best educated in the world capitulated with dismaying readiness to the leadership of dervishes. Russian education remains a puzzle to us. Its achievements in applied science have been spectacular, in some areas outstripping our own. But even if these achievements were greater than they are, we should probably still be skeptical about them. Why? Chiefly because doubts would still linger about the sort of man produced by the Soviet effort. Is he a mind that can play free in the humanities and politics as well as forge along in his specialty, or has he been living in a mental and political straitjacket that has ossified the cartilages of his mind? It is on the answer to this sort of question that judgment must be based in the end.

All this implies that we have in our own mind some view, however dim, of the kind of man an education should produce. And since, if I am right, this implicit ideal is the rod by which we must measure education, it may be useful to try our hand at sketching it. I do not know whether my own ideal figure will look like yours, and since he is too elusive and wraithlike to sit still for a portrait, I can only draw him from fugitive glimpses and hope he will be recognizable enough to allow you to accept or disown him.

Look at him first on the intellectual side. Here his chief characteristics will be two: he will have intellectual interest, and he will have sound judgment.

## INTEREST

All of us are interested, and strongly interested, in some things—the broker in his stocks, the mother in her children, the stamp collector in his stamps. But outside the circle of these interests, awakened by utility or instinct or accident, our minds may be pretty bleak, so that when the broker talks to the mother or the stamp collector, both sit in uneasy silence, groping about for some common ground. There is a great difference, as Chesterton noted, between an eager man who wants to read a book and a tired man who wants a book to read. Breadth of interest is necessary even for the plain good citizen. How is one to vote responsibly with no interest whatever in foreign aid or foreign trade? How is one to give discriminatingly or play one's local part if one has no concern about public health, delinquency, housing, hospitals, or schools? At present we are kept going by the interest in these matters of a precious fraction of the citizenry.

True intellectual interest will run beyond even these bounds. It will be the interest of a citizen of the world, eager to be at home in it, intrigued and invited by it not merely because the knowledge of it is useful, but because of the intrinsic fascination of exploring it, of understanding it, of watching its expanding frontiers. If our time is one of political chaos and a population explosion, it is also the time of an unprecedented explosion of human knowledge. This has shifted the center of educated interest in the direction of science. The Roman Terence thought nothing human alien to him, and this has been cited a thousand times by humanistic scholars as a model of breadth of vision, though it makes no mention of the world in which the physical scientist lives. Dr. Thomas Arnold, headmaster of Rugby, said: "Rather than have physical science the principal thing in my son's mind, I would rather have him think that the sun went round the earth, and that the stars were so many spangles set in the bright blue firmament." Sir Charles Snow has reminded us that we can no longer afford such indifference, and that unless we

5

recover from it we may shortly be gathered to our fathers, with the Russians, who are far from indifferent to science, ruling in our stead. The educated man I am sketching needs no such reminders. The thought that the physical world he lived in as a boy has dissolved before his eyes and that matter itself has now become, to use Russell's words, mere "waves of probability undulating in nothingness" will carry an excitement of its own. I am not suggesting that he will be interested only or even chiefly in science; revolutions have been going on not only in men's theories of nature but also in their views of human nature and of the supernatural. Freud, for example, pioneered a revolution in psychology; and Karl Barth changed the theological climate of Protestantism. It does not detract from the interest of these two figures to realize that if one of them is right, the other must be wrong; there is a special fascination in the conflict of such gladiators. The person who is bored in the modern world shows that he is in no full sense a member of it.

## JUDGMENT

The second characteristic of the educated mind is sound judgment. Can we say anything useful about such judgment generally, whether displayed in business, law, or morals? I think we can. It seems to have two chief bases. The first is reflectiveness, in the sense of a settled habit of seeing things in terms of their consequences. It is the opposite of impulsiveness; it is the trait of the man who looks before he leaps, and trims his plans and beliefs to accord with his prevision. Good judgment in chess requires the foreseeing of what a move will probably entail on the part of one's opponent; good judgment in a businessman requires a sense of what will happen if he moves his store to a new site, or cuts his prices, or raises his wages; good judgment in mathematics or philosophy requires that the thinker see any theory proposed to him in the light of its implications. Military strategy is a particularly good field in which to study what good and bad judgment mean, since the moves and their results stand out so clearly. Field Marshal Lord Wavell once prepared a list of the great commanders of history, based upon their ability to take into account all the factors, military, personal, and political, on which decisions should be based. It surprised many. The meteoric Napoleon stood sixth on the list. First came

Marlborough, the embodiment of versatility, then Belisarius, the great Byzantine of the sixth century, then Wellington, Frederick of Prussia, and Lee, distinguished even in defeat. All were masters of the sort of prevision that suited imperfect means to large ends.

Now this capacity to see things in the light of their consequences may itself have different bases. Sometimes it is mainly a gift of Providence. Whatever the doctrine that all men are born equal may mean, it does not apply to their intelligence; imbeciles and geniuses are born, not made. Some minds can see effortlessly and at once how to solve an equation, how to escape from a maze, what to do about a fire or an accident, while others with a like experience behind them have to sit down and think it out. These latter, who perhaps include most of us, have the other kind of intelligence, which is based on effort and habit. They may go farther in the end than competitors with a higher I.Q., for what is commonly called intelligence is very largely character. A normal person can make himself intelligent in this very important sense by discipline; indeed, the providing of this discipline is the main work of higher education. Such intelligence is far more important than knowledge. Mere catholicity of interest may fill one's mind over the years as full of information as one of our government granaries is full of surplus grain and with as little profit to the owner. What turns knowledge to account is the habit of trained reflection; Pascal said that most of the ills of the world were due to the fact that men could not sit in a room and think. If philosophy, as someone has said, is the process of thinking about everything else philosophically, we all need to be philosophers. And we all need to be scientists, not in the sense of being experts with computers or microscopes, but in the sense that we have acquired the habit of observing things accurately, thinking about them, developing our thoughts into their consequences, and checking these against the facts. Indeed, good judgment in matters of fact *is* just scientific method converted into habit.

### The Training of Judgment

No one academic subject is essential to this sort of discipline. Mathematics has often been put forward as the great whetstone of the mind, but work of much power and exactitude has been done by the mathematically incompetent—in archeology by Wallis Budge, in philosophy by F. H. Bradley, in history by Macaulay

7

who, according to Sir Richard Jebb, "seems to have regarded every mathematical proposition as an open question, a theme for lively debate." History has often been thought the ideal educational subject as combining scientific with humanistic interests, but if we discovered that Darwin and Einstein were historically ignorant, would that affect our respect for what they did? I should be happy to plead the cause of my own subject, philosophy, but I should have to admit that if that means the philosophy of the specialist as opposed to the reflective habit, most men get on pretty well without it; indeed, Emerson remarked: "Who has not looked into a metaphysical book? And what sensible man has ever looked twice?" No, trained and critical reflection has not been patented by any single subject, and a first-rate teacher can exemplify what precision, order, lucidity, and self-criticism mean in teaching anything from cytology to numismatics.

The fact is that trained intelligence is not only not the perquisite of any university subject; it may be achieved without any help from college or university. Science is common sense refined and rendered self-critical, and with sufficient dedication that refinement can be achieved by one's own effort. It is well for us academics to remind ourselves occasionally that neither Washington nor Lincoln, neither John Stuart Mill nor Herbert Spencer, neither Franklin nor Faraday nor Edison, neither Marlborough nor his great descendant and biographer ever attended a university, that neither of the Wright brothers had so much as a high school diploma. What is important, whether in a university or out of it, is the power to identify first-rate work when we see it, enthusiasm for it, and the appropriation of its standards in one's practice. If a young man clearly sees the quality of *The Wealth of Nations* or *The Origin of Species* or the essay on *Liberty* and feels the urge to go and do likewise, he has the root of the matter in him; indeed, he has gained, whether by himself or not, the best thing that a university could afford.

### Judgment of Good and Evil

I suggested that good judgment has two bases, one of which is the reflectiveness that sees beliefs and proposals in the light of what they imply. But there is a second element in good judgment, the sense of value. The first without the second has often been a menace to mankind; think of the intellectual power that German generals and scientists threw into the service of Hitler. There are lawyers of great gifts who are not above using them to smirch innocence and condone wrong. Some large American fortunes have been built on a well-mixed concrete base of shrewdness and callous inhumanity. Indeed, the commonest criticism of our culture as a whole is that it combines a large control of the means to the good life with much dimness as to what the good life is. If judgment is to be sound, it must be able not only to calculate consequences, but to weigh the good or evil of those consequences.

Now what makes experience valuable is the fulfilment and satisfaction of human needs. Some of our activities—the daily buttoning and unbuttoning, the routine of commuting to our work—are trivial, however necessary, because they do not realize our powers in any satisfying way, while others—the achievement of a new understanding or friendship, a new response to Mozart or Wordsworth—do somehow fulfil and enlarge us. We are sometimes told, of course, that there is no such thing as the really good or bad in art or morals, that it is all a matter of taste, and taste is arbitrary. This I disbelieve. There are some poems—for example, Gray's "Elegy"; some novels—for example, *War and Peace;* some plays, like the great Shakespearean quartet of tragedies, that are good by general suffrage; they are good because they speak not to something peripheral in human nature, but to its central interests and longings, because they help us to see ourselves in perspective and to be ourselves more fully.

The vision of good and evil calls for imagination, and this is why the humanities are so essential a complement to merely intellectual discipline. The humanities are the soil in which imagination grows. Authors in inventing Captain Ahab and George Babbitt, and we in understanding them, are trying out in idea varying ways of life, and because we have entered into them, we shall make our own future choices with relevant experience behind us. Many people, when they have rejected new adventures of the mind, have done so because they did not know what they were rejecting; it is hard to believe, for example, that the Puritans in rejecting drama, or Mr. Ford in describing history as "bunk," really knew what they were forgoing; they were judging from too narrow a base. Many persons in our own society, which has the highest living standard

9

ever known to man, have achieved wealth and efficiency over the years by hard, unremitting application, only to find at the top of the ladder an inward void, and to realize too late that the rigors of the climb have left them fitted for nothing but going on with the climb, however pointless now. This applies to the intellectual as well as the practical life. Scientists, whose techniques are becoming more technical and demanding, have realized that science is too thin and cerebral a diet for "human nature's daily food"; our medical and engineering schools are insisting that both as raw material and as products they want men, not high-powered human computers. "The Science of the nineteenth century," a British writer says, "seemed to expel poetry with a brandished test-tube; the Science of the twentieth re-opens the door to her with a bow."

## RATIONALITY IN PRACTICE

We have been looking at our ideal university product on his intellectual side, and we have found that he will have two marked traits, breadth of interest and good judgment, the latter resolving itself in turn into reflectiveness and the perception of values. Happily we can touch the nonintellectual side of him more lightly, since this is not the university's prime concern. It will be enough to say one thing: his emotions and his impulses will be under rational control. It is a strange fact that a towering genius may be an overgrown child, full of tantrums, self-pity, and irrational hatreds. This sort of genius, though insufferable to live with, is more interesting to read about than mere dull reasonableness, and so much is made of it in print and on the screen that some young people have drawn a wrong inference about it. They have concluded that eccentricity is a part of genius, so that if one lives like Scott Fitzgerald or Dylan Thomas, one is showing some kinship with their creativeness. It does not follow. One is copying their weakness, not their strength. Romantics do not like rational bits and bridles; "Those who restrain desire," said William Blake, "do so because theirs is weak enough to be restrained." But one may restrain passion not because one feels less, but because one loves sense and reason more. And "it is by no means self-evident," as T.S. Eliot notes, "that human beings are most real when most violently excited." Education, on its

10

emotional side, is discipline in the art of adjusting feeling to its object. The only feeling excluded by this discipline is feeling that is ill-tempered or intemperate.

As for impulses, they too can be disciplined, for they are the raw material of an educated will. But universities can hardly undertake this sort of education, which must be turned over, for the most part, to the more ruthless school of life. Unhappily, a person who is both reflective and sensitive may be thoroughly flabby of will. A French writer said of someone, "Il pense comme un homme, il sent comme une femme, il agit comme un enfant." That could be said, I suppose, of many persons of stature—of Coleridge and De Quincey, for example, who for all their scholarship were ill regulated and ill-disciplined characters. What wishy-washy creatures they seem by the side of the old Iron Duke, Wellington, who once said that having found there was no point in lying awake, he never did. Universities cannot generate wills of this kind, but they ought not to discourage them, as I sometimes think they do. Men who earn wages or run a business have to keep themselves to their task and get things done on schedule; students often get by with a degree of self-permissiveness that would ruin them in an office or a regiment. The habit of seeing things through, of doing quietly and promptly what has to be done, is one that can be acquired, and whether acquired in a university or not, it is one of the marks of a really educated man.

Well, there is the rough picture of this man that I find in the back of my mind. Perhaps when he is thus sketched in the abstract, there will be little debate about him. Everyone nods assent to the suggestion that a life is better for breadth of interest, good judgment, and the rational control of feeling and impulse. But I should hope for more than the automatic assent to an abstraction. I should like to think that embodiments of this abstraction, if set before us in flesh and blood, would be really liked and admired. Do such embodiments actually exist? If so, we shall know better how we feel about the ideal I have been describing when we look at its incarnations.

Happily, there have been such people, not perfect examples, of course, or they would not be human, but at least instructive approximations to it. I will not take living examples, which are likely

11

to be invidious, nor will I take examples from our own country, for the rather distressing reason that it seems harder to find here the kind of examples I want. My impression is that they would also be hard to find in Germany, though somewhat less so in France. Whether it is through ignorance, prejudice, or insight that my choice falls on England I am not sure, but the English universities do seem to have been more prolific of the type than others I happen to know. This may be partly because the British universities skim a thicker cream off the general population than those of other countries, and partly because Britain, for all its residual class system, has a generous tolerance for marked individuality. But no doubt it is also due in part to the fact that the older British universities were founded and organized to turn out not merely "squares" but persons in the round. Let me name three men who were so nearly contemporary that they all knew each other and so nearly contemporary with us that I knew the first, saw the second in action, and might have known the third.

## THREE EXAMPLES

Gilbert Murray seems to me to offer about as good a pattern of the educated mind as one could hope to find. He was of course a scholar, so brilliant indeed that within about a year of taking his B.A. at Oxford he succeeded Sir Richard Jebb as professor of Greek at Glasgow. But more important than his knowledge of Greek was the fact that he *was* a Greek in mind and temperament. As a discerning friend said of him,

> he had, in a degree far exceeding that of most modern scholars or modern men . . . that central serenity and self-sufficiency . . . which [ancient philosophers] so commonly made it their object to attain. . . . I doubt if Murray ever acted, except on the spur of the moment—and such moments occur to every man—without first asking if what he proposed to do were just and considerate. This is the teaching of Greek moralists and indeed of Greek literature in general; *audi alteram partem* is characteristic of all their best writers, and is what enabled them to create Greek drama and science and philosophy. Murray was like them in this, that his appeal was always to reason and humanity. . . . He said at the end of his long life that for many years there had never been a day when he failed to give thought to two things: Hellenism and the work for peace. [British Academy, *Proceedings*, **43** (1957), 256, 257, 254.]

Little by little it came to be recognized that the Regius Professor of Greek at Oxford was not only a rare spirit but a power in the land. He was made head of the League of Nations Union; he was the courageous president of the Society for Psychical Research; he was chairman of that Committee on Intellectual Co-operation that did so much to save the scholars of Europe in Nazi days; he served as Norton Professor of Poetry at Harvard and very nearly as British ambassador to the United States. Though an Australian by birth, he was awarded the Order of Merit as one of the greatest of Englishmen; though a rationalist in religion, he was buried (when he could no longer protest) in Westminster Abbey. He was a humanitarian as well as a humanist, and though the gentlest of men, had a passionate hatred for two things, cruelty and injustice. One passing remark of his I find revealing. He and Rudyard Kipling knew each other as boys, and indeed planned to write a huge epic together. In later years, a friend asked him how he liked Kipling. "Not very much," he answered; "I remember that he threw a stone at a cat."

The second man was a better friend of Murray's, and one whom he always revered, Herbert Henry Asquith. He too was a brilliant classical scholar who retained his interest in the classics to the end. But he was a Roman, not a Greek. He went into politics and proved more impressive in Parliament than he had been in the university, quickly becoming home secretary and then prime minister. Even among prime ministers he stood out, for the quality of his mind and character raised the level of British public life. He had "the best intellectual apparatus, understanding and judgment," said Lord Chancellor Haldane, "that I ever saw in any man." One of his inveterate opponents, Lord Birkenhead, after comparing him to no less a figure than Julius Caesar for his quiet, impersonal, universal adequacy, went on to say: "Mr. Asquith's character is a national asset. He fights cleanly, wins without insolence, and loses without rancour." It is natural enough that such a man should succeed as jurist, bishop, or professor, but that he should have preserved in the rough and tumble of politics the clarity of a logician, a style that was the admiration of scholars for its purity and economy, and a complete freedom from professional envies, personal animosities, and all the little vulgarities that are almost forced upon politicians, is amazing.

What is the secret of it? The answer is, I suppose, that in his case education really "took." In an address to university students he left on record what he thought a university should try to produce, and what his hearers must have thought it had produced at least once.

> It is not enough [he said] that a university should teach its students to eschew narrowness in the range of their intellectual interests and slatternliness in speech and writing. It should put them permanently on guard against the Dogmatic temper. . . . To be open-minded; to struggle against preconceptions, and hold them in due subjection; to keep the avenues of the intelligence free and unblocked; to take pains that the scales of the judgment shall be always even and fair; to welcome new truths when they have proved their title, despite the havoc they make of old and cherished beliefs—these may sound like commonplace qualities, well within every man's reach, but experience shows that in practice they are the rarest of all. [*Occasional Addresses* (London: Macmillan & Co., 1918), pp. 94-95.]

Asquith was sometimes thought to be a human iceberg, a massive gleaming intelligence without feeling. His daughter Violet, who was very close to him, gave me a very different picture of her formidable father. He was a man of intense feelings, great sensitiveness, and wide interests; he loved poetry, biography, and fiction, which he read in his dressing gown for two hours every night before going to sleep. But he detested feeling, when irrelevant, as bad taste. He had the standards of a Stoic and an iron self-control. It was not without reason that he was called the last of the Romans.

The third figure in my trio, John Buchan, was junior to the others, a pupil of Murray's and a friend not so much of Asquith as of his brilliant son Raymond, who like so many others of that remarkable but doomed generation never returned from the war. John Buchan was also a classical scholar of distinction, who, when he read modern poetry, philosophy, and history, did so with Sophocles, Plato, and Thucydides approving or murmuring over his shoulder. He was in a sense a Jack-of-all-trades, as he has made clear in his autobiography, *A Pilgrim's Way*; he was in turn a publisher, a mountain climber, a South African administrator, a historian (he wrote a twelve-volume history of the first war), a novelist (he wrote some twenty-five successful novels), a biographer of Augustus and Cromwell, a member of Parliament, and a governor-general of Canada. Here certainly was a man whose contact with the world was made on a wide perimeter. But through all these activities there was an interior unity, a firm core of standards, which showed themselves clearly enough when he dealt with the shapeless fiction and impenetrable poetry that have been so fashionable in recent decades. Of these standards he wrote, "one was a belief in what the French call *ordonnance*, the supreme importance of an ordered discipline both in matter and style. Another was a certain austerity—I disliked writing which was luscious and overripe. A third was a distrust of extreme facility; a work of art, I thought, should be carved in marble, not in soapstone." It is reassuring that so discerning a critic should have written:

> You have to go to America, I think, for the wholly civilized man who has not lost his natural vigour or agreeable idiosyncrasies, but who sees life in its true proportions and has a fine balance of mind and spirit. . . . They are a people in whom education has not stunted any natural growth or fostered any abnormality. They are Greek in their justness of outlook, but Northern in their gusto. . . . As examples I would cite, among friends who are dead, the names of Robert Bacon, Walter Page, Newton Baker, and Dwight Morrow. [*A Pilgrim's Way* (New York: Houghton Mifflin Co., 1940), p. 271.]

If you know these names and prefer them to the three I have taken, I shall be content. They were all hewn from the same rock.

Here, then, are some samples of what I have sketched as the ideal university product. All were men of catholic interests. All were habitually reflective and notable for their judgment—intellectual, aesthetic, and practical. All had a touch of Stoicism in the firmness with which they had themselves emotionally in hand. All held administrative posts in which they proved that they could act as well as dream. This, I suggest, is the type of man that a university should aim at producing. He is an intellectual without being a prig, a scholar undrowned in his own erudition, an academic who is, or can be, a man of the world, a mind that has not only contemplated in its ivory tower the subtleties of the philosophers and the visions of artists and poets, but has allowed itself to be permeated down to the last fibers of its being by that love of reasonableness which is the most precious distillation of any study. A nation whose pattern of life was set by men of this stamp would be the model and envy of the world.

## THE CENTRAL QUESTION

Is our culture producing such persons? Certainly it has an impressive machinery for doing so. No students ever had access with the same freedom as ours to the world's store of knowledge. The belief in education is almost a religion for Americans, and as John Buchan says, the education they believe in is a rounded one; they have the Greek ideal of the healthy mind in a healthy body. A larger proportion of the people, for all their numbers, are in institutions of higher learning than is true anywhere alse. It has never been so easy for ability to find subsidy, and our graduate schools are models for the world. And it is surely undeniable that our universities are in fact turning out men of light and leading. What broader-gauge diplomats could reasonably be asked for than George F. Kennan, John J. McCloy, and Frank Graham? What more variously cultivated journalists could be found than Walter Lippmann or James Reston? What more judicious administrators of wealth could be found than the heads of our great foundations? We need not worry about affairs committed to such hands as these.

Granted this, it remains true that we are producing fewer such men than we ought. Since we do in fact produce a small crop, year by year, of these humane and well-equipped minds, there can be nothing in our educational system that necessarily blights them. Yet it produces so limited a crop of them, and with such effort and expense, as to suggest something inhospitable in the American soil. What is this? There is no simple answer. A swarm of moles and beetles of many different species has been gnawing away at our cultural roots, both inside and outside the universities. I will try to ferret out a few of them.

### Apathy

First is the fact that intellectual distinction receives so little honor in this country. I am not thinking about monetary reward, though much could be said about that, too. I am thinking of spontaneous interest, respect, and admiration for work of the first quality in the humanities, for example. In his farewell address as commissioner of education, Dr. Sterling M. McMurrin declared that the nation's culture was "pervaded by the decline in respect for the intellectual quality of men." For two years I sat on a committee of the

American Council of Learned Societies charged with the pleasant task of selecting nominees for ten splendid awards of $10,000 each. They were to go to the ablest humanistic scholars in the country in recognition of distinguished work completed or in process. Our committee spent much time, pains, and discussion in winnowing out a group of scholars in literature, history, religion, philosophy, and art, who, if they had lived in Germany, would have received the honor paid there to the most eminent of its professors, and if they had lived in France or Britain, would have been elected to the French or British Academy. The selections were made with the advice of leaders in the scholar's own field, so that the choice would be as near as possible to an accolade from massive authority. It seemed to me that this crowning of ten leaders of American thought should be on page one of newspapers and magazines throughout the country, that it was almost as important as the choice of a bathing beauty queen at Atlantic City or the escape of a convict from Alcatraz. In fact, the news struck the public with the detonation of a dropped pin. The *New York Times*, committed to presenting "all the news that's fit to print," did include an item about it somewhere in the middle of its Sunday edition, but even Argus-eyed *Time* did not deign to notice it, and the hungry cameras of *Life* found nothing of interest in these intellectual faces. Now mind is not so hardy a weed that it will grow anywhere at all. It needs not only a soil of opportunity but also an atmosphere of encouragement and a little of the sunshine of heartfelt honor. We provide the soil with unexampled generosity. But we are niggardly of air and sun.

### Disproportion of Return

Second, there is very little relation between quality of work and the quantity of economic return for it. Perhaps I may illustrate again from my own limited experience. In war days I had a telephone call from Washington saying that an attempt was being made to enable men in army camps to go on with their own education and that the army needed a philosophy book which would further this laudable purpose. The book was wanted in about three months, and four philosophy teachers were being asked to collaborate on it; would I serve? I did. Of course it was done hastily

17

and I am afraid superficially in off-hours, but it went into paperback and was picked up after the war as a textbook. I found that a casual left-handed product of this kind was far more profitable than books that cost six to fifteen years of work; indeed, if the three of this latter kind that I have laboriously produced were put together, they would leave me well in the red. The moral is clear. If economic return is important to you, don't put quality first; give that place to textbooks or to immediate popular appeal.

If you do not do this, you may well be a gentleman, defined as a man without visible means of support, but you will hardly be what is called a success. On the other hand, if you do catch the ears of the many, your success may be fabulous, for America is the richest of all markets; one best seller may bring wealth. But quality and success remain two different things. Augustine Birrell remarked that "*Charley's Aunt* had made more money than would be represented by the entire fortunes of Sir Walter Scott, Thackeray and Dickens all added together." Sometimes a scholar has the courage to use the success of a second-rate work as a springboard into work of higher quality, as Will Durant did with his *Story of Philosophy*. But that is not the general pattern. For persons who can do both kinds of work there is a continuing temptation, and sometimes a relentless economic pressure, to do the kind that taps the widest range of purses, the more irresistible because the reward of success may be so overwhelming. In short, economics lines up with popular interest to back the second- or third-rate mind rather than the first, and to make the first run under handicaps.

### Overdifferentiation of the Sexes

Third, there is the curious fact of the overdifferentiation of the sexes in this country. At first glance the fact seems quite the opposite. Education at all levels means increasingly coeducation; politically and legally, men and women are equal; women are now doctors, lawyers, ministers, and powers in business; indeed, they own the larger part of the country's wealth. True, but what of the images of the two sexes in the public mind? Here history has played a trick on us, aided and abetted in recent times by the glossy magazines and Hollywood. They have conspired to make American women too sweetly feminine and American men too toughly

18

masculine. Youth, romance, and the bloom of beauty have been so played up that the woman who has moved beyond them, however much a person, is apt to feel forlorn, and the spectacle of Russian women working in the fields and almost monopolizing the medical profession strikes the American as somehow unnatural. On the other hand, as H. G. Wells pointed out, the ideal American man is a square-jawed, two-fisted fellow, cool in crises, ungiven to words, but much given to deeds that spring straight from a heart of gold. This ideal is a heritage of the frontier; indeed, it is inherited from much farther back; all men in a sense are Walter Mittys, compensating in dreams of this kind for the drabness of the gray flannel suit and the unglamorous daily round. One reason why Hollywood has been so preoccupied with the frontier is that it gives this side of us a rich and swashbuckling release.

Now this extreme differentiation of men and women has had an unhappy cultural effect. It has tarnished the gentle lives of the scholar, the thinker, the poet, and the artist with a suspicion of unmanliness. Such men are not, as a rule, of the two-fisted type, and to that type there is something a little effete and decadent about them. The three men I have mentioned as the finest sort of university product were all of them sturdy physically, but they were not of the square-jawed type, nor were they much interested in competitive sports; their interests, even in youth, ran to literature, philosophy, and politics; they loved poetry, and read the classics with enthusiasm, and distinguished themselves for devotion to exact scholarship. One cannot help wondering whether a boy with these interests in a Jonesville high school or college would not be regarded as a "square" and a "queerie." So far as I know, such interests are untouched by any stigma of effeminacy in France or England, perhaps because the tradition still lingers there of an aristocracy that respected them, whereas our aristocracy has been of another kind, in which force and business drive have been more prized. For a boy interested in the humanities, our frontier tradition is still something of a hurdle.

He finds a further hurdle in his own ignorance. He probably does not know that boys develop more slowly than girls on the linguistic and appreciative sides, and that he is not really as unpromising here as he seems. Too often and too early he is pushed by these impalpable forces away from humanistic studies into others that seem more masculine and more practical—engineering, medicine, economics, science, business adminstration. I do not complain about the strengthening of these useful professions. I do deplore the resultant watering down of that precious cultural component, the quality of mind and spirit, which is contributed by education to public life.

### The Pressure Toward Uniformity

Fourth, there are all the powerful pressures toward uniformity in American life and education. These are the penalty of our size. When individuals move in masses, their edges get rubbed off, like those of the pebbles on a beach, and the larger the mass, the smoother they are and the less important they seem to themselves and others; in overpopulated places like India and southern Italy, one can feel the dispiritedness in the air. The same holds in education. In a class of five, the student is, or may be, an active participant; in a class of five hundred, he relapses into a notetaker. Now the class of five is hardly practicable in America, for when millions must be educated, mass methods are inevitable. Our vast educational machines tend, therefore, to grind out graduates as like each other as their diplomas. And the pressures toward uniformity still surround them when they have left the college gates. Little by little local journals of opinion and discussion are being mowed down by such weeklies as those of the Luce empire, with their incomparable coverage, photography, and power of suggestion; everything the American hears on radio or television is interlarded with psychologically skilful touts about what he should eat, drink, and wear. We seem to be verifying Emerson's remark that "society everywhere is in conspiracy against the manhood of every one of its members." We have been called a land of status seekers surrounded by hidden persuaders.

With all this din in our ears it is hard to think or to have an inner life that is genuinely our own. But think we must if thought is to go on at all. Crowds cannot think, nor journals nor radios nor even universities. Only individuals can think, and only as the habit of such thinking is encouraged and kept alive has education really succeeded. No doubt that is why William James broke out in a letter to a friend:

20

I am against bigness and greatness in all their forms, and with the invisible molecular moral forces that work from individual to individual, stealing in through the crannies of the world like so many soft rootlets, or like the capillary oozing of water, and yet rending the hardest monuments of man's pride, if you give them time. The bigger the unit you deal with, the hollower, the more brutal, the more mendacious is the life displayed. So I am against all big organizations as such, national ones first and foremost. . . . Give me individuals. . . . [Ralph B. Perry, *The Thought and Character of William James* (Little, Brown & Co., 1935), II, 315.]

The three men I have taken as examplars were all intensely individual. You could not mistake any of them for any other, in spite of their common interest in truth and reasonableness. Their voices were not echoes; their thought and feeling had the freshness of authenticity.

### The Complexity of Modern Life

Among the enemy miners and sappers we must note, fifth, some of the material conditions of modern living. It is hard to maintain in the midst of them that citadel of quiet reflectiveness which should be there as our strength and our refuge. The three men I have named were born in the Victorian era, when domestic life was largely based on personal service. There were maids to make beds and get meals; there were handymen whose wages one could afford. The vacations of these men, as college students, were not filled with hard physical work, necessary to earn one's way through. The kind of mind I have sketched may be achieved in the unhurried freedom of the English squire; but his class has hardly existed in America; and even in England increasing taxes imposed from above and increasing wages required from below have all but destroyed it; men—and still more, women—must do for themselves what used to be done for them.

It may be answered that a world of gadgets has taken the place of human service and that the work day is growing shorter. But the gadgets have now so multiplied that they have become themselves a care. The speeding car, the buzzing telephone, the complicated toys for Junior, the coughing and expiring power mower and the anxious do-it-yourself kit, the weary commuting to work of our increasingly urban people, the mountains of mendicant mail, the recurrent struggle with income tax, the protracted niggling necessary to finance a college education for all one's brood, regardless of their powers, the shoals of newspapers and magazines that call for attention if one is to keep abreast of the times—in a word, the sheer complexity of modern life, seems to make the ideal of serene thoughtfulness a rainbow in the clouds. The very perfection of those techniques that pile the news of the world on our doorsteps, almost at the hour of its happening, is more calculated to enlarge our information than to give us a philosophy, a standard of value, or a habit of reflection. And information without these is not education at all.

### The New Demands of Science

I must mention, though hesitantly, a sixth and final danger to our liberal education. In recent years and for obvious reasons the claims of science in education have been forced upon our notice, and indeed forced down our throats. There is no doubt that we need more science. If Sir Charles Snow and the secretary of defense say that we need it for national safety, I accept what they say, though I should add that we need it anyhow; the scientific way of thinking is part of the equipment of any educated mind. But if anyone says that a scientific education by itself is a liberal education, and just as liberal as one in the humanities, I beg leave to differ. My reason is that science, for the most part, ignores persons and their values, and persons and their values are the most important things in the world, indeed, the only things that are intrinsically important. Mathematics is concerned chiefly with classes as such, and whether they are classes of poets, popes, or pebbles is irrelevant. You could read many volumes of physics and chemistry without running across a suggestion that there is such a thing as consciousness in the world. Since consciousness is not public and observable, as good scientific objects are supposed to be, even psychology deals with it in a slightly shamefaced way. But consciousness, with its loves and hates, its idealism and despair, its visions and its villainies, is the sole residence in the universe of good and evil.

In view of the pressure put upon us for more and more science, it is well to know where we stand, and perhaps I may be permitted to say with dogmatic brevity where I stand myself. First, from a utilitarian point of view, science is essential. Second, it affords an admirable intellectual discipline. Third, that discipline is no better than an equally rigorous discipline in history or philosophy; indeed, I incline to regard these latter as better, for the reason that they engage our prejudice, and straight thinking in them is therefore an exercise not only in logic but in objectivity, in intellectual ethics, in the detection and control of wishful thinking. Fourth, even if this advantage is an illusion, it will be conceded that art and literature provide food for imagination and feeling which a scientific diet can hardly supply. And for the estimation of the goods and evils of life, imagination is of more use than logic. Finally, if world opinion were consulted at this moment, I suspect that we should be told quite bluntly that what we most need, as a people, is not so much more science as more of that humane wisdom required to use aright the tools that science has piled around us. I am not belittling science, which would be a stupid thing to do. I am saying that the educated mind must have qualities of sympathy and taste which science is not well calculated to supply, and that the substitution of a scientific for a humanistic core in liberal education would for us be a mistake.

These considerations may be felt to be "airy nothings." Granted that the test of a university is the sort of person it produces, granted that this person is of the kind I have sketched, granted all these difficulties in the way of producing him, is not the real question what we should do about it? What do you propose, I may be asked, about a new production belt for turning such persons out in satisfactory numbers? On that very different question I propose to say nothing. Not that I take no interest in educational engineering and in getting public support for it. These things are immensely important. No one could think the mechanics of education unimportant who worked, as I did for many years, under that remarkable Swarthmore pioneer, Frank Aydelotte, who did so much with his system of honors seminars to break the educational lockstep and set the abler students free to move at their own pace; and I would commend to your attention not only that experiment but all the other devices canvassed in John Gardner's book on *Excellence*. I am much in favor of state aid to education and on an enlarged scale, though not for sectarian purposes. We need more junior colleges;

our teachers need more money; our teaching methods, particularly in the languages and the sciences, need revision. These things are important, I repeat. But they belong among the means of education, not its ends, and one of the chief American temptations, here as elsewhere, is to confuse ends with means. A mammoth high school, a crowded campus, a football team with all wins and no losses, an expensive faculty, a B.A., a Ph.D.—these are not ends in themselves; they are tags and devices that take such value as they have from the persons they label or help to produce.

Some persons are in a position to forward American education by munificent gifts, and the tradition of giving to education in this country is a splendid one. Most of us cannot greatly aid in this way. But there is one way in which all Americans can aid who have been through a university's doors. They can justify their alma mater by valuing what it values, and by trying to be the sons and daughters it deserves. The most convincing witness to the value of education is a living, breathing human being whose habitual speech and action are invested by distinction of mind.

In giving that witness, we in America have to resist the inverted snobbery that makes the educated man feel uneasy if he is not like everyone else. He is too often afraid that if he uses the language more sensitively than other people, if he interests himself in Eliot's criticism or Tillich's theology, if he tries to embody his own taste in his dress or the layout of his house, he will be accused of being "high hat." Now education has surely failed if it leaves us like everyone else. Our graduates should not simply dissolve and disappear in the democratic melting pot; they ought to lead in every community, not as a result of their own pushing, but as a result of gravitation to the top by minds and characters that belong there. Of the three men I have mentioned as university types, I am particularly drawn to the politician among them, Asquith, because on this point he never compromised. In his political campaigns he may have kissed babies and milked cows (though I doubt it), but he always argued with the knowledge and urbanity, thought with the relevance, and spoke with the distinction of the gentleman and scholar. I remember feeling the same admiration for Woodrow Wilson when as a middle western youngster I heard him make a campaign speech; here was no man's copy, but a mind speaking to plain men and most persuasively in the unmistakable accents of the scholar. "The rule for every man," Wilson once said, "is not to depend on the education which other men prepare for him,—not even to consent to it; but to strive to see things as they are, and to be himself as he is. Defeat lies in self-surrender."

So it does. Surrender to the mass mind is one of our chief dangers. That we should bear our individual witness is all the more important because, as education becomes more widespread, the dead weight of numbers may pull it down; its attractive power may no longer be sufficient to pull them up. No expenditure and no legislation will ever give it this power. Only one thing will. That is the potent magnetism of living examples scattered about the land, minds of light and sweep, persons that we can admire and envy and seek to emulate. James Russell Lowell said to Harvard at its two hundred and fiftieth anniversary that the ideal of the college should be "a man of culture, a man of intellectual resources, a man of public spirit, a man of refinement, with that good taste which is the conscience of the mind, and that conscience which is the good taste of the soul." Whether or not it produces such men is the test of a university.

# 2
# The Uses of a Liberal Education

Our higher education has two types. One of them is represented by schools of engineering and law, medicine and journalism. The other is represented by the liberal arts colleges. About the first I am going to say almost nothing, since for most of us professional studies need no defense. But liberal studies, the sort of studies that are pursued for their own sake rather than for their utility, do stand in need of defense. To put it bluntly, if they have no use, what is the use of them? Each wave of students, considering how they are to budget their lives, must ask that question anew. On the answer they give to it will depend not only the course of their education, but very possibly the course of their lives. Furthermore, it is a question on which there are two sides. Many people take the view that in these days when the getting of a living is so sternly competitive a business and in all the professions there is so much to learn, liberal studies should be regarded as merely the parsley on the roast, or if you prefer, the frosting on the cake, or the sugar coating on the educational pill. The dean of a well-known medical school told me that he would be just as happy over a good halfback among his applicants as over a Phi Beta Kappa in the liberal arts.

Such studies in his view did supply a buttonhole bouquet which, worn with a careless grace, might help a young gentleman through conversational evenings, particularly if the talk happened to veer toward T. S. Eliot or Jean Paul Sartre. But he regarded them as decorative merely. They did not supply the vitamins and calories of the educational feast; they were something added as garnishing.

I want to raise the question whether he is right. He certainly has a case. And in order not to be unfair, I will begin by stating and stressing some of the arguments commonly used against liberal education.

First, there is an argument that often stirs as a vague protest in the subliminal mind of students, the argument from the price you have to pay for it, not merely the price in money, though that is high and going higher, but also the price in freedom. For many young people the opening of college is the time when shades of the prison house begin to fall, when life must be abjured for books. Four years of it, too! Four years when the sap is rising in one's veins, and adventure calls, and the urge to do things is at its strongest, given over to the companionship of—whom? Primarily not human beings at all, but books—dusty books, dead books, by authors dead and dry as nails. Four years of forcing a reluctant attention, of sitting in dreary classrooms, of dragging the academic ball and chain, while beyond the prison walls the skies are blue and open roads are inviting to the larger world where things are happening.

And what are the books about? Perhaps economics, described by Carlyle as the dismal science, in which all men are supposed to be scrambling for wealth at the expense of their neighbors. Or mathematics, described by a great mathematician as the science in which nobody ever knows what he means, or whether what he says is true. Or history, which is the record, according to Dean Inge, either of events that probably never happened or of events that do not matter. Or philosophy, defined by one practitioner as the finding of bad reasons for what we believe on instinct, and by another as an inverted filter into which whatever goes in clear comes out cloudy. Now people have been known to offer themselves a living sacrifice because they thought that sooner or later a reward would be conferred on them for their high disregard of the flesh, as St. Simeon Stylites chose to divorce himself from the world by living on top of a pillar where normal comforts and contacts were out of the question. But who believes nowadays that one must buy the abundant life with asceticism? Youth was not made for gazing at print through premature glasses; it was made for action and high spirits. We your teachers would vote for the books, but of course with a professional bias—and besides just look at us. The poet's voice is more understanding:

> Gather ye rosebuds while ye may,
> Old time is still a-flying:
> And this same flower that smiles today,
> Tomorrow will be dying.

That is the first argument, the argument from the dreariness of academic drudgery. The second argument is stronger. If the drudgery brought proportionate rewards, it would and should be borne in patience. But it does not. These years of the treadmill, it is said, are on the whole wasted effort. To be sure we hear on all sides that a college education is the condition of getting on. In some fields the statement is plausible. If one is going to be a physician or dentist or engineer, one needs a technical training, and if one wants to form connections with future secretaries of state, experience reveals that it is the part of prudence to go to Yale. But even in fields where the argument seems strongest, as in engineering, there seem to be plenty of contrary cases. Robert Fulton, Thomas A. Edison, Henry Ford, have left firm footprints on the sands of time, but those footprints never passed across the threshold of a college. And if even a technical degree can be dispensed with, how much more readily can one in the liberal arts, which hardly pretend to usefulness. One can no longer take the high line of the Cambridge don of story, who, after demonstrating a very abstruse mathematical theorem, added: "And the best of this, gentlemen, is that this theorem is pure theory with no sort of application anywhere." But if John Dewey is right, there are still fossil remains among us of those academics of old time who thought of an education rather as an aristocratic adornment than as a thing of utility. The Greek aristocrat and the young gentleman of Victorian Oxford had no need to bother their handsome heads about earning a living; a liberal education was for them an aid to the graceful employment of leisure; and some people seem to conceive it so still.

We no longer feel happy about such a view, but the critics tell us that we really have little more to offer. They point out that the classicists staved off the inevitable for a while by insisting that their subjects had transfer value, so that the habits formed in studying them could be applied to other subjects. But the psychologists have undercut this argument by showing that habits are far less transferable than was supposed. And the suggestion that these subjects are widely applicable is met by the critic with an embarrassing insistence that this be shown specifically. You are studying mathematics, for example, often described as a tool subject. Just how often in the past year, or in all your years, have you had occasion to use a trigonometrical theorem or an algebraic equation? And even if you have done so occasionally, was the advantage worth some hundreds of hours of work? You are proposing to study French. How often in the future do you expect to be in a position where the information or ideas you need are inaccessible in English? You are studying Spanish. What is the likelihood of your taking up residence in Spain or in South America, where Spanish will be necessary? You are studying history. Do not even the historians now admit that not one law can be derived from history that will make possible the prediction of any single event? How well have historians done in prophesying American depressions, war, or elections? As for philosophy, the utility of that distinguished subject was suggested very early when the first Western philosopher, Thales, wandering about with his head in the clouds, fell into a well, to the mirth of his more practical neighbors and all their derisive progeny. They have put their view on the matter in the proverb that philosophy bakes no bread. And so of the other subjects. If you ask your father and mother how well they remember and how often they have used the physics and chemistry, the political or economic theory, the astronomy or zoology, the knowledge of *Beowulf* or *Paradise Lost* that they picked up in college, the answer will be strangely hesitant.

The skeptic could say more if we let him. He could point out that students' interest even in Shakespeare may be dulled by en-

30

forced study, so that they never read a page of him later; that some of the humanities, poetry for example, are better grasped in maturity than in youth; that college puts off the apprenticeship in practical life which will in any case be necessary; that a passing grade of seventy is ill preparation for a world of competitive business where you will go under with less than eighty. But I have said enough to indicate the main line of attack. It is simply that a liberal education calls for a great outlay in time, money, and effort, for which little or nothing useful is gained in return.

What is to be said on the other side? Unfortunately the argument in defense of liberal studies is harder to state. But I will try to put it in the following steps. To begin with, I will ask you to examine with me what usefulness really means. When we have got clear about this, I will argue that the studies in question are enormously useful in three ways. First, they are useful *directly* because they satisfy some of the deepest wants in our nature. Secondly, they are useful *indirectly* through enabling us to borrow the best insights and standards of others. Thirdly, if taken seriously, they may permeate with their influence all our thought and feeling and action.

First, then, let us ask the critics a question. You are insisting that the college prove its usefulness: just what do you mean by usefulness? You imply that a thing is useful when it contributes to success, but how do you measure success? Is it success, for example, to make a great deal of money? That is certainly not the whole story, for money is not an end in itself; it too is prized because it is useful, that is, because it is a means to something beyond. Money in itself has no value. If you were on an island, cut finally off from civilization, and your pockets were bulging with bills of large denominations, what would the money be worth? A little, perhaps; it would save one the trouble of gathering leaves if one wanted to build a fire; but that would be about all. Money is literally not worth keeping; its only value is that we can get rid of it in exchange for other things. Well, what are these other things? A better house, we say, a better car, the chance to travel. But then we prize these too for their usefulness, for the something further that they bring us. The ampler house brings us comfort and rest and quiet and a sense of freedom and dignity; the car brings to our family the pleasures of the open road, and their pleasure is reflected in ours; travel enriches us with new impressions and ideas. These are the ulterior things, the self-validating things, that make money and possessions useful. Comfort and quiet and richness of mind are not good because they are good *for* something; they are simply good, good in their own right. And you will notice that all these values are goods of the spirit, goods that lie not in things but in the minds that enjoy them. In the end all useful things are useful because they produce these useless goods that are valued for nothing further; or if you wish, it is precisely the useless things of the world that in the end alone are useful, since only they will give us what we want.

We are now ready to deal with the question whether a liberal education has use. It is clear that the issue is not whether an education will increase our income or our efficiency; it may very well do that; but if it fails to do so, it is not thereby proved to be useless. The issue is a deeper one. It is whether an education does or does not contribute substantially to those ultimate goods on which all usefulness depends. I do not think many of us would hesitate here. It contributes enormously.

It does so in the first place by satisfying directly some of our elemental hungers. One of these is the hunger to know. To be sure, I have sometimes wondered how elemental this is when I have observed how skilful some students are in avoiding the banquets spread before them. "The love of truth," said A. E. Housman, "is the faintest of human passions." And there is no doubt that much that passes as the love of knowledge is really something else, such as the love of finding some place off the beaten track where one can excel, or a mere hobby like that of a friend of mine who collects languages, or a frankly avowed means to a further end, as it is in the subscriber to the *Wall Street Journal.* But when all the impurities have been washed away, there remains, I think, a genuine golden residuum of interest in truth itself.

I am a teacher of philosophy, which is commonly held to be one of the most difficult as well as most useless of all fields of study. Students prowling about in search of what they may most painlessly devour have often asked me what was the use of studying the subject. I have come to see that when they do, it is a radical blunder to stutter out something about how helpful philosophy is in solving business and personal problems. I do not for a moment deny that it is thus helpful. But that is not the real reason why men philosophize. They philosophize because they want to understand the world they live in. I believe that, in some degree or other, everyone wants this. Everyone is a budding philosopher, not perhaps in the sense that he wants to spoil a great many pages with very large words, but in the sense that he is genuinely interested in the great metaphysical problems.

Take one or two of these at random. The old question of free will is the question whether, if I knew all about your body and mind at this moment, I could tell what you would do or say five minutes from now, or whether, so to speak, you could double-cross me by doing something incalculable. One of the clearest heads that ever wrote on the problem, Henry Sidgwick, said that a solution one way or the other would make no practical difference; and yet the problem has fascinated men's thought for thousands of years, and, if Milton is to be believed, is eagerly canvassed by the angels in such spare time as they have. Or take body and mind. I find it impossible to doubt that at the present moment something called ideas in my mind are causing movements of tiny particles in the cells of my head, which movements in turn cause messages to be sent down to my lips and make them move. But how is it done? How can an idea, which has no mass or shape or motion, push solid particles about in a very solid head? If any student can write a paper on this which gives a tenable answer, I should be glad to propose him for a Nobel prize.

Of course if one has no interest in questions of this kind, the effort to answer them will be a dreary business. But the dreariness will belong less to philosophy than to one's own soul. Certainly the great thinkers have not found philosophy a dreary business. As Josiah Royce said, "You cannot think the truth without loving it; and the dreariness which we often impute to metaphysics is merely the dreariness of not understanding the subject—a sort of dreariness for which indeed there is no help except learning to understand." This desire to understand rises in some persons to a passion. Professor Montague of Columbia remarked that "man began to think in order that he might eat; he has now evolved to the point where he eats in order that he may think." Perhaps not many of us

33

could say that of ourselves, but certainly some people can. I like the story that Alcibiades tells in Plato's *Symposium* about his companion in a military campaign, a strange ugly soldier whose immense physical strength was matched only by the delight he took in the play of ideas. "One morning," says Alcibiades, "he was thinking about something that he could not resolve, and he would not give up, but continued thinking from early dawn until noon—there he stood fixed in thought; and at noon attention was drawn to him, and the rumour ran through the wondering crowd that Socrates had been standing and thinking about something ever since the break of day. At last in the evening after supper, some Ionians out of curiosity . . . brought out their mats and slept in the open air that they might watch him and see whether he would stand all night. There he stood all night as well as the day . . . and with the return of light he offered up a prayer to the sun, and went his way." The Western world has never been quite the same since this strange figure stood that way in thought. He showed men an ideal city and gave them the key. Even the tough campaigners who poked fun at him did so with a puzzled respect, for they knew that he had the freedom of that city, and in an instant, from the midst of business or the crowd, could go for refreshment to far places where they could not follow.

But the field of truth is as wide as the world, and philosophy is only one part of it. The mind that wants to know can find fascination along a hundred avenues. Darwin will spend countless fascinated hours in watching the behavior of earthworms, Heisenberg the behavior of atoms, Shapley the behavior of nebulae, Jane Goodall the behavior of apes. One of the most remarkable lectures I ever heard was given by Karl von Frisch, the Austrian zoologist, whose particular interest was bees. He discovered that when a bee finds a new bed of flowers, it is able to report its find to the hive and to supply its colleagues with accurate directions as to the distance, the direction, and the kind of nectar to look for. Von Frisch set out to solve the intricate problem of how it did this, and was able to prove beyond doubt that it was done by a dance that the discoverer performed for its neighbors, in which it indicated the point of the compass by dancing in the right direction, the distance by the number of wiggles, and the nectar by supplying whiffs from a specially collected sample. If you were to ask these scientists what was the use of such knowledge, they might reply, as Faraday did to the person who asked the use of his early studies in electricity, "What is the use of a child? It grows to be a man." But probably in their own minds they would silently register one more philistine. If one wants as much as they do to know the secrets of things, one would not need to ask the question; if one does not, their answer would be unintelligible. Knowledge was their profession; and it has been said that while a trade is something one follows in order to live, a profession is something one lives in order to follow.

This passion of the scholar and the scientist, this love of truth for its own sake, is a quality beyond price. "To love truth for truth's sake," said John Locke in his wise old age, "is the principal part of human perfection in this world, and the seed-plot of all other virtues." This may appear extravagant praise. There seems to be nothing very heroic in ferreting out the facts about bees and earthworms. But put this same pure light, this love of uncolored truth, in one of those fields that are rendered murky by human bias, and "how far that little candle throws its beams." "Things and actions are what they are," said Bishop Butler, "and the consequences of them will be what they will be; why then should we desire to be deceived?" But apparently we do. "We are past masters in the art of throwing dust in our own eyes." How many of the millions who read about Women's Liberation or black militancy can look at the issue with an eye wholly single to the truth of the matter? How often does one find a person who can see in perspective not only the cruelty and intolerance of the system behind the Iron Curtain, but also that which makes it so seductive to millions the world over? A man or a society with a genuine interest in truth is like a gyroscope that may wobble crazily for a while, but will right itself in the end. What seems to some of us most sinister in the reports from behind the Curtain is not so much the suppression of mercy, heavy-fisted as that is, as the suppression of objectivity, the discouragement of the very desire to see things straight. When it is decreed that the issue between Lysenko and Mendel, or between the religious man and the atheist is to be settled by an appeal not to the facts or to reflection, but to the party line, the love of truth itself becomes an offense. And when the love of truth is banished, justice and honor too are on the way out. Archbishop Whately was right that "it makes all the difference in the world whether we put truth in the first place or in the second place."

Now the true defense of the educated mind is that it alone has at once the desire and the discipline to see the truth. This truth may or may not have applications in practice; that is not the test of its value. We even have it on good authority that he that increaseth knowledge increaseth sorrow and makes men sadder as well as wiser. Even so, would you, if you had the choice, prefer to be happier at the cost of living among illusions? You have come to see, perhaps, that the theory of evolution is true, and that its truth renders impossible your old interpretation of Genesis and of much else that you once believed. With the passing of those beliefs there has gone something of your old assurance and peace of mind. But would you be willing to buy back that old assurance at the cost of the knowledge you have gained? I suspect not. There is something wrong with the man who would sell his intellectual maturity for the sake of a return to childhood with its irresponsibilities. "In the long run," as Augustine Birrell says, "even a gloomy truth is better company than a cheerful falsehood." The mature mind, the mind that has escaped the straitjacket of prejudice, superstition and ignorance, the mind that knows the truth about itself and its world and by knowing the truth has been made free, is itself the highest value that education can confer. The courageous clinging to that value by a comparatively few men—Socrates, for example, Galileo, Erasmus, Newton, Darwin—brought our Western intellectual world into being. The Irish poet "AE" has given us their quiet injunction:

No blazoned banner we unfold—
One charge alone we give to youth,
Against the sceptered myth to hold
The golden heresy of truth.

I have mentioned only one of the direct satisfactions that liberal studies bring us, the satisfaction of an understanding mind. But of course there are many others. We are told that a thing of beauty is a joy forever, and many people have testified to this in the province of beauty that they have made their own: the province of poetic speech, or of line and color, or that purest of the arts, music. Again, one of our deepest desires is to be liked by other people. There are no classes in college on the art of social intercourse, yet every day of college life provides discipline in that high art. Oscar Wilde said of Bernard Shaw that he had no enemies, but was much disliked by his many friends. College will not teach you how to avoid enemies; such avoidance is hardly open to one with the strong convictions that an educated mind should have. But it will give you a hundred lessons in the important business of making friends and keeping them.

In theory it is possible to satisfy all these hungers, hungers for the best that has been thought and said and acted and painted and composed in the world, without going to college at all; indeed it has actually been done. John Stuart Mill was one of the best-educated men of his century, but he was never entered as a student in school, college, or university. But it is sad to think of how few Mills there are, how few people succeed in educating themselves merely by efforts after hours. They find that the noblest and purest pleasures are the result of an acquired taste which itself must be won laboriously. That is what college is for: to help one acquire the tastes that make possible the deeper delights. Those who can really hear Bach—and their numbers are not great—tell us that they are transported by him into another and serener world; but to hear Bach is not a matter of walking into a concert hall and sitting down; it is a matter of years, not minutes. So of all truly fine art. Probably much that nowadays passes as such has a streak of charlatanry in it; but only those who have served an honest apprenticeship in these things have the right to bring the charge. And even if Eliot and Picasso are all that their admirers say they are, we shall not find it out by approaching them jauntily and demanding that they stand and deliver. We cannot see till we have eyes to see, and perhaps also some mental spectacles. "Mr. Whistler," said a lady to whom the painter had shown one of his pictures, "I never saw a sunset like that." "Madam," he answered, "don't you wish you could?"

But it is not only the direct enjoyment of the greater values of life that a liberal training gives us; it is also, and secondly, a large indirect enjoyment. Other minds are sounding boards that enlarge our own powers of response. The psychologist William McDougall reminded us that it is an exciting experience to sit in the grandstand with ten thousand other people through the wind and rain of an autumn day and watch a football game, but that if you had to watch that same game sitting in the grandstand in wind and rain alone, it would be a dreary business. Indeed many things remain simply invisible till we see them through others' eyes. This was brought home to me vividly when I first visited Venice. Venice is by any estimate an extraordinary city, but by a double stroke of luck it became for me an enchanted city. The small pension where I was staying happened to be a house where John Ruskin had lived when he was writing *The Stones of Venice*, and on one of its shelves was a battered old copy of this wonderful book. It was just what an unobservant descendant of Thales needed, and from then on I went gaping about the streets of Venice with the book open in my hands, gazing at the Doge's palace and St. Mark's and the Rialto through eyes many times more discerning than my own. Thanks to Ruskin, Venice has been to me ever since a sort of fairy city.

Fortunately, it is not only others' sense of sight that we can borrow, but also something more important, their sense of values. Education, someone has said, is a process of learning to like the right things. Our likes, then, should change as our education proceeds. It is natural that a boy of eight should regard Superman as the creation of genius; if he holds this opinion at eighteen, he is suffering from arrested development; if he holds it at fifty-eight, he is suffering from premature senility. Unhappily, the growth of a formed and independent taste calls, in this country, for exceptional courage and self-reliance. One reason for this, whose relevance is perhaps not at once plain, is that America is the largest market in the world. A company that can produce the right refrigerator or cookbook or washing machine for the average American family has its fortune assured, for the two hundred-odd millions of us are mainly average people with average income and average tastes. This means that America is the paradise of mass production; Dr. Stringfellow Barr has said that mass production is one of our two main contributions to civilization, the other being the idea of a federal union of states. Now mass production is an admirable thing, which is here to stay; but its results are not equally admirable in all fields. In the field of taste it is a catastrophe. The artist or novelist or Hollywood producer who has original gifts knows that if he consults his own idea of what is first-rate, he is not unlikely to wind up in bankruptcy, while if he can manage to hit the dead center of taste, he may make a fortune. No doubt there are persons who, like Henry Clay, "would rather be right than be President," and get their choice; but the pressure on an American artist to compromise his integrity is almost irresistible.

The result is what we see all around us; moving pictures, for example. Our moving pictures alone might make us believe Professor Terman's pronouncement that the average mental age of American adults is fourteen years. What do Americans read? Dean Mott of the Missouri School of Journalism reminded us some years ago of the name of "the most popular author in the annals of American publishing." What would be your guess as to that name? Not Hawthorne or Melville or Henry James, of course, but perhaps Mark Twain or Harriet Beecher Stowe? No, it would take you several guesses more. It was Mrs. E. D. E. N. Southworth, nearly all of whose fifty novels sold more than 100,000 copies, and two of them more than 2,000,000 each. What, one wonders, are the standards of a reading public that would place books of this kind on such a pedestal? Sentimentality, sex, and excitement find it all too easy a business to palm themselves off as artistic worth. Nor is it only in art and literature that counterfeits are common. President Davidson of Union College spoke wisely, I think, when he said, "Americans need to be warned about . . . words and ideas which look much alike, but have different effects. For example, Americans often confuse size with importance, . . . speed with progress, . . . money with wealth, . . . authority with wisdom, . . . religion with theology, . . . excitement with pleasure. . . . " Goethe once spoke of "was uns alle bändigt, das Gemeine," of what enslaves us all, the commonplace. Commonplaceness, the surrender to the average, that good which is not bad but still the enemy of the best—that is our besetting danger.

The danger is the greater because it is so largely invisible and connected so intimately with what is best in American life. In our country the common man rules, and until we can achieve the Platonic utopia, that is perhaps as good a plan as can be devised. But it is fatally easy to go from the proposition that political power should follow the majority to the proposition that taste should follow the majority, a conclusion both false and fallacious. If you accept it, even implicitly, the probable result will be the drowning out of any budding distinction or individuality you may possess. In the great volume of voices you cannot, as the saying goes, hear yourself think; and before long you cease to have any thought worth hearing. How is one to escape mass suffocation? One must get outside the mass to some point from which it can be looked at in detachment. And the best and highest of those points is one that we shall never reach unaided, because the only guides that can take us there are those great spirits of the race who themselves hewed out the trail.

When we look back from such a peak, we see what little lives we were living. We begin to see ourselves as we are. Nobody who has read Meredith's *The Egoist* sees himself again in quite the same light. Nobody can take his motives at face value after reading Freud. Nobody can place himself at the same point in the moral scale after following the long slow advance toward purity of heart in the Old and New Testaments. Of course if the change in perspective meant a disillusionment with the old with no compensating devotion, it would be better to go on with the bleak life of the wasteland. The snob and the pedant are restless creatures because they can neither like what other people like, nor get much from their own sterile idolatries; Sinclair Lewis's Mrs. Dodsworth gives the type. True advance in taste or morals is that in which one falls in love with something better, and therefore is no longer tempted by the old. If you want the doctrine worked out on its moral side, you will find it in a classic sermon by Thomas Chalmers on "The Expulsive Power of a New Affection." Many years ago, when I was doing an obscure turn with the army in France, we had a song that was not quite refined in some of its interpretations, but enormously popular in spite of, or perhaps because of, that. It ran, "How're you going to keep them down on the farm after they've seen Paree?" There is philosophy in that song. Podunk and Zenith do look different as seen from the porches of the Louvre.

This brings us to the last value in liberal studies that I set out to remark on. They give us great direct satisfactions. They serve us indirectly by enabling us to share the insights and standards of first-order minds. Finally, they infuse a new quality into our thought, feeling, and action. It seems to be implied in the ditty that once you have seen Paree, you are ruined as a farmhand. Many people think of a liberal education as a means of escape into a white-collar job and otherwise useless. How often have I been told that all you can do with philosophy is to teach it! Now it is true that to rest the defense of philosophy or history or literature on applicability, in the sense that the theory of gas engines is applicable, is to blunder badly. The main value of philosophy and history and literature lies in what they supply directly, a deeper understanding, a wider knowledge, a finer power of response. But to say that this is their main value does not imply that they lack values in use. These they have abundantly.

The reason they have such uses is that a mind is built, not like a rockpile, but like an organism. If you can add a stone or a thousand stones to the rockpile, none of the original stones will take the least notice or perhaps stir one inch from its place. But you cannot add to your mind an understanding of Plato or Milton or modern Europe and leave the rest of your mind what it was; everything you think or feel or do will be affected by it. It is said that Mendelssohn was once scheduled to give an organ concert, but was delayed; a local organist took his place and did what he could against a sea of inattentive conversation in the hall. Mendelssohn at last arrived, and, slipping unobserved onto the organist's seat, took over the piece he was playing. Suddenly the conversation was hushed and the audience was all ears. It was the same instrument and the same score, but there was one great unmistakable difference. Mendelssohn was at the keys.

I like to think of that incident which, according to Vasari, brought to light the genius of Giotto. The Pope wanted a supreme craftsman to help in making the old church of St. Peter a thing of beauty. He sent his envoy round to the studios of the Italian painters asking for samples of their work. When his envoy came to Giotto in Florence, so the story goes, the painter halted his work briefly and told the envoy to watch. Taking a large sheet of paper, he drew a perfect circle on it with a single stroke of his hand. "Take that to the Pope," he said; "he will understand." The Pope did un-

41

derstand, and Giotto got the appointment. Both knew that genuine mastery can reveal itself not only in a vast spread of painted wall, but in the drawing of a single line.

Now the educated mind is the mind that has achieved mastery of its own powers, and such mastery is reflected through all the detail of one's living. A liberal education impractical? Why there is nothing in the range of our speech or thought, our feeling or action, that it leaves quite as it was! Because the educated man knows the difference between knowledge and opinion, his thought on everything—on his business, on his creed, on the devaluation of the dollar—will be more self-critical and more precise. Because speech is the reflection of thought, his talk on all these matters will have more point and precision and weight. Again, right feeling is largely a matter of right thinking; if a man is honestly convinced that racial discrimination is wrong, the struggle for right feeling is two-thirds won. And besides, feeling is as educable as thought. The person who has really entered into "Rabbi Ben Ezra" or Burns on the field-mouse, or Stephen Benét's *John Brown's Body* can never feel about old age, or four-footed things, or black people, as he did before.

And if his thought and feeling are affected, so surely will his action be. I have been reading lately Thornton Wilder's *The Ides of March*. I felt about his hero, Julius Caesar, though with some reservations, as I felt long ago in reading Froude and Mommsen, that there is something not only fascinating but almost frightening in the man. That extraordinary intelligence so permeated everything he did that the ablest statesmen and generals of his time, when they tried to oppose him, looked as you or I would look if we played chess against Bobby Fischer. He was a great man of action, but he was so because his action embodied the precise and lucid mind that wrote the *Gallic War*, a mind that saw every detail, saw them all in perspective, seized the essential as if by instinct, and conducted a campaign with the economy of a superb artist. And through it all there was so little sign of strain that Caesar almost seemed to be lounging through life. With that serene intelligence sitting on the inner throne, he was not only adequate, but almost effortlessly adequate, to every situation. To corner him was not to defeat him; it was only to give his infinite resourcefulness its chance.

To educate a human mind is not merely to add something to it, but to do something to it. It is to transform it at a vital point, the point where its secret ends reside. Change what a man prizes and you change him as a whole, for the essential thing about him is what he wants to be. Samuel Butler said that there were two rules about human life, a general rule and a special one. The general rule was that everyone could make of himself what he wanted to be, and the special rule was that everyone was more or less an exception to the general rule. Yes, but only more or less an exception. It remains true that as a man thinketh in his heart, so is he. He may cut a wide swath socially, financially, politically, and be a midget. He may be a humble doctor of black people on the rim of the African jungle and be, in the opinion of discerning people, the greatest man alive. What is significant about a person or a people is the invisible things about them, the place where they keep their treasure stored, the unseen sun behind the clouds that determines the orbit of their lives. And curiously enough, it is these unseen things that are most nearly eternal. The educators of the West were those restlessly active people, the Greeks. But not one ship or bridge, not one palace or fortress or temple that their impatient activity erected has come down to us except as a ruin; and the state they built so proudly was already a ruin two thousand years ago. Does anything of them remain? Yes, the Greek spirit remains. The thought of Plato remains, the art of Sophocles, the logic and ethics of Aristotle. Literature, it has been said, is the immortal part of history. No doubt there were hardheaded practical men in Athens who stopped before the door of Plato's Academy and asked what was the use of it all. They and their names have vanished; the little Academy became a thousand academies among nations then unborn. There is a moral, I think, in this history. It is the usefulness, the transcendent usefulness, of useless things.

# 3

# *Education as Philosophy*

Shortly after the Second World War I served as a member of a commission from whose work I gained a great deal of light. It was a commission appointed by the American Philosophical Association, and its assignment was to report on the place of philosophy in American education, both the place it actually held and the place it might ideally hold. We solicited opinions from colleagues in all parts of the country; we received hundreds of letters of advice, complaint, and analysis; we held conferences in Boston, New York, Baltimore, Chicago, San Francisco, Los Angeles, and New Orleans. We listened to ardent Deweyites who would make education more practical, and to Robert Hutchins, who would make it more rigorously intellectual. We got opinions in speech and writing not only from teachers of philosophy, but from businessmen, clergymen, high school teachers, scientists, adult educators, and deans. I want to go back to some of the criticisms of college education that we heard most often, for they were fundamental criticisms; they are perhaps more in order now than they were then; and if they are to be met, it must presumably be in the same way.

In the minds of the people we conferred with, there was a great and justified pride in what our colleges have achieved. At the same time, there was, and still remains, an uneasiness about their product. The young men and women who carry away our degrees are an attractive lot, less attractive indeed in appearance than those of ten or twenty years ago, and rather more self-permissive, but generous, sensitive, alert, and socially concerned.

What of their intellectual equipment? That too is in some ways admirable; for in spite of President Lowell's remark that the university should be a repository of great learning, since the freshmen always bring a stock with them and the seniors take little away, the fact is that our graduates have every chance to be well informed, and usually are so. Yet the uneasiness persists. When it becomes articulate, it takes the form of wishes that these attractive young products of ours had more intellectual depth and force, more at-homeness in the world of ideas, more of the firm, clear, quiet thoughtfulness that is so potent and so needed a guard against besetting humbug and quackery. As the critics warm to their theme, their complaint tends to resolve itself into a bill of three particulars. First, granting that our graduates know a good deal, their knowledge lies about in fragments and never gets welded together into the stuff of a tempered and mobile mind. Secondly, our university graduates have been so busy boring holes for themselves, acquiring special knowledge and skills, that in later life they have astonishingly little in common in the way of ideas, standards, or principles. Thirdly, it is alleged that they reveal a singular want of clarity about the great ends of living, attachment to which gives significance and direction to a life. Here are three grave charges against American education, and I want to discuss them briefly. My argument will be simple, perhaps too simple. What I shall contend is that there is a great deal of truth in each of them, and that the remedy for each is the same. It is a larger infusion of disciplined reflectiveness, of the philosophic habit of mind.

The first charge is that the student's studies are too scattered and fragmented, that they are in need of integration. This charge is a witness to the fact that our knowledge is outrunning our wisdom. In Bacon's day, a man could take all knowledge for his province without exciting open laughter. In our grandfather's day, he could still take a whole college curriculum as his province, and indeed there often was not much to this beyond mathematics and classics. Today a small college will offer a richer variety of courses than the great university of a century ago; and to try to master the offerings of a present-day university would be like trying to put Sears Roebuck and Company into one shopping bag. The Columbia student who was provided a legacy so long as he remained a student—and decided to stay on permanently—knew that he could do so without repetition till his beard became gray. When he tired of the principles of physics, he could go on to the principles of advertising, and if principles of any kind seemed a bore, he could take courses in newspaper practice or debating. What is the student to do in the face of these pitilessly accumulating mountains of courses? If he specializes, he loses much that he feels he should know. If he scatters himself over the curricular landscape, he ends in universal superficiality.

The instrument that the college has traditionally placed in his hands for dealing with this problem is the elective system, under which the task of selecting and unifying his studies is left to him. The vast vogue of this system in America is due to something very like an academic instinct of imitation. When President Eliot introduced it at Harvard in 1872, it was only for the senior class, and was designed to give science a fair field in competition with the strongly entrenched classics. In 1879 he extended it to juniors; in 1884 to sophomores; ten years later the only requirements left were English and a modern language, and the idea was sweeping the country. There was something large and generous and democratic about it; there were no longer any privileged subjects; there was to be a fair field for all and special favors for none. Since those days we have amended the system in this way and that, but within its general design our colleges and universities still live.

Now, that this system has not been a mere failure is clear enough. Turn any hungry young mind loose in the lush pasture of the contemporary curriculum, and he is bound to get nourishment. But he has so often got indigestion too that doubts about the dietary have troubled the rest of countless baffled deans. The very premises of the elective system are now freely called in question. What are those premises? There seem to be three of them; and the curious thing is that when they are brought out and looked at, they do seem plainly false.

The first premise is that the subjects and courses of the curriculum are of approximately equal value. Well, they are not. The main aim of a liberal education is to give understanding of nature, human nature, and society. In the understanding of nature, physics is more important than meteorology. In the understanding of human nature, psychology is more important than comparative linguistics. In the understanding of society, ethics and political theory are incomparably more important than railroad management. To introduce democratic notions of equality into this sphere of values, to suppose that because two subjects appear in the catalogue with equal hours and credits and equally skilled and devoted exponents, they are therefore of about equal educational value, may be natural enough for openhearted youth. It is nonsense, and costly nonsense, none the less.

Secondly, the elective system assumes that you can compound an education out of hours and credits. Now hours and grades and credits are convenient things. They keep registrars busy and happy, just as appendices do surgeons, and they have forestalled endless adolescent mischief. If anyone were to set down as of no account a diploma guaranteeing that a student had been corporeally present through forty courses and 1,600 hours while we of the faculty talked, I should prefer that he smiled when he said it. But does the fact that a student has swallowed these forty capsules mean that he has so assimilated them as to have become a mobile, mature, and well-knit mind? That does not seem to follow, and if it did, the credit-hour system would not measure it. What it measures is an accumulation of piecemeal achievements, in which the mind of depth and power and scope may come out well below the gradgrind.

Thirdly, the elective system assumes that the student is competent himself to fix the pattern of his education. The trouble with this is that it attributes to him at the beginning what, with good fortune, he can hope to get only at the end. If someone who had brooded long and deeply over human experience were turned loose in the Harvard or Chicago curriculum, he could presumably bypass

48

some hundreds of courses and make straight for the essential few. But freshmen, in my experience, have not habitually done such brooding; they are far too healthy. And there is nothing in the healthiest of mere instincts that will tell one that Plato is better reading than Norman Mailer or Dale Carnegie. The student or someone else must try them and see. If the student does it for himself, he will spend much of his time in sifting chaff. Have we any right to ask him to do that, or his parent to subsidize him while he does it? We have not. The business of a college is to put at the student's disposal the best possible models of good thinking and good taste. As Professor Montague of Columbia has said, each student at the start is "intellectually and culturally naked. Why should we expect him in the name of 'individuality' and 'self-realization' to repeat all that the race has learned by generations of trial and error?"

The elective system thus presents the student with a vast variety of subjects at a time when he lacks the means of selecting or coordinating. The problem of selection is being solved by a return, not so much to required courses as to alternative programs, each prescribed in its main outline. But the problem of coordinating knowledge cannot be solved by manipulating courses. What is wanted is not a closer juxtaposition of hard round pellets, but something intellectual, organic, and inward, the sort of unity of command that a seasoned mind has over its resources, a unity based on the habitual reflective cross-fertilization of the parts. Integration of knowledge does not mean that one remembers the facts of political science when one has gone on to economics, and of economics when one takes a course in ethics, but that one understands political movements as modified by economic laws, and both in the light of those moral ideals which serve as a dynamic and corrective in every field of practice.

Now what this demand for the integration of knowledge amounts to, I suggest, is a demand for the philosophic mind. To philosophize is to try to understand; to understand is to explain to oneself; to explain is to relate. When any fact is reflected on with a view to understanding, it sends out tendrils to other facts, and since these reciprocate, they all tend to be woven into one firm extended fabric. There is no subject that does not, when the life of reflection

49

gets into it, begin to stir uneasily in its little hard academic pot and send feelers over its side. Physics burgeons into metaphysics, poetry into psychology and aesthetics; to the reflective mind "there are no islands any more." It has been the traditional business of philosophy to take the world as a picture puzzle and try to fit the pieces together; it is in that attempt that its classic problems arise. We all believe in physics, for example, and that means that for every movement of our body there is a physical cause. We also believe that we sometimes go to movies or attend concerts because we want to; and a want is not a physical cause. How are you going to put those things together? We all believe in psychology, and that means that for every mental event, including of course our choices, there is a cause, given which it must happen as it does. Most of us believe also, when we send a thief to jail, that he could have chosen otherwise, and we treat him as if he could. How are we going to put those things together? The capacity of the average man and even the college student to live in a honeycomb of unconnecting little cells is marvelous. A student will be an expert biologist on six days of the week; on the seventh he will go to church and recite "I believe in the resurrection of the body" without even a sense of difficulty. He will study economics and accept its conclusions about tariffs, monopolies, and taxes; he will then go home and cast a cordial vote for candidates whose views are the contradictories of his economic convictions.

You may say that he doesn't need to be a philosopher to avoid this; all he needs is an interest in thinking things out coherently for himself. I answer that that precisely is what I mean by philosophy. I am not arguing that Professor X's desiccated teachings about the syllogism or fusty old Professor Y's lectures on Descartes-to-Kant are going to save education. I am not thinking of philosophy as courses in philosophy or even as a subject exclusive of other subjects. I am thinking of it in its old Greek sense, the sense in which Socrates thought of it, as the love and search for wisdom, the habit of pursuing an argument where it leads, the delight in understanding for its own sake, the passionate pursuit of a dispassionate reasonableness, the will to see things steadily and see them whole. It is a bent and temper of mind that can show itself in any field; indeed some distinguished educators have held that philosophy would do its work most effectively if the department were abolished and all teachers taught philosophically.

This does not mean that the teacher of poetry should give up poetry for theory and that the teacher of history should retailor himself into a second-rate metaphysician. It means that if a student has a teacher of literature like A. C. Bradley or a teacher of history like R. H. Tawney, literature or history, without ceasing to be itself, will become a liberalizing agency of new power. Philosophy should not be a competitor of poetic and historical teaching; it should be part of them; they should be shot through with it. Just as English is every teacher's business, so it is every teacher's business to awake the questioning mind, to argue things out with all who wish it, to justify his tastes on demand or even without demand, to regard fact at every point as an invitation to theory. Whether this activity is called philosophy is of small account. But unless it is present in this pervasive fashion, not as one academic loaf ranged on the shelf beside others but as the yeast in all of them, the integration that is so much needed will never be achieved.

Now for the second current criticism made of our educational products. I state it in the words of Walter Lippmann:

> There is no common faith, no common body of principles, no common body of knowledge, no common moral and intellectual discipline. . . . We have established a system of education in which we insist that while everyone must be educated, yet there is nothing in particular that an educated man must know.

In the light of the judgments commonly passed upon us by foreign visitors, this criticism seems strange. What they usually complain is that we are all so much alike. "The distinction of America," wrote Lowes Dickinson, "is her absence of distinction. No wonder Walt Whitman sang the 'Divine Average.' There was nothing else in America for him to sing." And if we have so painfully much in common as our foreign critics say, how can we have so little in common as Mr. Lippmann says?

The answer is that Mr. Lippmann is not thinking about the facades of our minds, but of what lies behind them. He is suggesting that educated Americans have not a broad enough cultural hinterland which they can occupy and explore together. When, after dinner, the physician and the engineer meet, only to

51

find that the physician knows nothing of turbines and the engineer nothing of serums, they can communicate, to be sure; but their communication is too often Yea, Yea and Nay, Nay; and when it is more than that, it comes too often of evil, or what they regard as such, taxes, operations, or the Mets. Each would like to make contact with the other, for they are both Americans and therefore well disposed; but they find that they must either meet on ground that is hardly worth occupying or else forgo meeting altogether. The great uncrowded spaces where joint exploration is always a significant adventure and the meeting of minds an excitement and delight, the spaces of religion and art and morals and literature and speculation, are too often half-mythical regions, thought of (if at all) with a passing wistfulness, rather than solid ground to be possessed and used. This is an area that educated men should own in common, a preserve to which the key should be provided by every B.A.—to say nothing of postgraduate degrees. "What do these letters mean?" said the small boy, poring over a university catalogue, to his father. "Here is M.D., D.D., LL.D." "I suppose," said the father wearily, "that they mean 'Mairzy doats, and dozy doats and little lambsey divey.'" One is tempted at times to think he was right.

Why is it that our degrees have not served to open a common preserve of the universal human interests? It is largely because the liberal theory of education is being superseded by another theory, the vocationalist. This theory says that education should be preparation for life, life here meaning one's lifework, or more briefly, one's job. It should be remembered that our higher education is on a scale that is quite without parallel or precedent. In 1970 we had 1,670 four-year colleges and universities, and the proportion of young adults with college degrees has almost tripled since 1940. The great surge of enrollment is obviously connected with the conviction that in our technological society an education is necessary if a job is to be assured. The pressure upon students from their homes, from their own impatience, and from a society in which everyone is trying to get on is all but irresistible, and they insist on appraising a subject in terms of how it will help them too to get on.

This vocationalist influence is felt in every department of study. Consider the languages. First the utility of Latin and Greek falls under suspicion and there is a flocking away to French and German, which is in turn succeeded by a flocking away from them into Spanish. The fact that French and German are keys to richer stores of thought and literature than Spanish seems to weigh little against the fact that Spanish may be of some conceivable, though remote, use in business with Latin America. In our universities the liberal arts college is being surrounded by more and more imposing professional and technical schools, whose long arms are reaching down into the college and recasting its curriculum. The tendency in many places is to leave the cultural subjects to women, and for the men, concerned about their professional future, to confine themselves to what seems to have practical bearing. Little by little the old liberal hub of the wheel is dissolving and flying off along the spokes. Is it any wonder that in becoming effective specialists, our educated men have so often paid the price by becoming defective human beings, who have lost the language, because they have lost the principles, interests, and standards, of the universally human?

I think that hub should be restored. I think it should be strengthened, and that philosophy should form a part of it. Why philosophy? Because in all times philosophers have been connoisseurs of unity in diversity. For example, in spite of the differences in what and how men think, they have been convinced immemorially that there are certain principles of evidence and proof that hold alike for every subject and every mind, and they have formulated these principles in the science of logic, which is, or should be, common property.

They have sought to do the same for art and conduct. The art world of today has gone beyond Dali's droopy watches and Warhol's regimented soup cans to what in many cases looks like calculated chaos. We have ingenious sculptures that look like eggs, but are really birds or ships or the Soul's Awakening; we have poems that, eschewing both sound and sense, awaken nothing but puzzlement. What we need, I suppose, is not to rail at these things or to Oh! and Ah! about them, but to judge them through understanding them; and to do that we must learn to think straight about what art is trying to do, which is the business of aesthetics.

Consider again the place of philosophy in our students'

thought about conduct. They read their anthropology and sociology books, full of piquant tales about human custom, which show, as Chesterton said, that

The wildest dreams of Kew are the facts of Khatmandu,
The crimes of Clapham chaste in Martaban,

and they find the inference tempting that there is really nothing right or wrong but thinking makes it so, and that anyone who at this time of day believes in objective standards is a bit of a fogy. In this they are vastly fortified by finding that some encyclopaedic but muddled people like Sumner and Westermarck agree with them. To generous youth this new blend of sophistication with infinite tolerance is very attractive. Of course, they have never really thought that the difference between fascism and democracy was a matter of arbitrary taste; and they are showing in the most convincing of all ways that whatever a little perverse philosophy may have done to their heads, their hearts are right. Now the best cure for a little philosophy is more philosophy. The great tradition of ethical thought that starts with Socrates says not only that there are moral standards as objective as the multiplication table, but that if we probe into men's minds to their ultimate intrinsic values, we shall find that they all agree. Just as there is no Chinese logic or American logic, but only logic, so there is no Russian or American scale of values, but only a real better and worse; and if we differ about them, as of course we do, what that proves is not that there is no real better and worse, but that one of us is still muddled as to what he means and wants.

Now if, as Mr. Lippmann says, we are in need of common principles and standards which will enable us to discuss our differences in belief and art and conduct with interest, mutual understanding, and some hope of agreement, where can we turn more profitably than to this great tradition of reflective thought about the nature and end of man? How can we better save ourselves from the centrifugal specialisms of our time than to come back to this common center of all reflective life, this inward light which is so objective and universal precisely because in each of us it comes from "the deep heart's core"?

But we must hasten on to the third and last of our current criticisms of education. To how many of our students has it given any clear faith for living, any set of reasoned convictions on what is ultimately worth while, any philosophy of life to which they can give themselves wholeheartedly?

Such a faith did flourish in this country once. The people who founded the country had it; the people who founded our older colleges had it. It is now largely dissolved away by "the acids of modernity." The book on which the faith of our fathers rested and which gave them guidance is becoming that well-locked thing, a classic. President Klapper of Queen's College reported that three out of five college seniors did not know what "the patience of Job" meant and pronounced the name "job"; he also reported incidentally that he found college students unable to list in chronological order Moses, Christ, Mohammed, and Luther, though none of them came within five hundred years of any other. The religious interest and the religious outlook of the older America is vanishing, and nothing has yet appeared to fill the void. Youth needs something to give a sense of direction to its life, to govern its major choices, to deliver it from cynicism and triviality, to give it freedom and scope and confidence. Where is it to get this? It once got it from the churches. The universities are replacing the churches as the real centers of light and leading. Do they supply such a faith for living? No.

That is the criticism. How are the colleges to meet the challenge implicit in it? Some would meet it by large compulsory doses of American history and American ideals. I suspect that most of us, without denying that more of such study would be well, would see in such a program too much of a replica of certain other nationalistic programs to make us wholly easy. The new design for living must not be provincial or even national; it must aim at the sort of validity that will carry suspicious and skeptical youth along by its intrinsic reasonableness. Is it any wonder that in this situation many are turning with an inquiring look to philosophy? Many indeed are turning to it in the hope of finding an external bolster with which they can prop up sectarian faiths. In this they are doomed to disappointment. Philosophy is, or should be, a single-minded pursuit of truth, and a philosophy that accepts briefs is therefore a contradiction in terms. The man who takes the road of reason honestly does not know where he is going to come out. There is no set of beliefs of which you can say, "This is what philosophy says," for philosophy, like life, is in course of growth and change, and no two philosophers quite agree. And if it has no agreed-upon creed or message, does it have anything important to offer?

I think it has something of the utmost importance to offer, something more important than any belief because it is the source of all true beliefs. That is the spirit of reasonableness. Edward Caird used to say to his students: It is important that a belief should be true, and it is important that it should be reasoned, but it is *more* important that it should be reasoned than that it should be true. A belief that is true but unreasoned is at the mercy of the sophistries of the day. A belief that is false but also reflective carries with it the means of its own amendment. To be sure, philosophy is skeptical; reason builds by first destroying; it is apt to start by pulling one's house about one's ears. But it destroys in order to rebuild, and perhaps it is better to live in a modest house of one's own, built by authentic insights and the sweat of one's own narrow brow, than in something more imposing that one has inherited without question from authority.

So when I suggest that philosophy lies at the heart of education, it is not *a* philosophy that I am urging on you, but the philosophic temper, the habit of criticism and self-criticism, the tying of one's self-respect to being reasonable in belief and behavior. It is not a temper peculiar to philosophers, who have sometimes been sadly lacking in it; and it may be a quiet, powerful force in business, on the bench, and at the bar, in literature, journalism, or any other profession, as well as in the academic life. It inspires confidence wherever it appears, because its interest is not in personal advantage but in seeing straight, in objectivity, in clear vision and fair judgment. This is the best fruit of education, not the mastery of some technical art or of an encyclopaedic knowledge, valuable as these things are. Without judgment the technologist is a philistine and the polymath a bore. They need that ancient advice of the Proverbs, "With all thy gettings, get understanding." Perhaps the rest of us do too.

# 4

# In Defense of the Humanities

What place should the humanities have in a liberal arts college? The answer depends, I suppose, on how much they contribute to the maturing of the student's mind. And how much they contribute will be appraised differently by persons with differing standards of value. If one appraises achievement by income bracket, one may consider business management important, economics less so, and history, with the first of the Fords, as "bunk." If one thinks that personal adjustment to others is the essential, one may be ready, like a friend of mine who was a professor of education, to relegate both the sciences and the humanities to the borders of the curriculum and place at its center the discussion of such things as inferiority complexes and marital relations. In short what we put first in education depends on what we put first in life. As T. S. Eliot says: "to know what we want in education we must know what we want in general, we must derive our theory of education from our philosophy of life."

That makes our problem difficult. Any appraisal of the humanities in education, if it is to carry real conviction, must rest its case on a philosophy. If we are to convince a doubter that music or mathematics or literature is important, we must be prepared to state and defend our standard of importance itself; for if you hold that music is more worth study than mathematics and I that mathematics is worth more than music, our differences are bound to come back to this in the end. Not that the values one assigns to music or mathematics are consciously deduced from any sort of principle, but they imply a principle nevertheless, and often the best way to clear the air is to bring this principle to light.

Now one of the major facts about present-day American life is precisely its confusion about standards of worth, and above all its confusion of instrumental with intrinsic goods, of means with ends. It may be helpful to illustrate this confusion from three areas where we are justly proud of our achievement—wealth, freedom, and leisure.

Everyone knows that the average American has more income, motorcars, dresses and suits of clothes, tinted bathtubs, and telephones, cubic feet of housing, and years of life at his disposal than anyone else. Our possession of these things is described as our high "standard of living." I would not depreciate them for a moment. Indeed I feel pretty sure that when peoples of less wealth and energy charge us with materialism because we are interested in such things, they are green with envy. But while observing the mote in other people's eyes, we may well grant that there is a beam in our own. It can hardly be denied that we often do take houses, cars, and gadgets as goods in themselves, while the truth is that they are not. If we say that they are, we are confusing means with ends. No motorcar, for example, not even a golden Cadillac, is in itself an end worth seeking. It may be a very fertile means to things that *are* worth having for themselves—refreshment, the delights of the open road, wider contacts with persons and things—but it is not something in which our aims can come to rest, and in working ourselves into thromboses in order to gather into our hands as many such means as possible, we may be only exemplifying Santayana's description of a fanatic as one who redoubles his effort when he has forgotten his end.

There is a like confusion about freedom. We are right in prizing freedom—freedom to think and say what we wish, to create as much beatnik poetry or formless art as we feel moved to, to proclaim the absolute truth of all the thirty-nine articles plus some fortieth one of our own. Nevertheless, freedom merely as absence of restraint has no value. It is of value because it is a condition of something else that it may lead to. If people can use it to advantage, it is a great instrumental good; if they are not ready for it, it may be their undoing. "Teacher," said the disillusioned little philosopher in the progressive school, "*must* I do what I want today?" We regard with dismay some of the newly emerging African peoples, who, with an opportunity to accept freedom on American lines, look the gift horse in the mouth. But there is realism behind their hesitation. They know that freedom may be, and has been, a means to anarchy as well as order. Bertrand Russell once wrote a book on *Roads to Freedom*. But he would agree, I suspect, that freedom is not the end of any road but a road itself which may lead to a larger life or to chaos.

We must say the same about leisure. The fact that so many look to it passionately as an end is a dreary commentary on the dullness of their work; mere escape seems heaven. That this is an old story is suggested by the fact that the Greek word for work, *ponos*, comes from the same root as the Latin word for sorrow, *poena*. In recent times there has been a steady pressure to cut down a twelve-hour to a ten-hour to an eight-hour day or less, a six-day to a five-day or even a four-day week. Less work, more leisure, is the great hope. It hardly becomes us academics, much of whose work we should want to do anyhow, to be critical here. We can point out, however, that the new leisure is generating an unexpected problem—what to do with it when achieved. Men who have worked all their lives for leisure get it at last on retirement, and too often find it a mirage. They have learned too late that what counts is not leisure merely, but something else which, to an active and interested mind, leisure may bring.

What is that something else? Suppose we have got rid of these confusions between means and ends and want to know what makes any experience in itself worth while; what is this essential factor? I cannot argue the matter out, as a philosopher should; there is no time for that. I can only give dogmatically my own often-repeated answer and hope for a tolerant hearing. First, the only thing in the world that is good in itself is experience. But that experience must be stamped with two marks: it must fulfil some natural capacity or demand of our nature, and it must come to us, as it normally will if it thus fulfils, suffused with satisfaction or pleasure. There is nothing new or heretical in this view; it is essentially Aristotle, though none the worse for that. It holds that human beings are bundles of impulses seeking fulfilment, and that the natural life as well as the good life lies in realizing these impulses as fully and harmoniously as may be. This is just as true for Willie Mays as for Einstein or Picasso. Since what their differing natures prescribe for them is different, the good life for them will be different in its content. But it will be the same in principle; it will be the fulfilment, and the happy fulfilment, of what nature has given them. This is not a doctrine of selfishness, for if fulfilment is good for me, it is also good for you; reasonableness will call for justice, and at times sacrifice.

If anything is to be intrinsically good, then, three things are necessary, and if any one of them is taken away, the value too disappears. For one thing, value lies in experience. If there is no life on Mars, there is nothing of value there, though there may be minerals and gases that might be means to value; and if minds were to cease on earth at this moment, nothing of intrinsic value would remain even in the Louvre or the British Museum. Secondly, if an experience fulfils no impulse, need or demand, it is valueless again. I recently asked an eminent philosopher of my acquaintance why he had not written on aesthetics, since he had written on nearly everything else in philosophy. He answered that it was because on this side of his nature he was congenitally defective; for example, he could never carry and could barely recognize any tune, even "God Save the Queen." For him the Fifth Symphony would be a mere noise, because there was nothing in him to which it could give expression; it was not really music at all. Thirdly, an experience bare of satisfaction or pleasure is without value. This does not deny that painful disciplinary experiences may be good as means, but it does suggest that people who deliberately seek these ends are morally confused. If you can take no pleasure whatever in the Fifth Symphony, it is idle to say that for you it is good.

I have gone through this long explanation because my case for the humanities depends on it. If one accepts it, the value of the humanities, indeed their overwhelming value, will be apparent. The aim of education is to help us, and through us others, to get the most out of life. Men get the most out of life only by the zestful fulfilment of faculty. Of all academic studies the humanities contribute to this fulfilment most broadly and most directly.

Are there any other disciplines that might be taken as serious rivals of them? Three have been suggested: technical or vocational training, the social sciences, the physical sciences. How serious are their claims?

As for vocational training: a respected teacher of mine, John Dewey, used to hold that any subject could be educative, that there was something absurd in saying that French irregular verbs liberated the mind while cooking and carpentry, intelligently taught, did not. Now I should certainly not care to enter the lists for everything that passes as a humanity, and I agree that there is a place for technical and vocational courses. But surely that place is not the liberal arts college. Why? Not because they are unimportant, nor merely because their content is so often better mastered on the job, but because they represent a different kind of interest from that of liberal studies—the interest in skills. Such skills are means rather than ends. They may, of course, be very sophisticated means to very valuable ends. Whenever I go to a dentist, I feel how important it is that someone should be able to extract teeth skilfully. Still this importance is not the same kind of importance as that of the illumination brought by the historian or the philosopher, or the enrichment of feeling brought by music. A liberal activity is one that is, and may legitimately be, pursued for its own sake; tooth extraction qualifies for much, but not for that. The two activities belong to different curricula.

What of the social sciences? They belong beyond doubt among liberal studies. No one can study the ways and attitudes of peoples remote from us in place and civilization without enlarged views of our own ways and attitudes. Anthropology is cultural travel, and like travel in the flesh, it brings us back with wider horizons; "what do they know of England who only England know?" Still, the social sciences, valuable as they are as a supplement to the humanities, are clearly no substitute for them. The reason is one often insisted on in their own circles, namely that their business is with facts, not with values, or at least with values treated as facts. The sex practices of the French or the Trobriand Islanders *are* such and such; the religious ceremonies of the Aztecs or the Hittites *were* such and such. How much better or worse they are than of those of Paris or Budapest, the social scientists commonly tell us, it is not for scientists to say. Nor is it for us to protest this self-denying ordinance. What we can say is that if the appraisal of attitudes and beliefs, as well as the knowledge of them, is central to the liberal arts, then the social sciences, essential as they are, will not be in the middle of the picture; they will be somewhere to the right or left of center.

The arch rival of the humanities in these days is neither vocational nor social study, but physical science. It has been pushed into a new importance by two circumstances that seem at first glance rather remote. For one thing, a powerful nation which has chosen to be hostile to us, but which we supposed far behind us culturally, has shown a mastery of the sort of science used in armament and space technology which, if ever used to implement their hostility, might destroy everything we prize, ourselves included. The Russians achieved this mastery by channeling masses of their best students into science, and exacting high performance from them. We are told that unless we can keep abreast or ahead of them on the scientific side, we cannot maintain military equality, and if we lose that, we may in time lose all. Hence we have had pleas from the government, with support from many foundations, for more science, and more rigorous science in our schools and colleges. Secondly, the 51 countries that formed the United Nations have grown to 130. Most of the newcomers are backward, poor, frustrated, clamorous for scientific and technological help from anyone who can give it. There are only two nations that can possibly give it in anything like adequate quantity, Russia and the United States. If we do not give it to them, Russia will, and as a result will come to dominate their economy and their minds. If we are to prevent that, we can do it only by giving a larger place to science in education and by vastly enlarging the number of our scientists.

Lord Snow has made us familiar with the idea that there are two cultures among us, the first a traditional one based on the humanities, the second a newer and smaller one based on physical science. As science grows more technical, the gulf between the two cultures widens. Even now they can hardly communicate with each other. Ask any group of college graduates what is the significance of the notable experiment by Yang and Lee in which they disproved the principle of parity, and you may draw a complete blank. Ask them what the second law of thermodynamics is (a question Snow considers to be for the scientist about on the level of "Have you read any work of Shakespeare?" for the humanist) and you will all too probably draw another blank. Even if you go to the very bottom and ask a question like "What is mass, or acceleration?" (the scientific equivalent of "Can you read?") you may still get only embarrassed silence. What all this points to, he thinks, is a shocking and complacent scientific illiteracy, which may have been excusable in the Victorian era but is shameful in the twentieth century and in the West. Unless the level of scientific interest and literacy can be raised, the needed number of scientists will probably not be forthcoming; unless the needed number is forthcoming, we shall lose the cold war, to say nothing of a hot one. Only by a concerted gigantic effort to give science a higher place in our interest and knowledge can we hope to save the future for the sort of society we believe in.

Lord Snow's case is a strong one. For those of us who have spent our lives in college teaching it is also a disquieting one, because we do not know how to deal with it. We are told that we must change our educational scale of values in view of a danger that we have no adequate means of estimating. We cannot enter the secret places of the Kremlin heart or head; we do not know the needed technical facts about our comparative military position; we do not know whether, even if we made an all-out effort to help the uncommitted nations, they would not still, for the sake of visionary ends, choose the more regimented way of life. We do not want to be unpatriotic; we do not want to be uncharitable; but neither do we want to gamble with our educational values in a game of Russian roulette. There are those who would draw from Snow's warning the conclusion that the humanities have had their day in the educational sun, that the wave of the future is with the sciences, and that it is high time we mounted that wave. Let us give history, philosophy, and literature a long-needed rest. Let us give our college programs a new intellectual tone and rigor by putting the physical and biological sciences, with their great instrument, mathematics, at the center of the curriculum.

With this reasoning I cannot agree. The humanists have long been beleaguered; I suggest they have retreated far enough; and that it is time for them to dig in and hold their line. My feeling about this springs largely from two convictions.

The first is that if the nation needs more knowledge of mass, acceleration, and thermodynamics, as no doubt it does, it also needs, and still more conspicuously, better values, more widely diffused. We need them even to achieve that influence outside our borders which the friends of science hold so essential. Many of us have been dismayed of late to find that uncommitted peoples, when given a chance to choose between the two great ways of life, have preferred not only neutrality, but a neutrality tinged with hostility. Of course much of this hostility is directed against a scarecrow with an imperialist head and grasping colonialist arms, manufactured in Moscow. Unhappily some of it has been conjured up by an image of America exported from our own shores—by Hollywood, with its adolescent drumming on violence and sex, and by a formidable list of writers from Nobel prizemen down. It seems to be the fashion among these writers to regard as a Pollyanna doctrine any supposition that men are pulled from ahead by high motives, and as clear-eyed realism the assumption that they are pushed from behind by their biology, which is very like that of goats. We in this country may not have met in our circle of friends Sinclair Lewis's Elmer Gantry, or Faulkner's neighbors of Yoknapatawpha County, or the shufflers along Tobacco Road, or Norman Mailer's men in uniform. But people who know this country only from abroad do not have our means of supplementing these pictures. They take them, together with the newspaper reports from America with their stress on gangsters, jail riots, political corruption, and the rates for murder and divorce, as reflecting the facts of American life. Naturally they are not greatly drawn by what they see.

What this suggests is that if we are to win the respect or emulation of other peoples, we must see to it that they have a less distorted picture of us. But suppose they had the picture in full color and detail, how attractive would they find it? I fear that even a sympathetic observer would carry away one overwhelming impression, namely that of the disparity between quantity and quality in American life. I have discussed that disparity in another talk of this series, but let me illustrate it. As one drives across the country, one finds that as a rule the most impressive buildings in the successive towns are the high schools—admirably constructed, lighted, financed, and equipped. But inside these very modern buildings we have a long way to go before we overtake the German gymnasium or the French lycée in rigor of teaching and seriousness of intellectual work. When one sees the sprouting television antennae on the lonely farmhouse, or the forest of them along even the poorer streets in our towns, one can only think how much this triumph of technology might do in lifting the general level of idea and feeling; and then one recalls the recent outcries of parents against the invasion of their living rooms by crime and brutality, to say nothing of the huckstering during dinner of laxatives and deodorants. Our newspapers, particularly the Sunday ones, are masterpieces of production and volume; an astonished English writer points out that "the Sunday issues *alone* of one American daily consume yearly the annual growth of a forest the size of Staffordshire (1250 square miles)." Are they worth the price? Irving Babbitt's answer, given when these papers were much smaller than they are now, was: "The American reading his Sunday paper in a state of lazy collapse is perhaps the most perfect symbol of the triumph of quantity over quality that the world has yet seen." Once more, we have foundations that give most generously to the support of artists. Have these artists anything to say that is commensurate with the support or the publicity they receive? Many excellent critics have questioned it.

There is no need to multiply instances. The conclusion they suggest is clear enough; we are long on technology; we are short on standards. We have tended to apply our democracy to values themselves, forgetting that to have values *is* to put some things above others. We have too often regarded the insistence on high standards as intolerant or presumptuous, and the serious pursuit of them as the business of the egghead. This has not always been so. A hundred years ago a college education was a rather rare and distinguished accomplishment, sought after wistfully by the young of high purpose. Now that it has become a commonplace, the pride in distinction that used to attach to it is largely gone, and one cannot assume in college graduates a disciplined taste or any special interest in things of the mind. Professor Douglas Bush writes: "In a survey made in 1956, only 17 percent of American adults were found to be reading books, as compared to 31 percent in Canada, 34 percent in Australia, and 55 percent in England; 57 percent of our high school graduates and 26 percent of our college graduates had not read a single book during the preceding year; of the college graduates, 9 percent could not name the author of any one of twelve famous books in English, and 39 percent could not name more than three; 45 percent could not name any recently published book." For those of us who think ourselves the best educated nation in the world, these are penitential figures.

If they are correct, the proposal that we de-emphasize the humanities in favor of science or technology is a prescription admirably calculated to make the disease worse. We need, not less of what the humanities can give us, but very much more. For we are suffering from a creeping standardless mediocrity, an almost universal, apathetic compromise with vulgarity.

Once in a while the lowly worm of taste does turn, and show what can be done by those who take values seriously; for example, when the lobbyists for Madison Avenue sought the privilege of plastering our new highways with beer and cigarette signs, the lovers of the American countryside rose and slew them. In sheer numbers the army of educated men and women in this country is overwhelming and irresistible; by a judicious use of its patronage it could force Hollywood to grow up; it could shame the tabloids off the stands; it could transform radio and television; it could make good bookstores flourish across the country; it could revive the lost art of conversation; it could give politics substance and dignity; it could do virtually anything at all. But as David Riesman has said, "While college education undoubtedly serves on the whole to raise the cultural level of America, there is also a countertendency in which the unprecedented millions who have demanded a college degree have not so much risen as pulled the colleges down." The salt may lose its savour if used to season too much broth. One cannot assume in these days that the college educated will stand together or stand for anything.

Now values are the special interest of the humanities; the study of the humanities is the best tried method we know of acquiring mature and critical standards. And my first reason for resisting the pressure to put anything, even science, in their place is that for a people already drifting away from the humanities to weaken their influence deliberately is to take just the wrong turning. We need the heaviest possible infusion of what the humanities alone can bring.

My second reason is one that has formed itself only slowly. It is that, regarded simply as education, the humanities are in advance of science. This is sometimes conceded by self-appraising scientists. Some years ago I attended a fascinating debate in the Senate House of the University of London, held before a convention of British physical scientists and presided over by the president of the British Association for the Advancement of Science, himself distinguished both as chemist and as classical scholar. The question at issue was the comparative educational value of the sciences and the humanities, and to my surprise the vote of this audience of scientists was heavily for the humanities. What their reasons were I do not know. Mine would be three.

First, the discipline supposed to be distinctive of science can be gained from the humanities equally well. It is commonly admitted that what counts in scientific study is not the achieving of particular results but the grasp of scientific method, the training in observation, in the forming of hypotheses, in working out their implications, in verifying them, and generally in thinking clearly, self-critically and precisely. That science gives valuable discipline in these things I of course agree. But except perhaps for observation, so does humanistic study. A good historical paper on why Britain and France invaded Suez may display as much exactitude, fertility, clarity, cogency, and general intellectual address as a good paper on the integument of the armadillo. There are beautiful examples of lucid and conclusive reasoning in Darwin and Newton, but there are equally beautiful examples, presented even more effectively, in

Burke's speech on *Conciliation*, in Mill's essay on *Liberty*, and in those models of philosophic thinking, Broad and McTaggart. Good thinking is not done in one subject matter only.

That brings me to my second reason. The subject matter of the humanities is much closer to ordinary life, and therefore to the kind of thinking that we shall later have to do, than that of physical science. The problems most of us will be engaged with are extremely concrete problems, many of them calling for ethical perception, personal tact, and resort to that probability which Butler said was the guide of life. We must run a lumber business or an insurance agency, deal with fractious children and temperamental colleagues, make up our minds what church to join, what party to support, what needy causes to give to, what books to read. I have no doubt that a laboratory discipline helps us in such decisions; I think that a discipline in literature, history, and ethics helps more. The physical sciences live and move on a snowy summit where there are no persons, and things themselves tend to dissolve into abstractions and equations. The humanities live and move in a world of persons, which is the world of common life.

Thirdly, in the sciences you are beyond the temptations of ordinary thinking; in the humanities you constantly face them. What the seventeenth decimal of pi may be, or the precise velocity of the moon, or the chemical components of rubber, are questions to which there are delightfully definite and important answers, but those answers do not have to be groped for through mists of passion and prejudice. As John Jay Chapman said, "Science neither sings nor jokes, neither prays nor rejoices, neither loves nor hates." In our common thinking we tend to do all these things. Try to reach any clear conclusion about God or freedom or immortality, about increased taxes or women's liberation, even about this very issue of the humanities versus the sciences, and you find yourself having to discipline and hold in check your own loyalties and prejudices. Now the thinking in the humanities is for the most part thinking of this kind. It is thinking about matters where our feelings are not only engaged, but engaged on one side, and it forces us to think about values as objectively as we can. It therefore prepares us in a special way for the thinking we shall actually do in household, religion, or politics.

For these three reasons I would give the humanities the supreme place among our disciplines in purely educational value.

It may be said that to assign superior educative value to any subject as such is misleading, that whether it possesses humane values depends on how it is taught. And it must be admitted that any subject—even mathematics, which is the most inhumane of disciplines in the sense of being most uncolored by human passions and prejudices—can be taught with regard to its history and applications and even to the personal triumphs and tragedies of Archimedes or Lord Russell. But the true mathematician would regard such embroideries as irrelevant. It is true, too, that the most purely humanistic of subjects, which I suppose is poetry, can be taught in scientific fashion. Humanists, stung by the charge that their students lack discipline and precision, have sometimes set themselves to outdo the scientists themselves in minute factuality. I gather that the Harvard English Department of a generation ago had a greater satisfaction in turning out scholars with a philological mastery of a second-rate middle-English poet than scholars with a luminous understanding of a first-rate modern one. Even the poet A. E. Housman, who was perhaps the greatest Latin scholar of his time, devoted much of his life to a minute textual study of a poet, Manilius, whom he would have scoffed at as a contemporary. Such studies seem to me to show neither the humanist's sense for importance nor the scientist's sense that facts should lead to generalizations. As attempts at crossing two different species, they are infertile, like the mule.

The true humanities are subjects that in their own nature involve reflection on, and appraisal of, values. Consider, for example, the study of art. Art is an attempt at perfection in expression, and its study calls for an effort to go beyond oneself into the feelings of more sensitive minds than our own, expressed with a power and delicacy above our own. To study painting as—to mention a name no longer popular—Ruskin studied it is to civilize one's feelings profoundly and to make one prize some things passionately, and passionately to dislike others. Is such discipline particularly needed among us? It seems to me to be needed desperately. Standards have become so vague that formless smudges pass as art. A similar chaos is invading music. How otherwise could we abide the caterwauling voices that assail us from radio, record, and jukebox? It is sometimes suggested that to deprecate such art is intolerant. But the very point of education in taste is to produce not only a love of what is good, but intolerance of what is bad—not, of course, in the sense of repressing it, but in the sense of avoiding it through seeing it for what it is.

History is another and more important example of a genuinely humanistic study. Exact minds have been known to jeer at history as a pseudoscience in which the main facts cannot be determined accurately and no generalizations are possible from those that can. "The Deity cannot alter the past," said Samuel Butler, "but historians can and do; perhaps that is why he allows them to exist." But accuracy, important as that is, is not the only thing in history. As Lord Acton said, history should be "not a burden on the memory, but an enlightenment of the soul." The power to give such enlightenment through making one relive the crises of the past is the special gift of some great historians such as Macaulay, Froude, and Carlyle. Good history, like good literature, of which it is one form, carries us out of ourselves, and takes us into other times and other minds. To follow with real understanding how the three chief revolutions of modern times, the American, the French, and the Russian, came into being and spent themselves is to enlarge one's understanding of the present as well as of the past. Human nature remains largely the same, and the elements of statesmanship may be studied with as much advantage perhaps in Pericles or Lincoln as in Churchill.

What should we aim at in the study of history? Not facts merely; not laws or predictions, for these are impossible. Two things, however, are possible, at least in degree, two things of high importance. The first is the understanding of the present in terms of the past. According to James Harvey Robinson, that is the chief value of history, and I agree. Take the American businessman; there is a complex phenomenon for you. How are you to understand him? Where, for example, did he get his religion? It is a combination of Calvinistic theology, of scientific skepticism, of high moral purpose, of innumerable and subtle social pressures; and all of these have long roots in the past. His ideal of education comes partly from Germany, partly from England. His political theory has flowed down to him from John Locke. His business ethics is a somewhat watered-down Puritanism. The main virtues emphasized by the American businessman are such austere old Puritan virtues as honesty, punctuality, prudence, and hard work. Dean Inge has said that if an American businessman is not the son of the ghetto, he is pretty certainly a grandson of John Calvin. Now if you are to understand the American businessman, it must be not metaphysically or scientifically, but historically. You can trace his lineage with surprising definiteness to the immediate and even the remoter past.

The other great purpose that history can serve is to project human nature on a large scale and in dramatic form on the stage of the world. Think of Carlyle's *French Revolution*. Here you see what human nature can do and what it inevitably will do, when, outraged by a sense of injustice and oppressed beyond endurance, it breaks out at the expense of its overlords. What we see by the smoky light of those flaring torches is not this or that angry Frenchman, but human nature itself; we see the great moral issues of mankind crystallizing themselves and working themselves out with the inevitability of a tragic drama. Indeed history in the hands of the masters is great drama, and has the sort of truth such drama possesses. Great drama of course is true. Othello, for example, is true. It is an account given with extraordinary imaginative accuracy of what jealousy will do when combined with simplicity and magnanimity of mind. It was the possibility of giving such an account, with all irrelevant detail excluded, that made Aristotle say that poetry was even truer than history. However that may be, history can and does supply us with this dramatic truth.

Of my own subject—to mention but one other—I cannot speak impartially. It is easy to deride philosophy as the search by a blind man in a dark cellar for a black hat that isn't there. But there is one argument for philosophy to which I do not know any answer, namely that it is unavoidable, and that if one must do it, it is better to do it well. Almost every issue we talk about runs out into philosophy in the end. We try to get clear what in a given case we ought to do, and the question arises how we know when anything is our duty—and that is ethics. We wonder whether we can hold to a certain religious belief, and the question arises how we know that any belief is true—and that is epistemology. We start wondering about the meaning of the great little words of the language—"I," "time," "space," "cause," "life," "mind," "God"—and at a step we are in metaphysics. The question is not whether we shall think about these things, but whether we shall think about them in a disciplined and responsible way or in a loose and hit-or-miss way. "Metaphysics," said Bradley, "is the finding of bad reasons for what we believe on instinct, but the finding of those reasons," he added, "is no less an instinct." Philosophy is not at enmity with common sense or science. It is the attempt to carry through to the end lines of reflection that arise in those fields inevitably.

To sum up: Our case for the humanities is a simple one. It amounts to this: Man is so made that he is not only a knowing mind, but a willing and feeling mind, and so far as he wills and feels, he is in the realm of value. To that realm, so important to the richness and quality of his life, the humanities are the best introduction that the college can supply.

# 5

# *What Is Education For?*

The subject of this talk is the very large one of the ends of education. What is it that we as students should seek to acquire from our education? What is it that we as teachers should aim at producing in our students? In short, what is education for?

Many aims have been urged on us as the right ones. It has been said that the aim is to adjust young people to their communities. But there are communities to which no educated person ought to be well adjusted, and we have all known morons who seemed to be beamingly well adjusted. It has been said that the aim is proficiency in what young people will be called upon to do. That may be a sound aim for an institute of accounting or a veterinary course, but if the value of poetry, philosophy, and art is to be measured by the added efficiency they produce, liberal study is a lost cause. It has been said that the aim is the most comprehensive knowledge of the world. But a man may acquire a stupendous body of knowledge and still be unintelligent and insensitive. It was suggested by the school of Thomas Arnold that the aim is to make men good, to turn out Christian gentlemen or ladies; "Be good, sweet maid," said Charles Kingsley, "and let who will be clever."

But in the modern world goodness is not enough, even if classrooms could produce it; the good heart needs to be guided by a reflective head. It is sometimes said that if all these partial aims break down, the remedy is to choose a wider one; let us aim at the all-round man and liberate all the powers and faculties of our young people. But this would be self-defeating. If one is to fulfil one's powers as a scholar, one must skimp one's self as an actor and an acrobat; and in any case, colleges are not equipped to turn out Jacks-of-all-trades.

I am not discouraged by all these failures, and am about to propose what may be another. But at least my suggestion is one that has been commending itself to me with increasing force for a long time. I suggest, then, that the aim of a liberal education is to produce reasonable minds. And by a reasonable mind I mean one which, in the varied situations of life, adapts its beliefs, attitudes, and actions to the facts of the case. The end of education is reasonableness.

The first point to note about such reasonableness is that it is a disposition or habit. Habit, not knowledge, is the main thing we can take with us from a college education; as someone has said, education is what is left when we have forgotten what we learned. When I think how hard my teachers must have worked to convey their riches into my own sievelike memory, I am ashamed to think how little I retain. I remember that I took courses in medieval history and economics; from the first, I have carried down the years the conviction that Charlemagne was crowned in 800 and from the second, that there is a law of diminishing returns; but apart from these impressive remains, standing out like Palmyra pillars among the ruins, very little is left standing of my conquests in those regions. Of course, people vary vastly in their power of retention. William Lyon Phelps, in his little book on memory, illustrates the extremes. On the one hand was his brother, who could recall what he was doing, and even the state of the weather, for every day of the preceding sixty years. On the other hand was the man who said, "There are three things I can never remember—first, I can't remember faces; second, I can't remember names; and—and—I can't remember the third thing I can't remember." No doubt a mind of the first type will carry away from college a more voluminous baggage of information than the second. But the first has small ground for elation and the second none for despair, for what is essential is not information at all, but the habit of reasonableness.

First, the habit of reasonableness in belief. The prime concern of a university, as Newman said, is intellectual; the disciplined intellect shows itself most surely in the truth, the clearness, and the consistency of its beliefs. The need of such minds today is obvious. We must manage to take a stand on countless complicated issues. We are probably all in some degree religious, and, as such, we have some sort of creed, perhaps unexamined and dead, perhaps examined and alive. We are called upon to vote for a new president of the United States. The party platforms consist of beliefs—dozens of them—and whether they shall become the national policy depends on us. Our day-to-day life calls for constant decisions in which our intellectual quality, such as it is, will display itself inevitably. How much insurance shall we take on our car? Shall we support the proposal of a black family to move into our block? John or Jane, who is an indifferent student, wants to go to college; shall we offer money and encouragement, or not? We complain sometimes that our place in life gives us no opportunity to use the powers that are in us. The truth is that the person of most modest lot among us has in the reasonable settlement of his problems a task that the ablest of us could hardly perform.

Now the logic of forming reasonable beliefs is laid out in countless excellent textbooks, and if anyone wants to know how beliefs are developed and tested, or what the law of excluded middle is, or the devices for excluded muddle, any amount of help is open to him at small cost, except of his own effort. I do not propose to compete with these books. I do want to suggest some attitudes or habits which seem essential to that reasonableness in belief which is the mark of the educated mind.

The first of these habits is skepticism. I do not mean by this the spirit that is reluctant to agree with anyone, like that of the man in the train who, when his friend remarked that the sheep in yonder field had been sheared, replied, "Well, on this side anyway." We have all known people who think that independence of mind consists in contradicting or correcting nearly everything we say, and who if they can manage to differ on something really important, like religion or morals, are in their element. This is a disease that may infect able minds. Bernard Shaw seems at times to have

75

proceeded on the maxim: "Find out what people think most important and unquestionable among their beliefs, and say that of course
this is nonsense." But surely that is *un*reasonableness. Common
sense is a philosophy that has been approved by centuries of rough
testing, and whoever denies it must accept a large burden of proof.
In the perpetual carper and village atheist Freud has taught us to
recognize not an exceptional love of truth, but an irrational compensation for inferiority.

The skepticism of the reasonable man is of a different kind. It
is the spirit that asks "Why?"—not to embarrass another or to score
for himself, but to see things as they are. Every belief that is true at
all has grounds which lie occasionally in its own self-evidence but
more often in the truth of something else from which it follows. The
educated mind is one to whom it is second nature to say to a proposed belief, "You may be true, but if you are there must be some
ground for thinking so; just what is it in your case?" The ideal of
such a mind is to give to every belief the degree of assent that the
evidence warrants—no more, but also no less.

This skepticism is necessary because we are surrounded by increasingly powerful pressures that are directed, sometimes in-
nocently enough, to deceiving us. Since Americans constitute the
choicest market in the world, and Madison Avenue is full of experts
at exploiting it, we are bombarded through radio, television,
magazines, and newspapers by an unremitting battery fire of
cozening solicitation. Our newspapers have become monsters
because they are used for advertising as they are nowhere else, and
our very forests are being depleted to keep them monstrous. As the
inspired poet sang:

> See that spruce against the sky?
> That is "Harper's" for July;
> And the poplar in the canyon
> Is the "Woman's Home Companion."

Now the purpose of advertising is not to judge a product, but
to sell it. And to sell it you need to maximize its virtues, and not so
much minimize its defects as omit or conceal them. Madison
Avenue studies our points of vulnerability; it knows that its best
defense may be offense, and that if something has a weakness or
danger, it may be good strategy to insist loudly on the opposite.

Whiskey is never associated with "alcoholics anonymous" but with "men of distinction"; cigarettes not with lung cancer, but with athletes; beer, lest it be thought a man's drink and a plebeian one, which I suppose is the fact, with a gay and dainty young miss waving at us from a picnic. Much advertising has made itself relatively harmless by gradually heightening our sales resistance, but where what is offered is drugs for sick bodies or prescriptions for sick minds, this resistance can hardly be too high.

It has lately been pointed out that skepticism is further needed if we are to avoid becoming "organization men." Society, remarked Emerson, is in conspiracy against every one of its members. Curiously enough, social pressure may be crushingly strong even in a democracy. In older countries, where the social strata are clearly marked, a young man may feel quite content to stay in his native stratum. A young American, if he has one, wants to get out of it, which implies that he will take on anxiously the coloration of thought and manner of the group to which he aspires. At the beginning, this may be an advance, but it may end by his being a fly stuck motionlessly in amber. No educated man's opinions should be predictable from his social level, his profession, his friends, or his age. All real thought is done by individuals, and the thinking of the so-called mass man is not thinking at all, but obedience to mass suggestion. "The third-rate mind," said A. A. Milne, "is only happy when it is thinking with the majority, the second-rate mind is only happy when it is thinking with the minority, and the first-rate mind is only happy when it is thinking."

In a democracy there is danger that the suggestion supported by the largest number should be assumed to be the wisest one, and that those who govern us should proceed on this assumption. All of us receive letters from time to time, asking us to write to our congressman and virtually telling us what to say; and it is hoped that if this harassed man has ten pounds of letters on one side and a hundredweight on the other, he will take the hundredweight as the weight of the evidence. He will not be dealing with us fairly if he does. He is sent to Washington to consider the truth about measures for public welfare, and to vote in accordance with this truth, not to be pulled about like a puppet by wires from pressure groups, even if those groups should be a majority. He, too, should be a skeptic, and a skeptic about us. One expert opinion is worth a thousand ill-informed letters.

It is often said that among youth conformity to mass pressure is stronger today than it used to be, and I think this may be true. When I was in college, those of us who wanted to take our own line were commonly socialists, though there was some conformity to fashion even in that; but the course of socialism in the chief land of its adoption has taken the heart out of the older radicalism. Whether anything more thoughtful and generous has taken its place I do not know. Among students there seems to be a revived interest in a Kierkegaardian religion, but since this attitude entails a denial that religion is an affair of reason, it carries small promise for those who, like myself, think that more reasonableness is needed everywhere.

Indeed, it raises an important question. I said that the reasonable mind would take proposed beliefs with a grain of salty skepticism. Many would say that this is all very well in science or in politics, but quite wrong in religion, that the right attitude toward religious belief is not one of inquiry whether it is true or not, but of faith regardless of evidence; "blessed are those who have *not* seen, and yet have believed." Those who take this view should be prepared to deal with two consequences of it. First, there are many religious groups whose beliefs conflict with one another, and such unquestioning acceptance would therefore commit large numbers of people to beliefs that are false. Secondly, is the religious man to be contented with a less exacting intellectual conscience than his scientific colleague? The issue is a complex one because religious belief is more closely bound up with conduct than is scientific belief. My own view, which I have time only to state, not to develop, is that there cannot be one ethics of belief for theology and another for science or philosophy, that if the attempt to equate one's belief with the evidence is legitimate anywhere, it is so everywhere.

A second habit that is a great help to being reasonable is that of reflectiveness. It is not an easy habit to acquire. Thinking is hard for everyone, even for those who are professionals in it; "When I am not walking," said Charles Lamb, "I am reading; I cannot sit and think. Books think for me." During the First World War Asquith confided to his journal about his colleagues Lloyd George and

Churchill: "They can only think talking, just as some people can only think writing. Only the salt of the earth can think inside, and the bulk of mankind cannot think at all." We have the right to ask of the educated man that he show some proficiency in this art; it matters less whether he practices it with his pen or his tongue, or merely with his brain, as Asquith and Pascal would prefer.

What is it to think? Dewey says it is to see a suggestion in the light of the grounds from which it springs and the consequences to which it leads; it is therefore the natural complement of the skeptical attitude we have commended. The reflective man is not confined to the immediate; he is always passing beyond the given into what it means or portends. Of course we all do that every hour of our waking lives; what we call seeing a house or a man involves going beyond what we literally see, and recognizing the object before us as having many unseen properties; this is what John Stuart Mill meant when he said that the drawing of inferences was the main business of life. Reflectiveness is just an extension of this habit. The plain man is related to the reflective man as Dr. Watson was to Sherlock Holmes: Watson would see a working man coming down the street; Holmes would see a working man the color of whose hands indicated that he was a tanner of leather and whose cauliflower ear indicated a pugnacity that required strategic treatment. To Peter Bell "the primrose by the river's brim" was nothing more; to a botanist or to Wordsworth, it is considerably more.

It is an ironic fact that surrender to the immediate, particularly in the way of youthful impulse, has come to be associated by many with a great name in educational thought that I have just mentioned, John Dewey. The fact is ironic because it is really the opposite of what Dewey was always insisting on, namely that our beliefs and choices should be made in the light of their reflective consequences. Dewey himself was the most complete embodiment of the reflective habit that I have ever known. It fell to my lot, many years ago, to spend a summer with him investigating conditions in a depressed area in Philadelphia. Some little fact about the community—a strike, a lockout, a political meeting—which would awake no response in most of us was enough to set the wheels of that brooding mind in motion; he would start pecking away at his battered typewriter, and next morning at breakfast he would have for our inspection an article for the *New Republic* which showed us how much there was to see if only one looked with the eyes of the mind.

We need more of that Deweyan habit of thoughtfulness. Events have conspired to make it difficult at a time when it is required. Too many of us are bred up to passiveness of thought. A child can sit for hours before a television set, a young man at a big league game, or both at a double-feature movie, without any sort of mental effort. A hundred years ago people beguiled their leisure by reading three-volume novels by Dickens or Thackeray. I suspect that from many of our young people, who can entertain themselves by the hour through turning a button, even a storybook of that quality and quantity would demand an unwonted intellectual effort.

Yet to be a responsible citizen calls for a more active and varied thoughtfulness in this century than in the last, for the obvious reason that our civilization is a vastly more complicated web, with its parts more subtly interconnected. A good test of how fully we are at home in it is our ability to read a newspaper understandingly. Can we read the financial pages, for example, in such a way as to see the significance of the facts they report for the health of our economy? I hope you can do this better than I. Can we read a court decision on the separation of church and state, and see what the decision means for religion and for education? Do we perceive as readily why an eminent scientist or theologian should be in the headlines, or on the cover of *Time*, as a $150,000 baseball player? We are not fully living in our exciting time unless we do, and we can do so only if we have attained some power of thinking independently. Of course we must have some information to start from, but that is no problem for any of us. "Culture," said Whitehead, "is activity of thought, and receptiveness to beauty and humane feeling. Scraps of information have nothing to do with it. A merely well informed man is the most useless bore on God's earth. . . ."

There is a third habit that seems to me essential to a reasonable mind. It is the habit of thinking *impersonally*. There has grown up a widespread disbelief in recent years in the power, and even the desirability, of impersonal thinking. Freud wrote near the end of his life: "I am sure only of one thing, that the judgments of value made by mankind are immediately determined by their desires for happiness; in other words, that their judgments are attempts to prop up their illusions with arguments." The philosopher is held to be the victim of his desires as truly as other people; "Philosophy is to history," Will Durant writes, "as reason is to desire; in either case an unconscious process determines from below the conscious thought." The teaching of our Yale anthropologist Sumner that "philosophy and ethics are products of the folkways" has, for many, become a commonplace. MacNeille Dixon declares in his Gifford Lectures that "there never yet was a philosopher, whatever they may have said, no, nor man of science, whose conclusions ran counter to the dearest wishes of his heart, who summed up against them, or condemned his hopes to death." D. H. Lawrence went further and frankly exulted in irrationality: "My great religion," he wrote, "is a belief in the blood, the flesh, as being wiser than the intellect. We can go wrong with our minds, but what our blood feels and believes and says is always right."

What makes this doctrine so dangerous is the breadth of its acceptance. Are not the leaders most generally admired men who think with their blood, and do we not tend to copy those we admire? The voices that are listened to, particularly in times of crisis, are voices vibrant with passion. In the First World War the comparatively stolid British people turned out the judicial Asquith whom we have heard praising quiet thought, and put a spellbinder—an able one to be sure—in his place. The Second World War followed the First because the people of a country that gave us much of our civilization surrendered themselves to a strutting mountebank, and because in the honored home of philosophy and scholarship, scholars and morons joined hands to troop after a dervish who knew how to play on their passions. And human nature does not change greatly in a few decades. Arnold Toynbee writes: "We are living in a madhouse. . . . Our descendants' expectation of life could be assured if the control over atomic power were made the monopoly of some single authority. Of course we are not going to do this. Rather than do it, we are going to continue to take the risk of bringing destruction upon our descendants together with the rest of the human race. . . . If this is not lunacy, what is?"

Happily one can agree with Toynbee that men are behaving like lunatics without conceding that lunacy is inevitable. It would be silly to say that we cannot think rationally, for the theory that we cannot do so is itself a theory supposed to be rationally arrived at, and therefore admits that we can at times see things as they are, and not as our emotions paint them. What Freud and others have shown is not that we cannot think straight, but only that it is hard to do so, and why. The explanation is, roughly, that we have very imperfectly emerged from the animal level and that reason is a sort of oil with which we have to control, as best we can, waves of impulse and feeling that come surging up from immemorial deeps. But now that we see what we have to control, we are in a far better position to control it. And it is the business of the educated man to exert that control, for only when he does so can he think truly or act justly. As Santayana says, "This love of bare truth, this intellectual asceticism, is itself a human passion and the secret of a regenerate life: so that the more I strip myself, the better I bring to light that something in me that is more myself than I am—the spirit."

I suggest that this control of passion in the interest of truth, this prejudice against prejudice if you will, should be part of the freemasonry of educated men, that it should be one of the conscious pillars of their self-respect. We are too tolerant of intellectual childishness. Goethe, who admired Byron's poetry, said of him, *sobald er reflektiert ist er ein Kind*, the moment he tries to think, he shows himself a child; yet Byron was a great hero to the sentimentalists of his day. A wave of similar sentimentalism has risen in our own time. Beatniks and hippies argue with lamentable logic: "Geniuses generally kick over the rational traces; hence people who do so evince a mark of genius." Neither statement is true, nor does the second follow from the first. What does seem to be true is that many gifted persons, particularly in the arts, have remained in some respects spoiled children, and that to people who feel the harness of reasonableness galling, there is a certain vicarious freedom in contemplating them. So there has been a spate of books in recent years about Van Gogh and Gauguin and Oscar Wilde and Scott Fitzgerald and Brendan Behan and Dylan Thomas and others of their numerous family. It is not quite without significance that the heroes of the two main branches of contemporary philosophy both lived on the outer borders of sanity—Kierkegaard and Wittgenstein. I do not say, of course, that this discredits their philosophy, any more than it discredits the painting of Van Gogh or

Gauguin. I do say that it was a dark deformity of spirit, not something to be prized or praised or in any degree copied.

The things on which university-trained persons have based their self-respect have varied curiously. An Oxford or Cambridge man of 1900 would hardly have forgiven the hint that he was not a gentleman. A Heidelberg man of the same era would have been proud of his scholarship, but equally proud of something called his honor, which was most effectively testified to by gashes on his face. Judging by the votes of some American collegians, the football captaincy outranks any intellectual honor in the gift of their institution. Now from a great distance I much admire football captains. But to suppose that theirs are the special qualities which a university should aim at does seem odd. The business of the university is intellectual. The true mark of its product is something that can be felt but not seen; it is an intellectual conscience, a special fastidiousness of mind, a gravitation toward the truth, a sense, for example, that one is being soiled and befouled if one indulges in mere name-calling, or judges another in anger or envy, or believes things in politics or religion because it is to one's advantage, or swallows or regurgitates gossip about another because one dislikes him, or generalizes when all one knows is a particular fact or two, or dogmatizes without ground. Dogmatism mistakes the emotion of conviction, which is of no significance at all, for the insight of the mind that can see for itself.

It is this independent, authentic, impersonal vision that is the true mark of the educated mind. Of course it has no necessary connection with degrees, ordinary or honorary; it is notoriously lacking in some persons with many diplomas, and conspicuous in some others like J. S. Mill, who reported that he had never suffered the handicap of a university education; and it may appear in either sex, in youth or age, or in any rank or race. Whether gained in a university or not, it is something one must win for one's self, for it cannot be poured in from the outside. But this sense of intellectual honor, this scrupulousness about truth, makes itself quickly felt when it is there. I have had the privilege of seeing it at work at fairly close range in some extremely different persons who, to me, were men apart because of it. One of them was Gilbert Murray, the classical scholar. Poets and artists often lack it, but you will agree, I think, that at least in his critical writing T. S. Eliot had it. The philosopher G. E. Moore had it almost to excess; if one's scrupulousness passes a certain point, it may become paralyzing. And just as one can feel its presence clearly in some men, one can sense its absence in others, even in men of great parts. Mr. Mencken, for example, lacked it; he is quoted as saying, "I don't want the *Mercury* ever to be objective. That's a horrible word anyway." Bernard Shaw in his later years lacked it; F. L. Lucas remarks that he "became in the end merely a kind of court-zany to the British public." If one wants to see its absence elevated into a habit and almost a principle, one has only to recall the newspaper columns of Westbrook Pegler.

Our thesis so far is that the aim of a liberal education is the reasonable mind, and that such a mind will be marked by a skeptical and reflective conscientiousness of thought. But reasonableness is not a matter of belief merely. The unreasonableness of a spoiled child or a Brendan Behan is nothing so simple as a mistake, or a defect in logic; it is a failure to bring one's impulses into line with what, in saner moments, one may see quite clearly. Why is it that so often, when we know the better, we do the worse? To me it is an impressive fact that the first great moral philosopher of the West, Socrates, simply denied that we ever do. He thought that the cure for all our ills was steady clearness of vision, that if we saw with full vividness that a certain way of behaving was wrong, we were never such fools as to choose it; and if we did choose it, it was always because we had allowed our eyes to wander. William James held a rather similar view when he said that the secret of a firm will lies in the control of attention. But whether the Socratic teaching on this point is right or not, I think you will agree that there is such a thing as reasonableness in feeling and action as well as in belief.

What does reasonableness in feeling mean? I suppose it means the adjustment of feeling to the true character of its object, just as reasonableness in thought means the adjustment of belief to the evidence. The person who flies into a rage when his egg is underdone, or falls into panic when he has a degree of temperature, is not being emotionally reasonable; there is nothing in the object to justify his passion. How is one to know when a feeling is justified?

Unfortunately, philosophers are here disagreed. The Stoics thought that in the end no feeling was justified at all. If you took the scientific view of things and saw that whatever happened was necessary, you would see also that to repine about anything, or storm about it, was absurd. Oddly enough, an influential recent philosophy of value says likewise that feelings cannot be rationally justified. The emotivists tell us that whenever we judge anything good or bad, that *is* a mere expression of feeling, and that to suppose there is anything good or bad in the object which could justify this feeling is naive. But to say that nothing is good or bad until we have feelings about it is to say that no feeling is more appropriate to it than any other, and on this point I remain among the naive. The feelings appropriate to a mugging are not those appropriate to a wedding ceremony.

We are not a phlegmatic people; our feelings are strong and quickly inflammable. It is a widespread belief among us that if an experience is exciting, that in itself is enough to justify it and make it significant. Professional entertainers and advertisers have caught this fact and taken advantage of it. They know, for example, that mere rhythm, the regular beat of a tom-tom or a band is exciting; the Greeks and our own Indians used to work themselves into a frenzy of excitement by the rhythmic stamping of feet and clapping of hands; even an inhibition-bound Yale professor admitted that he never heard a band without being swept off on a wave of emotion. Now American amusements are showing a curious reversion to the primitive. Consider what is popular in music. A respected friend of mine, on a trip to Europe, had the pleasure of being invited to lunch by that great man, Albert Schweitzer, on vacation from his labors in Africa. After lunch, Schweitzer said to my friend, "You like yahtz?" Without having the least idea what was meant, but wishing desperately to be agreeable, my friend assured him that he liked yahtz very much. Whereupon the eminent authority on Bach took him into the next room, sat down at his organ, and played him some *jazz*. He assumed that if you were in American, you would naturally like jazz. And what is jazz? I am no musician, and friends tell me that much fine music passes under this name. But much else that is so called seems to me essentially primitive music which acts directly on the spine without reaching the cerebellum. I have seen

on the screen some of its best-known exponents sweating, grimac-
ing, and writhing in paroxysms of excitement, without having the
faintest notion of *what* there was to be excited about. It was apparently excitement for its own exhilarating sake. Indeed, it is entirely possible to get excited merely by acting as if one were excited.
This is a secret well known to that uniquely American phenomenon, the cheerleader. He—and she—are not content to let us
shout and wave our hats for a touchdown; we find ourselves, at
their suggestion, roaring in unison before a team has appeared on
the field.

This faculty for excitement over little or nothing has been ex-
ploited by contemporary art. A few months ago in London I went to
two exhibitions of contemporary art, one of Russian art, the other of
American. The Russian works were along traditional lines—ikons,
portraits of Tolstoy, dramatic incidents of the war, peasants gathering in the sheaves. It was technically competent, pleasing, and intelligible, though hardly novel. In the American exhibition all was
novelty; the break with tradition was complete. The paintings
*represented* nothing; they were expressions of how the painter felt.
We have learned from clinical experience with Rorschach tests that
even a shapeless blot may be expressive and diagnostic, in the sense
that whether it suggests an angel or a gargoyle may reveal
something important about one's state of mind. But these paintings
were not offered, I understood, for the sake of the meanings or images they suggested, still less as tests of abnormality; the shapes
were supposed to be exciting in themselves. Abstract and nonobjective painting have been converging toward a strange result—the
deliberate exclusion of meaning from their content, the concentration on the meaningless as that which alone is aesthetically pure.

I venture to think that for most people that sort of artistic diet
is too austere to arouse any appetite; it is like living on pills after
steaks and salads. The art that Ruskin talked about so eloquently
seems to the modernist painter a hybrid and mongrel affair in
which truth and morality were hopelessly mixed up with the pure
form that should be the prime concern of the artist. Still, the art
that Ruskin looked at, confused or not, engaged a large area of the
mind, and he wrote about it in such a way that one understands his
excitement and shares it. The painters in the London exhibition
tried to do that, too. They distributed a printed catalogue in which

they elaborately explained what they were doing and why. To me at least, that was a mistake. Naive as I am with my eyes and ears, I have had forty sad years' experience in identifying nonsense in the written word, and here was indubitable nonsense. I came away convinced that much of this ambitious work was that of earnest but pinched minds, trying to persuade themselves that they had found something rich and succulent in cactus.

A friend of mine who is an art historian tells me that he finds the new art fascinating because now everyone can be an artist. Even I, who cannot draw a flagpole, am an artist, he assures me; I need only put a stroke on canvas, and go on from there as my spirit or elbow moves. This assurance had the unintended effect of deepening my skepticism. For I am sure that what I did in that way would have no worth at all, and if someone tells me it is fine art, what that shows is not that I am an artist, but that he lacks standards. The standardlessness of contemporary art is to my mind disquieting.

Five years ago a London mother complained that some exhibitions accepted paintings that might have been done by a child of eight. Since she had an eight-year-old daughter who had recently done a sketch of her doll, she decided, by way of testing her view, to enter this sketch for competition at the annual show of the New Burlington galleries, headquarters of the Royal Academy. It was accepted and hung along with the work of some of the most distinguished British artists. Of course this child may have been a supergenius. But that can hardly have been true of a seven-year-old named Betsy about whose nonobjective paintings there was a pother at a lesser art show in Berkeley, California. Betsy's paintings had been selling, it was said, for $25 to $50 a canvas, but there was some question of their admissibility under the bylaws. The technical difficulty was that Betsy was a chimpanzee.

Lest it be thought that painting is in a unique position, I may add that poems about practically nothing arouse in some critical quarters an equal enthusiasm. You will remember the two prank-loving Australians, Corporal Stewart and Lieutenant McAuley, who concocted a new poet named Ern Malley by putting together odds and ends from books they had lying around. The first three lines of one of Malley's masterpieces were taken from an American government report on the drainage of breeding grounds for mosquitoes. A literary magazine devoted some thirty pages to Malley as "a poet of tremendous power" who "worked through a disciplined and restrained kind of statement into the deepest wells of human experience."

Of course this is an extreme case. It leaves me uneasy, nevertheless. Could such pranks succeed if the literate public had any secure standards by which to distinguish sense from nonsense?

I do not want to be a wet blanket or a Sad Sack. I am all for excitement and enthusiasm if it is a by-product of an interest in something worth being excited about. But much in contemporary music, art, and literature is not worth being excited about, and feeling for itself and apart from the worth of its object is not a rational end for anyone; if it were, the manic case in the hospital should be the envy of us all. What counts is whether we are excited about the right things. In Plato's *Phaedrus*, Socrates asks a young man with whom he has been pursuing a discussion of ultimate truth whether they shall go on with the inquiry. "Should we, do you say?" replies the young man. "Are there any pleasures worth living for like these?" That was a remark that would come more naturally perhaps from a Greek than from an American student. But it is occasional remarks like this that give heart to the university teacher. A young mind will suddenly discover Gibbon, or the essay on *Liberty*, or Marcus Aurelius, or Shelley, and feel that for him there is a new heaven and a new earth. That is as it should be. The education of feeling is a long, slow discipline in unliking what is childish and coming to like things in which our thought and feeling can rest. There is an old address by President Eliot called "Life's Enthusiasms" in which he argues that admirations are the measure of a life. "Note what the great admired," says Thackeray; "they admired great things; narrow spirits admire basely, and worship meanly."

What the standard of reasonableness is in this matter of liking and disliking I cannot discuss here, important as that is; I shall be content if you agree that there are such things as reasonable and unreasonable enthusiasms. Can we say the same of actions? I think we can, and that in the ideal of reasonable conduct we have another side of the true end for the educated man.

Many people would complain that being reasonable is too pale and neutral an end for a man of action. Love or hatred will really move people, but reasonableness—what juice is there in that? May I point out in answer, first, that reasonableness is not an alternative to love or hatred, but the principle of their regulation. The reasonable man will love and, more rarely, hate, but his distinction will not lie in these things, which after all he shares with the animals, but in his way of ordering them. F. L. Lucas says: "Imagine the greatest man you can think of, in a bad temper—does he still, at that moment, seem great? No. Not even were he Alexander. Real greatness implies balance and control." Secondly, any motive may be deadly unless it is ordered by reason. Of hatred that is obvious. But it is true even of love. St. Francis was a man of profound and universal love if ever there was one. But when a poor friar wanted to take just one book with him on a journey, Francis, who had no interest in knowledge, sternly forbade him; and the good man's way of dealing with an epidemic, as Russell reminds us, was to call the people together in church to pray for deliverance from it, which spread it most efficaciously. Love not in accordance with reason may destroy the thing it loves.

It is sometimes objected, again, that to be reasonable is to be dull. There is some force in the objection. We have seen already that the people men like to read about and flock to see are not those eminent for reasonableness. One wonders whether there has ever been a play or novel whose characters were all reasonable men and women, and if so, whether it had any readers. If a prima donna can manage a few tempestuous flurries, if a moving picture star can manage three or four bizarre marriages, the lines at the box office seem to lengthen. But it must be added that there are minds who find these tempestuous persons themselves boring. Owen Chadwick, in his inaugural lecture at Cambridge University, said: "The world may be divided by temperament . . . into those who like it warm, and those who like it cool; into those who naturally sympathize with Luther and those who naturally sympathize with Erasmus." I belong to the party of Erasmus. I can neither forget nor easily forgive Luther's reference to "the harlot reason," or his remark that "philosophy is an old woman that stinks of Greece." It is told that at a time of crisis in our own Civil War, President Lincoln sent an important message to Stanton, his secretary of war. The messenger returned in embarrassment to report that Stanton had torn up the letter and called the President a fool. There was a moment of silence. Then Lincoln began to laugh. "Well," he said, "if Mr. Stanton says I am a fool, I must be one. Mr. Stanton is generally right." I find this response of a rational man more interesting than anything that a prima donna might have done at that inflammatory moment.

It is sometimes said, again, that reasonableness would kill the gusto of life, and once more there is something in the charge. We noted that the reasonable man will be habitually reflective. Now to reflect is to look before one leaps, to see one's act in the light of its consequences, and if one does that, one may never leap at all. The reasonable man, it is held, will suffer from chronic Hamlet's-disease; he will be intellectually inhibited and muscle-bound; his impulses will be "all sicklied o'er by the pale cast of thought."

> The centipede was happy quite
> Until the toad, for fun,
> Said "pray which leg comes after which?"
> Which wrought his mind to such a pitch
> He lay distracted in the ditch
> Considering how to run.

It is true that excessive analysis, especially if it comes too early, may kill the freshness of impulse; if you want a case history, read Mill's *Autobiography*. But there are two comments to be made. For one thing, I have noted very few of my own students who stood in great danger from being too reflective. The trouble with most men is that they think too little; it was the sober Bishop Butler who said that the world would be a happier place, even if men were more selfish than they are, provided only they were reflectively selfish, not impulsively and stupidly so. Secondly, to complain of the restraint placed on impulse by reason is like complaining that there is a premium on an insurance policy; the premium may be a nuisance, but it is the price of protection against disaster.

What we want of a man of action is responsibility. What we want in a soldier or a mayor or the head of a business is someone who is reflective enough to see what needs to be done, and ready in translating thought into action. The first quality, the intellectual one, is probably rarer than the second. No two businesses, and no two occasions in the same business, call for quite the same decision, so that a vigilant flexibility of mind is a requirement for the executive.

It is seldom that the two qualities meet in full measure in the same person, but in one remarkable figure, the two-thousandth anniversary of whose death we commemorated recently, tradition has it that the two did really meet as perhaps never in anyone else. What has fascinated biographers of Julius Caesar over the centuries is the strange ease with which he gravitated into the control of the civilized world. He never seems to have been under inner strain, never to have displayed temper or even temperament, always to have seen with a calm clearness what needed to be done in each situation as it arose, and to have done it. Perhaps the picture of this extraordinary man has been touched up in the course of the centuries; and a good man in our sense he was not. But the legend, true or false, puts before us once and for all the type of the great executive, great because a flexible intelligence was at the instant service of an inflexible will.

These formidable men of action may be, and often have been, a curse to the world. If so, that is because intelligence may be one-sided. Whitehead has distinguished two types of rational man, Plato and Ulysses; "the one shares reason with the gods, the other shares it with the foxes." But the craftiness of the criminal is not rationality; it is cleverness about means in the service of irrationality about ends. That is the chief threat to the modern world. We are face-to-face with a political system that cultivates the wisdom of the fox while sternly repressing the Platonic wisdom, the wisdom that comes of sustained free thought about the ends of life. And some of our educators have been frightened into the view that we must follow suit and make our colleges institutes for the wisdom of foxes. But would not that be defeat already? We shall not score an educational triumph by producing a race of superlative technicians with nowhere to go but the moon. The educated man, who—I am maintaining—is identical with the rational man, is not only skilful in his means but reasonable in his goals.

We are often told in these days that reason itself is a fickle guide; that as appealed to by a Russian or Chinese, it will give one answer, and as appealed to by a Frenchman or American, it will give another; that there's nothing right or wrong but thinking makes it so; that the mores can make anything right. I cannot argue the matter here, but I am convinced that this is a mistake. Put two Americans together who are undisciplined in thought, feeling, and impulse, and you will get hopeless disagreement; put a Russian, a Chinaman, and an American together who have a common pride in reasonableness, and through differences of nationality, religion, and race, their judgments will gravitate, like the planets, toward a central light. When an American president says to a Russian premier that something is right, or wrong, or unjust, or unfair, I cannot doubt for a moment that there are equivalents in Russian, and that the premier will know what they mean. The terms of the moral life are a universal coinage, and as the presence of a common reason is more strongly felt, they tend to be applied in the same way. The present upsurge of the underdeveloped peoples is not a rebellion against what we stand for; it is rather an implication of it, a by-product of what we have taught them; they see that there is not one justice for Africans and another for Caucasians, there is only justice, appointed by a reason the same in all men.

I must close. I do not know what you are going to say about these remarks of mine, but one thing you cannot well say, namely that there was anything new in them. The doctrine I have been preaching about the end of education is in essence as old as Aristotle, and while I can keep hold of that giant hand by a finger or two, I feel that I can walk in some safety. Two thousand years before Darwin or Freud, Aristotle saw, with those strangely clear eyes, what sort of creature man was; he was a vegetable that had sprouted animal proclivities, and one proclivity that was even more than animal: he could think. That was what made him human; that was his distinction and his glory. It followed that to educate one's self was to be more completely human, to give this distinctive faculty dominance and free play. If one did this, what would be the standard of the educated man? As respects beliefs, adjustment to the evidence. As respects feeling, propriety to the object. As respects action, making the most of one's self consistently with the general good. In sum and in short, in all things be reasonable.

I do not echo this counsel of the master as a prescription for success. In a country where Jimmy Hoffa can be an idol, and attacks on UNESCO make thousands cheer, one can hardly rely on reasonableness as a winning card. But then success in the ordinary sense is not what education is for. The business of education is to show that nothing fails like success if that is achieved with inward emptiness, and that nothing succeeds like failure, if that is purchased by integrity of mind.

The case for being reasonable is not that it will make one successful, still less that it will make one spectacular, but that without it everything else is apt to turn to ashes in one's mouth. Reasonableness is hard because it means keeping our human nature at all points in check. When Ruskin was called on for an epitaph for his businessman father, he prepared one that he thought almost extravagant in its praise: "Here lies an entirely honest merchant." It would be high praise for any of us, when he has finished his course, to have it said, "Here was a fine scholar, a good soldier, a great executive." In the light of what human nature notoriously is, it would be praise still rarer and higher if it could be said of us, "Here was a really reasonable man."

# 6

# *Education and Values*

In the midst of the universal clamor for more and better technology, too little is heard about the place of values in higher education. No one can doubt the importance of technology. But technology is important only because it is itself a means to values that lie beyond it. Uncontrolled by values, it is like a car that is running wild. Life without what technology has given us would no doubt be a far more pinched and meager affair than it is, but by way of getting the perspective right, we may profitably remember that technology as we know it was unknown to Buddha and Socrates, to Sophocles and Aristotle, to Virgil and Dante. Their lives were not quite bare of value, nevertheless. In the campaign for a good life, technology is the O.S.S., the Office of Strategic Services, not the G.H.Q., which sets the objectives of the campaign. And it is these objectives, these overall ends or values, and how education can help us gain them, that is my theme.

What do we mean by a value? To define the term is surprisingly hard; many thinkers have thought it impossible. But it is easy enough to give examples. As examples of minor values, we could cite such experiences as toasting one's toes before a pleasant fire, having a good dinner after missing lunch, watching a world series game on television, and taking a cool plunge on a hot day. As examples of major values, we could cite the love of Damon for Pythias or of Darby for Joan, the hearing with full understanding of Beethoven's Fifth Symphony, the experience of Keats on first looking into Chapman's Homer, the experience of Schweitzer in ministering to his African patients. Is there anything that all these values have in common? Yes, three things, I think.

In the first place they are all experiences. You may say that there are many things that are valuable besides experiences, and it is true that we commonly talk that way. For economists anything has value that can be exchanged for something else one wants—for example, money or a diamond ring or a grandfather clock. But why should anyone else want these things, and why should you want things they will exchange for? The answer in both cases is the same. It is because these things are means to experiences that are wanted for their own sakes. If somebody wants your grandfather clock, it is because he can set it in his front hall and look at it and gloat over it. Things are always wanted for the sake of experiences, never experiences for the sake of things. For, strictly speaking, things have no value at all. Suppose some comet were to switch its poisonous tail across our planet and asphyxiate us tonight; would there be anything of value left on the earth tomorrow? The books would still stand in their rows on the library shelves, and the pictures would still in some sense be there on our walls. But would they have any value? None. Only if there were people to take knowledge of them or delight in them would there be any worth in them, and even then it would be the experience of knowledge and delight that had the value, not the books or pictures themselves.

Secondly, these values are not only experiences; they are pleasant experiences. I am inclined to think that every experience valued for its own sake is suffused with a flush of agreeable feeling. This does not mean, of course, that hard work, mental and physical, or even the acute suffering of a bad illness or a bad conscience is not good in a sense; only it is good in a different sense. If we call these things good, it is not because we seek them out for their own sakes, but because they are the means to later states of mind that *are* thus sought; in short, they are instrumental, not intrinsic goods. We admire people who can face suffering with Spartan firmness in the interests of a cause. But if we found a man who cultivated illness or pain for its own sweet sake, we should choose our gambit warily in approaching him; we should assume that he was a crank, and not improbably a psychopath. Indeed, I doubt whether even psychopaths attain this pitch of oddity. To be sure, we hear of masochists who find pain good in itself. I doubt whether there are such people. Those so called are probably persons who, for reasons discoverable by a psychiatrist, get satisfaction as a *result* of enduring pain, which is a different thing from finding the pain itself good. However that may be, can you think of any experience that would retain its value for you if you felt no satisfaction in it? Suppose you had the musical ear and experience of a Toscanini, but felt no pleasure in music; would music be any good to you? Suppose that in physics you had the flair of an Einstein but never felt the slightest glow of happiness over solving an equation or making a new discovery; would research have any value for you? I think the answer in both cases must be no. Pleasure, the feeling of satisfaction, is a component of everything that is intrinsically good.

Our conclusion so far is that all goods involve pleasant experiences. Is there anything more that is essential to them? I think there is. And perhaps the best way to see it is to take an example which perplexed John Stuart Mill, one familiar to all students of ethics. He began by saying that pleasure, and pleasure alone, was what made anything good. But he was brought up short by reflecting on the comparative value that this doctrine would assign to the lives of Socrates and a pig. Take first a month in the life of a pig, and make it no ordinary pig but a porcine gourmet whose every gustatory whim is satisfied with the most exquisite dainties of the trough. Then take a month in the life of Socrates, and make it a month in which the good man is tormented by doubt, taxes, and Xanthippe. Which life would Mill rather live? Being a singularly honest man, he voted for Socrates, thereby making untold trouble for himself. For he was by no means certain that Socrates' life was a pleasanter life, while he had no doubt at all that it was more worth living. There must, then, be something other than pleasure that makes it more worth living. What was this? I will not remind you of Mill's answer because, by pretty general agreement, it was wrong. The right answer, I suggest, is this: Socrates' life was better because, whether more pleasant or not, it involved a completer fulfilment of powers. Grant the pig as generous a gastronomic capacity as one wishes, still one must admit that its intellectual, moral, and aesthetic horizons are limited, while those of Socrates are all but unlimited. What gave Socrates' life its value was the free play of a magnificent mind, the fulfilment in thought, feeling, and practice of a great intellect and a great heart.

This gives us the clue, I think, to the third component of all values. Besides experience, and pleasant experience, there must be fulfilment of natural faculties or powers. What we take as good always fulfils some need of our nature, some urge, drive, or impulse; and if the impulse is not there, we are cut off from value in that direction. Some great men—Lamb, Macaulay, Asquith, and Dean Inge, for example—have admitted that most music was mere noise to them, that they had a congenital lack of capacity for this form of experience. If this is true, fulfilment in this sphere is for them impossible, since there is no impulse or capacity to fulfil; strictly speaking, there is no such thing as music for them, and to try to educate them musically would be cruelty, as it would be to force a blind man to study painting. "Our aims," Emerson said, "should be mathematically adjusted to our powers." Values are not adventitious to human nature. A value is a value because it speaks to our condition, answers our need, meets and completes some demand of our nature. And the more central and fundamental the demand, the greater is the value attaching to its fulfilment.,

In the light of all this, we may describe a value as an experience that is at once pleasant and fulfilling. And our question now is, What is the place of values, so conceived, in education?

The answer is that they should form the polestar of education. For the aim of education is to secure a more worthwhile life, in the first instance for those who receive it, in the second for others affected by these; and a more worthwhile life is one that is richer in values. But while education should aim at the production of values, it has two branches that serve this purpose in very different ways. The aim of *liberal* education is to qualify us directly to realize such values; the aim of *technological* education is to qualify us for them indirectly. Since the latter is nowadays the talk of the town, let us look at that first.

Technological education is training, discipline in doing things, the acquirement of a degree of mastery over an art or craft, whether that of building bridges, pulling teeth, or setting type. There is an ancient dispute about whether this should be called education at all. Humanists have often argued that a man may be the most expert of all practitioners in setting bones or setting type and still be ignorant, bigoted, and provincial; technical proficiency is not enlightenment. On the other hand, our most eminent philosopher of education, John Dewey, held that a technological education, rightly conducted, was every whit as good as one in the humanities. If we think otherwise, he said, it is because for twenty centuries the West has been deluded by the Greeks. Plato and Aristotle were aristocrats who thought that hewing wood and drawing water, however expertly done, were the work of slaves, and that the natural business of free minds was the contemplation of unchanging truth. Dewey believed them mistaken—mistaken as to the nature of thought itself; for thought is not really contemplation, he held; it is itself an instrument for getting things done. That is why he called his theory instrumentalism. It is ironic that Dewey, a champion of technological training, should now be held responsible by many for schools that turn out too few technologists. But our question is whether he was right in holding that technical training contributes as directly or richly to values as the study of the humanities.

I do not think he was. He was a philosopher who carried his attack on philosophy, as traditionally conceived, to an untenable extreme. The attack was popular because his stress on activity, on doing things, was typically American, and a thinker who proclaimed that a hypothesis, a philosophy, or a religion must be appraised by the difference it makes in practice seemed to be saying what, for a philosopher, was surprisingly sensible. But this was hardly the sort of teaching of which we stood in most need, at least those of us who were adults. To be sure, Dewey did much to dispel the dreariness of the little red schoolhouse by insisting that life consisted chiefly in doing things, that education should be a preface to life, and that the child could learn by doing, even by playing; we are all pragmatists from five to ten. But I incline to think that a person who is still a pragmatist at forty is suffering from arrested development. A person who limits the fruits of the spirit to those that can be tested in action is not so much freeing himself from an older dogmatism as fettering himself by a new one.

In justice to Dewey, we must remember that technology has many levels and that he was talking about the higher levels, not about routine plumbing or repairing. When my car breaks down—here I speak with the authority of broad experience—I take it to a certain garage where there is a kindly staff of mechanics. I always hope that a particular one will be there, a big, cheerful, grease-stained Boanerges whose mastery in his field fills me with envy. When I last presented myself on a bitter day, complaining that my radiator was so sick that it could not hold even Prestone down, the first man who came peered about beneath the hood in helpless bewilderment. Then Boanerges sauntered round. He poked a grimy head under the hood, scoffed at the childish notion of a leak in the radiator, and announced in some thirty seconds that one of the plugs in the manifold casing must be loose. He was right, as usual. To me this was sheer wizardry. Here was a master of his craft, and because of this an obviously happy man; and here was I, a master of—well, what?—who had been thinking about free will for thirty years and was confused about it yet. Still, when in my dealings with Boanerges the conversation becomes general, my envy abates. His head is always in that hood; his world seems to be bounded by it; and when he ventures outside it, the master craftsman becomes as awkward and floundering as a puppy. The hood of a car is not, after all, a stately mansion for the soul. The number of things that can go wrong with a car is limited; you can get to the end of them; and when you have got there, the next fifty years of the same looks less appealing.

Dewey would object that this is very primitive technology, that the true technologist is a man whose reflection is continually challenged by fresh problems and whose horizons are always expanding; if an example is wanted, take Edison, or Kettering, or Langmuir, or Wernher von Braun. And we must agree that the services of these men to society have been immense. Their electric lights, motorcars, and nuclear energy are transforming the physical side of life. But that is not the point. The point is whether

100

technological education on a high level opens the mind to values as humanistic education does. The answer is that it does not. We may gain great satisfaction, to be sure, from solving puzzles about how iron or hydrogen behaves when compressed, or frozen, or heated to a million degrees, and from harnessing the more mulish forms of matter and making them work for us. But technology, even at these exalted levels, remains a complicated game of chess, in which, though you pit yourself against nature and play for very high stakes, you are still in essence pushing physical pieces about; and pushing pieces about, even under the most complicated rules, is not a general liberation of the spirit. The objection to a complete preoccupation with matter is that matter is dead. In material things, even in the most perfect of mechanical men, there is nothing to call out our love or admiration or sympathy or emulation or even dislike. The ideal technologist is an infinitely subtle brain at work on an infinitely subtle puzzle. He needs curiosity and endurance; but any appreciation of human goodness or artistic beauty, of what is funny or tragic or sublime, any sense for music or religion or justice, would be for him, simply as a technologist, superfluous baggage. Emerson somewhere deplores our modern tendency to become specialists, so that a man, if truly seen, would appear as a great nose, or a vast mouth, or perhaps a gigantic ear. In such a world, a pure technologist would be a hypertrophied cerebrum connected to a pair of mobile hands, but without any attached heart, glands, or spleen.

Now there is a difference between a technologist and a scientist. What is this difference? Presumably, that the technologist studies nature for the sake of controlling it, while the scientist studies it for the sake of understanding it. Thus the horizon of the scientist is wider than that of the technologist; for if a certain kind of knowledge gives no promise of application, the technologist's interest fades while that of the scientist may remain as lively as ever. Indeed, Bertrand Russell says that "Faraday, Maxwell, and Hertz, so far as can be discovered, never for a moment considered the possibility of any practical application of their investigations"; and Whitehead points out that mathematics was studied for at least two thousand years before anything important came of it "except the intrinsic interest of the study." Science, pursued in this untrammeled way, is now held to form a part of liberal education; indeed, we are being urged to make it the chief part. Let us ask, then, what return in the way of values a young man or woman may expect from this pursuit.

There is, of course, first, the satisfaction of *knowing* something of physics or chemistry or biology. How great a value is this? We may appraise such knowledge for either its illumination or its discipline. To begin with the first, what makes knowledge illuminating? Surely the light it casts upon the world at large, the extent to which it helps to make that world intelligible. Scientific study and research may be a mere grubbing among details, as one could show in a grisly way by citing some of the Ph.D. subjects in any of our graduate schools. But from time to time there appears on the scientific scene a man who shows us afresh what science can do in the way of illumination. For him the details are push buttons which release a flood of light on nature or human nature. Isaac Newton was one of these minds. He saw that if he could explain the fall of an apple he could probably explain the deflection of the moon from a straight line into its orbit around the earth, and if he could explain that, he could explain the movement of the earth around the sun, and if he could explain that, he would have the ground plan of the universe. He believed that he had the formula for the apple, and he tried it on the moon. It did not work, and he laid it aside for years. Then, learning from a French astronomer that he had been mistaken as to the size of the earth and therefore its pull, he tested his formula again with the correct figure. Result after result seemed to come out right. It is said that as he approached the end of his calculations, and the great generalization came almost within his grasp, he became so excited that he did not trust himself and turned over the final audit to steadier heads.

I suppose the only name in modern physics that can stand beside Newton's is that of his challenger, Einstein. And Einstein, so far at least as a layman can follow him, tells us the same story as to what it is that makes science significant. Michelson and Morley had tried what seemed like a rather trivial experiment to check the speed of light. They set up a platform with a beam projected from one end and a mirror at the other end. They then measured the time it took for the beam to go to the mirror and back, first when the beam was traveling in the direction the earth was moving, and then when it was traveling at right angles to that direction. The distance it had to travel in these two cases was different, and they assumed that the time taken would therefore be different. But they found that it was exactly the same. They were surprised and baffled. Einstein was also surprised, but declined to be baffled. Just as Newton had seen in the falling apple the clue to a universal law, so Einstein saw that what this odd result entailed was nothing less than the reconceiving of all measurement and ultimately of the relation of time and space. The little beam of Michelson and Morley he enlarged till it illuminated the physical world.

It is the same with the social sciences. While Einstein was puzzling over the experiment in Berlin, a Vienna doctor was puzzling over such unlikely details as slips of the tongue, bad dreams, and the inability to remember things. For most students, these were quite unconnected facts and not very significant ones. Sigmund Freud insisted on understanding why a slip of the tongue occurred, why one dreamed in one way rather than another, why one could recall some unimportant details and could not remember some shocking ones. He pursued his clues unremittingly until he had a theory which not merely unified the explanation of all these facts but altered our conception of human nature.

It may be said that science, studied in this spirit, is hardly distinguishable from philosophy. I agree. There is no sharp line between the two; they fade into each other. They are parts of one enterprise and are necessary to each other; if philosophy without science is empty, science without philosophy has too often proved to be blind. Philosophy, science, and what we call common sense are all stages of our endeavor to understand the world. By common sense I mean the great body of judgments that we take for granted. These judgments include much dubious metaphysics, such as that grass is green and snow is cold even when nobody is about, and much moral philosophy in the form of proverbs, often of dubious consistency, such as "Be not penny wise and pound foolish" and "Take care of the pence and the pounds will take care of themselves." Now science does not turn its back on common sense; it starts with the earth, trees, and sky that we all accept and tries to make its judgments about them more general, precise, and consistent; it is common sense extended and refined. Philosophy I take to be simply more of the same. It *is* science, concentrating now on its ultimate results and its initial assumptions. This means, on the one hand, that philosophy goes on after science ends; it takes the main results of the various sciences and tries to put them together into a consistent picture of the world. It means, on the other hand, that philosophy begins before science does, in the sense that it subjects such ideas as space, time, and cause, and such assumptions as that nature will behave tomorrow as today, which are not commonly questioned by science, to critical analysis. Philosophy is the attempted completion of science at both ends. I should follow Plato, then, in holding that this makes it the crown of education on its intellectual side. But lest it be thought that this disparages science, I hasten to add that by philosophy I mean science become self-conscious about its beginning and its goal.

The notion of science has now broadened in our hands to mean the attempt to lay hold of principles in any field of study, and it will include the reflective study not only of the natural sciences but also of sociology, economics, psychology, and history. The great point is that education, on its intellectual side, is the quest not of knowledge, not of facts, but of illumination or understanding. Facts, of course, are important, but their retention is not what our minds are for but what the *Britannica* is for. I admire and envy a man who, like Asquith, has the sort of flypaper memory which enables him, if the subject of horse racing happens to be broached, to name all the Derby winners since the race was instituted; but I recall also that Asquith's great antagonist in the Commons, Balfour, had so faulty a memory that if he wanted to quote a single line he had to take it with him on paper. Yet Balfour, by general consent, was one of the best-educated minds in Europe. Quickly seizing the essential points in any issue, he would discuss it with a philosopher's eye for principle and the logic of a master debater.

This brings us to the second of the two values to be found in the liberal pursuit of science, taken in the broad sense. The first was illumination. The second is discipline. Our education ought to supply us with a habit and a method of attacking problems, a habit of orderliness, clearness, persistence, and precision. How often we must endure performances by persons, too often with degrees after their names, which require an agonizing reappraisal of their being educated at all: political speeches without form, and void; radio sermons full of sound and fury, signifying nothing; after-dinner oratory in which the point, if there is one, is fathoms deep in half-relevant anecdotage! And what a satisfaction it is, when we are hunting for light on some complicated issue, to find an article that puts the issue simply, offers its evidence economically, faces difficulties fairly, and draws a firm conclusion! The ability to do that is one of the most infallible marks of the educated mind.

How is it attained? There are plenty of prescriptions for it on the educational drug counter. We should take more mathematics; we should hone our wits on the tough abrasives of symbolic logic; we should study scientific method; we should be exposed to philosophy; since language is the great deceiver, we should study semantics. I do not doubt that we could profit by any of these courses. But there are people of excellent intellectual practice who have never taken any of them, and plenty of muddlers who have taken them all. The common error of such proposals is to assume that there is only one royal road to sound intellectual practice. But the effective use of intelligence is confined to no one field, and it may be acquired in any. How? I venture to think that it is usually gained in two steps: first by admiring it as shown in some particular person, and then by copying it at least once.

Consider the first step. As a teacher, what seems to me distressing is that so many students go through college without contracting any enthusiasm for intellectual artistry, and that so long as we fail to arouse their enthusiasm, we shall accomplish relatively little by force-feeding and stern drills. To be sure, first-rate work does sometimes break through to the student in spite of us if not through us. When I was a high school student I was taught Burke's "Conciliation with America" by a teacher who seemed to have no conception of its quality. But that marvelous speech had its innings in spite of all the teacher could do. I thought it wonderful and, young prig that I was, went around mouthing Burke. I had never met a human being who talked like that or could think like that, but here was the thrilling fact that one man actually had. Not that I understood Burke; no teenager could; but that did not prevent my contracting a bad case of hero worship, and I have never quite recovered from it. In my little cabinet of masterpieces, the speech on conciliation still stands on the same shelf with the Fifth

Symphony. I shall always be grateful that, as a raw youngster in a middle western high school, I caught sight of a distant, unforgettable mountain peak.

The second step in acquiring good thinking habits is to do for oneself in a single case what a good model does. It is far more significant for our education to write one good essay than dozens of mediocre ones, for that one essay means that we have standards, and what we have done once we can presumably do again. No one does eighteen holes of golf in seventy-three by accident; you know that if anyone does that just once, he is a master of the game. A student who has carried through one piece of responsible research in history or biology or anthropology, so that it will stand intensive criticism for its cogency and its style, has had the ideal discipline for future work. It may be objected that discipline does not carry over from field to field. Of course there is something in this, and it makes me a little skeptical about precisely those subjects that have been often thought highest in disciplinary value, namely mathematics and a purely formal logic. In these subjects clarity is achieved *for* one rather than by one, since the concepts are perfectly definite from the beginning; one's conclusion is either completely necessary or false; and the issues are so abstract that personal feelings are not engaged. That is not the sort of thinking we do in politics or religion or even in natural science. When we are discussing liberty or democracy, half the trouble may be in the woolliness of the concepts. Rigorous demonstration will probably be out of the question; judgment will be constantly called for on degrees of importance and relevance; and impartiality may be under test at every step. I am inclined to think, therefore, that for general intellectual discipline good work in an inexact science is more valuable than in an exact science. It may be said that even this kind of discipline does not carry over. Here I can only beg to differ. Caution, clarity, precision, orderliness are the same traits in all the sciences of fact, and though eminent minds are not exempt from foolishness, I think journalists and plain men display a sound instinct when they listen with respect to anything a Toynbee or a Sherrington has to say.

We have been considering the disciplines that aim at knowledge. But what about the study of literature, music, and art? These are now a recognized part of liberal education, and their primary aim is plainly not knowledge. Their aim is to satisfy and educate feeling. We sometimes forget that feeling is as educable as intelligence and that, so far as happiness is concerned, its cultivation is even more important. What does the education of feeling mean? Someone has given the answer in the remark that culture is the adjustment of feeling to its objects and that education is learning to like and dislike the right things. Such education is one of our most conspicuous needs. Americans are a people of strong feelings, freely expressed; they have been called the Latin branch of the Anglo-Saxon family. Many of us seem to like excitement for its own sake, and if there is insufficient outward occasion for it, we are adroit at generating it ad hoc. When Shriners or Legionnaires get together, or a birthday or the New Year is to be celebrated, Americans have an inexhaustible repertory of first aids to excitement: brass bands, paper hats, ticker tape, horns and whistles, snake dances, fancy costumes, and drum majorettes; and at big games there are trained cheerleaders to work up our emotions and give them organized vent. Of course exuberance and high spirits are excellent things. But this hardly implies that the value of an experience depends on how exciting it is. May I quote two or three wise sentences from the philosopher A. E. Taylor? "The mere identification of *any* fundamental activity of the human spirit with emotion, cut loose from a *specific* object, is the degradation and, in the end, the paralysis of the emotion itself. Emotions of all kinds so manifestly derive their value for human life from the character of the object on which they are directed. Emotion inappropriate or disproportionate to the objective situation by which it is evoked is the bane of life."

Now, emotion inappropriate to its object is a chief bane of American life. It shows itself in the scale of admirations felt by the American public. Let me catch a few straws from the wind. When Mr. Nixon, then Vice President, came home from one of his trips, he was met by his small daughter, Patricia, who told him that she had started piano lessons. "And do you like to practice?" asked her father, who used to be fairly adept at the piano himself. "Yes," said Patricia, and went on to give a pointed little lecture to her father: "You know, Daddy, if you had practiced a lot, you would have gone to Hollywood. And you know what would have happened? You would have become famous and everybody would remember you, and they would bury you in a nice place." I hope that moving into the White House did something to mollify Patricia. But to my somewhat naive mind the likings of the American public are puzzling. On my desk is an attractive advertisement for a new *Encyclopedia of Jazz*, which informs me that since it contains the birthdays of 1,065 jazz artists it "provides an invaluable tool for . . . school jazz groups, etc." Consider this revealing sentence by a reviewer asked to write an advance notice of a new novel for the *Retail Bookseller*: "Savage as *The Hucksters* . . . rough, tough, and violent, it looks like a best seller." To be sure, the stage and television aspire at times to higher things. The producer Mort Abrahams ventured to put on his television program, "Showcase," a novel version of an old thriller called *Romeo and Juliet*. It didn't do badly, and Mort is reported to have commented happily: "This boy Shakespeare is a real comer: I'm going to use a lot of him."

If these things seem comic, there are numberless people who do not find them so, and that makes them also tragic. In the sphere of science we can protect ourselves fairly readily from quacks and frauds; there are consumers' unions, pure food and drug acts, and often simple tests of one's own that will serve to eliminate the worst in the way of soaps and cold remedies. But there is no kind of litmus paper that will show vulgarity as what it is except the inward kind called education. And by education I do not mean, of course, a college degree; I mean living in the presence of the best till one understands and likes it, till the ways of feeling of fine minds become one's own, till one catches their health by contagion as one catches other people's disease, and develops a general immunity to the viruses of cheapness. "Moral education is impossible," says Whitehead, "without the habitual vision of greatness." "The way to acquire a good taste in anything," says Sir Richard Livingstone, "from pictures to architecture, from literature to character, from wine to cigars, is always the same—be familiar with the best specimens of each." One of the blessings of our time and country is that this kind of education is open to any determined boy or girl. There are plenty of good guides to reading, and plenty of libraries and cheap editions available to anyone with a real desire for the best. It is salutary for us academics to recall occasionally that

Chaucer and Shakespeare, Keats and Browning, Jane Austen and Dickens, Mill and Shaw never went to a university.

The strange thing is that the very democracy that was supposed to diffuse acquaintance with the best is serving in unexpected ways to prevent this. Our literate public is the world's greatest market. Publishers depend on sales and Hollywood on the box office; both therefore are tempted to appeal to the lowest common denominator, the level on which we can all meet, which is not that of ideas but of crude emotions: fear, anger, sex, and self-glorification. The standard formula is to mix these up into one potent brew, varying slightly the proportions of the ingredients, and to serve it up over and over. That is what we shall get as long as we go on patiently accepting it. Many have come to think of tolerance as a virtue that extends equally to values and beliefs; I cannot agree. Not that we should suppress vulgarity any more than we should suppress mistaken ideas, but that the very notion of values implies that there is a good and a bad, and that democracy among values is a contradiction in terms.

If we really love what is good, we shall despise what is bad and say so. There are courageous critics who show us the way in this. I was reassured some time ago to find J. Donald Adams telling the house of Scribner to its austere old face that in publishing James Jones's *Some Came Running* it was issuing a book on "the intellectual level of a retarded adolescent" and that it ought to be ashamed of itself. Dean Robert E. Fitch of the Pacific School of Religion has spoken out against what he calls the *mystique de la merde* in our fiction, a phrase variously translated as "the deification of dirt," "the apotheosis of ordure," and "plain mud mysticism." He says that writers like Jones and Norman Mailer and Tennessee Williams and, at his worst, Hemingway would have us believe that what sadistic sergeants and moronic prostitutes blurt out in their cups is somehow truth and reality, while thoughtful and kindly people are too dull to be worth listening to. I will not try to appraise this; I am not well read enough. But of some of the things I have read it rings true.

It may be said that in these matters no grounded preference is possible; and we are sure soon to hear that *de gustibus non est dis-*

*putandum.* But matters of taste are precisely what people argue about most vigorously, and if there is any force in what we have said about the nature of value, there are objective betters and worses and it is simply silly in Bentham's fashion to put pushpin beside poetry. The Greeks saw that in great tragedy one somehow fulfils oneself and becomes a new and larger man, with a new sense for the central and the trivial. What troubles me as a college teacher is that so many students leave college with apparently no sense at all of what is central and what trivial. College courses have exposed them to greatness, but it has somehow left them cold.

This is partly our fault as teachers. It is all very well to say, "we needs must love the highest when we see it"; the trouble is that without help the highest may be as hard to make out as Mount Everest is from Darjeeling. The teacher of literature must make his students see the subject with his eyes and, if he can, feel for it some of his love. Overworked jade that he probably is, he must manage to remain on fire with his subject, for only so can he light fires under anyone else. Fortunately, to do that he does not need to be a great writer or critic himself. William Lyon Phelps was neither, but he was one of Yale's most valuable assets nevertheless, for he had the happy faculty of turning out lovers of literature in droves. How did he do it? Chiefly by a joint enthusiasm for literature and for youth. "When I wake up in the morning," he said, "I lie in bed and think with delight of my first class." Is it any wonder that the class repaid him in kind?

We have considered values of the intellect and values of appreciation, but have said nothing about the values of conduct or practice. Is not life largely action, and should not college prepare us to act as well as to think and feel? Now if action means mere behavior, the play of arm and leg, there are no values of action, for values are in the mind. Still, we all know that the man of action—the Napoleon of the army or industry or public life—is a distinct type from the thinker or the artist, and a vastly important type who is often lost in the shuffle when education is under review. Can a college turn out such men, or even do much to help them? This is my last question.

Of course there are schools of business administration and welfare work and diplomacy, but no college can reproduce the conditions in which the man of affairs is going to work. So when liberal arts colleges are criticized because their graduates on entering business have to learn it from the ground up, the charge is both true and negligible. No curriculum ever devised will guarantee a Churchill or a Henry Ford. But that a college can do something even here is suggested by the fact that little Merton College, Oxford, with less than 150 students, produced, if I remember rightly, seven archbishops of Canterbury in one century, and that Balliol under Jowett poured out administrators to every part of the empire.

The chief points about the office of the college in training men of action seem to me to be these. First, a training of intelligence *is* a training of will. As William James pointed out, a firm will is largely a matter of controlled attention, of fixing our thought firmly on what must be done, and hence a discipline of thought is itself a preparation for action. Secondly, college life on the practical side is not wholly divorced from the rest of life. It exacts hard tasks, it sets deadlines, it requires the ordering of one's time and the budgeting of one's energies. Teachers are sometimes slack and indulgent about these things, as doting parents are, but the student ought not to be so toward himself. He is enjoying a great privilege which he ought to take most seriously, and if he keeps himself to the mark, that alone will equip him to meet the deadlines of the world. Thirdly, American colleges, rightly I think, value athletics; and the participation in competitive games, if wisely conducted, gives an admirable discipline in taking success modestly, in taking defeat and hard knocks uncomplainingly, and in developing respect for justice, since sportsmanship is justice in play. If Yorktown was lost, as has been alleged, on the playing fields of Eton, at least Waterloo was something. Fourthly, as in the realms of intelligence and appreciation, so too in the realm of action college can marshal models across the stage for whom we feel a self-revealing repulsion or affinity. Here history is the chief resource, not so much social or constitutional history as the old-fashioned kind that makes it largely the biography of great men. We all find it intelligible that General Eisenhower, traversing Napoleon's field of action, should have remarked, "I'd have liked to tangle with that fellow," or that he and Montgomery should have gone over the field of Gettysburg together and come up with a reappraisal of Lee. What is more surprising is that such people as Goethe, Hegel, and Emerson should also be fascinated by Napoleon; that Mommsen, Froude, and

Thronton Wilder should have been fascinated by Caesar; and that Carlyle should have worshiped at the shrines of Cromwell and Frederick. These men of action had deep moral flaws, but they were, after all, among the "quarto and folio editions of mankind," and to know them is to expand one's ideas of what a mere human being can do. Finally, education not only can inspire action, it can give it perspective and goals. How different the world would be if Napoleon and Hitler had been just and cultivated minds instead of being the one an outsized Corsican brigand and the other a guttersnipe of genius!

We have reached the end of our argument, and it proves to be as simple as it has been long. Values, we have argued, are experiences that are at once satisfying and fulfilling. The purpose of education is to make us creators and centers of value. Technological education does that indirectly by supplying us tools for the exploiting of nature. Liberal education on its intellectual side provides the values of understanding, which makes us at home in our world. Liberal education on its appreciative side makes us responsive to the best that has been said and painted and built and sung. Liberal education on its practical side puts the wind of emulation in our sails and gives direction to our voyage. Values are the stars by which education may and should steer its course.

# 7

# What Should We Get from College?

What should we get from college? One student will tell you very definitely what he wants. He wants to take all those subjects, and only those, that will help him get into a medical school; or knowing that a job awaits him in his father's firm, he wants to become an engineer as quickly and painlessly as he can. In contrast with him is the man, who I suspect is in the majority, whose only definite aim is to discover some definite aim. He doesn't yet know what he wants to make of himself and hopes that college will help him to find out. He wrote a short story once for his high school paper that everyone praised, so he has a vague idea that he would like to write; the awkward thing is that to write you have to have something to write about, and on this his mind is a blank. Or he is just an embarrassingly average man who never gets above B even in English and never falls below C even in mathematics, who has never stood out in anything and therefore doesn't know what he is good in, who has never flunked anything, and therefore doesn't know what to avoid. So he uses college as an experimental laboratory, hoping, like Mr. Micawber, that some cue will turn up.

Now I think that students in both these extreme positions are in a rather bad way. The student who, with a definite idea of what college has to give him, orders it to stand and deliver, usually finds it rather poor pickings. One of the best things that an education has to give is an instructed expectation of what to ask of education and of life; it ought to give us much more than we can definitely plan for at the beginning. The student who has it all plotted in advance is like the man who motors through the Yellowstone with his speedometer set at sixty and his eyes fixed on the road. He sees less of the countryside than the man with no goal at all. The trouble with this latter gentleman is that he may never arrive anywhere, which after all is important too. I recommend to you the unexciting middle position. It seems to me that in beginning college work, or in resuming it year by year, one should have some idea of where the protracted business is leading, and that it is perfectly possible to be clear enough about this to prevent wasting one's own time and one's father's balance at the bank without taking a college education merely as the shortest distance between two points. One ought to have a *general* idea from the outset of what one wants from education, an idea that specifies itself as one goes along, and particularly as one approaches the great decision what to do with one's life. My question, then, is: What is it that any of us, beginning or resuming higher education, can sensibly ask that it should do for us?

For one thing, we may surely ask of it what the more modest of these student types requires of it, namely that it help us define our own aims, by revealing what we can and cannot do. Education is a voyage in self-discovery. William McDougall used to say that each man was not so much one self as a federation of selves. You are not, for example, a poet, *or* a mechanic, *or* a lawyer; you are a unique synthesis of sixth-rate poet, second-rate mechanic, fourth-rate lawyer, and perhaps first-rate performer on the trombone. Now it is the root of ten thousand tragedies that Smith, who arouses everyone's delight and admiration when he plays the trombone, and is awkward and commonplace when he does anything else, is convinced that playing the trombone is beneath his dignity and practicing law is a noble profession, and therefore becomes a lawyer hunting vainly for briefs and playing the trombone wistfully of an

114

evening. I am not saying that playing a horn is as great an achievement as mastering the law; I am saying that if one is, by endowment of nature, a first-rate horn player and a fourth-rate follower of the law, it is best to be oneself, that is, one's dominant self. That self, though perhaps a poor thing, is your own; and though your own, it can be discovered only by trial and error; indeed, if not given a chance to grow, it will probably die. John Stuart Mill was right in saying that there are those who, "by dint of not following their own nature, . . . have no nature to follow." The efficiency and happiness of your life may well depend on your deciding rightly what that nature is.

In making this decision, three somewhat different kinds of courage are needed. The first is the humble sort of courage needed to stick at a task till one can take one's own measure in it. It is a great mistake to suppose that if one is good at something, this is bound to show itself in the first day or the first month of one's work in it. Students sometimes think that if they have a gift for a subject, it will announce itself in the manner of Oscar Wilde on his first arrival in this country. When asked by the customs officer whether he had anything to declare, he replied, "I have nothing to declare but my genius." There is an impression in the minds of some that if they have an affinity for economics, say, or chemistry, it must reveal itself instantly as, according to Hollywood, heaven-made and eternal affinities reveal themselves in a flash when boy meets girl, whereas interest, like love, is as a rule the gradual result of association. If success depends on interest, interest also depends on success, and success in most subjects and for most people comes by hard work.

Capitulation before an early lack of success would have cost the world many of its leaders. One of the most distinguished logicians of the last century was F. H. Bradley, but I have been told that Bradley almost flunked the Oxford entrance examinations in elementary mathematics. In his own generation, probably the finest Latin scholar in the world was the poet A. E. Housman, but while Housman did succeed in getting into Oxford, he never left it by the front door; he failed flatly in his degree examination. Or consider Bernard Shaw, a genius by others' vote as well as his own. It is tempting to think of him as virtually having been born with the Shavian style. The fact is, so he tells us, that before he found his true vein his writings had the distinction of having been turned down by every publisher of note in England. I suppose Alfred Adler would construe such cases as evidence for the doctrine that nothing succeeds like failure. While that is an overstatement, it remains true that many a man has failed to discover the vein of gold in the depths of his own nature because he has been put off by the hard work of the digging.

The second kind of courage is the courage to see and avow when one is beaten and to give up a bad job. There is a conviction rife in this country that every healthy and ambitious boy or girl is somehow entitled to a higher education, and if given the chance, would take a degree almost automatically. The tendency of such a belief is to lower our standards everywhere. Higher education should be for the able, and not everyone is able; most of us are not; and no one is able in everything. The college is not doing its duty by most of us unless it plants unequivocal signs in appropriate spots: "No road this way." To be sure, I am still waiting for the day when a student will approach me with heartfelt thanks for flunking him in a course, but I suspect that some should have done so, and that I should have given far more of them an opportunity to do so. If your education does for you what it should, it will reveal to you a set of *in*capacities and blind spots, perhaps in the very region where you thought your powers lay; and then the courage and honesty of cheerful renunciation will be needed.

What these things mean you could hardly learn better than from Charles Lamb's little essay called "A Chapter on Ears." Lamb was a lover of the arts and, enjoying strumming on the piano, he would have liked to think of himself as something of a virtuoso in music. But he came slowly to realize that, even on its humbler levels, music was not for him. He discovered that, with all his sensitivity in other directions, he lacked an ear. "Sentimentally, I am disposed to harmony. But *organically* I am incapable of a tune. I have been practising 'God Save the King' all my life; whistling and humming of it over to myself in solitary corners; and am not yet arrived, they tell me, within many quavers of it." Instead of hiding his incapacity, and trying to clap in the right places by following others, Lamb reported with engaging candor what was a simple matter of fact and no disgrace, namely that he could not distinguish a soprano from a tenor, and that in consequence Haydn and Mozart, Bach and Beethoven, were to him insufferable bores. He had no desire on this point to interfere with others' pleasures, but neither would he delude himself about his own. What a mass of futile, struggling unhappiness would be averted if people could achieve the gay courage of renunciation of that "Chapter on Ears."

The third type of courage needed is the obverse of the second, the kind celebrated by Emerson under the name of self-reliance. It is the courage to choose and be oneself. "There comes a time in every man's education," says Emerson in the great essay, "when he arrives at the conviction that envy is ignorance; that imitation is suicide; that he must take himself for better for worse as his portion. . . . The power which resides in him is new in nature, and none but he knows what that is which he can do, nor does he know until he has tried. . . . A man should learn to detect and watch that gleam of light which flashes across his mind from within, more than the lustre of the firmament of bards and sages." A college course should be a hunt for this gleam. The gleam may take any form; and because the American university is less singly intellectual than the European, it gives wider scope for the search. For the American student, it is part of his university experience to try his hand not only at trigonometry and poetry, but also at baseball, debating, dramatics, talk, and the college paper. This is as it should be. Such ventures are important experiments in the confirmation or elimination of hope.

May I recall as examples of this courage of loyalty to one's own line two men who were fellow undergraduates with me? When I was a sophomore at the University of Michigan, I was a substitute catcher on the sophomore literary baseball team; this represents nearly the high-water mark of my athletic distinction. Our team once had to play a freshman engineering squad that had on it a young man newly arrived from the great open spaces, and the engineers put him in to pitch. The result for the sophomores was as utter destruction as this goodly sport permits. This freshman stayed on the mound, if I recall correctly, for seven innings, and of the twenty-one who faced him, twenty went down on strikes. I remember yet the absurd things a ball seemed to do, in the way of flouting physics, when it left his prestidigitating arm; a baseball in his hands seemed like a pingpong ball in anyone else's. We naturally inquired about him. He was reported to be a modest and likeable youngster, not conspicuous in the classroom, but with serious ambitions as an engineer. In the course of his self-exploration, he was making the odd discovery that, though commonplace enough in everything else, he was, in one little line, namely throwing and hitting a baseball, as unquestionably a genius as Edison and Emerson were in their own loftier lines. This was his gleam, such as it was, and he decided to follow it. He did so with honor to himself and as long as his health lasted, with success. His name, George Sisler, is not a name that will ever appear in our best-known Hall of Fame, but it does appear in a humbler hall of fame at Cooperstown, which would perhaps be equally difficult for most of us to enter.

The other man took longer in discovering his gift. When I knew him, it was in a foreign university and he had his Harvard degree behind him; but he was apparently still groping for his métier. He was a struggling student of philosophy and I remember how, when we went off on a reading party, he used to sit hour after hour contemplating rather wanly the pages of *Principia Mathematica*. His heart, and sometimes his thoughts, seemed to be far away. But where? None of us knew. What struck us about him was an aloofness, detachment, and impersonality, as if he had never been young and impulsive, as if he were already above the battle, viewing the human scene with a disillusionment precocious and overmournful for one in his twenties. He had a gift for languages and had used them for a wide reading; he had already read most of Plato in Greek. When our ways parted, I lost sight of him for some years and wondered what had become of him. Then there appeared in an American magazine a strange poem in a new style, charged with a brooding melancholy and variegating a curious restrained eloquence with echoes from Greek, French, and Italian literature. It was called *The Wasteland*. T. S. Eliot had come into his own. He had found the mood and the medium in which he could say what was in him to say. Neither matter nor manner seemed likely to catch the public ear, but by his depth and sincerity he caught that ear none the less. Here was a clear new note, and it was plainly no man's echo.

One thing, then, that we may hope to gain from our education is a set of clues to such self-discovery. That is one of the two great services that our college years can render us. Now for the other. Besides self-discovery, it may give us self-discipline. It may impose upon us a regimen, intellectual, aesthetic, and practical, that will enrich our spirits and add to our force, wherever our special calling.

I say, first, *intellectual discipline*. Cardinal Newman said that the aim of a university education was as solely intellectual as the aim of trade was profit. If this is an overstatement, at least the *distinctive* aim of the university is intellectual; its main concern is to produce the formed mind. But if you ask what a formed mind is, you get very different responses. Some people appear to mean by it a *full* mind, a mind whose cellars and attics are crammed with learning; the aim, they think, is to *know* a great deal. It was said of Macaulay, who was the perfect example of this educational ideal, that the test of his power was his readiness to embroider any subject even when not introduced by himself. Macaulay once said, not in boasting but in mere report of fact, that he read a book as fast as others skimmed it, and skimmed it as fast as others turned the pages; he would read two or three books of his Greek *Iliad* on an afternoon walk. And he added to this speed of absorption a flypaper retentiveness, so that when he reached maturity the literature and history of Europe were at his finger ends as they have perhaps never been at anyone's before or since. He was the sort of person whom it was hard to catch out on the kings of England, the major or minor prophets, or the Popes of Rome, and who undertook to restore *verbatim*, if they were lost, *Pilgrim's Progress* and *Paradise Lost*, the sort of man whose volume of knowledge on every subject was so great that when he chose to pour it out, as he often did, his friends were fairly drowned in it. One of them, Sydney Smith, expressed his gratitude for Macaulay's occasional "flashes of silence."

Now it would be absurd to deprecate learning. The power to retain great masses of detail is a most enviable gift, of real importance to the lawyer, the academic lecturer, the scientist, or the historian. I once heard Norman Hapgood challenge a company to name one man who had done first-rate things in the realm of mind without a good memory, and the company had difficulty in meeting the challenge. Still, that mere learning is not enough is suggested by Emerson's remark about Macaulay that no one ever knew so much that was not worth knowing. What is important is not quantity of information, which the *Britannica* can always supply us on call, but something else, which is almost as much a function of what we have forgotten as of what we still retain, the power of judgment. A distinguished philosopher of our day has said that all the first-rate philosophers have been marked by a "massive common sense," which is not learning, not cleverness, not dialectic skill, not practical sense—though most of the great thinkers have had all these—but the sort of judgment that enabled them to see what was absurd as absurd, and what was probable or reasonable for what it was. As President Butler remarked, it is fairly easy to be clever and tremendously hard to be right. The first result of an education on the intellectual side is the sense of when an assertion is made out and when it is not. And to see that, we must not only be able in a given case to discern what is relevant evidence and whether the evidence at hand gives proof or probability; we must understand that some beliefs require a wholly different kind of evidence from other, while some require none beyond themselves. The ideally educated man is the one who, as Locke suggested, is able to give to everything proposed for his acceptance precisely that degree of assent which the evidence warrants.

Does that seem a tame achievement? If so, this itself shows how much we need it, how much we have been victimized by the temper of our time with its demand for the violent, the exciting, and the spectacular. Any Hollywood moron can be exciting; but I suppose no one in history has succeeded in being quite reasonable for as much as a single day. Consider what such a feat would involve.

We open our newspaper of a morning and look at the headlines. On page 1, in the right-hand column, is a statement by the secretary of state that between the soviet and democratic ways of life there is an irreconcilable conflict. How much truth is there in this? To know the answer would require not only that we should grasp a vast mass of fugitive evidence, but that our appraisal of it should be undistorted by slogans and headlines, by personal prejudice or popular feeling. What is wanted to deal with such an issue is more than knowledge, though that is essential, and more than cleverness, though an eye for remote implication is also essential, and more than a sound sense of the important and the unimportant, though that too is indispensable. What is wanted is that rare combination of these things called wisdom, which is the common sense of the cultivated mind.

But education, I suggested, is not a purely intellectual affair. We have a right to ask of it not only that it should polish our powers of reason, but that it should enable us to like and dislike the right things. There are some kinds of experience that men who have had them have always reported to be singularly rich and rewarding and have preferred unhesitantly to others, some writers who do not brook our question, some workers in sound or color who are masters beyond all cavil. About these there is small disagreement. To be sure there are always those who have blind spots for greatness. Darwin, you will remember, found Shakespeare unreadable, just as Samuel Butler thought Darwin a fraud, and Malcolm Muggeridge thought Butler a fraud. But in the long run such judgments are more commonly taken as evidence of limitations in the critic than of littleness in his victim. When Darwin said that he could find nothing in Shakespeare, he added with his usual honesty that he had lost the imaginative nerve ends which would enable him to feel what was undoubtedly there; and when Bernard Shaw returns to the attack—well, you would hardly expect pure prose in the person of Shaw to respond very adequately to pure poetry in Shakespeare. Some artists have a range on the keyboard of human nature, a depth and richness and complexity of the chords they strike that send one away with a new perception of

> How good is man's life, the mere living, how fit to employ
> All the heart and the soul and the senses forever in joy.

Some years ago in London I saw the production by Olivier and Leigh, first of Shakespeare's *Antony and Cleopatra* and then of Shaw's *Caesar and Cleopatra*. Now I greatly admire Shaw; I never fail to get pleasure and stimulation from his dialectical and linguistic acrobatics. But if you happen to have seen these two plays, I suspect you will agree that one ought not, as I did, to see Shaw *after* Shakespeare. It was really chalk after cheese; and that is hardly good enough, even if the chalk is the best chalk and the cheese not the best cheese. There is a vast difference, after all, between cleverness, even when raised to the *n*th power, and true greatness of soul, imagination and style. It is not that Shakespeare did better what Shaw tried to do; it is rather that he lived in a world of more dimensions, and has the power of taking us home with him, of making us feel over and over again

> Like some watcher of the skies
> When a new planet swims into his ken.

H. W. Garrod, who was professor of poetry at Oxford, complains in one of his essays of the loss among recent writers of what he calls "magnificence of mind." It is not hard, I think, to catch what he means. It is the sort of thing that distinguishes Michelangelo from Brancusi; Bach (so they tell me; I am incompetent here) from Edward MacDowell; Milton with all his faults from e. e. cummings with all his virtues. There are many people who prefer the second in each of these pairs to the first. The question of real interest is whether, not many people, but anyone at all, who has entered with equal completeness into the experiences which these artists open to us, would not report that what the first of them gave was more fully and richly satisfying than that of the second. The issue is difficult, perhaps impossible, to put to the test, but for my own part I should doubt whether there are any such persons at all. Nine-tenths or more of the disagreement about values is due, I suspect, to the fact that one party or both are looking at them in blinkers and simply not seeing what is there. The business of education at this point is also simple enough; it is to take the blinkers off so that we can see and judge for ourselves. And that is a long process. For seeing here means not only seeing and hearing, but also feeling; the chief value of the study of art lies in the education of feeling.

Education we have conceived, so far, as a double affair, a quest of more expert reasonableness and of a more discerning taste. Many people would be willing to let it go at that. I think that in doing so they ask too little of education, for there is another and most important side to it. There are plenty of persons on record of splendid intellectual competence and very fine sensibility who have done much less than they ought because they were never able to get themselves in hand on the *practical* side. Two or three summers ago, I had the pleasure of visiting a cottage in the English Lake Country which will be known as long as English literature endures, because it had been the home successively of Wordsworth and De Quincey, and the scene of frequent visits to both by Coleridge. Of these three remarkable men, I suppose it is the first who holds the highest place in literature, although perhaps he was the least gifted of the three. There is something satisfying about Wordsworth's life, because it was moulded, ordered, and unified by an immense firmness of character. Beside him De Quincey and Coleridge were imposing ruins, and ruins because they lacked character. De Quincey was in a sense a wonderfully educated man; his Greek tutor at Oxford said that the boy could harangue an Athenian audience as easily as he himself could an English one. And yet I could not help remembering, as I stood in his study at Dove Cottage, that for a succession of miserable years he had sat helplessly in this room increasing his dose of laudanum from 1,000 to 2,000, 3,000, 6,000, 8,000 drops a day to dull the sense of his own feebleness, while his devoted young wife grew prematurely old. Coleridge was in some ways a profoundly educated man; he was one of the most remarkable talkers on philosophy and literature of whom there is any record. But I wonder if you can properly call anyone educated if you have to add that nobody can ever rely on him for fulfilling any engagement. Little by little people learned about this brilliant man that they could not count on him for getting his articles in on time, or returning books he borrowed, or meeting his debts, or paying his rent, or even for supporting his children. One of the finest poets and critics of Europe ended at last in the house of a friend as an object of charity, talking of course with fluent brilliancy to the last.

Coleridge and De Quincey had disciplined minds and undisciplined characters. With all their immense gifts they were imperfectly educated men. Character, the power of conceiving a program and sticking to it, is obviously a central condition in the ordering of a life, and it is as truly educable as either intelligence or taste. Many people have thought that while a building covered with ivy is a very good place to shape intelligence and taste, we must depend for the formation of character on struggle in a larger world. As Goethe put it:

Es bildet ein Talent sich in der Stille,
Sich ein Charakter in dem Strom der Welt.

Talent is shaped in silence,
Character in the turmoil of the world.

Indeed one is tempted to think at times that our colleges do an actual disservice in this vital respect. Some employers declare that they would rather *not* have college products. We professors are sinners here. We announce that papers are due on Friday, October 22; when we discover that a half-dozen have not come in, we beam through paternal spectacles and follow a policy of appeasement; we are so sorry you had trouble in finishing the paper; yes, there *was* a big game on Saturday; yes, there *was* a good deal to read; yes, it *is* hard to write with a headache; so sorry you were under par; next Wednesday will do after all. A student who knows he can get away with this is only too likely to do it, and what is worse, to do it in other things, to form the habit of getting by in this way without putting anything properly through. Don't let us spoil you in this. You are not winning at our expense when you do it; it hurts you far more than it hurts us, for you are still laying foundations, and we are only too probably ruined already. Whatever may be the motive of this advice of ours, I wish it might stick in your memory as a sign I once saw sticks in my own. It was thirty-five years ago on the walls of a military unit overseas that I saw it, and I have often thought of it gratefully when I was tending to grow slack. The sign read, "This office wants results, not explanations." Of course one can always find such explanations if the results are not forthcoming, but the mark of what I am calling character is the disdain either to use them or to get oneself into holes where one needs to use them.

I wish I could pass on to you the secret of this great art of getting things done. But if there is one, I don't know what it is. There is a vast yardage of literature designed to stiffen the spines of the people who can't get up, and can't get to bed, and are always late, and don't answer letters, who burn brightly in college dramatics and then sputter slowly out for fifty years. These persons often know their own weakness, are miserable about it, and try to cure it as Carlyle said Coleridge did, even in his conversation, by assembling at the outset "elaborate precautionary and vehiculatory gear." If they have a task to do, they make a great fuss about the proper foundations for preparing to begin to commence. If action is called for, the man of the hour is not the person who first gets involved with himself and then gets sorry for himself; it is the man who, without fuss or friction, does what is needful.

Perhaps the nearest thing to a secret of the art of putting things through is the suggestion made independently by two very wise men, Aristotle and William James, that character is a matter of habit. It is a commonplace that if something has to be done, the best chance of getting it done is to appeal to the busiest man around. The power of putting a long program through depends on the power of putting a short program through, and that simply on doing what needs to be done from moment to moment. No one has stated the case better than William James:

> The hell to be endured hereafter, of which theology tells, is no worse than the hell we make for ourselves in this world by habitually fashioning our characters in the wrong way. Could the young but realize how soon they will become mere walking bundles of habits, they would give more heed to their conduct while in the plastic state. We are spinning our own fates, good or evil, and never to be undone. Every smallest stroke of virtue or of vice leaves its never-so-little scar. The drunken Rip van Winkle in Jefferson's play excuses himself for every fresh dereliction by saying, "I won't count this time!" Well, he may not count it, and a kind Heaven may not count it, but it is being counted none the less. Down among his nerve-ends and fibres the molecules are counting it, registering it, and storing it up to be used against him when the next temptation comes. Nothing we ever do is in strict scientific literalness ever wiped out. Of course this has its good side as well as its bad one. . . . Let no youth have any anxiety about the up-shot of his education, whatever the line of it may be. If he keep faithfully busy each hour of the working day, he may with safety leave the final result to itself. He can with perfect certainty count on waking up some fine morning to find himself one of the competent ones of his generation. . . . [*Talks to Teachers* (London: Longmans, 1899), pp. 77-78.]

It follows that these bouts of college days with intractable assignments, witless classmates, and professorial ogres are not mere shadow boxing. They are the means of finding yourself and thereby finding your niche in the scheme of things. They are the means of acquiring that art of thinking without which our world is becoming an increasingly insoluble puzzle. They are the means of learning to like and dislike intelligently and therefore rewardingly. They are the means of moulding persons who can act with firmness as well as think with point and judge with taste. Like the men in the scriptural story, you are given talents, some one talent, some two, some perhaps five, and then left to your own devices for four crucial and testing years to see what you will do with them. On what you do with them depends what the world will do with you.

# 8

# *Can Men Be Reasonable?*

One of the most significant changes that have occurred in recent decades is the decline of faith in reason. It is true that in the years before 1914, now so quiet in their appearance and so remote, there were deep divisions in most departments of thought, but it was not supposed that they were beyond remedy; it was taken for granted that there was an objective truth to be found, and that if it was looked for patiently and persistently it could be brought to light. However far men fell short of reasonableness in thought and practice, they did not doubt that there was such a thing as a reasonable way of looking at things and a reasonable way of life, and that, so far as they could, they should make them their own.

In those days the dominant philosophy was idealism, which held that the real was rational and the rational was the real. The dominant psychologies were those of Wundt, James, Titchener, and Ward, all of them brought up in this rationalistic philosophy and respectful of it even where they did not follow. The dominant logic was that of Bradley and Bosanquet, whose view was that thought in its very nature was an attempt at rational system. The dominant ethics were those of Sidgwick, Moore, and Rashdall, who held that the test of right and wrong lay in the self-evident rational insight that $x$ was better than $y$. The most influential political theory was one which found in a rational and general will the justification of the state. In religion the voice of the time was liberalism, which said that God revealed himself to men in the degree to which they achieved a coherent experience of goodness, beauty, and truth.

All this has now changed. Reason has had a pelting from every side; even in its own field of philosophy it has been jostled and on occasion jeered at as if it were some rude interloper. The idealist systems, where they have not bowed themselves out, have become hesitant, vague, and apologetic, and the splendid vision they inherited from Plato of a reason freely following its own law is put down by naturalists and pragmatists alike as a mirage. Psychology has been invaded first by Freud, who finds all rational consciousness to be controlled by reins that come up from an irrational unconscious, and then by the behaviorists, who profess to doubt whether consciousness exists at all. In logic, the most conspicuous present-day school denies that the sort of insight that rationalists have been seeking is even possible; no necessary connections exist except in logic, and there they are tautologies. The rising vogue in ethics is for a relativism beside which the relativism of Sumner and Westermarck is naive; it holds that "moral judgments" are not judgments at all, but exclamations which, as expressing nothing but feeling, are neither true nor false. In the political sphere the theory that international differences are incapable in the nature of the case of any rational decision and can be settled only by force came within a very narrow margin of imposing itself on the civilized world. In religion, to name but one more province, the massive theology of Karl Barth represents the claim of reason to apprehend religious truth as an impertinence.

If these views were really acted upon, I do not think the results could be accepted complacently. For these results would include defeat in philosophy, an overstress in psychology upon the animal nature of man, a retreat toward verbalism in logic, a thoroughgoing skepticism in ethics, anarchy in politics, and irresponsibility in religion. Just as there is nothing more practical than reasonableness, so there is no sphere of practice that will not have to pay a heavy ransom for the abandonment of reason as its authority and guide.

But having pointed this out, I am going to pass it over. I do so partly for reasons of strategy. One of the things that must strike any student of the recent revolts against reason is the curious practical unconcern so often displayed in them. An acute young writer will propose an ethical theory from which, for example, it follows that the claim of democracy to superiority over fascism has no objective ground whatever, and being acute, he must have seen this; but it is apparently of small interest and receives no mention. It seems to be a matter of pride to leave all such things to others and to keep strictly to one's analysis, like a scientist perfecting his formula for botulinus toxin. That the sole practical importance of this toxin is its capacity to destroy 180 million lives per ounce is a consideration which after all is irrelevant to chemical theory. To anyone who works in this spirit, arguments from practical consequences cannot be expected to carry much force.

I do not find this unconcern about the human consequences of theory an attractive trait. But I suppose one has to admit that the implied logic of it is sound. To be sure, if the question were whether a course of conduct was right or wrong, the character of the consequences would be relevant in the highest degree. But if the question is whether a piece of analysis in logic or in psychology is correct, that is not to be proved erroneous by recounting the undesirable consequences that would follow if it were accepted. And the question whether reason is in fact the slave of the passions, or whether men ever do in fact grasp a necessary connection, is a question of this second kind rather than the first. The conclusions of the irrationalists do seem to me practically disastrous, and those who hold them ought to be alive to these. Nevertheless, if these conclusions are to be overthrown, it must be not by insisting that they are dangerous but by showing that they are incorrect. And I am convinced that, in the case of the irrationalisms most conspicuous today, that can be shown quite clearly.

But first as to the issue. The really pressing question raised by the attacks on reason is not whether the world is in the last resort rational or whether it is wholly open to human knowledge, or any other such tremendous question, but the nearer and comparatively humble one whether we ever can in fact be reasonable. If we can, there is hope for us, both in philosophy and in practice. If we cannot, the outlook is not bright in either.

What do we mean when we call a man reasonable? We mean at least this, that in his thinking and acting he shows objectivity of mind. And what is that? It means being realistic, impartial, just; seeing things as they are rather than as fear or desire or prejudice would tempt one to see them. The reasonable person will suit what he thinks and claims to the facts. He will be ready to give up an opinion if the facts are against it, and adhere to the opinion in the face of inner and outer pressure if the facts require it. His claims against others and their claims against him he will view impersonally and with detachment; he will not ask more for himself than is just merely because he is he; nor will he allow himself to be put upon for the like reason; he bases his self-respect upon respect for the sort of justice that is itself no respecter of persons.

Now, if such reasonableness is to be possible, two further things must be true. In the first place, there must be a set of independent facts to be grasped. It would be senseless to try to suit our opinions to the facts of a case if there were no such facts to suit them to; and if justice consisted in following our own interest or desire, then, as Socrates and a hundred other philosophers have shown, there is no such thing as justice at all. To be reasonable either in thought or in act requires bowing to an authority beyond ourselves, conceding that there is a truth and a right that we cannot make or unmake, to which our caprices must defer. If I have a pet theory in science and am to be reasonable about it, I must be ready to trim it, recast it, or give it up, as an impersonal logic demands; nonconformity here is not heroism but suicide. As McTaggart said, no one ever tried to break logic but logic broke him. It is the same, of course, with morals. Reasonableness in conduct implies wearing a yoke and walking a line; it implies that if you and I differ about our rights, there is an answer to our question waiting there to be found, and that we are doing what we can to find it and conform to it. To say that there is nothing right or wrong but thinking makes it so is to say that there is nothing for thinking to discover; and to say that is to deny all point in trying to be reasonable. If all our beliefs are reasonable, then none of them is.

Thus the first condition of being reasonable is that there be an independent common rule. The second condition is that this common rule should at times control the course of our thought. We must sometimes be able to say: If I thought as I did, it was because my mind was under the influence of an independent pattern, the pattern of an objective truth. This is only to say that thought, if it is to be reasonable, must be like perception when it is accurate. Suppose we look at a checkerboard. If there is to be any such thing as accurate perception at all, there must be, in a sense "out there," a certain number of squares related to each other in a certain way. That corresponds to our first condition. Secondly, we must be able to say: If I see them in this way, that must be because they *are* this way, because that independent order acts upon my mind and makes me see it so. If this arrangement presents itself, not because it is there but because my mind is being pulled about by wires from within, then there are no grounds for believing that we ever do or can see accurately; if we did, it would be sheer luck. I am happily not concerned with the mechanism of perceiving, but with a principle. If, when we perceive things, we never perceive them so because they are so, then perception is a cheat. Similarly in thinking, unless at times we think as we do because the real relations of things are controlling our thought, laying it under constraint, governing its movement, then knowledge must be an illusion from first to last.

Let us proceed with these two conditions in mind. To be reasonable implies at the least that there is an objective truth and right which we can at times apprehend and that, if our thought follows a certain course, it is because it is laid under constraint by the objective pattern of things. If these conditions are granted, reasonableness is so far possible. If either is denied, it is not possible. To show either that the pattern we seem to find in things is not there, or that, although it is there, thought can never surrender itself to the control of that pattern, is to put reasonableness beyond reach.

Now, it is by denying these conditions that the case against our power to be reasonable proceeds. They may be denied in many ways. They may be denied indirectly and by implication by persons who do not realize the bearing of their theories and who in most of their own thought and practice are models of reasonableness. Indeed this holds of all the theories we are to examine. They are not, as attacks on reason so often are, the manifest products of disillusioned or conceited crankiness; they are the considered views of men of distinction in both philosophy and science, to whom we owe much. But of course that makes them the more formidable. I propose to examine three current positions that seem to me inconsistent with one or the other or both of the conditions of reasonableness that have just been laid down. I choose them partly because they seem to me fundamental, partly because they are so ably advocated as to have received a wide assent.

The first of these positions is that the movement of thought is explicable in terms of processes in the cortex. This view is widely held among those who describe themselves as naturalists. The second is that the movement of thought is controlled by nonrational processes within the thinker's own mind. This is an ancient theory which has been given new life in recent years by the psychoanalysts. The third is that the very ideal of rationality, conceived as the following of an objective and necessary truth and right, is an illegitimate one. This is the view of the logical positivists and their numerous legatees. It is, of course, impossible to discuss these positions generally or adequately within the compass of one paper, and I make no pretense of doing so. But I think it will be found in each case that the limitations imposed on reason rest upon distinct and special grounds which can be isolated without difficulty. Let us look at the three positions in order.

The first, or naturalist, theory rests on facts which physical science has led us to accept as commonplaces. We are asked if we do not concede these to be facts; we admit readily that we do; and then, as we follow out the inferences from what we have conceded, it begins to appear that we have conceded also our rational birthright. How naturally we are led on from what seem to be the most innocent facts to a conclusion that is far from innocent will perhaps be clearer if we construct a little dialogue. The physiologist interrogates us:

"When you step on a tack and feel pain, you would agree, would you not, that stepping on it is the cause of the pain?"

"Yes, of course."

"The immediate cause?"

"No, a remote cause only. The change in the nerve ends, so I've been taught, induces an impulse which is carried to the cortex and induces a further change there. It is this change in the cortex that is the immediate cause of the pain."

"Correct. And you would take the same view, would you, about other sensations, and about affections and emotions?—that is, that their immediate cause or condition is a cortical change?"

"Yes, there seems to be no doubt about that. It is true, isn't it, that one can produce sensation artificially by stimulating the cortex?"

"Yes, and we are even learning what precisely to do to produce different kinds of experience; we can put the brain through its paces. We can turn your world yellow by giving you santonin; we can increase or diminish your anger by adrenal injections; we can lift cretinism into normality by small doses of thyroxin; and if we reduce your body's secretion of this by about a hundredth of a grain a day, you will slide down into imbecility. It is true we haven't found out much about the cortical correlates of ideas, but I don't suppose you would doubt that they are there too?"

"No, there seems to be no escaping that. If sensations and affections are brain-conditioned, so must ideas be. One could hardly chop a mental state in two and say that half of it—sensation and feeling—is brain-conditioned, and the other half, involving the use of ideas, is a sort of will-o'-the-wisp, with no roots in the brain at all. If some forms of consciousness are brain-conditioned, presumably all of them are."

"Good, I'm glad you see that so clearly; we can't make an exception for ideas. Now suppose that one idea is followed by another; each of course is brain-conditioned?"

"Yes."

"And the thought sequence is conditioned by the sequence in the brain?"

"Well, since we have agreed that each thought is brain-conditioned, the explanation why one follows the other must lie, I suppose, in the explanation why one brain state follows the other."

"Obviously. And the reason why one brain state follows another is to be found, I suppose, in a physical law?"

"Since both are physical, that must, of course, be true."

"Then the reason why one thought follows another is also given in physical law?"

"Yes, that seems right enough."

"Thought, then, is under the control of physical law?"

"Yes, that does clearly follow."

133

"Well, we seem to agree perfectly. If you are a philosopher, you are at least an unusually sensible one."

I wonder if others have, as I do, a sense of doom closing in as this dialogue unfolds. The concessions do not seem extraordinary; nine out of ten natural scientists would grant them without hesitation, and, unless in a mood of unwonted suspicion, probably most philosophers too. That is just what makes this first argument so effective. You seem to be doing nothing more than conceding obvious facts and drawing obvious inferences. And yet I believe one can show, also by obvious reasoning, that this account cannot be correct, and that if it were, it would mean nothing less than disaster for our rational life.

Let us look at the matter more closely. I said a moment ago that, if we are to be reasonable, we must be able to follow the argument where it leads, which means that thought must at times be governed, not by secret strings within but by the pattern of what it knows. When we say that our thought is objective, we mean just that, that it is moving under the control of the object. Of course there are processes often called thinking that are not so controlled; I may sit down to a geometry problem and think first of the weather, then of my dinner, and then of my headache; but that is not thinking. Thinking proper means reasoning; and reasoning means surrendering one's attention to the logic of the case, moving to one's conclusion because the evidence is seen to imply it. Success here, as the experienced know, demands a wise passiveness; the best thinking is the least free, in the sense that it is most completely laid under compulsion by the course of objective necessity. If my inference moves from step 1 to step 2 and from step 2 to step 3, that is because, when I am really thinking, the facts that 1 implies 2 and that 2 implies 3 make a difference to the course of my thought; the inference takes the line it does because it is following, and is influenced by, a line of necessity that is there before it. This is what it does, for example, when, starting from the postulates of a logical or geometric system, it spins out the theorems that follow; and the account holds equally whether the necessity linking the steps is conceived as synthetic or analytic.

Indeed this is what always happens when our thinking is at its best; its course is then governed and guided by the requirements of the evidence. Our conclusions are not arrived at by leaps in the dark, then checked against the evidence and found to hold by miracle; it is rather that, starting from the evidence, our thought moves to the conclusion it reaches because the evidence requires this, in both senses of the word; the objective entailment controls the movement of inference. If this never happens, then strictly speaking, we never reason. For if, when we pass from premise to conclusion, the premise's entailing the conclusion has nothing to do with our reaching it, then our reaching it as often as we do, indeed our reaching it at all, becomes incredible luck.

It will now be a little clearer why to explain thinking by cortical change is not to explain it, but to explain it away. The subjective process of deduction is, when really deduction, governed by an objective implication, but when one distribution of particles follows another in the brain, what we have, so far as can be seen, is not implication, but cause and effect. The sequence of brain state B upon brain state A is as little governed by any visible implication as the sequence in motion of Hume's billiard balls. I should not deny that between the brain states correlated with the steps of inference there is more than mere conjunction; but how far this is, as we know it, from anything like implication is shown by the facts, firstly, that, if for one of these states there had been substituted any one of a hundred others, we should have accepted the causal relation no less readily; and secondly, that between the sequence of states in the brain that serves as the correlate of a demonstrative process and that which serves as the correlate of the loosest association there is no detectable difference. Physical causality is one thing, logical necessitation another. If therefore you say that what controls the passage from A to B in inference is physical causality, you are saying that even in reasoning at its best and clearest, where we seem to see most plainly what we are doing, we are being grossly deluded. We suppose we think as we do because the evidence requires it; we now learn that this never happens. What really happens is that a sequence of distributions of material particles, or, if you prefer, of stresses and strains, or levels of energy, each connected with its successor by nothing nearer to logical necessity than the succession of waves on a beach, produces a series of mental efflorescences which turn out by some incredible chance to bear the relation, each to its follower, of ground to consequent. That this nexus among the objects of thought exercised the slightest constraint upon the course of our thinking must be set down as illusion. The fact that A is evidence for B had no influence at all in making us think of B, or in making us accept it. The purer reasoning seems to be, the deeper is the illusion, since, speaking strictly, we never reason at all.

Must we accept this view? I do not think so, and for two reasons. First, when our thinking is at its best and clearest, our certainty that it is controlled by necessity is greater than that of any physiological speculations that can be set on the other side. Take a simple train of reasoning and observe what goes on when you follow it. Two is to four as four is to what? Four is to eight as eight is to what? Eight is to sixteen as sixteen is to what? How do you manage to hit upon the answers as you move along this series? The natural reply is, Because the dominant rule of the series logically requires that each successive proportion should be completed in just this manner. I believe that this, which is the natural account, is also the true account. There are dozens of directions in which thought might wander off at any step in the series, and I believe that if it declines these wanderings and remains in the groove, it is because there *is* a groove, because thought is laid under constraint by the logic of the process. We not only see when we reach the end that this constraint did operate; we may be aware of the constraint as we proceed. And to my mind there is something fantastic in brushing aside such empirical evidence for the sake of a flight of physiological speculation. Some persons, to be sure, are so much in the habit of prostrating themselves before physical science that they are ready to ignore their clearest insights if such science has shown itself cool to them. Let us recall, therefore, that what we are offered here is conjecture, not established fact. No competent physiologist professes to know exactly what happens in the cortex when any conscious state occurs, nor exactly how any cortical event leads on to another, nor exactly what is meant by parallelism between the two series—still less to have verified in detail any hypothesis about their relation. To set a theory at once so vague and so tentative against the clear, immediate assurance of the reasoning mind is not properly science at all, but the sort of philosophy bred by an uncritical idolatry of science.

But there remains a more cogent reason for denying that physical causation will account for the sequence of thought. The view is self-refuting. How is it arrived at? It is an inference from observed sequences of mental and bodily change. Now, the inference to this conclusion has either been constrained by the evidence or not. If it has, the conclusion is refuted by the mode of its own attainment; for something more than physical causality was at work in attaining it. On the other hand, if the inference is not under such constraint, why should we respect its result? For then nothing more is at work in it than in the equally good causal processes of woolgathering or derangement. It may be replied that, though rational and irrational processes are equally matters of physical causation, we can see by later reflection which are necessary and which are not. But this is again self-refuting. For even if I do, in a flash of later insight, see that the conclusion was required by the evidence, I do not have this insight because the necessity is objectively there, but solely because some change in my cortex has made it appear to be there. Given the physical change, I should have "seen" it whether it was there to see or not; and hence it is the physical change, not the presence of the necessity, that makes me think I see it. This is to make all apprehension of necessity illusory, and all attempts to prove anything vain, including this one.

It is curious that the disaster implicit in the physiological account of reasoning has been so seldom noticed. But there is one school of psychologists that has seen it and explicitly sought to deal with it, the school of Gestalt. They have said boldly that there are mental processes that cannot be explained in terms of traditional natural science; that it is futile, for example, to explain a course of reasoning in terms of habit or conditioned reflexes, or even association, and that if we complete a syllogism as we do, it is for the same reason that we complete an imperfect circle as we do, because the law of structure of what is before us makes its specific demand upon us. For this insistence, at a time when psychology is threatened with ruin by technicians without vision and without philosophy, we can only be grateful.

But their theory is now being developed in what seems to me a dubious direction. Having broken with a strong tradition of natural science by finding necessity in mental sequences, they make it up to such science by putting this necessity back into the physical realm. When we reason syllogistically, we *are* under the control of necessity, but this necessity is literally in the brain. They have argued with some cogency that when we perceive a square or a circle there is actually a field of similar structure in the cortex. They hold that when our thought is carried along the line of necessity there is a gradient of force in the cortex, a physical tension and its resolution, and that between the physical and the conscious necessity we can detect, if we look sharply, an identical "requiredness."

My chief difficulties with this are two: First, try as I will, I cannot see that the necessity which moves us in reasoning *is* the same as physical compulsion, however abstract and schematic we make their allegedly common element. What the necessity is that links premise with conclusion I do seem to see; and I also seem to see that it is something different in kind from what the physicist means when he talks about a flow of energy from higher to lower potential. To say, then, that what moves me is really the latter is to say once more that when my thought is at its clearest I am under an illusion as to what is directing it. And I do not see how you can say that without discrediting reason generally.

Secondly, the Gestaltists would agree that between the conscious and the cortical state the parallelism is not concrete and detailed, but isomorphic merely, that is, identical only to the extent of a highly abstract and formal pattern. But is this the necessity that works in consciousness? The Gestaltists themselves have taught us that it is not. They would hold, for example—and I believe with sound and important insight—that there is a necessity in music which constrains a composer to continue a melody in one way rather than in others. This necessity is one which holds among the sounds as heard; it takes its character from the terms it relates, namely, these phenomenal sounds in this concrete phenomenal field. But these sounds, as the Gestaltists agree, are not themselves cortical events. Any pattern, then, that is common to brain and consciousness would have to leave them out. But a pattern in which phenomenal sound plays no part is not the pattern that works within experience. Everything depends on which pattern is to control. To say that it is the first, the abstract isomorphic schema, is to say that what really governs the musician, the painter, the moralist is not what he believes to govern him, but something extremely different; and this seems to me in effect to discredit our actual thought in the field of value. To say that what governs is the second pattern, the pattern that takes its character from the phenomenal sounds, is to concede control by what cannot be found in the cortex.

It is time to turn to the second of the contemporary theories that imperil the life of reason, a theory that to most men is more familiar and more persuasive than the first. Even if our thinking is not in servitude to nonrational forces in the body, it is still, we are told, in servitude to such forces within the mind. Man is not primarily a thinker, he is an actor, for the reason that he is still an animal, with far more animal ancestors than human clamoring in his blood. His business, and that of his forebears, has been to fight for a foothold on the earth, first by instinct, then by cunning, then by intelligence; and of these, intelligence, the latest to arrive and not yet fully mastered, is as truly as the others a tool to ends selected for it and not by it. Man thinks to live; if he sometimes lives to think, that only shows that his mind, like his body, is subject to distortion. Thought sprang originally, and still springs, from practical need; it is maintained by a feeling—interest—and tested by another—satisfaction; its goal is not knowledge, for knowledge itself is only a means to survival and success. Little by little the beliefs that seemed to be the products of pure reason are being shown by subtle analysis to be the daydreams of frightened men who need to be comforted, or compensations for defects that cannot well be admitted, or rationalizations of the plainly irrational bribes paid to the forces of unreason for letting us hug self-respect a little longer. Man likes to boast that he is a rational animal. How better disprove the claim than by pointing out that even in these latter years he has continued to make it?

There are people who believe all this to have begun with Freud. It would be less formidable if it had. The truth is that it is the undercurrent of all philosophic history, a strain in minor key that can always be heard if you listen attentively, even when the trumpets of reason are sounding most confidently. At the very moment when Plato was heralding a reason that was the impartial spectator of all time and all existence, Protagoras in the same city was declaring, "Man is the measure of all things," and Callicles was teaching that the doctrine of justice was convention only. While Plotinus was saying at Alexandria that reason was the highest emanation of Deity, Tertullian, farther along the coast, was saying: *Certum est quia absurdum est, quia impossibile est.* No sooner had St. Thomas completed the edifice of his rationalism than Duns Scotus was undermining it with the doctrine that even in God the will is primary and that it manufactures truth and right in accordance with inexplicable impulse. While one great Frenchman was building rationalism into the temper of France, another was protesting: *Le coeur a ses raisons que la raison ne connaît pas.* Spinoza wrote a great book to show that the good life lay in progress in reasonableness; and before it was published Mandeville appeared in England to preach that goodness is the offspring that flattery begets upon pride, and to hear an echo from Scotland proclaiming that reason is and must be the slave of the passions. When Hegel announced at Berlin a series of five-o'clock lectures on reason in man and the world, a young gentleman named Schopenhauer set another series at precisely the same hour to show that in both man and the world the primacy belonged, not to reason, but to blind will. While Bradley in Merton was thinking out the dialectic of the *Appearance*, Schiller just over the wall in Corpus was teaching that "our knowing is driven and guided at every step by our subjective interests and preferences, our desires, our needs, and our ends." So it goes; so apparently it has always gone. And thus if Freud and his philosophic disciples have been teaching, each in his own way, that belief is the puppet of feeling, it is not as if their doctrine was something new under the sun; it is only a new form of one of the oldest protests against reason.

Before commenting on its claim to respect, perhaps I may be permitted a remark on its political relevance. No doubt the tidal wave of World War II that threatened to wash us and our studies into the discard was inspired by no one philosophy, if indeed it was tinctured by philosophy at all. But there are those who, to the amazement of some of us, have sought to link this wave in spirit to those who have made most of reason. The thinkers of the great tradition have held that our thought, if it was to be reasonable, must bow to a logic the same for all of us, absolute in its requirements and independent of desire; some of them have gone on and said that in such a logic we had the key to a world which, if we knew it fully, would be found intelligible through and through.

This view is called at times absolutism. Perhaps for that reason some persons have professed to find in it the seeds of political absolutism. To set up logic as a final authority; what is that but authoritarianism? To bow to a truth that exacts recognition regardless of our desires—is not that surrendering liberty to a metaphysical Moloch? A philosopher of repute was advocating not long ago a view in which, to use his own words, "logic ceases to be a bully, and makes an appeal to our better instincts." The argument seems to be that rationalism appeals to a kind of authority, the authority of reason, that totalitarianism also appeals to authority, and that both are therefore authoritarian in the same sense.

On the virtuosity of this performance as an argument I shall not comment. What is important is that its conclusion is worse than untrue; it is the opposite of the truth. The authority of reason is about as congenial to authoritarianism of the political stripe as an atomic bomb; it would shatter all such claims. One feels that there is something absurd in calling the appeal to reason authoritarian; the term usually implies a claim to authority that is more or less arbitrary, while most men feel in their hearts that in the authority of reason there is no trace of arbitrariness; indeed the very meaning of "arbitrary" is found in divergence from its standard. Authoritarianism in all its forms distrusts the intellect and with a sound instinct fears it; for in reason it recognizes, and knows that the world recognizes, the most dangerous of its enemies, an authority without caprice, an absolutism that does not tyrannize, and a master in whose service there is freedom.

But to return to the argument: thought, we are told, is under constraint from within. It reflects not the outward pattern of things, but our hidden loves and hates, desires and fears. In *The Future of an Illusion* Freud explained religious belief as due to the persistence of the infantile need for a father. According to Westermarck, what is expressed by our moral judgments is no character in the act, but our emotional attractions and repulsions. Indeed, according to a distinguished exponent of Freud, Professor E. B. Holt: "The entire history of philosophy is little else than a tiresome and futile series of pictures in which each philosopher has imagined what he most yearned to have in his own 'best of all possible worlds.'" "This," he adds, "is levity." Such skepticism about

141

reason, though anything but new, has perhaps never been more popular and more formidably supported than in recent years. What are we to say of it?

The first thing we must say of it is a commonplace. It is that if the argument is pushed through and made general, nothing further is called for; like so many other attacks on reason, it disposes of itself. If it is true that we are always governed by nonrational pulls, then of course our conclusion that we are so governed is also produced by nonrational pulls. But if it is, why should it have more respect than any of the other illusions produced by such pulls? Surely the attempt to prove by rational processes that rational processes are irrational is the last irrationality.

Perhaps the reply will be made: "I admit the inference; and hence I offer my theory only as one which expresses and satisfies my own feeling and may turn out to have the advantage of rival theories in better expressing the feeling of others also." But the reply will not do. First, to say, "I admit the inference," is to say, "I accept it because I see that it follows," and to say that is already to have abandoned the view that beliefs *need* be governed irrationally, since this one is not. Secondly, the theory is plainly not offered merely as something that pleases its maker; it is offered as true, as conforming to fact, and because it does so conform, as sounder than rival theories. If it is not so offered, why offer it? If it is, then the offer is inconsistent with the theory offered, for it offers as governed by fact the theory that, owing to subjective pulls, our theories are *never* governed by fact. And thirdly, when anyone says he is content to have his theory take its chances with other theories, it is hard to believe that he is really proposing to test it by its appeal to popular feeling. He is saying that as people come to know the facts better they will see that these facts exclude the other theories and require his own. That implies that the minds to whom he takes his appeal are not puppets of feeling, but are to this extent reflectors of fact.

The truth is that in this generalized form the theory does not make sense. It says that our thought is inevitably distorted by feeling, and it is ready to say pretty precisely, as Freud does in discussing religion, where thought goes off the rails. Now, you cannot recognize that another has gone off the rails unless you know what it means to stay on them. If Freud can point to the mote in other people's religious vision, it is because he is confident he has cast out the beam from his own. He is sure that in the main he is thinking straight when he thinks about religion and about the crookedness of most people's thought about it. What he has proved, then, is not that thinking straight is impossible—a proof that could not get under way without assuming the falsity of its conclusion—but only that thinking straight is hard, which we knew before. To say that we can never think straight is to expose oneself to that charge of fatuity which has now stood for some thousands of years against the sort of person who rises to remark that he knows he knows nothing.

I am, of course, not offering these few observations as an appraisal of the work that has been done by the students of man's irrationality. We owe them a great debt. McDougall said that Freud threw more new light on the workings of the mind than any other psychologist since Aristotle, and I should not care to deny that he is right. All I am concerned to deny is the conclusion often drawn from these researches—that the mind is so controlled by pulls from within that it is never under the control of the objective pattern of things, or follows the thread of an impersonal logic. The observations I have offered, slender as they admittedly are, do seem to me to settle that point in principle.

We now come to the third of the current criticisms of reason. It is a far more technical criticism than either of those we have considered, and its importance is chiefly for the theoretical rather than the practical uses of reason. But it is a peculiarly formidable criticism, because it comes not only from within the camp of the philosophers but from a part of that camp in which clearness and accuracy are cultivated with laudable care. The attack is formidable, again, because it calls in question the very end and goal of reason as we have described it. That end is to understand, and to understand is always to follow an objective pattern or order. What kind of order is this? If it is to satisfy reason, it must be an intelligible order, and what is that? It is an order that never meets our question Why? with a final rebuff, one in which there is always an answer to be found, whether in fact we find it or not. And what sort of answer would satisfy that question? Only an answer in terms of necessity, and ultimately of logical necessity, since of any answer that falls short of this the question Why? can be raised again. When we reach an answer that is necessary, we see that to repeat the question is idle. Of any statement of merely causal necessity, such as the law of gravitation, or Ohm's law, or Boyle's law, we can intelligibly ask why things should behave in this manner. But when we see that things equal to the same thing are equal to each other, we cannot sensibly ask why, because we are at the end of the line to which such questioning can take us. We have already reached the logically necessary.

Now, if the world is to be the sort of world in which reason could even in theory reach its end, it must be one in which intelligence finds an answering intelligibility. I see no way in which it can assure itself beforehand that this is what it will find; I only wish I did. It may be that when we ask such questions as Why does the sun attract the earth in accordance with the law of inverse squares? we are asking a question to which no answer that satisfies reason will ever be forthcoming, and this not because the answer is beyond our reach, but because there *is* no answer, because the connections of things and events are nonnecessary, and therefore in one sense nonrational and unintelligible. If this is true, the attempt to understand is doomed to defeat from the outset. But I see no way of proving this either.

Here is where "logical empiricism" comes in. It claims to have evidence that in entering upon such a program reason is bound to fail. The argument is as follows: Thought must live and move among propositions, for it is intent upon grasping what is true, and only propositions are capable of truth. Since the material with which it directly deals is thus always propositions, a review of the kinds of proposition open to it will throw light on what we may expect of it.

Now, when we review the possible kinds of proposition, we find that they are all reducible to two. On the one hand are necessary propositions, such as those of logic and mathematics. Because of their necessity, they have always given delight to the rationalistically inclined. But unfortunately they are all tautologies; they unfold our own meanings only and give no knowledge of the actual world. On the other hand there are empirical propositions: this is a table; American robins have red breasts. These do assert of the actual world and, if they are true, tell us something about it. But then they are never necessary; they never report that S *must* be

P but only that SP is the case. And if the positivists are right that these two are the only kinds of proposition that ever present themselves to thought, then the program of reason as we have conceived it is clearly impracticable. That program was to penetrate through into the intelligible structure of things. This we now see that we can never do. For though we can indeed know necessities, these necessities are never links that join actual facts; and though we can know facts, these are never necessary. The world of existence is unintelligible.

The case of the positivists or logical empiricists against our program thus rests on two contentions: that all necessary propositions are tautologous and that all factual propositions are contingent. It is important to see more precisely what these mean.

It may be supposed that the first contention, all necessary propositions are tautologous, means what Kant meant when he said that analytic propositions were tautologous. These, he said, merely set out in the predicate what is already contained in the subject. Positivists reject this account of tautology as resting on psychological grounds; it places the test, they say, in subjective intension, in the accident of how one happens to conceive of the subject named. The test they offer instead is whether the proposition in question can be denied without self-contradiction; it is necessary if it cannot. Now, they admit that there are large numbers of propositions which are in this sense necessary; and if so, why should we take offense or alarm at their theory? Do not all these necessities stand for just so many intelligibilities in the nature of things, and are not these precisely what we are seeking?

Unhappily, the positivists will not let us read them in this way. They insist that the necessity here exhibited has nothing to do with the nature of things, that the contradiction involved in its denial means incoherence, not in nature, but in our own linguistic usage. According to Professor Ayer necessary propositions "simply record our determination to use words in a certain fashion. We cannot deny them without infringing the conventions which are presupposed by our very denial, and so falling into self-contradiction. And this is the sole ground of their necessity." (*Language, Truth and Logic*, 2d ed. [London: Victor Gollancz, 1946], p. 114.) A necessary proposition of the form "S is P" tells how we propose to use S. A necessary proposition of the form "P implies Q" illustrates a definition of implication which has been adopted arbitrarily, and which stands, not for a nexus in nature, but for a convention of our own. Let us look at these two types.

A necessary proposition of the form S is P, which in former days would have been said to state a necessary relation between concepts, is now said to state how we use, or propose to use, S. I think that what this amounts to, after all, is that such propositions are analytic in Kant's sense; the predicate sets forth, in part or in whole, how one conceives of the subject; the addition to the older theory is that this predicate is arbitrary. Regarding this doctrine I should hold as follows: (1) the view that all propositions of this form are analytic is untrue, and (2) the addendum that the predicate is arbitrary is equally untrue.

(1) "Whatever is red is extended." This seems to me a necessary proposition, and most positivists would, I think, agree. By saying this they mean that its contradictory would be self-contradictory. Why would this be true? Because in our first proposition we merely set forth in our predicate part of what was meant by our subject. This analysis seems to me incorrect. What I mean by extension is not what I mean by redness, nor is it part of this; the two are quite distinct. If when I think of a billiard ball as red, the extension of that red is part of what I mean by red, then when I think of another billiard ball as white, the extension of the white will be part of what I mean by calling it white; and I shall then have to say that the balls are similarly colored, which is absurd. Being extended is, to be sure, so intimately connected with being red that if a thing is red it must be extended also; the one entails the other. But surely that is the way to put it. It is quite incorrect to say that when I call a thing extended I am defining the meaning of red. Though I am asserting a relation of entailment or necessity, it is evident from inspection that that relation is not one of identity, either in whole or in part. And if so, necessities are not always tautologies. I should myself maintain that in actual thought they never are, but that is another point.

(2) To the contention that such propositions are analytic, the positivists add, as we have seen, that they are arbitrary, in the sense that they state or illustrate a convention which might have been different. Mr. Ayer writes as follows: "If I say, 'nothing can be coloured in different ways at the same time with respect to the same

part of itself,' I am not saying anything about the properties of any actual thing . . . I am expressing an analytic proposition, which records our determination to call a colour expanse which differs in quality from a neighboring colour expanse a different part of a given thing. In other words, I am simply calling attention to the implications of a certain linguistic usage." (*Language, Truth and Logic*, p. 104.) Now I suggest that when we call two differently colored patches of a rug different it is because we see that they are and must be different, and that this, which we mean to assert, is wholly independent of linguistic usage. If it were really a matter of usage, the adoption of a different usage would make a difference to what I assert. Would it in fact? Suppose we decided that when we saw two differently colored patches we should henceforth call them the same patch; would that which we meant to assert be different from what we meant to assert before? I think not. We should still be asserting the parts to be different, because we see that they must be, and if we used the word "same," it would now mean what we meant by "different." The fact is—to repeat—that we call two differently colored parts different because we see that they are so, and must be; they are not so, nor are they seen to be so, because we have adopted the convention of calling them so. Language adjusts itself to the observed nature of things; the nature of things does not wait on our language. These are truisms which I am almost ashamed to set down deliberately. And yet when we are offered statements of the kind I have quoted as the final result of exact linguistic researches, a few truisms may come as a relief.

I have been dealing with necessary propositions of the S-P form, that is, propositions which assert a connection between subject and predicate. I come now to assertions of the P-implies-Q type, which assert a necessary linkage between propositions themselves. The positivists treat these in essentially the same way as the others. They would argue as follows: when we assert that a proposition, P, implies another, Q, we are, in the first place, asserting what we have asserted already, and in the second place, asserting a relation to hold that belongs, not to the nature of things, but to our own set of conventions. As for the first point, when we say that P implies Q, we find that we always know, or think we know, certain things about the truth of P and Q. Of the four possibilities—both true, both false, P false and Q true, P true and Q false—we know that one or other of the first three holds. But in knowing that, we know already that P implies Q, for that is what the statement *means*. At least that is what it means to us. For, secondly, say the positivists, you are at perfect liberty to mean by it something else if you wish. You may mean by it what, following the *Principia*, we have just offered, i.e., either P is false or Q is true, or what C. I. Lewis means by it, that P's truth is inconsistent with Q's falsity, or any one of a large number of other things. Which of these you choose is not determined for you but by you; it is a matter of convention. All that is required is that once you choose your conventions you adhere to them, that once you have defined implication in a given way you mean this by it consistently; otherwise you stultify yourself.

Now, the first of these points, that implication is tautologous, depends on the second, that it is a matter of convention; for, in the position we are examining, what implication shall be is conventionally determined. The question before us, then, is whether it *is* so determined.

It seems to me that there is one simple argument which shows that it is not. This argument is that of all the various definitions which are offered of implication, we can sensibly ask, Does this give what I really mean or not? We can not only sensibly ask that question; we can see that the various answers miss or approach what we mean in various degrees. Thus we can see that the Russell-Whitehead formula of material implication misses what we mean by a wide margin, and that Lewis's strict implication approximates it more closely. This shows that we have something in mind to which all the conventions must come for testing, a relation conceived as holding *independently* of our usages and conventions. When we say that the premises of a syllogism imply its conclusion, or that being extended implies being divisible, we do mean something definite, however difficult to hit with words; and this is what gives the target at which our definitions aim. If there were no target there at all, how could we tell, as in fact we can, that some definitions strike close to the mark and others go wide of it? Of course our definitions are arbitrary in the sense that to the word "implication" we can attach any sense we want. But to argue from this that any sense we attach to the word will equally fit what in common use we mean by it is surely confusion. When we dispute over the nature of "justice" or "number" or "truth," are we really free to define the term as we please? Do we not assume on both sides that we are trying to run down and capture the same thing? When we argue with each other as to whether an inference is to be admitted, is there no bar, in the form of a common understanding of what "follows" really means, to which both of us must take our appeal? If there is not, argument is futile. If there is, positivism is wrong.

This consideration is to my mind decisive, and those who hold logic to be conventional have not, I think, wholly escaped it. It is true that from differing definitions of "P implies Q" there follow "alternative logics," in the sense of differing sets of basic logical propositions. (If, for example, one defines this, not as meaning "material implication" [either "P and Q," or "not-P and Q," or "not-P and not-Q"] but as meaning "either 'P and not-Q,' or 'not-P and Q,' or 'not-P and not-Q,'" a sort of logic would follow in which a true proposition implies and is implied only by a false one.) But so far as I can see, when one says that such things follow, one means by "follow" what all the rest of us mean by it. The concept of following is common to all the alternative logics; to that there is apparently no alternative. Once more, if logic is wholly conventional, there should be logics in which the principle of contradiction is replaced by an alternative. So far as I know, there is none such; without this principle the sort of distinction required by all logics in common would be impossible. But a convention that is necessary to make all other conventions possible is not in the same sense a convention itself.

I have been dealing so far with the first position of the positivists, which would make all necessary assertions mere statements about usage. It may be asked: If not about this, what else? You would not hold, would you, that they are statements about the actual world? I answer: Of course I should. "That apple yonder cannot, in the same part and under the same conditions, be colored in different ways." I believe that, when we say that, we are saying something about the apple. "X cannot at once have Y and not have it." The positivists take this as meaning, "I do not propose to *call* both that which has Y and that which hasn't by the name of X." Bradley takes it as meaning that nothing that is real is self-contradictory. Which is right? Of course if one says, as positivists do, that all assertions except those about usage are assertions about

149

sense experiences, Bradley is talking nonsense. There is no space here to discuss this curious and interesting revival of sensationalism. All I can say is that after an inspection of my own meaning, I wish to make it clear that I am talking Bradley's kind of nonsense.

We turn now to the second position of the positivists, which must be dealt with in the briefest way: All factual propositions are contingent. What are we to say of it? I think that even if factual propositions are defined in the straitest positivist fashion, the statement must be set down as untrue. Before us, for example, is a series of colors arranged in order of their affinities. We perceive that in this series orange falls, and must fall, between red and yellow. Is this an assertion about elements given in sense? Yes, and it is therefore a factual assertion. Is it a contingent assertion? No. Things are related contingently when they might be related otherwise than they are. But the relation I am here asserting could not be other than it is; if orange were not related as it is to red and yellow, it would not be orange. The Gestaltists tell us that when we "see," as we often do, that to continue a melody in the right key we must proceed thus and not thus, we are laying hold of a genuine requiredness; and I think they are right. Here again the *must* holds among the given sensory elements; the insight is at once factual and necessary. And if one breaks with the narrowly sensory interpretation of "factual," as one should, many other types of factual necessity are admitted. When I say that my present toothache is bad, am I saying that the badness is accidentally conjoined to it, so that the pain could be what it is without the badness? Clearly not; I am asserting a predicate that belongs to its subject necessarily, though that subject is an existent. When I say "I cannot doubt that I am now conscious" I am reporting that a present fact excludes, and necessarily excludes, a predicate suggested of it. Personally I should be ready to maintain, in respect to each of the positivist positions, not only that it is false, but that the truth lies in its contrary. I think that in the end all necessary propositions must be taken to assert of existence and that no factual propositions are altogether contingent.

But it is no part of my design to argue for these positions. My aim is sharply limited; it is merely to help clear the ground of some objections to our power to be reasonable, taking this term in one very important sense and of profound significance for the emergent civilization. Is this all shadow boxing? It may be said that when people are moved to be unreasonable in thought or practice it is not because they have drawn irrationalist inferences from such theories as we have examined. True enough. But that is not the point. The point is that among present-day systems of thought some of the most widely influential would make the pursuit of the reasonable impossible, that if these systems prevail their implications will tend to be realized, accepted and acted upon; and that these implications are disastrous. If any one of the theories I have discussed is true, philosophy has no future except perhaps "the future of an illusion." If our reasoning is in truth the shadow cast by the irrational displacements of matter, if it is only the bobbing of corks on the surface, pulled about from nonrational depths, if it is really a play with syntax, signifying nothing, then we should face the truth and, as Cromwell said to the cleric, we should "cease our fooling."

On the other hand, if these things are not true, it is the philosopher's business to brush them out of the way, not by alarms but by analysis, and so help men to get on with their work. If he succeeds, the first gainer will be philosophy, which stands in need today of some of the high and hopeful adventurousness of the great pioneers of reason. But the influence will not stop there. What the philosophers and men of science conclude today the public is asking about tomorrow and taking as a matter of course the day after tomorrow. There is such a thing possible as a "sentiment of rationality," a popular trust in reason, a pride in its private exercise, a general demand that the issues between man and man, race and race, nation and nation, be settled in accordance with it. Such a spirit is coming to seem less utopian than merely necessary, and to help prepare the way for it is the most practical service that any philosopher can render.

# II
# *Corollaries*

# 9
# Quantity and Quality in American Education

A British Minister of Education, H. A. L. Fisher, reported after a transatlantic visit that America was a land of many churches and one creed: all Americans believed in education. In this he was surely right. I suppose that no other people on record has had anything like so many schools, so many students, so many colleges and universities, so much money to support them, so universal an interest in getting what schools have to give. Since I am talking about quantity and quality in our education, it may be well to begin by getting some of the quantitative facts before us.

In 1970 the nation had 1,670 four-year colleges and universities, which means an average of more than 33 per state. Although our population has swelled in the last century like a rising tide, our college population has risen about thirty-five times as fast. In the single decade from 1941 to 1951 the number of college students increased 78 percent. A Census Bureau study shows that the population of young adults with college degrees has almost tripled since 1940. The proportion of those with at least high school diplomas has risen from 38 to 75 percent. The number of college students mushroomed from 4.6 million in 1964-65 to 7.4 million in 1969-70.

The extent of change within a generation is suggested by the fact that the fathers of nearly two-thirds of our present college students did not go beyond high school.

I suppose there has been nothing like this experiment in mass education in the history of mankind. Even in advanced countries there seems to have been nothing like it. It was pointed out a few years ago that the state of Illinois had about twice as many college students as Great Britain and the state of New York three times as many.

It is not merely by the masses of students that our belief in education is attested, but also by the massed wealth that pours into our educational coffers. Americans have acquired a habit that, so far as I know, is theirs uniquely, of grateful and persistent giving to the colleges that nursed them. It would be impossible for the Sorbonne or Heidelberg or Oxford or Cambridge to maintain itself without government subsidy; in this country the oldest and most distinguished of our universities have received their hundreds of millions of endowment almost wholly from private givers. Since World War II this habit of generosity has taken a new turn. Through the appeals of statesmanlike men of business, such as Alfred P. Sloan, the world of industry has been awakened to the needs of education; and to the mere professor, operating on his slender budget, the response of American business has been breathtaking. The imaginative gifts of Du Pont, the General Electric Company, and many others were capped by a donation from Ford of half a billion dollars in a single stupendous package. Along with these came a similar flood from the cornucopia of government. What would the culture of the West have been like, one wonders, if this habit of munificence had been established earlier? You may recall that in 1728 that great philosopher and human being, George Berkeley, set out on a voyage to the new world to establish "a college for the spread of religion and learning in America." For this enterprise Parliament had voted him 20,000 pounds. For some three years he waited hopefully in a Rhode Island farmhouse for the money to arrive. It never came. On second thought, Parliament considered the sum too great to be approved. An enterprise that would have affected the course of American education for centuries was abandoned for want of an amount that would run the present Yale or Harvard for little more than a week.

We live in better days. Wherever the traveler goes in America, the evidence of public care for education strikes his eye. How often, in driving across the plains, one passes through some little Gopher Prairie of a town where the wooden houses are ramshackle, the stores shabby, and the filling stations too many and too loud, only to find that, after all, the town has one impressive modern edifice, which turns out to be its public high school. And education, as conceived by our schools and colleges, is not, as in Europe, for the mind only, but also for the body. Our young men, disciplined in well-equipped gymnasiums and trained to speed and sportsmanship on the diamond and in stadia of Roman proportions, have won the Olympic games, up to the last one, with monotonous regularity. The idea of *mens sana in corpore sano*, originated by the Greeks, was inherited by the English, and from the English by the Americans; judging by the physical fitness of our students, there is ground for thinking that our country has bettered its instruction.

At this point in the recital, some of us may begin to be uneasy. Do we not find here, it may be asked, a good example of that confusion of quantity with quality which is the standing danger of American education? This is a doubt I want to explore with you. And yet I have put first this recital of facts because I want to make it clear that in placing quality high I am not placing quantity low. It is only a dull imagination that would fail to see the light that shines through such statistics. The shift of a statistical pointer may record an immense change in human happiness; consider what it means, for example, that since 1900 our average life expectancy has increased by twenty years. Consider what it means to you and me to be able to read and write, and then what it means in a country to have a literacy of 95 percent rather than 45 percent. America is often criticized, particularly perhaps in the East, for her materialism, for her excessive preoccupation with what can be measured by statistics, like the outlay for clothes and cars and kilowatts. It is a criticism with which I had less sympathy after two years in the Far East. If the good life is to be lived with any fullness, it normally needs health of body and training of mind, and these things call for that unfortunate crass necessity, money. Here quality is more dependent on quantity than we may wish to think. Sir Arthur Quiller-Couch, after listing a dozen of the great poets of the last century, pointed out that nine of these were university men, with the background of means that this implies, and that of the remaining three, Browning was the son of a prosperous banker, Rossetti had a private income, and Keats, the only one without any sort of backing, died, broken with the struggle, at twenty-five. I must frankly confess that when I think of those high schools dotting the prairie, of those 1,670 colleges, of those well-appointed gymnasiums and big playing fields, I gloat. The business of the state, said the philosopher Bosanquet, is not to produce the good life, which it cannot do, but to hinder the hindrances to the good life. That is what we are doing with these things that can be put into statistics. We are using our material means to fertilize the field for quality.

Are we getting the qualitative return that we ought to get from so prodigal an effort? That, I doubt. To be sure, in certain areas where energy and technical skill are important, such as engineering, architecture, and dentistry, American work is supreme; there are few such dams, skyscrapers, and bridges—whether of the kind made by civil or by dental engineers—as are to be found within our borders. But what about the pure science on which the triumphs of practice ultimately rest? There we are less secure. In respect to Nobel Prizes, which are usually given for this kind of service, we have won about one in ten of the prizes awarded. That is no mean achievement. But it makes one pause to discover that for the first quarter of this century at least, the University of Cambridge alone produced more Nobel scientists than all our universities put together, and that the theoretical foundations of the new world of science were laid almost entirely by non-American hands, by Rutherford and J. J. Thomson and Neils Bohr, by Planck and Heisenberg and Einstein. I am told that we have only one name to place alongside these intellectual frontiersmen, that of Josiah Willard Gibbs, who walked for the most part unrecognized among us.

Have we fared better in literature? Opinions will differ. So far as Nobel prizes go, our record is about the same as in science—roughly one in ten. Whether Sinclair Lewis and Hemingway will last as interpreters of the human spirit is hard to say. What one would like to find as one looks back over recent decades is writers who have brought ideas to bear in a fundamental way in the criticism of their time, writers like Shaw, Wells and

Chesterton, Russell, Inge and Toynbee in England. Edmund Wilson, Walter Lippmann, and Lewis Mumford will perhaps sustain comparison. It may be said that Mencken was a host in himself, but, apart from his work on language, was he not almost wholly negative? We have produced one man of high originality both as poet and as critic, Mr. Eliot, but like our most reflective novelist, Henry James, he found a foreign atmosphere more congenial than that of his own country, and left us early.

In music the situation is curious. We are exporting in quantity, and to increasingly wide and eager markets, but the exports consist chiefly of jazz and other forms of popular music. Significant musical creation we leave chiefly to others—to Shostakovich and Prokofieff, to Stravinsky and Bartok and Hindemith. We have splendid orchestras, led for the most part by conductors whose names are revealing—Ormandy, Fiedler, Mitropoulos, Stokowski, Kostelanetz. With voice and instruments we do better, but it is surely suggestive that a good middle western tenor named Benton should turn up in New York as Bentonelli.

In speculative thought the story is similar. Quantitatively, our philosophic wealth is incomparable; we have more than a thousand philosophers in the American Philosophical Association, including many superb teachers, able analysts, and competent writers. But I think most of my colleagues would regretfully agree that there is no one among them of the stature of Russell, or Moore, or Broad, or Whitehead, all products of one foreign university. Or consider theology. Here we have had a challenging name in Reinhold Niebuhr; Tillich was a German and German-trained. But able as Niebuhr was, his theology is not so much an original growth as a transplanted stock, for whose seeds we must go to Luther, Kierkegaard, and Barth.

The conclusion from this sampling is that the quality of our cultural achievement has hardly kept pace with our quantitative achievements. But we must try to make this contrast more precise. When quality is set over against quantity, two different things may be meant by quality. One is quality as such, as opposed to quantity as such. The other is higher quality as opposed to lower quality. When I suggest that quality should have more stress in our education, I mean that it should have more stress in both senses of the term. Let us try to get clear about each.

First as to the distinction between the quantitative and the qualitative as such. Here what is quantitative means what can be studied by natural science or can be measured and publicly observed. Further, what can be thus publicly observed is always physical; most commonly it is the movements of material things or of the particles composing them. The realm of the quantitative, the realm of natural science, is that of matter in motion. On the other hand, in the realm of the qualitative are placed those events that cannot be thus observed, such as thoughts, feelings, and desires.

Now it is a strange but significant fact about America that there are many people among us, many able and thoughtful people, who doubt whether any such distinction can in the end be drawn. They doubt it because they have fallen so completely under the sway of natural science as to question whether anything it fails to recognize should be recognized at all. Some of our psychologists, in their desire to be natural scientists, are reducing the study of mind to the study of bodily movement. Think, for example, of B. F. Skinner, whom many would name as the most influential American psychologist of our time, and whose recent book *Beyond Freedom and Dignity* has been a best seller. The essence of Dr. Skinner's psychology lies in the bypassing of consciousness, the confining of his science to the study of bodily responses. He not only declines to admit that our purposes, in the ordinary sense, make any difference to what we do, or that our ideas make any difference to what we say; he denies that purposes and ideas, as distinct from bodily changes, exist at all, and holds that a science which deals with them is placing itself in the company of alchemy and astrology. Man is an elaborate machine which, like other machines, has no inner control; to suppose that he has is the illusion of "freedom and dignity." He is controlled as completely from the outside as any slot machine. The secret of education and social advance alike is therefore to order man's environment in such a way as to elicit the kind of bodily behavior wanted, and in Dr. Skinner's utopia all of us would be conditioned by a central directing agency. But conditioned to what end? How will the agency judge what conduct is to be promoted and what not? At this point Dr. Skinner and all other behaviorists I have read prove bankrupt. For if they are to answer that crucial question, they must say something about values, and for values their system has no place. Happiness, knowledge, beauty, moral goodness are not forms of bodily behavior that can be observed and measured, but conscious experiences, and such experiences are precisely what behaviorism has dismissed. In the effort to reduce everything to what can be treated with quantitative exactness, the whole realm of the qualitative is thrown overboard.

Most psychologists have not followed Skinner to these lengths. They would probably agree with the old jest that this type of psychology, having lost its soul, had now lost its mind as well. Some critics have acidly remarked, with Count Keyserling, that behaviorism was the natural psychology of a people without inner life. Still, the influence of the school has been great. There are many psychologists who describe themselves with pride as behaviorists and who, even when they reject Skinner's conclusions, do so reluctantly. They stay as closely as they can within the bounds of his sort of natural science, and feel uneasy when they stray outside it. This seems to me significant. It reveals in the study of mind itself a stress that is felt more strongly still in other areas of American life, a stress on the outward rather than the inward, on facts rather than values, on the quantitative rather than the qualitative order.

Consider some of the ways in which this emphasis shows itself. Though there has been a wave of impatience with science and technology over the part they have played in costly armament and pollution, the man of science today stands on a pedestal. Particularly since Einstein's great discovery, this pedestal has risen notably, and its occupants have been invested with a kind of wizard's mantle. Plain men did not know what to make of the strange little German dominie and his bizarre announcement that we were living in a new world which was governed by the formula $E = mc^2$, but when, aided by the magic of such formulas, there began to issue from the laboratories packets that could blast whole cities in a moment, they could only bow to a magic they could not in the least understand. We are at the mercy of these scientists, and we know it. They stand for something before which we are helpless, as we are before the surgeon with his scalpel and his masked face.

And their authority is extending itself to their lesser colleagues. Have you noticed how often there appears in advertisements the figure of the man in the white coat peering through his microscope or into his test tube; he is the chief threat to the pretty girl as

161

the means of casting the desired aura over the product. Have you noticed, again, how advertisers are aping the quantitative exactness of the scientists, whether it makes sense or not; we are assured that a soap will eliminate so many percent more bacteria; I learned recently, as I listened to my radio, that if I used a new shampoo, the brightness of my hair would be increased up to 35 percent. We find every sort of cause or product urged upon us in language that seeks to borrow prestige from its use in physical science; and imitation is the sincerest flattery.

Now the curious thing is that while we are busy pushing the scientist up to his giddy throne, the scientist himself is protesting that about values he has nothing at all to say. If we happen to want bright hair or red hair or curly hair, he can help us (though unfortunately not if what we want is just hair); but if we want to know whether it is of any *importance* to have one kind of hair or another, if we want to know what is *worth* reading, or feeling, or doing, if we want to know about the *ends* of life as opposed to the means, we find him silent. He is not only silent; he is deliberately and even ostentatiously silent. His business, he says, is with facts, or with laws, which are general facts. He can tell the practical man how to make fissionable material explode, and with the aid of his lieutenant the technologist he can explain how to make planes and submarines, rockets and guided missiles. If you ask him whether it is well that we should have these things, he shrugs his shoulders and says that physics has nothing to do with such questions. The psychiatrist prefers not to talk of right or wrong, good or bad; these are not impartial scientific terms; they are loaded; the delinquent may be "emotionally disturbed" or "maladjusted to his social environment," but anything beyond that is "subjective evaluation."

This tendency to draw a sharp line between fact and value and to insist that knowledge or intelligence, virtually identified with scientific method, has no concern with value, has been fortified by developments in the philosophy of science. Such influential writers as Russell, Carnap, and Reichenbach agreed that judgments of value are not really judgments at all; they are neither true nor false, and therefore do not fall within the province of intelligence or knowledge; they are merely expressions of pro- or anti-feelings, or at most of commands to behave this way or that. Since they do not assert anything, they cannot be made out by reason; they are expressions of the nonrational part of our nature. When you call anything good or bad, the reflective man may interest himself in the cause or effect of your thus exploding into speech, but to consider whether your remark is true or not is to mistake the business of intelligence.

I believe that this view about judgments of value is bad philosophy, but there is no time to argue that out. What I do want to stress is the implication of the view for education. Education is supposed to be chiefly a training of the intelligence, and if intelligence has nothing to do with values, it follows that education, in its chief function, has nothing to do with values either. This conclusion seems to me disastrous. The realm of values is bundled up by the scientists and other custodians of knowledge and left like an unwanted child on the doorstep for some passerby to pick up. And who is going to pick it up? The churches? But there are millions of our people that the churches never reach. The parents? But with our juvenile delinquency rates among the highest in the world, parents are proving pretty frail reeds. The press, television, the movies? But their values, as we shall see in a moment, are those of the box office. If American education, with its vast resources and its all-pervasive reach, is not to undertake the inculcation of values, who or what is?

Indeed, we have it on good authority that a disciplined sense of value is the most important product of education. Plato says: "It is not the life of knowledge, not even if it included all the sciences, that creates happiness and well-being, but a single branch of knowledge—the science of good and evil. If you exclude this from the other branches, medicine will be equally able to give us health, and shoe-making shoes, and weaving clothes. Seamanship will still save life at sea and strategy win battles. But without the knowledge of good and evil, the use and excellence of these sciences will be found to have failed us." (Plato, *Charmides*, Steph. 174.) And Dr. Conant writes: "To the extent that education ceases to be concerned with 'value judgments' in art, in literature, or in philosophy, it ceases to be of service to the free way of life—it ceases to uphold the dignity of the individual man." Of course neither this philosopher nor this scientist is decrying scientific knowledge; they value it highly not only for its own sake, but for the sake of the mastery it gives us over nature, and the vast fruits of that mastery in wealth and health and military power. But they see that wealth and health and military power are not in themselves goods at all. There have been people who had all of them and lived very meagre lives; there have been people who had none of them whose lives have been full and rich. The fact is that the measurable things of the world—its dollars and ships and refrigerators—are of value only as they contribute to nonmeasurable things, such as justice and happiness and love and poetry and laughter. In the end the usefulness of useful things lies in the help they give us in getting these useless things.

Does this seem like a paradox? If so, a moment's thought will make it almost a platitude. Suppose you ask a college student why he came to college. He is likely to answer, "Because it will help me to succeed in my job, whatever it is." You ask him why he wants to succeed in his job. If he has patience with what seems like a silly question, the not improbable answer will be, "Because it will give me a larger income." If he is then asked why he should want a larger income, he says, "Because then I can have a house with modern improvements, I can have a Cadillac if I want one; my fiancée, if she wants to, bless her, can be the grandest lady in the Easter parade, and we can send our children to Yale."

But in spite of the inspired climax, doesn't that sort of thinking go round in a squirrel cage? He wants an education for the sake of success, this for the sake of income, this for the sake of Cadillacs, and this for the sake of education one generation removed, which is supposed to start all over again for the sake of success, for the sake of income, for the sake of a two-helicopter garage. That is a vicious circle, education for gadgets for education, and how is one to escape from it? Not by crying out that things are in the saddle and ride mankind, or trying to live like Gandhi or Thoreau; it is too late in the day to secede from civilization. No, the only feasible escape is to make quantity subserve quality, to accept this vicious circle as a ring that provides a solid setting for a pearl of incalculable price. For my own part I think that our gadgetry is one of the glories of our culture and should serve as a proclamation of emancipation into a fuller life. It is surely not for nothing that our science and technology are shortening our working day in about the same proportion that they are lengthening our life span. But what will it profit a man to gain this new world of gadgets if he wears the bloom

164

off his soul in getting them? It is only too possible that wealth should accumulate and men decay.

Will you carry out with me another little philosophical experiment? Imagine successively three kinds of world. First, our modern world with all its gadgets, and scattered around them its notable men and women, Churchill and Charlie Chaplin and Eleanor Roosevelt and you and me. Secondly, imagine a world with all our modern gadgets subtracted—with no electricity or steam or motors or railways or radios or telephones, with no printed books or newspapers, no means of preserving food, no anaesthetics, no science of medicine or surgery, no sewing machines, reapers, typewriters, even spectacles. One feels at once that such a world would be shrunken and impoverished, for so much that we are and do is made possible by these things. Would life in such dreary poverty be worth living at all? Well, let me remind you that this *was* the world of Socrates and Sophocles and Aristotle, of Virgil and St. Augustine and Dante. There was nothing poverty-stricken about these minds; indeed it is to these minds precisely that men in other times turn when they want to escape from their own poverty. Carlyle once raised the startling question, Which would be the greater loss to England if it had to part with one or the other: Shakespeare or India? With all respect to India, how that question lights up the worth of one great spirit!

But now imagine the third world. Instead of subtracting the machinery of civilized life, let us leave it all standing, or rather multiply it to the limit, with superskyscrapers on every horizon and, within them, push-button resources for every want. And let us subtract just one thing, consciousness. It is a paradise of gadgets, lacking only persons. And the question I want to ask is, What would be the value of such a world? The answer is, nothing at all. Without its persons the worth of the world would vanish utterly. It is for persons, for better and more sensitive persons, for the knowledge and love and goodness of persons, that all the machinery of civilization exists. There may be great persons with little or none of this machinery. There can be greater ones, I am convinced, with the aid of this machinery. But the machinery without the persons has a value of precisely zero.

My conclusion is that the machinery of civilization is to be justified only so far as it contributes to the qualities of persons. Now colleges are an important part of this machinery. We could make them, if we tried, into efficient factories, mass-producing efficient robots, themselves the most efficient of machine tools, who would whir us along toward *1984* and Aldous Huxley's *Brave New World*. Some think that is essentially what they are doing already. That keen observer, Lowes Dickinson, wrote home from this country: "Colleges are an investment to Americans, and educate only as a means to getting on." Professor Sir Walter Raleigh wrote home even more sourly, "There are no persons in this country." I am afraid that in both cases what is speaking here is dislike. Yet dislike may have keen eyes. And here it may remind us that the prime business of the college is not to enable a youth to "get on," but to become more of a person; "Reflect on the difference," said President Wriston, "between the 'gain wisdom' of Solomon and the 'get wise' of today." It may remind us that scholarship itself may be dead and mechanical. Ivor Brown has remarked that "there are naturalists without wonder, scholars without awe, theologians without worship, economists without anger, historians who never laughed or hated or despaired. They may be wise, but who is jealous of their wisdom? It is possible to know everything and understand nothing."

Important as it is not to confuse quality with quantity, it is still more important, and far more difficult, not to confuse second-rate quality with first-rate. It is difficult because there are so many pressures in a democracy that make for this latter confusion, and important because it is the prime business of liberal education to resist it. Let us look at these two points.

Consider how strong the forces are that make the good the enemy of the best and the commonplace the enemy of the good. The first, to use a phrase of W. C. Brownell, is "the immense extension in our time of what may be called the intellectual and aesthetic electorate." More than 95 percent of Americans can now read and write. This is an unparalleled national achievement, and there have been reformers who would have thought of it as ushering in Utopia. But Arnold Toynbee has questioned whether the extension to everyone of the capacity to read has not lowered values generally by enlarging the demand for the vulgar. It is easy to see how this could happen. Economically, we are still a society in which production is determined by profit. The man who is producing books knows that his profits depend on circulation; the man who is producing movies knows that his profits depend on the length of the line at the box office. Now if what is wanted in both cases is the largest number of buyers, the proper course is not to appeal to this or that group, with this or that taste, but to the largest possible group.

And how is that to be reached? The answer can be given in mathematical terms—by appealing to the lowest common denominator. And where is this common ground to be found? Hardly in thoughtfulness, or in moral or psychological acuteness, or an interest in delicate portraiture. It is found rather in what is primitive about us, in sex and fear and anger, in sensation in both meanings of the term, and in those infantile daydreams of ourselves as princesses or supermen that all of us have when young and some of us never lose. Hence publishers find it profitable to fill the racks in airports and drugstores with paperbacks celebrating violence. The consumption of comics, both in newspapers and in book form, is portentous.

If our fiction does not run to coarseness and violence more than it does, we probably owe it to American women, who form our chief audience for fiction. Unhappily the same selection by mass appeal is at work among them too. I trust you look occasionally, as I do, into some of our incomparably illustrated women's magazines. What strikes one in the pictures is that nearly all American women are aged eighteen; what strikes one in the stories is that those who are not are expected to spend so much time brooding on the emotional involvements of those who are. Now of course it is a tragic thing to realize that one will never be eighteen again; I have been carrying that bitterness with me for many a downhill year; but I can attest that even when the larks of spring are no longer singing and fresh romance has long abandoned its station round the next corner, life may with resolution be borne.

There are journals, indeed, that make small concession to either sentiment or sensation, but the *New York Times* is no competitor in circulation with the *Daily News,* and in our superb illustrated journals you see in vivid form the effect of mass appeal in confusing values. Side by side with remarkable studies of religion, or art, or the cultural advance of man, there will appear some shapely nitwit or the sprawling corpse of some gunman.

167

*Corollaries*

A more effective witness still to the leveling effect of mass appeal is the movies, which now constitute a large part of television also. That Hollywood can produce admirable things I was reminded recently when I went to see a double bill. But following the excellent "Oscar" film there came a second of the sort that producers apparently depend on for their income. The photographic and other technique was of course perfection, but the hero and heroines (for there were three of these) were apparently based on the conclusion of the early mental testers that the mental age of Americans was, on the average, fourteen. The hero was a young man who showed his immense virility by nonchalantly piloting airplanes over the Rockies, knocking through a window a notorious brawler with a foreign accent, and downing endless glasses of bourbon on the rocks. Many of our movie heroes are incarnations of what a critic has described as "ferocity modified by fatuousness." The heroines were all dolls of faultless face, form, and costume, mammoth wealth, and total absence of ideas. Here were great sums of money and consummate technical expertness spent on embodying the daydreams of the boy behind the soda fountain and the girl behind Woolworth's counter. Those dreams, like those people, are all right in their place and for their years. But why, for their sake, must we all pretend to arrested development?

The profit motive is not the only leveler of values. Democracy itself is a powerful leveler, with its massive majority pressures toward conformity. It is sometimes thought that these pressures have been overcome by the recent revolt of youth against the establishment. And it does seem true that a separate youth culture is developing among us which is notably different from the older culture. But does this mean the choice by a young man or woman of a life style that truly expresses his own insights and powers, or does it mean that another pressure group has arisen among us which appoints for its members their length of hair, their style of dress, and their attitudes toward the powers that be? From what I can observe, there is still too much conformism about it.

Of course we have heard much of American individualism and self-reliance, and we are proud of it. Schopenhauer once defined society as a collection of hedgehogs driven together for the sake of warmth, and we rather like the idea of ourselves as bristling and prickly with individuality. But that is rather an ideal than a

168

historical fact, and it is not the impression we give to visitors from abroad. It was something of a shock to me to hear Sir Ernest Barker addressing an American club in England on his experience of teaching in an American college and entitling his address "The Tyranny of Conformity." He warmly liked American youth—as who that knows them does not?—but he felt a looming danger that our young people should graduate from high school, and even college, with minds as much alike as their diplomas.

Why are the pressures curbing individuality stronger here than in some other countries? Surely part of the reason is this, that we have no social classes in this country whose members, merely by belonging, are given a feeling of security. Most Americans are immigrants, one to three generations removed, who have been thrown willy-nilly into the melting pot. The standards of their parents or grandparents quickly go; where are they to get others? Some never get them at all; hence in part our inordinate crime rates. The majority get them from their schoolfellows and neighbors on whose liking they must depend for their acceptance into the new culture. Hence there has developed in this country an almost passionate desire not to forfeit this acceptance by being too different from other people. This is so deep-going that, as Van Wyck Brooks says, "the desire not to be of the herd is in itself a herd desire. It is a recognition of the herd of which the original man is incapable." On this pressure toward conformity depends the vast assimilative power of America, and its results must be admited to be often excellent.

It may be said that the melting pot shows one great failure: we are not assimilating our blacks. I am not so sure of that. Granted that there is a new insistence among them on their difference; granted that there is much protest, and much defiance, much even of apparent separatism; still I do not think such attitudes can be taken at face value. The blacks are telling us by means of them that we have not let them live like the rest of us, and that they passionately want that privilege. And fairness is likely to prove infectious. Some years ago there was admitted to Yale a young black man who not only made the football team, but went on in his senior year to be elected, with the fairness of youth, to the captaincy of the team and to various secret and honor societies. When he left the university, some proud members of his race told him they wanted to give a scholarship to Yale in his honor. He was delighted. The scholarship, they said, would be earmarked for a young black man. No, no, he would not have that. A scholarship in his honor must not discriminate against those whose fairness had made him what he was. It is a happy fact about America that pressures for uniformity may level up as well as down.

Still, my main point about them is Emerson's point when he said that society is in conspiracy against every one of its members, and Goethe's point when he complained of *was uns alle bändigt, das Gemeine,* of what shackles all of us, the commonplace. We sometimes think of primitive communities where there is no law or police or government as singularly free, whereas it is precisely in such communities that everyone is most tightly imprisoned, like so many raisins in the cake of custom. There are many groups and persons in this country that seek to make it, in this respect, a large-scale primitive community, or even like those herds of animals that turn upon a sick member and attack it because it is different and they do not want such a creature about. They dislike the exceptional man or woman, because such a person is a challenge to their own standards and ways of thought. We all feel the tug of this impulse; Bernard Shaw has remarked that "the best of us is nine hundred and ninety-nine percent mob [Mr. Shaw was no mathematician] and one percent quality." But some groups are more passionate levelers than others. We have our American Legion clamoring against UNESCO; we have had a congressional committee attacking those foundations whose business it is to seek out and encourage the unconventional mind, precisely because they have encouraged such minds; and we ought not to forget the witch-hunts of the fifties, with their attempts to tar all liberal thought with the brush of subversion.

Since these repressive attitudes are likely to be directed against difference as such, they operate against good as well as bad; indeed the nonconformist intellectual, described as an egghead, is particularly suspected because he touches the springs of fear and envy. Charles Kingsley reported an interview with a newspaper editor in this country who said to him, "Mr. Kingsley, I hear you are a democrat. Well, so am I. My motto is, 'Whenever you see a head above the crowd, hit it.' " Now whenever a man stands for the first-rate in quality, his head is bound to be above the crowd; "Whoso

170

would be a man must be a nonconformist," to quote Emerson again; and he will therefore offer an inviting target for the philistines around him.

There is another and related force that makes against the first-rate. It is the curious conviction, more often felt than clearly formulated, that the very notion that some persons and subjects are better than others is undemocratic. Some schools have abolished grades in their reluctance to report that one of their students is brighter or duller than another. Some student bodies have tried to do away with prizes and honors, and some scholars have declined Phi Beta Kappa as likewise undemocratic. The elective system in our colleges went upon the assumption that it was dogmatism to say that some subjects in the curriculum were of more educative value than others. The result is that very odd characters, in the way of new courses, have crashed the academic party, both downstairs and upstairs. Two high school courses that particularly take my fancy are "Orientation to the School Building," and "Progress in Democratic Smoke Abatement." There are parents who refer to their children's courses as "Concentrated Beanbag" and "Advanced Sandpile."

The universities have their own courses in beanbag and sandpile. When I was teaching in a state university, I had as a house guest a distinguished foreign philosopher who came as a visiting professor of aesthetics. When he went to his first class, he found that there had been an unfortunate confusion and that he was confronting a large and eager group that had come for the psychology of advertising. I remember his incredulous astonishment that there could be such a course, and his speculations on the varieties of titillation and bamboozlement that were apparently canvassed in it. I am afraid some very respectable anthropologists have given aid and comfort to the false doctrine of democracy in values by their teaching of "cultural relativism." According to this seductive teaching, since each moral code must be authoritative for its own culture, there is no ground for saying that any code or culture is really better than any other; and some of my students who have worked in sociology seem to think it the last word in sophistication to say that since value is a matter of mores, the wary man will avoid judgments of better and worse. Democracy for practical purposes does count each man's vote as of equal weight with every other, but this does not mean that John Doe's opinion is of the same weight as the Chief Justice's; if it were, I should hope the Justice would be sacked for incompetence.

As for orders of merit and distinction, we need more of these rather than less. The French Academy, the British Academy, and the Order of Merit, in which true quality is singled out and publicly honored, have a few pale parallels in this country, like the Pulitzer prizes, but there ought to be more, and of greater weight. Americans so dislike snobbishness that they sometimes sniff it unfairly in the man who seeks distinction of mind or prefers to associate with it. Snobbishness, to be sure, is an unpleasant trait. But so is the inverted snobbishness that resists as priggish the suggestion that some types of manners, mind, and morals are true titles of nobility.

At this point a question is sure to arise. It seems always to arise when anyone talks about the first-rate in education. Some years ago we had Sir Richard Livingstone at New Haven to speak about education, and since, when he did that, he always talked about the importance of quality, I could see what was coming. One of our brighter and more articulate boys would surely take the first chance to rise and put a triumphantly awkward question. Sure enough it came, and ran something like this: "You are talking about the first-rate. But who is to tell us what is first-rate? One expert says one thing, another another. So when you ask us to seek the first-rate, you are really asking us to accept what you happen to prefer. And isn't that dogmatism?"

Sir Richard had a standard answer to that question, which was this: "For all practical purposes you know the answer already. There may be disputes about who is better than whom on the level of the third-rate, but there is surprisingly little dispute about the figures at the top."

May I try another little experiment with you? I am going to name several fields of academic study and ask you whether there are any names that come to your mind at once as supreme in these fields. Take first the field of poetry. Suppose you were asked to name to yourself one figure, not from American or European annals only, but from the whole history of poetry, would any name come to mind? Now think of music in the same way; is there anybody about whom you would say without question that he stands for

172

superlative quality? Now take the field of science; is there any name that stands out here likewise as unchallengeably great? Very well. Now I should like to know whether in answer to the first question, you thought of Shakespeare. In answer to the second question, did the name of Bach or Beethoven or Mozart come to mind? In answer to the question about science, did the name occur to you of Newton, Darwin, or Einstein? If the answer to these questions is Yes, then the question, Who is to tell me what is first-rate? is academic. The judgment of the world has sufficiently settled that for us. If we want work of supreme quality, we know already where we can find it.

You may be disposed to answer, These are classics, to be sure; but has not Dr. Hutchins defined a classic as a book so great that nobody reads it? To ask ordinary students, that is all students not at St. John's College, Maryland, to live with these people, still more to emulate them, would be like asking a moth to wing its way to a star. Is it not notorious that when education has tried to get students to drink draughts of quality straight, it has generally failed? Are there not people without number to whom the name of Shakespeare or Caesar suggests chiefly the boredom that surrounds a dog-eared high school textbook which they want never to open again? Our Yale Professor Phelps said that he never realized, while reading his Latin, that Caesar wrote sense, not sentences. It is all very well to indulge in commencement commonplaces about high ideals and quote Tennyson to the effect that "we needs must love the highest when we see it," but all this comes to is very little unless education has some way of *making* students see it.

I have much sympathy for this objection. It is of no use to hang golden apples beyond a student's reach if there is no ladder by which he can get to them. The point I would emphasize is that putting the ladder in place is chiefly the student's business rather than the teacher's. Unless the student has a genuine specific levity which carries him upward, some authentic interest, ambition, or enthusiasm, the teacher has nothing to work with. "You cannot get golden character out of leaden instincts." If some enthusiasm is there to start with, even a misguided enthusiasm, there is hope, for there is a drive that you can direct and modify. I would rather have a boy who was enthusiastic about Allen Ginsberg than one who did mere lip service to Shakespeare. And if I were advising students about their programs, I would say, watch your enthusiasms; keep them alight; only by letting the flame grow brighter will you ever do anything first-rate.

Take an example or two. Our college students are constantly accused, and I am afraid with justice, of using their mother tongue, in both speech and writing, clumsily, loosely, and flatly. Businessmen when they employ a college graduate hope to have somebody who can draft a report or state a case with clearness, conciseness, and precision—in short, in English of some distinction. Needless to say, they are often disappointed and begin to ask whether the teachers are earning their stipends. No doubt there are many of us who do not. But I should like to point out that mere good teaching has never produced a writer of distinction and never will. We can compel students to write monthly themes, or weekly themes, or, as Barrett Wendell did for many years at Harvard, daily themes; we can struggle over them half the night; we can do as I have done in the unbearable ennui of these piled-up essays, and have quantities of rubber stamps made with the most frequently repeated strictures, or again, as I have done, have a sheet printed with forty needed comments ready for the appropriate check marks. A teacher can bring to bear all the tricks of the trade for years, and the boy still writes English that is as flat and tasteless as cold porridge.

Then something happens to the boy that means more than all the years of the teacher's slaving: he reads an essay by Macaulay or a preface by Shaw, and with a glow on his face says, "What a man! Think of being able to write like that, perhaps even to talk like that! What wouldn't I give if I could do it?" That moment is the turning point in the boy's literary life. He has caught a gleam. He has felt at first hand the force and economy of fine prose. He begins to read it because he likes it, to feel the dullness of his own stuff beside it, to leave out the big dead words that made his essays wooden, to write firm sentences instead of the old shapeless ones, to write letters that convey himself. He buys Fowler's *Modern English Usage* and begins to take pride in achieving precision without any loss of ease. He begins to sample styles, to feel the force and coarseness of Mencken, the sloppiness of Dreiser, the music of De Quincey, the refinement of Newman. Then some day you see a piece in a journal and realize that a new writer has arrived, a writer of idiosyncrasy

174

and power and grace. You, the teacher, have not taught him those things. Like so many others, he has found himself by falling in love; he has had an affair with English prose. He has achieved with delight and by himself a quality that no amount of instruction could convey.

All this about style may leave you cold. Very well; take a more important example, and only one. It is a firm conviction of mine that the characteristic which a college should aim above all to produce is reasonableness. What does reasonableness mean? Not skill in reasoning, though it is always the better for that. It is not even wholly a matter of the intellectual side of our nature, though a trained intelligence is essential to it. It is the pervading habit and temper of a mind that has surrendered its government to reason. On the intellectual side it shows itself as reflectiveness, the habit of examining the meaning of a proposed belief, and looking to its grounds and consequences, before accepting it. On the practical side it is justice, a scrupulous regard for the rights of others as well as of oneself. On the emotional side, it is partly good taste—such an adjustment of feeling to its object that one is never wrought up over molehills nor cavalier about mountains, and partly, again, that equanimity of mind which comes of having made one's peace reflectively with the best and worst that life may bring. Reasonableness, in this complex sense, seems to me the finest flower of an education.

How many of us achieve it? I fear, none of us at all. Though college studies can refine and inspire our thought, they can do little directly about reasonableness in feeling and act; education, even the finest, cannot guarantee greatness of mind. But it can do the next best thing; as Whitehead reminds us, it can supply the vision of greatness for those who have eyes to see.

In this matter of the reasonable spirit, the business of education is to put pictures on the wall and point at them, and then hope that in our sluggish hearts and minds admiration will begin to stir. None of the pictures it holds up can show us fully what reasonableness is. But when it holds up Plato, for example, we can see in the play of that clear and all-encompassing intelligence what reflectiveness means at its best. When we turn to such figures as Marcus Aurelius and Abraham Lincoln, we see the reasonable mind in another aspect, the aspect of imperturbable justice and

175

magnanimity. As for reasonableness in feeling, we have on the one hand the long line of entries from Longinus through Goethe to Eliot, from whom we may learn sobriety of taste, and on the other the long line of saints from Buddha to Schweitzer to tell us the secrets of inward peace. Qualitative existence means living in the presence of these people till we find ourselves thinking as they do, feeling as they do, and walking in their farsighted ways.

It is a great thing for a university to turn out engineers and doctors in quantity. It is a fine thing to have given engineers and doctors a mastery of their technique. But the highest tribute to a college is not to have produced masses of technicians with a perfect technique. It is to have stamped on its sons and daughters the imprint of the reasonable mind. Just one such person—thoughtful in his judgments, fair in his dealings, unruffled of temper, fearless because he has looked before and after and made his terms with life and death—just one such person may give light to a whole community. His spirit is beyond price because you cannot buy quality with any amount of quantity. And if he lives at an altitude hard to reach, we may remind ourselves, with Spinoza, that all precious things are as difficult as they are rare.

# 10

# *The Specialist and the Humanist*

It is a great thing to belong to the community of scholars, not only for all it means as to wealth of mind, but also because this particular fraternity is worldwide. Men are deeply divided in their religions, in their national loyalties, in their customs, in their tastes; but when the scholar or scientist from Berkeley or New Haven meets his fellow from Paris or Belgrade or Moscow, they meet on common ground. They are united by their respect for fact, and for standards of evidence that are the same the world over. There is no Russian mathematics, no Chinese physics, no American botany, no standards of history that are exclusively French; there is only mathematics, physics, botany, history. Intellect is without nationality. It carries a passport from and to all nations.

Nevertheless there are rifts in the community of scholars of which Lord Snow marked the widest in his essay on *The Two Cultures*. In view of the vast extent of present knowledge, scholars seem increasingly content to stake out small claims, and not to look over their fences, still less to look beyond the horizons of their scientific or humanistic preserve. "That's not my subject," they say, and turn again to their specialties. There are plenty of literate humanists who hardly know the difference between the second law of thermodynamics and the second amendment to the constitution, and feel no vocation to learn it. There are plenty of competent scientists who, if asked whether there was any difference between the styles of Henry James, O. Henry, and Henry Louis Mencken, would say that this was beyond their province, probably beyond their depth, and certainly beyond their interest.

Now there is something to be said for this voluntary ignorance. In these days of accelerating and almost exploding knowledge, we cannot hope to master more than a tiny fraction of what there is to know, or even of what is known already. No chemist can know chemistry as a whole. Every new day complicates the life of the historian; no one can really keep abreast of current events; by trying to do so, as F. L. Lucas has pointed out, "one may degenerate into a fretful midge, a rootless will-o'-the-wisp, dancing fitfully across the morasses of modern life." "Reading maketh a full man," said Francis Bacon. "Yes," commented Dean Inge, "but the full man suffers horribly from indigestion."

I have been told of a New York intellectual who set out to read through the Sunday *Times* week by week, and completed it by reading continuously from Sunday morning till Tuesday night. But, of course, by then he was three days behind. Since this is a game one cannot win, it is better not to play. A scholar is not just an intellectual magpie; he must be selective if he is to achieve competence or preserve sanity. But that seems to mean specialization, and then we are back in the old dilemma: the more knowledge proliferates, the more necessary it is to specialize; but the more we specialize, the more we lose the advantage of this proliferating knowledge. Science, said Professor Lovatt Evans in a presidential address at the British Association, is becoming a tower of Babel, in which specialists are finding it harder and harder to master their own fields or to talk to those in others. "Will there have to be abstracts of abstracts," he asks, and "reviews of reviews? How will the results of special investigations be brought to common grounds if no great unifying principles come to life? . . . If they do not, will the progress of science be brought to an end by the accumulation of its own products?"

It is this dilemma on which I want to offer some comments. The first comment is suggested by something I learned long ago in elementary logic, that when you see a dilemma bearing down on you with horns extended, you can sometimes, if you are agile enough, leap between them right onto the back of the charging beast, and ride away in triumph. I think we can do so here. It is not true that our choice lies between being a mole and being a water spider, between burrowing blindly in a little hole and scurrying about on the surface of things. There is a middle way. The specialist, by limiting himself, is not cutting himself off from other provinces of the mind; he is in fact equipping himself in the most effective way to deal with them.

To suppose that specialization is the work of the mole is to misunderstand the nature of research. No doubt there is a molar kind of specialization that does little for the inquirer and less for the world. To count the number of times the enclitic "de" appears in Homer, or to list the place-names in sixteenth-century Shropshire, may be about as rewarding as to study the average number of syllables per name in the Brooklyn telephone directory. It is not truly research; it is intellectual featherbedding.

What is it that distinguishes true research from such scholarly frivolity? It is not practical usefulness, for some very good research has had very little use. Perhaps the most impressive of all researches were carried out by Newton, Darwin, and Einstein, and though they had some utility (in the case of Einstein much disutility too) we should never think of measuring their value by either. They were great pieces of research because they cleared up important problems of theory, and the importance of such problems turns on how central they are to the great task of understanding the world. If research helps in this task, it is sound, whether it adds to utility or not; if it yields neither light nor utility, it is a waste of time.

Now when I speak of specialization, I mean research in the true sense. And research in that sense always carries one beyond the question of the moment. It is a discipline in inquiry, in the sustained attack upon a problem, in self-critical reflection; and the general pattern of such inquiry is much the same, whatever its field.

At first glance, there may seem to be nothing in common between determining the cause of an irregularity in the orbit of Uranus and determining why Salem had an outbreak of witchcraft in 1692. In truth, the two inquiries, if properly done, have something of the first importance in common, namely their form.

They must both proceed by specifying precisely the issue to be settled, by framing all the theories for settlement that the data admit of, by developing each into its implications, by checking these implications against the facts, and then comparing the theories as wholes.

The man who does this about a swelling on an orbit cannot do this, of course, about the Salem witches without knowing the special facts about them; no one could. But if he has acquired what he ought from his research in astronomy, namely sound intellectual standards, he can deal with the witches far better than a man who knows a thousand facts about them but lacks such standards. He cannot carry over facts from his own field, for the facts are different. But facts are often the easiest thing to come by in an investigation, and never so much so as today.

What he can carry over is the orderliness of his attack, the rigor of his self-criticism, the ideal of clarity, precision, and cogency—in short, everything that belongs to intellectual style. "Every man," said James Bryce, who was one of the best educated men who ever lived, "ought to be thorough in at least one thing, ought to know what exactness and accuracy mean, ought to be capable, by his mastery of one topic, of having an opinion that is genuinely his own." We can see here in passing the difference between learning, training, and education. The learned man is the man who knows many things; but he may be learned without being either trained or educated. The trained man is the man who is practiced and adept at some particular process, such as blowing glass or repairing transistors; he again may be excellently trained without being learned or educated. The educated man is the man who has mastered the most flexible of his tools, his own intelligence; and if he has done that, these other and minor masteries are likely to come of their own accord, so far as he needs them. Given a problem, he can quickly acquire the relevant knowledge, and if he cannot so quickly acquire new skills, he knows how to tap the skills of others.

We in America are haunted by two confusions, one of which confounds education with learning, the other with technological proficiency. These two substitutes are attractive and relatively easy; but neither of them entails education, nor does education imply either. For education is intellectual address, the power of dealing with difficulties generally, not by this bit of knowledge or that bit of skill, but by the one technique that is universally applicable, that of disciplined reason.

We have often been told that there is no such technique, that thinking in logic or mathematics or Greek is as different from thinking in economics or politics or religion as its subject matter is. There is some slight color in this contention, but it is on the whole untrue. Any economist who reads Mill's *Logic* would, I think, be persuaded that if a mind with these habits applied itself to economics, it would illuminate the subject; and if he then turned to Mill's *Political Economy*, he would find his expectation confirmed.

Mill's godson, Bertrand Russell, once said that if a young man wanted to catch the general ear, the way to begin was to write something massive and formidably technical; after that, he could afford to be popular because people knew that he didn't have to be. The remark was not merely facetious. That was the way he and Whitehead did begin; their *Principia Mathematica* is one of the most impressive intellectual feats since Aristotle. The result was that whenever either of these men applied himself seriously in any field at all, his opinion was listened to with respect by the community of scholars. Practiced intelligence, whatever its field, is never negligible in any other.

This is perhaps less true in the sphere of action, but it tends to be true even there. I have gone back lately, by way of blowing on the embers of a fading scholarship, to that high school bogey, Caesar's *Gallic War*. I remembered it as the essence of dullness, and to anyone whose ideal of biographical interest is Brendan Behan or Dylan Thomas, it will remain monumentally dull. In his writing, as in his life, Caesar seems never to have raised his voice; he is never whimsical or wayward; he maintains the even tenor of the judicial spectator. But that very impersonality, so unlike the flamboyancy of most popular heroes, is so remarkable that I find myself coming back to him again and again.

Though he was a child of his age, and at times a ruthless barbarian, he is also one of the most striking examples in history of intelligence in action. It is as if, in his first campaign, he had penetrated to the universal principles of tactics and strategy, and from that time on, while his opponents were sunk in the harassments of the particular case, his mind was playing free above the battle, surveying it in the light of every possibility. The result

181

was a military mastery that was almost uncanny. The situations constantly vary, but you come to feel that the outcome is bound to be the same. The enemy may surround him completely, they may have ten times as many men; they may be commanded by a Gallic chieftain or by the great Pompey; no matter; they are pitted not merely against flesh and blood, but against a mind that will discern their point of weakness if they have one, and exploit it like fate itself. There is no reason to think he would not have shown similar power in civil life if he had lived. For that power lay in neither learning nor training, but in an elastic intellect that, by singling out the essential in any situation, could do the one thing needful. To achieve that sort of intelligence is the aim of education in the sphere of practice.

What I suggest, then, is that specialism of the right kind is universalism. The rungs on its ladder may be the facts about earthworms or Aztec remains or the customs of New Guinea, but if one climbs them faithfully, they should carry one up to a point where one can see something of the ground plan of nature, and realize that in exploring it, the logic, the lawfulness, the pattern of discovery, is everywhere the same. In short, what is important in education is that one master the grand strategy of the intellect, even while engaged in little skirmishes over earthworms and Aztecs.

Is it really true, however, that this strategy remains the same? There are many who admit that it does so long as one moves in the sphere of fact, but would add that the most important problems of life are those not of fact but of value. And what can science do for us there? Two physicists who agree entirely about the theory and technique of bomb production may flatly disagree about its morality, and have no idea how to settle such a dispute. Many a keen mind, bent on fact, would consider questions about the style of Henry James to be as far beyond his interest and perhaps capacity as a connoisseur of James would a book on thermodynamics.

The trouble is not merely that the scientist and the humanist take so little interest in each other's provinces, though that is sad enough, but that these provinces are so often regarded as alien and even hostile countries of the mind, where neither has anything to learn from the other, and where distinction in one may go with moronia in the other.

This mutual foreignness has been promoted of late even by theologians and philosophers. Religious persons have been assured by Karl Barth that their faith need fear nothing from science, since science and faith, reason and religion, have nothing to do with each other. If a scientist shows interest in morals or art, he is assured by an influential school of moralists that he may indulge his tastes freely, since judgments on matters of value are purely expressions of feeling, which need no rational defense, nor indeed admit of it. Thus, however fully the specialist may master the strategy of the intellect in his researches, this mastery will give him a passport only to the other states in the federation of fact; it will give him no entry into the great domains of art or morals, literature or religion.

Is this true? If it is, we must agree that in the kingdom of the mind there really are two cultures, with a rift between them that will all too probably grow.

We must admit, I fear, that the two cultures are really different. The ultimate reason is that insight into values is a very different kind of insight from the grasp of fact. When you say that a painting is three feet square, and was done in oil by Rubens, you are making one kind of judgment; when you add that it is a good painting, you are entering a new region, where what you say neither refers to, nor can be tested by, any sort of sense perception or measurement or historical knowledge. You might know every fact about the picture, you might know every fact in the *Encyclopaedia Britannica*, and still be incompetent to pass that kind of judgment.

To be sure, there are those who tell us that all one needs, even here, is scientific method. But this sounds like propaganda. Scientific inquiry starts and ends in observation, and there is no possible observation that will establish a judgment of value. As Hume said long ago, a geometer may point out many qualities in a circle—its even curvature, the blackness and thickness of its line—but if he adds that it has beauty, he cannot point that out. For beauty is not in the same sense a fact at all. Facts and values do thus fall apart.

Again, the responsiveness to fact and value must be separately trained and kept alive, and exclusive devotion to either tends to dry up our response to the other. Two celebrated cases are those of Darwin, who, after many years among plants, earthworms, and butterflies, confessed that even Shakespeare nauseated him, and

183

Herbert Spencer, who, after a few books of the *Iliad*, wrote: "I felt that I would rather give a large sum than read to the end." Science is not an adequate introduction to poetry. On the other side may be cited a recent archbishop of Canterbury who said he added a column of figures by first adding them downward, then upward, and taking the average of the two results. Religion is hardly an adequate introduction to mathematics.

Granting, however, that the cultures of science and value are different, are we to say that they are wholly different, so that education in one means nothing in the other? We have said that discipline in one province of fact carries over to others; does it also carry across this greater divide?

Surely in some measure it does. It has often been pointed out that the pattern of invention in art is strikingly like what we have called the pattern of discovery in science. There is the same initial attempt to formulate the problem, the same gestating of ideas in the subconscious, the same burst of what looks like intuition, the same working out of alternative suggestions, the same slaughter of the innocents among them when they prove to be misshapen, the same demand for coherence with nature or human nature. Study the process by which Poincaré made his discoveries in mathematics, or Newton in astronomy, and you find a movement of mind similar in many respects to that reported by Bach and Brahms in composing music, or by Coleridge and Housman in composing poetry. The subject matters are about as different as they could possibly be. But the line of attack, the order of advance, the principles of mental strategy are still largely the same.

Again, though fact and value cannot be equated with each other, neither can be pursued without appeal to the other. To be sure, some forms of art seem to flourish with a minimum freightage of ideas. There have been exhibitions in which the work of chimpanzees and schizophrenics has been mingled with that of other artists with an embarrassing lack of identification. But I still think that art is more than explosion of feeling or a surrender to impulse.

I am not thinking merely of the technical knowledge of materials, light, and perspective that an artist needs; I am suggesting that the art that matters most has always, without detriment to itself and indeed with large advantage, held ideas in solution, that there is meaning as well as color in the frescoes of Raphael and the lined faces of Rembrandt, that Dante and Chaucer and Shakespeare would not have been what they were, even as artists, without their knowledge of human nature. It is a tragedy of recent art that meaning is being extruded from it as something alien and expendable, and that so many poets and painters have in consequence lost touch with the public and speak only in corners to connoisseurs of the esoteric. If artists are to speak to the many, they need some breadth of base in the way of sympathy and understanding.

Just as the artist cannot escape the pull of fact, so the scientist cannot escape the pull of value. He is seeking to know the truth, and though truth is not a value, the knowledge of it is. What is it that makes anything valuable in itself? Three things, I think. First, it must be an experience; nothing in the world but experience has intrinsic value. Secondly, it must be, not just any experience, but one that fulfils some drive or urge of our nature. Thirdly, it must be not merely fulfilling; it must bring some pleasure or satisfaction with it.

Now in value so defined the life of the scholar or scientist is rich. The desire to know is a deep and ancient human hunger, and its appeasement is an experience that brings fulfilment and delight. "The intelligence of every soul," said Plato, "rejoices at beholding Reality, and, . . . gazing on Truth, is replenished and made glad." And Plato's great pupil, described as the "master of those who know," in the only passage in the range of his writings in which he shows any strong emotion, speaks of the life of the thinker as the most enviable of all lives, since his vision is at liberty to sweep with delight over all space and all time. "Sir," said Dr. Johnson, "there is nothing I would not rather know than not know." He would probably have agreed with Whitehead that the very "justification for a university is that it preserves the connection between knowledge and the zest of life, by uniting the young and the old in the imaginative consideration of learning." Indeed the life of the scholar gives room for all three of those values traditionally regarded as the central values. It is, of course, a search for truth. But in its higher ranges, particularly in mathematics, truth and beauty almost merge; "Euclid alone has looked on beauty bare." And throughout

185

its whole gamut, scholarship is an exercise in the austere morality of the intellect, in which accuracy and fairness are categorical imperatives.

So these two great countries of the mind, fact and value, are not, after all, wholly alien. If the mind of the scientist is not fueled by a dedication and zest that run beyond pure intelligence, the machinery of his intelligence will grind to a halt. And unless the humanist has a practiced and self-critical eye for truth, his product is too likely to be froth.

For all that, the fact remains that the two cultures are widely different, and that one may travel some distance in either with a minimum baggage from the other.

In which kind of specialism lies the greater danger? It has perhaps most commonly lain in a humanism without science. Think of medieval religion with its grotesqueries about angels, demons and witches—poor old women whose queerness was dealt with, not by the psychoanalyst but by the stake. Think of Victorian education, with such warped products as Rossetti, boasting that he did not know whether the earth went round the sun or the sun round the earth, and the great headmaster of Rugby, Dr. Arnold, writing in similar vein: "Rather than have physical science the principal thing in my son's mind, I would gladly have him think that the sun went round the earth. . . .Surely the one thing needful for a Christian and an Englishman to study is Christian and moral and political philosophy."

Those days have gone. The Victorian hierarchy has been turned upside down. In the course of one short century, science has exchanged the apron of Cinderella in the kitchen for the robes of a queen on an undisputed throne. Governments have been showering scientists with largess; the laboratory with its man in a white coat among his forest of rêtorts is coming to be our authority in thought as well as in advertising. His present charismatic exaltation dates, I suppose, from Hiroshima. The world suddenly realized that what has taken many centuries to build could now be wiped out in a few days or hours, and that the people who knew how to do it were a little group of wizards with equations, working in secrecy at Los Alamos. But those equations were of course communicable, and young scientists in Russia, France, China, and Israel quickly mastered them. Which will spread faster, science or sanity, no one knows.

The new position of science gives us much to think about, not only as respects what science may do *to* us, but also what it might do *for* us once unharnessed from bombs. Educators have a further point to consider, namely the effect of specialism upon the scientist. College students well know that the science curriculum leaves little time for browsing in the humanities, and that as it becomes more technical, such time becomes even harder to find. The prospect is that science will claim an increasing number of our ablest students, and put them through a more rigorous and more exclusive scientific regimen. The rigor is to be welcomed. But what of the exclusiveness? Is it desirable that science should wholly dominate any life? Devoted admirer as I am of the scientifically disciplined mind, I do seem to see perils in it.

First, there is the fact that physical science deals only with *things*. Things and their laws are immensely important to us, but always indirectly, as means to something other than themselves. They have no intrinsic value—not even diamonds and Rembrandts—though the delight they can produce may have it in full measure. Nor do they have any intrinsic *dis*value, not even H-bombs or poison gases, though the human misery they may occasion is beyond all reckoning. The importance of any material thing, or political project, or way of life depends on the intrinsic values of what it leads to, and if we are to appraise such values rightly, we must be familiar with them, able to think in terms of them, able to weigh them against each other. Indeed, we must try our hand at this every day in choosing books, newspapers, churches, friends, political allegiances.

But we shall not learn how to do it from the study of *things*. Sound, for example, as studied by the physicist, is the motion of molecules, and nothing could be further away from it, in spite of having the same name, than the sound we hear, except indeed what the musician creates when "out of three sounds he frames not a fourth sound but a star." With this I think the physicist would agree. His physical world is kept deliberately and antiseptically free from all values but that of knowledge, and it is idle to try to milk stones.

187

Secondly, people who work among physical things exclusively may come to have eyes for these only, and if anyone claims to see anything else, may deny that it is there at all. We have entered the age of computers. They work out payrolls, review taxes, control air traffic, diagnose diseases, and even compose a kind of poetry and music. These remarkable machines are taking over more and more of industry. They are doing something else: they are convincing many people that man himself is one of them. I have a friend—an engineer of distinction—who says that if a machine could be invented so full of feedback and other mechanisms that it reacted as a man would, it would *be* a man; and he is unmoved by the paradox of saying there is nothing in St. Francis or Keats or Gandhi that falls outside the province of the cybernetic engineer. The curious little detail about human nature that it is *conscious* does not worry him. And it seems negligible not only to some engineers, but strangely enough to some psychologists. At both Harvard and Oxford—of all places—leading students of the mind are currently teaching that mental processes are really bodily processes, and that when we seem to find a mind in them in some other sense, we are seeing "a ghost in the machine."

Surely this is scientific philistinism. It says to the human spirit, "Either you are something that can be dealt with by my methods, namely public observation and measurement, or you are nothing at all." That is an attempt to fit reality to our methods rather than our methods to reality. And this scientific fundamentalism takes on a sinister look when it enlists in the service of commerce. The aim of applied science is the control of nature, and if man is just a complicated mechanism, he is a part of nature, to be controlled like other parts by manipulating the right levers.

So Madison Avenue goes in for "human engineering" and, with the help of statistical studies of how the human animal reacts to varying stimuli, tries to find how its resistance can be lowered to toothpaste, aspirin, and cigarettes. One device of these gentlemen is to confer the aura of science upon their product by the free use of quantitative statements; 23 percent less boys using the product develop tooth decay; better than 90 percent of doctors consulted use it; since everything deadly is kept by a filter a nice clean quarter-inch away, all is well. Education is a favorite subject for these exercises in measurement. For example, there is a triumphant item from the Education Newsletter of San Diego, which points out that the volume containing the Education Code of California has grown from one inch in thickness to 3 1/8 inches in eighteen years, an increase in less than two decades of approximately 212 percent. This is taken to show something about California education, though it might be debated what this is.

The cure of scientific fundamentalism is the same as that of religious fundamentalism, namely exposure to a richer culture in which dogmatism dissolves. "Dogmatism," said Dean Inge, "is the maturity of puppyism." So it is, but full maturity comes only when that too goes and reality is seen as it is. Science is the finest of all disciplines for seeing *things* as they are. But reality includes more than things. It includes man. And "what a piece of work is man!" The scientist who would be a realist must be a humanist as well.

Of course, I do not mean that the scientific specialist is to be saved for the larger life by adding a few more humanistic courses to his curriculum. That might help; agreed. But it is part of the very attitude I would protest against to suppose that a mechanical arrangement can guarantee a quality of mind. And many courses in the humanities are more desiccated humanistically than most courses in science. One danger of exalting science is that humanism itself tries to ape it.

What is needed is a tradition in our universities and educated public as to what education means. It is not information; it is not skill; it is disciplined and flexible intelligence, ready to apply itself anywhere with clarity and precision. "I call, therefore, complete and generous education," said John Milton, "that which fits a man to perform justly, skilfully and magnanimously all the offices, private and public, of peace and war."

The sum of the matter would seem to be this: a sound intellectual strategy may be acquired in any field, even deep in the mine of the scientific specialist, where our graduates will increasingly work. The miner in those deeps may see so little of the green fields of value that he forgets how to play in them and hardly remembers they are there. If he is to avoid a shriveled spirit, he must take his own education in hand. He must learn to move freely not only among things, but among persons and causes and values. To do that realistically, he must be a humanist, even if self-made. "Every man ought to have outside of his work," wrote William James as a young man, "a chance to cultivate the ideal. I ought to be able to read biographies, histories, etc. a couple of hours every evening, for I think a professor in addition to his *Fach*, should be a *ganzer Mensch.*"

That is just what James became, a whole man. He began as a physiologist; but he saw that to understand bodily processes fully, he must go on to the mind they served; so he became a psychologist. Then he saw that to understand the mind rightly, he must go on to the ends and values it was seeking; so he became a philosopher and the sort of humanist to whom nothing human was alien. He did not cease to be a man of science in entering this larger world; he could now speak with both the discipline of the scientist and the humanist's sympathies. This is the sort of pilgrim's progress to which every young specialist may well commit himself as he walks out through the university's gates.

# 11

# Some Current Issues in Education

Since World War II I have wandered rather freely about the American scene, visiting over a hundred colleges and conversing with many hundreds of colleagues. The major impression I have brought back with me is of the overall health of American education to be sure, the standards vary enormously. In the private universities of the Northeast and the better state universities of the Middle West, the level of faculty scholarship and student qualification is high. In some of the smaller sectarian colleges, gasping to keep alive in the rising tide of costs, with little or no endowment and an overworked staff, the standards and the atmosphere are less happy. Still, the general impression is one of vitality. Nearly everywhere I went, I had the same sense of dedication on the part of the staff and of eager receptiveness on the part of the students.

What are the issues in education that are stirring discussion on these campuses? I do not mean such practical issues as faculty salaries, rates of tuition, and means of luring government subsidies, or the common bones of contention in student unrest, but issues of educational theory and policy. There are many of these—too many even to list here. But I noted that a few kept cropping up, and it may serve a useful purpose if I mention some of them and venture a comment or two on each.

### Hesitations about Science

First there is the old debate about the place of science and the humanities in the liberal arts curriculum. For the past fifteen years the humanists have been increasingly uncomfortable about their weakening position. Their alarm began with Sputnik I, was deepened by Lord Snow and his widely read book on *The Two Cultures*, and kept on deepening as the government poured funds into scientific research, got entangled in a remote war, and committed itself to vast programs in the exploration of space. In such activities scientists were conspicuously important, scholars and philosophers conspicuously not. Indeed in a culture dominated by technology, humanists do not find it easy even to state their case, and begin to feel a little apologetic for cumbering the ground at all. The kind of utility that belongs to scholarship, speculation, and the arts is so nebulous in comparison with that of the chemist, the physician, and the engineer that the humanist begins to have doubts of his own value. And Lord Snow is surely right that in a civilization where life and efficiency depend so largely on science, we ought to have a far greater understanding of it than we commonly have.

Yet the curious fact remains that most young men and women are reluctant to go into science. A survey made in 1958 indicated that nearly 40 percent of college-educated persons in this country had not taken a single course in physical or biological science. It was thought that after the first cry went up about Russian superiority in space, young scientists would come trooping in, but the cry was met on the whole with apathy. Engineering schools, which had already shown a decrease in enrollment, continued to decrease. Senator Ribicoff, then Secretary of Health, Education and Welfare, reported in 1962 that the percentage of freshmen entering engineering schools had dropped for three years in a row. In the universities, the sciences still lagged far behind the humanities as the subjects of major study, and many students who came to college with the intention of making science their chief pursuit turned away from it, after their freshman year, to history, literature, or economics. In a book of 1964 on *The Student and His Studies* by

President Raushenbush of Sarah Lawrence, there occurs this suggestive passage:

> In a highly competitive urban college, 572 students were reported as having changed their majors during college. Of these, 213 left science. Only 24 moved into science from other fields. The records of a class in one of the best of the small private colleges for men show during these same years that over 21 per cent listed science and engineering as their career choice in their applications, which dropped to 17 per cent when they became freshmen, and to 4.3 per cent by the time they graduated.

Congress undertook to prime the scientific pump by legislation and fat subsidies; foundations poured out money; universities gave new fellowships; the connections of science with patriotism, prestige and income were proclaimed. These efforts had some effect. But it was a strangely uphill fight.

Why all the hesitation? Partly, no doubt, because students soon discover that science is hard work. These same students can work hard enough at their summer jobs; they can make exhausting efforts and take Spartan punishment on the football field; but the habits of intellectual exertion formed by the American high school are not exacting. To the ordinary American student the regime of a French lycee or a German gymnasium would seem like a course of boot training. But grim application is the only known road to proficiency in such fields as mathematics or chemistry. It may be said that the same is true in all other subjects. I do not think it is. Anyone who can read the *New York Times* with understanding can read and understand Macaulay's *History*. An intelligent youth can do the reading for a course in the English novel with enjoyment and a pipe in his mouth. It is surely untrue to say that he can absorb calculus or Mendelejeff's periodic table as he would Macaulay or *Tom Jones*. And most boys have an uncanny compass inside them for detecting the path of least resistance.

Another deterrent to their flight into science is what they see farther along the road. If they could see themselves on the lofty peak of an Einstein or a Rutherford, if they could look forward to being an inventive wizard like Edison or Kettering, or a large-scale benefactor of their kind like Salk or Fleming, they would pay the price readily enough. But looked at through colder eyes, their

193

future seems more likely to be that of a man commuting in a gray flannel suit from the suburbs to the chemical works; and there is no great magnetism in that. The work of the scientist out on the frontier, or even of the scientific administrator—a Tizard or a Lindemann—is one thing; that of a private in the ranks is another. And you can hardly do scientific speculation or invention and live by it, as you occasionally can, if you are good enough, in literature; you must normally do it on company time and succeed anonymously. That is not romantic, and youth is.

Another breakwater against the student surge into science is the ineffectiveness of introductory scientific teaching. In my forty years as a pedagogue in institutions of various sizes, I have heard this complaint so continually that I can only believe there is something in it. The common defense offered by scientific colleagues is that they are sitting on the horns of a most uncomfortable dilemma. If they aim their introductory work at the students who are to become specialists, they must pitch it at a level that drives other students away; if they aim it at the nonspecialists, the best students are denied the discipline they need. The choice is thus to be either rigorous and ostracized or popular and mushy. I remain unconvinced. I do not think a rigorous course in science, if skilfully taught, is of necessity unpopular. I am told that in the fifties Amherst developed such a course in physics and mathematics, which was required of all freshmen and which carried them into calculus by the end of the first semester, and that the majors in science, instead of dropping off, grew from a fifth to a third of the student body. The same point seems to have been proved for chemistry by Professor Cassidy's work at Yale.

It is harder to invest science with excitement than it is literature or history. These subjects deal with persons, and carry a built-in appeal to feeling and imagination. Science is impersonal, and if excitement is generated, it must come from the instructor's own internal battery and be communicated by contagion. That is difficult. But it can be done, for it has been done. Such teachers as Huxley, Shaler, and Agassiz achieved it in days when science had far less prestige than it has now. Students are more open than ever before to the seduction of science. Many more of them could be won over if academic scientists paid more attention to the humble art of communication. In that art I should include a familiarity with the philosophical and human importance of their subjects, some acquaintance with the strategy of lighting up abstractions by timely examples, some sense for the order of logic and the order of difficulty in developing their theme, and some feeling for its dramatic possibilities. To these needs I should add one about departmental organization: the scientific chiefs of staff should be ready to deploy more of their top brass for service in the front lines, namely the elementary courses. Young teachers are inclined to ride intellectual hobbies, to be on the prickly defensive, to lack perspective. In any field of study the main points settle out only with the years. If I may cite my own experience again, it took me thirty or forty experiments in teaching an introduction to philosophy to get it where I wanted it, and then I found myself giving it for the last time.

## Science versus the Humanities

We have been asking why students drag their feet about science. But the more important question is whether they have good grounds for dragging their feet. As between the sciences and the humanities, does either set of disciplines hold a marked advantage simply as an educational instrument? If the student is yet uncommitted as to his future work, this is the question he wants answered. And the question takes one straight into philosophy. As T. S. Eliot said, "To know what we want in education, we must know what we want in general, we must derive our theory of education from our philosophy of life." If you hold that music is more worth study than mathematics, and I that mathematics is worth more than music, we must be prepared to state and defend our standard of value itself. That would be a fascinating undertaking, but too large for my present concern. I shall have to state without argument the chief assumptions I am making.

I am assuming, first, that only experience has value, that the only value of a rose or a symphony, for example, lies in seeing or hearing it. I am assuming, secondly, the distinction between instrumental value—the value of anything as a means, and intrinsic value—the worthwhileness of something in itself. It is intrinsic values that are important for our purpose, since the instrumental ones come back to these in any case. Thirdly, and most controversially, I am assuming that what makes an experience valuable intrinsically is the presence in it of two characters, the fulfilment of some drive or impulse of our nature and the presence of the satisfaction or pleasure that normally accompanies such fulfilment. Both must be there, and they are equally essential. If a man is tone deaf and can make no response to music, he will get nothing from it; and even the man who can respond will still find it ashes in his mouth if, through some veto imposed by circumstance he can take no pleasure in it. Experience, to be intrinsically good, must fulfil and satisfy. (This theory has been developed and defended in my *Reason and Goodness* [New York: Humanities Press, 1960].)

The main aim of a liberal education, I should hold, is to enable its students over the years to achieve experience that is in the above sense fulfilling and satisfying (and to aid others in doing the same). Studies are to be valued in the degree to which they subserve this end.

### The Double Value of Science

Science and the humanities both subserve it, though in differing ways and degrees. Science does so both directly and indirectly. That it does so indirectly is a point that needs no enlargement in these days. It is science and its applications that make modern life possible. Health, longevity, food, transportation, comfort, communication, the whole vast machinery of civilized life depends on it, and there is something futile and pathetic in the Tolstoys and Thoreaus who would resign from their age rather than live with the machinery that is an unavoidable part of it. Only through science and its technology can nature be mastered, and only through the mastery of nature can the good life be made possible for mankind generally. The plain fact is that we cannot have too much of it.

Scientific grasp is an intrinsic value as well as an instrumental one. The desire to know is an authentic and central drive of human nature, and though Dewey thought the philosophers had made too much of its distinctness and intensity, it is clearly there and its fulfilment is one of man's greater goods. Its aim, as I conceive it, is not to accumulate details, but to penetrate through to the network of law that renders the details intelligible, in brief, to understand its world. The aim in understanding is quite distinct from the aim in application. "Scientific discoveries," says Russell, "have been made for their own sake and not for their utilization, and a race of men without a disinterested love of knowledge would never have achieved our present scientific technique." (*The Scientific Outlook* [New York: W. W. Norton Co., 1932], p. 153.) And there is no fixed relation between the value of a discovery as illumination and its value in practice. The discoveries of Freud have been of great benefit to the race through transforming the treatment of mental abnormality; Planck's discovery of quanta, through making possible the fissioning of uranium, may yet lead to the destruction of the race; Einstein's theory of relativity is of neither help nor harm in practical life. But all alike are important theoretically, from their contribution to the understanding of nature. The student who can enter into the inheritance opened to him by modern science, whether he can add to it or not, has enriched his mind invaluably.

### A Case for Humanistic Studies

On the importance of science, both theoretic and practical, there will be no great difference of opinion. It is on another issue that the debate with the humanist arises. Considered simply as educational instruments, as disciplines preparatory to a full life, does the advantage lie with the sciences or the humanities? (For the sake of a clear issue, it is perhaps best to restrict "the sciences" here to the physical sciences, since the social sciences fall somewhere between the extremes.) My own conclusion, for what it is worth, favors the humanities. It is hard to say anything in support of this conclusion, however, without seeming to disparage scientific study, which would be absurd. Indeed I would myself subscribe to almost the whole of Mill's classic defense of mathematics and physics against Sir William Hamilton. (J. S. Mill, *Examination of Sir William Hamilton's Philosophy*, Chapter XXVII.) The scientific method of attack on a problem, with its precision, its clarity, its caution, its distinction between certainty and probability, between confirmation and proof, and with its insistence on total honesty and objectivity, provides a model of intellectual procedure which it is surely a main part of liberal education to fix in the student's mind.

But these same benefits are also by-products of the humanities, if rightly taught and studied. The most useful kind of clarity, for example, may be even better learned from the humanities. Though clarity is demanded in the sciences, it is probably easier there, since the concepts with which one is dealing are sharply defined at the outset; the notions of number, space, and time, of motion and velocity, of weight and temperature, offer no great opportunities for confusion to the moderately clearheaded. But the main ideas used in humanistic study are so enshrouded with fog and confusion in their ordinary use that one can win through to clearness about them only by a determined process of discrimination; the notions of freedom, right, good, beauty, justice, tragedy, intelligence, religion, are standing intellectual challenges. To get clear about these notions requires a harder effort of analysis than to achieve a corresponding clarity about the common notions of science.

Furthermore, the kind of thinking done in the humanities is nearer to that of ordinary life than the thinking done in the sciences. Granting that the scientific regimen is essential for those who enter science professionally, most students have other prospects; they become businessmen, housewives, lawyers, ministers, salesmen, administrators. The thinking involved in such work is usually at a far remove from that of the laboratory. It calls for decisions as to what is fair, tactful, or prudent, the appraisal of character, the judgment of better and worse, sensitiveness to the varieties of human motive and feeling, foresight of comparative advantages for oneself, one's family and one's community. It is the kind of thinking, taken in its highest exemplification, that is done by the statesman. Essential to it is the taking account of goods and evils, with which scientific study does not concern itself, and for which exclusively scientific study may even serve as a disqualification. I heard not long ago an address on rational choice by a philosopher of science for whose competence in his field there is universal respect. But his way of conceiving the problem was this: given an end that one wants to achieve, what is the most rational method of choosing among the means to this end? But if that is all science can tell us about rational choice it does not take us far. The choices of actual life are not merely between means to predetermined ends; they are also choices among ends themselves, between better and worse among values. Thinking in the humanities forces us to envisage these values, and to compare and appraise them.

What about objectivity? We have just acknowledged that science provides a model of objective thinking. But this too needs a qualifying clause. The best discipline in objectivity is to be gained where there is a temptation to be less than objective, that is, in fields where passions and prejudices are likely to be engaged. Now there is no doubt that science does at times engage one's prejudices. When a scientist has committed himself to a thesis on which his reputation depends, objectivity is difficult; Darwin admitted that for a long period he could hardly think of the development of the eye (which seemed inconsistent with his theory) without its making him sick; it is said that Newton was so strongly involved emotionally with his final calculations about the gravitation of the moon that he turned them over to other hands; and Kammerer, when his gullibility about the inheritance of acquired characters was exposed, committed suicide. But these are extreme cases. The atomic number of plutonium is not normally an emotional issue, nor the rate of acceleration of a falling raindrop, nor even the speed of a neural impulse. What answer is given is indifferent, so long as it is factually correct.

This is not true with humanistic problems. Were the mental quirks or the Fascist affiliations of Ezra Pound of any relevance when we are estimating him as a poet? Is freedom of will a condition of morality? Is Nietzsche's attack on Christianity valid? Is religion, as Arnold thought, really morality touched by emotion? Is Norman Mailer or jazz music or "the theatre of the absurd" or Kierkegaard or the "God-is-dead" theologian getting more attention than is deserved? These questions raise hackles. They are fascinating, widely discussed and important, yet one seldom or never hears them discussed with objectivity; that is an intellectual and moral feat of which few minds seem to be capable. But it is precisely this sort of objectivity, the sort that can move with fairness and sympathy in the vast field where values are involved, that is today most urgently needed.

I have spoken of the intrinsic value of scientific understanding, and it is well to ask how this compares with the intrinsic value of humanistic study. Here the beam tips strongly toward the humanistic side. History, art, biography, and literature have their own cognitive satisfactions, like science, but they open a large range of satisfactions that science explicitly forgoes. Men are full of loves and hates, heroisms and pettinesses; they have their

Churchills, Hitlers, and Al Capones. The humanities are imaginative adventures among such people. They enlarge our range of election among ways of living; they enable us to enjoy vicariously flights of imagination and feeling that we should never have been able to achieve alone; they refine and fulfil by catharsis battalions of impulses that would otherwise be starved; they sensitize us to the varieties of good and evil and discipline us in appraising them. And it is precisely in these regions that Americans are most widely considered deficient. Great numbers of students from Britain and France come to this country to study American science and technology; comparatively few come for instruction in the humanities; and the general belief outside the country, not wholly without foundation, is that our standard of living has completely outstripped our level of general cultivation. We need more science and more technology; I have nothing to say against either; but our most obvious need is for more of what only the humanities can give.

### Publish or Perish

Another educational issue that is being widely canvassed at present, particularly among the younger faculty in our colleges, is whether publication as opposed to teaching is being overvalued in appointments and promotions. Incidents at Tufts, at Yale, and elsewhere in which philosophers have been let go whom the students regarded as exceptional teachers have aroused agitated discussion.

There is no doubt that a mechanical requirement about quantity of publication would be unjust to the point of absurdity. Should the candidate for a chair or for tenure have published a book? That requirement would have excluded some of the men who, as professors at Oxford and Cambridge, have been leaders of contemporary thought; many of these men have made their contribution through relatively brief articles. Besides, in America where the size of classes puts a premium on anthologies, a man may edit a large and useful book without exhibiting anything more than a judicious taste in selection. Very well, should the requirement in the way of publication be limited to a certain output of articles? But it is notorious that if quality is considered, one article will often outweigh a dozen others, and that in some fields a long publication list is comparatively easy. In view of these difficulties, some persons have thought it unreasonable to place any stress at all on publication.

Here I cannot agree. In philosophy particularly, if a young man is thinking independently and vigorously, he will naturally take to writing; that is probably the best way of finding out for himself how clear, precise, and thorough his thinking is. It is also the best way, and often the only way, in which he can assure others of these qualities. What is important is not the publication but the writing, and not the bulk of the writing but its quality. In some cases an unpublished doctoral dissertation will give all the assurance needed that here is a man of mature achievement in analysis and argument. But some assurance in the way of writing there must be. I have heard the remark repeated that a doctorate is merely a "union card" for the prospective teacher, and is no more than a tiresome formality. It is nothing of the kind. Philosophy *is* an attempt to think things through exactly and persistently, and the only public evidence that one can do this is the evidence one gives on paper. Department heads looking for quality are entitled to such evidence, even though they would be mistaken in insisting on any one form of it. It may be said that there are first-rate teachers of philosophy who have no gift for such writing. But surely a teacher of philosophy should himself be a philosopher, not simply a purveyor of other people's notions. And how are you to determine his power as a philosopher except through work that will stand up under detached and critical appraisal? Someone has objected that under such a requirement Socrates would never get an assistant professorship in an American university. But a Socrates who, with all the modern facilities for writing at his disposal, could still do nothing but talk would not be Socrates.

With some qualifications, then, the university has a right to say "publish or perish." But is the sort of power shown in publication, whatever its quality, an adequate index of teaching? Unfortunately not. Scholarly productiveness and skill in the classroom are not functions of each other. I once heard a man who had studied under the two greatest physicists of his time say that there was only one worse teacher of physics in Europe than Kelvin in Glasgow, namely Helmholtz in Berlin. Such lack of classroom effectiveness may make little difference in the graduate school, where sheer competence in one's specialty is the great essential. But students in the liberal arts college have a right to demand some skill in communication, and administrative heads to make it a condition of advance. I doubt if there is any difference of principle here. No department or college head I ever knew would regard a first-rate undergraduate teacher as anything but a pearl of great price, to be kept, praised, and even coddled if his scholarship also passed muster. The real difficulty is in appraising this classroom skill. The head of a large department cannot solicit or honor student gossip; he has no time for extended sit-ins on the classes of his subordinates, and if he descends on them occasionally like an Assyrian on the fold, he may only induce a glottal stop in his young instructor. In the small college the problem is simpler. There the young man will probably have courses of his own, not merely discussion sections, and in a few years it will become plain enough by the implicit vote of student enrollment whether he can teach or not.

Here a note of warning may be in order. Undergraduate opinion, if I may judge by my own recollection of it, is something of a weathercock. Students love campus characters who titillate them with melodramatic antics, but they can often see in looking back on such a teacher that he had a larger following than was merited by either his instruction or his example. In general, students have a good nose for what profits them in philosophy, and the teacher who relies unostentatiously on clearness and order generally gets his reward. Unhappily the harlequin sometimes gets it too.

While we are on this matter of student opinion, I may perhaps be allowed an aside of my own. Granting that this opinion should be regarded, I do not hold with student sit-ins, picketing, and protest marches. These have their place, but it is not on the campus. Academic administrators, at least in my own limited experience of them, have been more anxious than the students themselves that justice be done and wrongs righted in the little kingdoms they reign over. Their very position as heads of an educated community commits them to an endeavor at openness of mind and reasonable dealing. Hence the attempt to coerce or publicly discredit them comes home to them more acutely than it would in a business dispute, and is likely to be felt as peculiarly unfair. If students feel strongly about the value of a given course or teacher or policy, as they are fully entitled to do, let them prepare a reasoned statement of their views, sign it, and submit it to the administration; I think they will find without exception that it will be heard with respect. If, after considering such a statement, an administration finds it inadequate, then it ought not to yield to any kind of coercion.

## Analytic versus Speculative Philosophy

A third issue that is currently much discussed is at once technically philosophical and of importance for the future of philosophy among the liberal arts. It is the question whether the emphasis should now be on analytic or speculative philosophy. By analytic philosophy I mean roughly the set of interests and methods introduced by the logical empiricists in the twenties and/or those of present-day linguistic analysis. By speculative philosophy I mean the attempt to answer such traditional questions as, "What is the nature of life, mind, the self, causation, truth, beauty, religion, moral obligation?" It may be said that between these schools there is no necessary opposition, that it is perfectly possible for an analyst to discuss these problems in his own way. That is true. But the two schools formulate their questions in ways which, though at first glance equivalent, are really different and lead to widely different answers. The traditional philosopher asked, "What is the nature of truth?" The analyst asks, "What does 'true' mean?" The one asked, "What is the nature of goodness?" The other asks, "What do you mean by 'good'?" or "How is 'good' used?" The one asked, "Does God exist?" The other asks, "What meaning, if any, does the word 'God' express?"

Now the importance of the new formulation is that if it is taken seriously, the speculative question often vanishes. According to Professor Ryle, philosophers have bemused themselves ever since Descartes by discussions of "the nature of mind" as distinct from "the nature of matter," because when they put things in that way, they were almost bound to suppose that they were dealing with two different kinds of entity, consciousness and the body. But if we study carefully the words in which we describe mental behavior, such as "intelligent," "bungling," "alert," "adroit," we see that these words are in effect adverbs describing different ways of responding bodily. Once we see this, talk about the nature of mind as a distinct existence becomes otiose. Similarly, if we start with "the nature of goodness," we shall assume that there is a character bearing that name which it is our business to examine. But if we begin with the meaning of "good," we shall find that the term has only emotive meaning, and that the character we were supposed to examine is an illusion. Does God exist? That depends on the meaning of "God." If it means an omniscient and omnipotent being, the "meaning" is really unthinkable; it is no meaning at all. The problem of the existence of God is thus a pseudoproblem which it is idle to discuss further.

This issue goes very deep. To use the language of the United Nations, it begins as a procedural question, but ends as a question of substance. If the analytic approach is adopted, at least as used by many of its exponents, problems that have hitherto lain at the center of philosophic interest will be set aside and the discussion of them by the historic philosophers will be studied chiefly as examples of how one may miss the point. Now it is obvious that the question at issue between the analytic and the speculative philosophers is far too large for discussion here. Not that I want to conceal my own conviction about it; I think that many of the conclusions reached by the analysts both about the test of meaningfulness and about the meaning of cardinal philosophic terms are mistaken, and I have tried to argue this out in detail in *Reason and Analysis* (La Salle, Illinois: Open Court Publishing Co., 1961). At the moment I can only make a comment or two as to the implications of the conflict, trying not to prejudge the main points at issue.

First, whether the analysts are right or not, no philosopher can ignore their work without heavy cost. Just as a Hegelian owes it to himself to read G. E. Moore, so a present-day rationalist or existentialist owes it to himself to read Ayer, Austin, and Ryle. He may not be convinced; certainly I have not always been; but his awareness of what he is doing will be intensified, and hence his alertness to obscurity and ambiguity. Moore made it more difficult to read Bradley and the Cairds patiently, which was a philosophic service; John Austin makes it more difficult to read Husserl or Heidegger patiently. The analytic standard of clarity is high, and it is salutary for a philosopher to have some gimlet-eyed hawks fluttering about his desk. The day of metaphysics is of course not over, though its demise has for long been eagerly announced; indeed it is already showing signs of renewed animation; and when it comes in fashion again, it will be the better for the long penance it has done.

Secondly, if the speculators should learn from the analysts, the salutation might well be returned. Philosophy did not begin in 1922 with the *Tractatus*, though one could cover large areas of analytic philosophy without suspecting the fact. A new paper by one of the acknowledged experts on language games or a posthumous paper by Wittgenstein, enlightening or not, is eagerly devoured; a criticism by Bertrand Russell may be paid the mute and sorrowful respect accorded to a lost leader; but the work of some of the ablest philosophers critical of the analytic tradition, such as H. J. Paton, C. A. Campbell, and A. C. Ewing, is almost wholly ignored. The kind of comprehensive and judicial reviewing that used to come from C. D. Broad and A. E. Taylor seems to be a vanishing art; many of the reviews in the analytically dominated journals are flip, spotty, and distressingly partisan. Attention to language apparently has nothing to do with literary form, and if one takes such form seriously, one is likely to be set down as rhetorical. All this is philistinism. The tide may now have turned; useful books have appeared from the analytic camp on Plato, Spinoza, and Bradley. But the reminder seems still in order that "the best that has been thought and said in the world," even in philosophy, did not necessarily begin with Wittgenstein II or even with Wittgenstein I.

Thirdly, the position of philosophy as an instrument of education in the liberal arts will certainly be affected as one or other tendency wins out. Let us suppose for the moment that linguistic analysis prevails, and indeed that it does so because it is right. Such success should be an occasion for rejoicing, since any fair-minded person would want the truth to prevail. Even so, one would have to agree that the importance of philosophy had been diminished. It could offer definitions of key words; it could study "the logic of science"; it could offer shrewd observations on how the misuse of language led to dilemmas and category mistakes; it could show that "if," "can," and "know" bristle with ambiguities. These are useful things to do. But they are not what Spinoza and Kant and Hegel and Spencer and James and Alexander were trying to do. It may be that these men were attempting the impossible. It may be that for a philosopher to set up as a critic of the assumptions of science and to attempt the synthesis of its results into a coherent account of the world is sheer presumption. Nevertheless it is precisely this presumption, if such it is, that has given philosophy its place, both in men's estimation and among the liberal arts. Students have pursued it in the past because it promised to give some answer to their irrepressible queries about man's place in the universe. If these queries are really confusions begotten by words, it is important that we should know that. But it is idle to say that philosophy would then retain the place it had when these queries were thought the most important one could raise, and when philosophy was accounted the oracle most likely to give the answer.

One further comment: a department owes it to its students to have both types of philosophy represented and effectively taught. In philosophy there is no orthodoxy and hence properly no heresy; any view that presents itself with a respectable show of reason has a claim to consideration. The value of philosophy as education lies largely in the examination of such claims and in the equipping of the student's mind to deal with them. He will best learn how to deal with them by working with persuasive advocates of diverse and incompatible views. An able candidate for a post in a large university told me that he had been informed by the department chairman that if he did not accept the approach of recent analytic philosophy, he might as well not apply. If the candidate had been the sort of Marxist or Thomist who thought that, having found the truth, he need waste no time in looking further, one could understand an insistence on more modernity of mind. But he was not; he had followed the reaction against metaphysics without being convinced by it. And it is surely possible for a man to examine Wittgenstein, just as it is Marx or St. Thomas, and responsibly reject what he finds. To impose philosophic shibboleths at the threshold of a department is not the way to build a department of educational variety and force. I think it was President Tucker of Dartmouth who said that the department in which James, Royce, Santayana, Palmer, and Münsterberg made friendly war on each other was not only the best department of philosophy, but the best department—period—in American history. Would it have been so if its members had all subscribed to the same creed?

Philosophy has lost ground with the public. Few books on philosophy are reviewed by such media as the *Saturday Review* or the *New York Times Book Review. The New Yorker* indeed published a few years ago a hundred-page article on the British analysts, but the interest was sustained largely by thumbnail personal sketches, and the public was impressed less by the importance of what the philosophers were saying than by the teapot character of the tempests they were stirring up. The scholars who have appeared in the pages of *Life* and on the covers of *Time*, and since World War II have drawn the largest audiences, have not been philosophers, but theologians—Karl Barth, John Courtney Murray, Reinhold Niebuhr, and Paul Tillich. That is understandable enough, for these men had something to say which, whether quite intelligible or not, seems to their hearers important. What the philosophers are saying seemed less important and their voices are drowned out by others that are more arresting or more strident. One would not wish philosophers to shout in order to be heard, still less to look around for causes that would catch the public eye or ear. Perhaps a fusion of speculative and analytic virtues would help to gain them a hearing. When the speculative philosophers achieve the clarity of the analysts, and the analysts acquire the speculators' sense of what is important and what is not, the voice of philosophy may become audible again.

# 12

## Limited Minds and Unlimited Knowledge

What are we to do in the face of the increase of human knowledge? What ought we to know in a time when the stores of accessible knowledge are almost infinitely beyond the range of any human mind? What should a college teach if it must limit itself to one-thousandth of what it might teach?

Let us begin by getting clear as to the main fact, namely, that the fraction of our intellectual capital which an individual mind can acquire is dwindling rapidly away. There was a time, not very remote in the history of man's life on earth, when an educated mind could know almost everything of importance known to anyone. Aristotle not only was acquainted with all the sciences of his day, but founded a goodly number of them himself. Bacon could take all knowledge for his province without a smile. A little later Leibnitz, a bachelor scholar who had no fixed hours for meals or sleep, used to sit in his chair and read and think till he became hungry, or sleepy, and then send out for a meal, and doze a while, resuming where he left off; he seems to have managed by this regimen to master the principles at least of all the existing sciences and the chief ancient and modern tongues.

Not long ago we celebrated the tercentenary of Leibnitz's birth. Three hundred years is not long in human history, and yet knowledge has so widened since his time that he now seems one of the dawn men of the modern world. In his day most of our present sciences had no distinct existence. It was in his lifetime that the fundamental natural science, physics, began under Newton's guidance a life of its own. From that time on new sciences prolificated with an accelerating fertility. About a century later chemistry reached independence in the humble laboratory of Priestley. In 1830 Sir Charles Lyell produced the first systematic geology. In 1859, that birth year of great things, came modern biology with Darwin's *Origin of Species* along with a set of remarkable babies, named John Dewey, Henri Bergson, Havelock Ellis, Samuel Alexander, and Edmund Husserl. In 1871 modern anthropology was born with Tylor's *Primitive Culture*. The sciences of sociology and psychology have had an independent place in our colleges only within living memory; the first man to hold a chair of psychology in America, James McKeen Cattell, died as recently as 1944.

One might think that with the establishment of a science, there would be a fixed body of knowledge that could be mastered once for all. But not so. Since the turn of the century, some of the most firmly based of the sciences have been digging up their foundations and moving to new ones, physics for example, so that those of us who learned our physics in days before the quantum have had to learn it over again. Other great sciences like medicine have been dividing by fission, so that the people who practice medicine generally are becoming proportionally fewer and are being replaced by specialists in urology, dermatology, and allergy. Still other sciences have been breaking into rival schools after the manner of psychology; to know psychology one must know functional and behaviorist and structuralist and Gestalt and "depth" psychology, which are disconcertingly different. The day is upon us when the smile that greets childlike innocence is given not only to the youth who would claim all knowledge as his province but also to the scholar who would claim to have fully mastered any division of it.

Let us take, more or less at random, one example. We are all interested in history, the study of how people and their institutions became what they now are. Every serious student of history discovers what Macaulay did in the course of writing his great work. He set out to write the story of England for 150 years. But when he came to the end of his sixth volume, which was also the end of his life, he found that he had covered only fifteen years of the period; to complete it in scale would have required about 135 volumes more. We sometimes think of the past as a closed account, with all its items conveniently frozen for our gaze. But the past, as actually studied, never stays still. It is not only that, moment by moment, it is growing at our end; it grows at the other end too. For hundreds of years the scholars of Oxford and Cambridge took it for granted that history began abruptly about six thousand years ago; Dr. Lightfoot, the Vice-Chancellor of Cambridge, fixed it on Friday, October 26, 4004 B.C. at nine in the morning. Little by little that date has been moving back. There seems to be at least one earlier date that is verifiable, 4241 B.C., when the Egyptians began to use the lunar calendar. And of course people who could do that belonged to a civilization that must have been old already. The men who made the beautiful drawings of bison in the caves of southern France appear to have lived about 50,000 B.C. A skull with a low forehead, found in a cave on the banks of the Neander River in Germany, was thought at first by the great physiologist Virchow to be that of a subnormal soldier of Napoleon's army who had got lost; but through the discovery of others at the same geological level it gradually became clear that he had gone into that cave not fifty or sixty years before, but something like twenty-five hundred centuries before. And even that is, to the new geology, relatively recent.

On the way to my classes in New Haven lies the Peabody Museum, an excellent place to enlarge one's time span and keep one's conceit in order. An exhibit that catches my fancy there is a big turtle with an injured flipper. He seems to have had a furious set-to with some other beast, who must have been a pretty vigorous specimen, since he weighed more than two tons himself. But then I reflect that no human being did or could have seen that memorable engagement. I asked the curator when it probably occurred, and he said that it might be put a few thousand centuries one way or the other, but the most recent possible date would be about 60 million B.C. If it is true, as a contemporary historian has said, that the business of history is the causal understanding of the present

211

through the past; if it is true, as another has said, that "evolution should be to the historian what dynamics is to the physicist," then the sphere of history has become almost overwhelming. Every culture and every institution has roots millions of years deep.

And these roots do not merely run deep; they spread out in all directions; and unless one is prepared to follow them wherever they lead, one cannot do one's historical job. Suppose you are studying the history of either of the world wars. What must you know if you are really to understand? Clearly you must know your geography well. You must know a great mass of economic facts and principles, if only to refute those who say that the causes were exclusively economic—the Marxists for example—or those who say it was all due to the munition makers, or international bankers, or the like. You must have a considerable grasp of political theory, of theology and the history of religion, and of philosophy, for both wars involved a conflict of ideologies. You must have a sufficient grasp of biology and ethnology to deal with racial conflict. You must have some acquaintance with normal, abnormal, and social psychology, and even some grasp of physiology. A historian has written, "It is probable that adrenalin played as large a part as Pan-Slavism in Sazonov's decision upon war in July, 1914." You must have an extensive knowledge of comparative politics. You must know something about business organization, corporation finance, the problems of transportation by sea, land, and air, the relative advancement of applied science and of the organization of labor in the various countries, the distribution of raw materials and the principles of military and naval strategy. Unless one knows all these things, and indeed many more, one will sooner or later break down in explaining the complex facts.

The precipitate retreat of the horizon which is occurring in history is occurring in most other departments of knowledge. One meaning of "the atomic age" is that man has shrunk to an atom, a tiny creature struggling for orientation in a known world unmanageably vast and an unknown world unimaginably vaster. Now the problem of education is precisely this problem of orientation; and it is a quite unavoidable problem, because to try to avoid it is merely to orient oneself badly. Of the stores of human knowledge now available to youth, some must be selected as what an educated

212

man should know and all but a tiny part discarded as unessential. On what principle of selection are we to proceed?

American education in this century has been experimenting with a number of such principles. I want to consider briefly three of these, each advocated by persons of authority in the educational field.

The first, the elective system, was introduced by President Eliot. It answers our problem of selection by saying: Leave the choice to the student himself. He is the one who will gain most by choosing rightly and lose most by choosing wrongly; and though the capacity of college students for childishness is beyond all fathoming, still the choice of their studies is one of the few fields where they tend to curb its exercise. Here at least they are serious. Not that an occasional snap course is not accepted in the spirit in which it is offered, but by and large the studies elected by college students are the ones reputed to be really profitable. Again each one has tastes of his own which no one knows but himself, secret yearnings perhaps after poetry, or Diesel engines, or retorts and test tubes, which taken at the flood may lead on to fortune. No two persons develop at precisely the same rate, and who but the student himself knows when his interest in something is ripe enough to bring a return from its study? Is it not notorious that what one is made to study when one's heart is far from it is never mastered anyhow? "You can lead a girl to Vassar, but you can't make her think," because thinking is an activity that proceeds from within and requires a will and an interest to sustain it. So it is suggested that we may as well capitulate at once to the elective system, for it is the system that will operate in any case. We may spread out before students not what they want but what we think they ought to want, but they will take away from it what they have an elective affinity for, and no more.

There is certainly some force in all this. Still, the plain fact is that after trying the elective system in various forms and degrees for more than half a century, American education is now abandoning it. Why?

For one thing because it has been discovered that the student is less interested in what is immediately interesting than in what is important, and that on this his judgment is uninstructed. The very

213

seriousness which the elective system assumes makes him discount his present interest and insist on what promises to help him deal with the world twenty years from now. That world is vastly complex; it is daily growing more so; and he knows that he has just four years in which to get ready for it. What knowledge will he most need? He knows that he cannot answer that question himself. It is idle to say that he can find the answer by trial and error, for the failure that might expose his error will not come till the error is irremediable. It is equally idle to say that on this matter of the comparative value of studies we have not accumulated a good deal of transmissible wisdom. The student has a right to share in that wisdom in order to save him from himself.

The second mistake of the elective system has to do not with the student's power to select but with the studies among which his selection is made. It may be called the fallacy of misplaced democracy. If the elective system is to work, the choice must be made among a number of units, and it has been found to simplify matters greatly if the various studies can be put on a numerical basis of credits and hours. It is felt that there would be something dictatorial in offering an election in which a course in literature were given six credits and a course in anthropology only three; so we have divided the world of knowledge into pieces each of which, with fine democratic impartiality, is awarded three hours and three credits. And if the teacher of ethics or of psychology protests that to attach precisely the same value to archaeology or astrophysics as to his own subject is to do it injustice, he is thought to be indulging in prejudice or propaganda.

Of course one is walking here on dangerous ground. One can hardly talk of *the* value of a study, for the value varies with the end in view. The study of literature, for example, is of small importance if one's eye is on what is called success; it is indispensable if one's aim is to know human nature. The question of the comparative value of college studies depends, then, on the prior questions whether college study has any ultimate end and, if so, what it is. To these questions I must venture an answer, and I do so at once. The end of a liberal education is richness of spirit. It is to enable the student to compass the largest amount of those values which make life intrinsically worthwhile. What are these values? On the intellectual side the great value is understanding, the understanding of the world for its own sake, the understanding, that is, of nature, human nature, and society. On the active side the great values are the moral values of love and loyalty, of duty and justice. On the side of feeling the great aim is taste, the sense for whatsoever things are lovely or finely conceived or finely done. An education that is truly liberal, that is, one that frees or enfranchises the mind, will introduce one to all these values. But it is the first of them, the intellectual values, that must have the stress in practice, partly because there are other institutions to cultivate the others, partly because it is the intellectual values that can be most readily taught.

We can now return to our immediate question. So far as one's aim is understanding, is it true, as the elective system seems to assume, that the values of the various studies are about equal? To that question there can be but one answer: No, they are profoundly unequal. For the understanding of nature, physics is of the first importance, and metallurgy, crystallography, geomorphology, and stratigraphy are not. For the understanding of human nature, the sort of psychology that deals with thought, emotion, and motive is important, and the learning processes of the white rat are not. For the understanding of human society, political theory and intellectual history are important, while drum and trumpet history, the marriage customs of the Melanesians, even social case work, are not.

I suspect that the father of the elective system would agree with this. When President Eliot introduced it at Harvard in 1872, his real concern was to give science, which was then playing Cinderella to Latin, Greek, and mathematics, its plain academic rights. He would have been horrified to learn that this innocent suggestion had been invoked in justification of counting toward the bachelor's degree "newspaper reporting," "copy reading," "retail advertising," "drugstore practice," "community recreation," and "elementary costume design," to name a few of the courses so used in one of our large universities. To introduce the idea of democracy and equal rights among college studies is to negate the very idea of education. The educated mind is precisely the one that refuses to put things on a level, that sharply discriminates the essential from the peripheral, the better from the worse, what is illuminating from what is informative, timely, amusing, exciting, or practical. The fact is that the very expansion of knowledge which brought in the elective system is in course of destroying it. The system had some plausibility when the choice lay between mathematics, classics, and natural science. It has no plausibility if it means roaming without chart or compass the limitless ranges of contemporary knowledge.

But if we cannot solve our problem of selection by leaving the choice to the student, where are we to turn? Many people have turned with reason to our most influential philosopher and weightiest educational theorist, John Dewey. His educational theory grew directly out of his philosophy, and that means that in both he was a pragmatist. And what is pragmatism? It is the view that only such knowledge or thought is significant as makes a difference in practice. If we want to know what thought essentially is, we cannot do better than ask how it first arose, for what it was then it is now. It arose as a means for surmounting a practical difficulty. Primitive man was chased by a bear and came to a river; that, as Professor Dewey would say, was a thought-provoking situation, since the man must either think or die. Let us suppose that necessity did in this case prove the mother of invention and the idea came to him of pushing out in the stream on a nearby log. What is meant here by an idea? It is in essence a plan of action, an instrument of behavior. Now pragmatism says that this is what thought always is; that is why Dewey called his philosophy instrumentalism. And it is this view of the nature of thought that provided Dewey with what is distinctive in his educational theory.

For the business of education is to train us to think more intelligently, and for Dewey intelligent thinking means intelligent action. What does this imply for the curriculum? It implies that the main studies of which education has traditionally consisted, such as mathematics and classics, will be demoted. It implies that culture in the old sense of cultivation of feeling and enlightenment of mind, of sweetness and light as Arnold called them, will no longer be an end. It implies that philosophy in its traditional sense of a pursuit of truth for its own sake will be abandoned, for it must submit to the test of results, and such philosophy bakes no bread. Well, what *is* to be included in the curriculum? Professor Kilpatrick, who was Dewey's leading educational interpreter, answered, "What one needs to know in order to do what one needs to do." "To learn," he said, "is to acquire a way of behaving." Education therefore should provide the ways of behaving that will be found most useful later

216

on. Hence in progressive schools learning was converted into doing. The young studied mathematics by keeping store, zoology by keeping pets, drama by writing and staging plays. Since activity not sustained by interest was likely to create distaste, pupils were encouraged to do what they liked; the idea of interest replaced the idea of discipline. The ideal, as one persuasive expositor said, was neither "the hard pedagogy of doing what you don't like, nor the soft pedagogy of doing what you like, but the new pedagogy of liking what you do."

The theory has been worked out much more fully in primary and secondary schools than in the colleges, but its influence has been felt on many campuses. That influence is in favor of placing technical and vocational courses on a par with, or above, courses in theory, and, since interest is so important, allowing the student great freedom in selecting his own studies and his own problems within those studies. The college is conceived as a laboratory of practical life in which the student learns not only how to manage himself and get on with others, but also, and not only at weekends, how factories are run, how elections are won and lost, and how to make effective stage sets. There are liberal arts colleges in which one can major in photography or the dance.

That this view of education is superior to many that have been respectable in the past I have no doubt. Dr. Leete, once headmaster of Eton, is reported to have said that any subject of study was good for a boy so long as he hated it. I prefer the pragmatic and "progressive" theory. It is better to have even a bouncing, bumbling, and undisciplined enthusiasm for scholarship than a cold and disciplined hatred of it. And I suspect that a "child-centered school" in which children are led to be interested in knowledge through finding its value in action is a far more cheerful and hopeful place than the little red schoolhouse was.

But I suspect too that it is in the lower schools that this theory really belongs. A student-centered kindergarten is a sensible proposal; a student-centered college or university surely is not. For one thing, it underrates the seriousness of student interest. We do not need to take college students by their little hands and coax them into history or economics by showing them what fun it all is, or showing them what practical difference it will make. Of course that can be done. If a young woman wants nothing in the world so

217

much as to be like Martha Graham, she may be led to take an interest in physiology, in anthropology, and in aesthetics by finding that they all bear upon the dance. True enough. But am I wrong in thinking that if her appetite for these things is so faint as to require such sugarcoating, she is scarcely ready yet for hardy college fare, and that if she is ready, she will be impatient of leading-strings? Certainly my own impression is that college students want to be taken by the shortest path to the heart of the matter, and that they will haunt the classrooms of even a teacher who is notoriously tough if that teacher—as they would put it—"knows his stuff," and has the clearness of head to make crooked things straight. I have a distinguished colleague who says that one trouble with American education is that we teach too well, in the sense that we are overconcerned about our students and underconcerned about our subjects. However that may be, it is clear that many a teacher who has worked himself gray in head and heart in cheering, counselling, and comforting his young charges has seen those charges turn away to some other teacher who, with nothing like his own sympathy and solicitude, is more obviously master in his field. If a teacher has understanding and the power to convey it, student interest will take care of itself.

There are persons who would reply that if a girl is encouraged to major in the dance, it is not as a means of arousing her interest in what is supposed to be more important; indeed the notion that theory is more important than crafts and techniques is the notion that must be got rid of. Here again I cannot follow, and on this point I think Mr. Dewey's views have done us a disservice. Of course the dance, like the other techniques of artisan and artist, is an admirable thing in its place; only that place is not the liberal college. For the business of the liberal college is to provide richness of mind, and for this special purpose to say that any crafts or techniques or vocational skills are on a level with the great achievements of the human spirit in philosophy and science, literature and religion, is untrue. It is untrue further to say that these things are to be estimated in terms of the difference they make in practice. That they do make a difference in practice is plain. But that is not what makes them valuable. What makes them valuable lies in what they are. Just to see what Plato meant, or to relive *Othello,* or to get clear where Marx was wrong and where he was right, or to creep slowly along after Einstein, is to become a different and larger person, a person moving about in worlds not realized by those whose minds are absorbed in getting things done. The present American need is not a gospel of action; we have had a surfeit of that already. What we need is a better sense of direction, a clearer view of the goals toward which our restless activities should be guided, a compass whose spiritual needle will still point firmly to its pole in the presence of Hollywood or Zen Buddhism, of dadaism or nationalism or racism, white or black.

The most incisive critic of Dewey's views on education was Robert M. Hutchins, who had an educational theory of his own. This theory he promulgated vigorously from his prestigious post as president of the University of Chicago, and it led to the radical revision of some college programs, notably those of Chicago and St. John's. In Hutchins's thinking the pendulum swung back from the elective system to the opposite extreme. He thought that the student mind was dispersing itself in so many different directions that college graduates had no common knowledge, principles, or standards, and even found it hard to communicate; when the man who took his degree in mechanical engineering met the man who had taken his in Spanish, they were reduced to some lowest common denominator, such as the weather. After two thousand years of study, Mr. Hutchins asked, was there no established scale of values, no body of ascertained truth that we could say was of central importance? Surely there was, he answered, and in order to make it the staple of higher education he would reorganize the college radically. He would break the present college course in two at a line between the sophomore and junior years. The first two years he would group with the last two of high school, and in that four-year period he would concentrate what he calls a general education. To the present junior and senior college years he would add one, and in these three years he would give a college or university education. What would be the content of the first course, or general education? It would consist of those books which by common consent ranked first in literature, philosophy, and science. The best protection against scientific faddism or literary counterfeit in the present was a taste formed on the best that had been said or

219

thought in the past; a classic Mr. Hutchins defined as a book contemporary with every age. What would be the work of the college
or university proper? Strictly intellectual discipline. All vocational
work, all majoring in photography or the dance, all training in dental or legal or medical practice, would be turned over to institutes
which might be connected with universities but would be no part of
them. The work of the college proper would be to give an intellectual mastery first of the principles of logic and metaphysics, which
are involved in thinking about anything whatever, then of the principles of nature and human nature as exhibited in the physical and
social sciences.

What are we to say of this program?

We must distinguish the essence of Mr. Hutchins's proposal
from all things that, in his presentation of it, were adventitious. Mr.
Hutchins's style, for example, which barks like a machine gun, and
his take-it-or-leave-it manner of advocacy were adventitious. The
proposal to divide the college period into two, and to distinguish an
earlier or general education from a later university education,
seems to me to have been also adventitious. So likewise, I venture
to think, was the list of great books that he and his colleagues drew
up, and the devotion of the earlier years to studying them. For
however strong the case for mastering poetry through Homer and
Dante, the argument for learning mathematics through Euclid,
physics through Aristotle, Galileo, and Newton, and physiology
through Harvey seems to me less than convincing. Even in
philosophy the case is not clear. The propositions that Kant's
*Critique* is a philosophical classic and that it is a good means of
making the student a clear and competent thinker are quite
different, and I see no straight path from one to the other. Once
more, when Mr. Hutchins, having insisted that metaphysics should
be central in higher education, comes to tell us what metaphysics is,
his authority and model appears to be St. Thomas Aquinas. I
prefer to take this too as adventitious. It must have been a distressing fact to Mr. Hutchins that when he offered an earnest and eloquent argument for putting philosophy in the middle of the
curriculum, the response from philosophers was so cool. But the
reason is not hard to find. Most philosophers think that their subject
has made immense strides since the thirteenth century, both in
methods and in insights, and that to take as one's model a system

developed before modern thought had begun was an equivocal compliment to philosophy as they know it.

Whether Mr. Hutchins would agree to strip these things away as superfluities is more than doubtful. But if he should, what we should have left, I submit, is a theory of the essential in education which is eminently worth considering. For what the theory amounts to is that in the great departments of human thought there are established and basic principles of truth, of value, and of method, that those which are first logically should be first educationally, and that if we seek them first, the other needful things will be added unto us. Mr. Hutchins thinks that the value of knowledge in education is to be appraised, not by its interest or by its utility, but by its aid in understanding the world. Here I cordially agree.

What is meant here by basic principles? One principle is basic to another if, given the first, you can understand the second, while given the second, you cannot rise to the first. Given the law of gravitation, you can understand the movements of the planets, but given the facts about the movements of the planets, you cannot leap to the law, unless indeed you are Newton. In physical science the general laws of motion, as exhibited in sound, light, and heat, are more fundamental than those of chemistry, important as these are. In the biological sciences, the theory of evolution is fundamental, because with it a million facts fall at once into intelligible order which without it remain mere facts. In the social sciences, ethics and social philosophy are fundamental. I know that many of our students, many even of our Ph.D.'s, are fascinated by the odd, pathetic, moronic ways of Australian bushmen, and conceive themselves as gaining a great and sophisticating light from the study of human diversities as such. But this light may be worse than darkness if there is no belief in a real better and worse, and no principle for discriminating them. Ethics and social philosophy attempt to provide such a principle. And so of all other spheres of knowledge; the aim of a liberal education should be illumination, provided through what is basic for understanding.

But education is not wholly a matter of content. President Jeremiah Day of Yale remarked in 1828 that "the two great points to be gained in intellectual culture are discipline and the furniture of the mind." We have said something about content or furniture;

221

what about discipline? There was a time not long ago when psychologists were telling us that the old claim for Greek and Latin that they provided a general mental discipline was false, since training in one field did not carry over into markedly different fields. There proved to be an uncomfortable amount of truth in their contention. But this much of the older theory seems to have proved irrefutable: that there are such things as mental habits of clearness, precision, and order which, once acquired, can be applied to any subject matter. A finely disciplined thinker like Descartes or Mill does not as a rule combine lucidity in one field with looseness and obscurity in another; whatever field he touches he lights up, because he is governed by an inward standard which exacts clarity everywhere. Now just as the liberal college cannot teach everything, but can teach the principles in the light of which other things become intelligible, so it cannot teach all techniques, but can instill those habits and standards that are the conditions of effective thinking in any field. There is no one road to such discipline; it may be provided by any subject; but some subjects lend themselves to it more readily than others. Mathematics is an example; I agree with Mill that formal logic is a still better example.

The great question before us was: What is the college to do in the face of the overwhelming increase in available· human knowledge? The answer is, of course, that we must select. But how select? By letting the student do it for us? No; the elective system has passed to its rest. By making the college a laboratory of useful arts and techniques? No; educational pragmatism is not for the intellectually adult. By a return to the ideal of the medieval schoolmen? No: except as they caught the permanent ideal of all seekers after light. And that ideal may have been better understood when knowledge was limited than today when it is unlimited and overwhelming. On the intellectual side, which is the special interest of higher education, the ideal is simple, even though exacting in the extreme. It is the understanding, through grasp of principle, of the world we live in. That ideal belongs to no particular age or school. It is not the property of Thomas Aquinas or of Robert Hutchins; it was the ideal of Socrates and Plato and Spinoza and Mill and Spencer and Whitehead. Understanding, they would all have said, is not to be achieved by exhausting an inexhaustible infinity of particular facts; that way lies distraction and defeat. But these facts, though infinite in number and variety, are not chaos. They are a tapestry shot through with threads of law; and the mind that masters the laws has mastered also the essence of the facts, namely their fixed explanatory pattern. Such mastery does not come by intuition or good luck. It comes only by the devoted labor of minds trained to sharpness and steadiness by disciplined reflection. To such minds the mass of accumulating knowledge presents itself, not as a crushing burden for the memory, but as the greatest opportunity man has had for the free play of his intelligence, for bringing order out of disorder, and reducing the many to the one.

# 13

## Sanity in Thought and Art

I have lived long enough to have seen both sides of a great divide. The First World War was a sort of watershed that separates everything on this side of it from the now strange and remote world on the other side. As I look back at that world before the deluge, it seems curiously static—as if fixed in amber and bathed in a gentle afternoon sun. Not that it felt like that to be in it; and no doubt the glow that it now carries is in part merely the illusion that memory always throws over the past. But it is not wholly that, I think. At any rate, for those of us who were academics, it had an intellectual serenity and stability that seem to have disappeared under the wreckage of two wars. The philosophers and scientists of those days had their problems, plenty of them, and they knew they had a long way to go; but they were fairly confident that they were on the right track and had only to remain on it to reach their goal; there was a broad straight road leading into the future. In philosophy, in morals, even in criticism, something like a consensus of opinion seemed to be in the making.

Let me recall to your mind first what was happening in philosophy. The time just before the first war was a rationalistic heyday. There is a picture extant of James on his New Hampshire farm wagging a finger at Royce and saying "Damn the Absolute," but Royce is smiling serenely, as well he might; for he knew that the pundits of philosophy were on his side and that James was looked on as a maverick and an amateur. In Europe the story was similar. There Bergson was the maverick, and the German system builders dominated the scene. When as a wandering student, traveling of course without a passport, I went to Berlin in the winter of 1913, it was Paulsen I wanted to hear, and though when I asked the porter at the gate where Herr Paulsen was lecturing, the answer was "Ach, er ist todt, er is todt," I found that Wundt was still lecturing at Leipzig, and Windelband at Heidelberg, and I went to hear them both. They were of course tremendous scholars, but they were more than that. Even a naive youngster could feel in them, as their applauding students did, a passion for reason, a passion for articulating in intelligible fashion the great mass of detail that their historical and social studies had accumulated, a conviction that, however dense the difficulties, reason could drive a Roman road through them if it would.

Across the Channel in England, James Ward was still lecturing at Cambridge, and Bradley at Oxford was still brooding in his rooms overlooking the Christ Church meadows. I sought them both out, as only a brash young American would; and being a student at Bradley's college of Merton with rooms a few steps away, I had an excuse for seeing something of him. It is hard to convey to persons of another generation what an aura his name carried in those days. He never appeared at meetings; he never lectured or taught; many of the philosophy dons at Oxford had never so much as seen him; but they were all aware of him and afraid of him; there was a sort of electric field around the den where the old lion was holed up. He was formidable not only because he wielded a slashing dialectic and a powerful pen, but also because he was in such deadly earnest about his thought; it was his religion and his life.

Bradley's conception of philosophy was the dominant conception of his time, but in essence it was not new; it had come, with some fresh flourishes, from Plato, Spinoza, and Hegel. The business of philosophy was to understand the world. The best way to do that was to start with the postulate that the world is intelligible in the minimal sense, and then go on to show how far it is intelligible in the maximal sense. The minimal sense is that the real is not self-contradictory. Bradley started with that as his test of truth and reality; what failed to pass it must be thrown out; and very little in religion, science, or common belief did manage to pass it. The maximal sense is that the world is an interconnected system of parts, in which everything is connected with everything else as necessarily as in geometry. The aim of thought from first to last is at system; understanding means placing things in a system—at first in a little one, as when a child grasps the function of the chain on his bicycle, later in a larger one, as when he sees why democracy must place limits on freedom, ultimately in a complete one, in which nothing is left out. Thought is an activity governed by an immanent end. That end has two aspects. One of these is completeness, the embracing of all things within our knowledge. The other is order, the grasp of that logical interdependence which all things have if the world is really intelligible.

This view made provincialism in philosophy almost a contradiction in terms. To test any piece of your knowledge, you had to go beyond it, then beyond the wider context to one still wider, like the ripples from a pebble dropped in the sea. Certainty lay at the end of an infinite expansion. Here Bradley the absolutist was in effect a relativist, while the traditional empiricist and rationalist were both by comparison absolutists, since both held that one could achieve certainty almost at the beginning of the process. The empiricist held that the judgment "that is my friend, Jones," could be known to be certainly true by its correspondence with given fact, while Bradley said it could be so known only by its coherence with further perceptual judgments about Jones's walk, dress, and habits, and these only by further judgments, which must stand or fall as a whole. The rationalist held, with Descartes, that no system could have more certainty than the axioms with which it started; Bradley held that even the axioms of mathematics were statements about the real, and must be tested, like other judgments, by whether they comported with our experience as a whole; the proof of the laws of identity and contradiction was that their denials would render any system impossible. Neither in knowledge nor in the universe are there islands any more. Science, history, and religion are all dependent on metaphysics for the testing of their assumptions and the synthesis of their results; metaphysics is in turn dependent on them for the material that it works with. Common sense, science, and philosophy are merely segments in one continuous effort of understanding, which is an effort to make everything intelligible through seeing its place in the system of things. The man who suffers from an intellectual cyst, that is, from any belief which resists criticism from his experience as a whole, is in that degree less than sane. When we start talking with a man in an institution, he may seem a very sensible fellow until he suddenly remarks, "I see I must set you right on one matter; you know I am really Napoleon." You may point out to him a thousand things that are inconsistent with his conviction; it is to no purpose; and if you corner him, he may be dangerous. His insanity lies in a loss of perspective regarding one of his beliefs. He is not wholly irrational; but neither is any of us rational altogether. Sanity, rationality is a matter of degree.

Bradley's philosophy made sanity in this large sense the end and criterion in the sphere of thought. There was a sense in which the ethics of those days was an attempt to introduce the same idea into the sphere of practice. In ethics Bradley and Green were neo-Aristotelians; for them the end of the practical life was the balanced realization of one's powers. In my student days this view was under attack by Rashdall and others as egoistic, and the prevailing ethics of the day was ideal utilitarianism, which held that our duty was so to act as to produce the greatest total good of all concerned. This good was understood to consist of results in the way of experience, for only experiences were intrinsically good or bad; books and flowers and pictures were not good in themselves; it was our experiences of them that were good. But then what makes an experience good? Moore and Rashdall wrestled with this problem and came out with an answer that seemed convincing at the time, but has not stood up well under criticism. They said that what made an experience good was a special quality of goodness, not a natural or observable quality like squareness or greenness, not even a quality that could be analyzed or defined, but a quality nevertheless, which could be seen to inhere necessarily in such states of mind as knowledge and happiness.

Leonard Hobhouse, that admirable but neglected thinker, here said no. The goodness of an experience was not a nonnatural wraith of this kind; it was something altogether natural; it depended on and indeed consisted in its satisfying human impulse. When someone expostulated with McTaggart for not shooing his cat

Pushkin out of the philosopher's own chair before the fire, McTaggart replied that he was quite happy where he was because he could think about the universe, while poor Pushkin could not. Metaphysics was a good for McTaggart, because it satisfied a faculty and thirst of his nature; it was not a good for the cat, because behind its narrower brow neither faculty nor thirst was there.

In his masterly book, *The Rational Good*, Hobhouse accepts in the main the ideal utilitarianism of Rashdall and Moore, but says that the good by whose production we are to judge the rightness of our conduct is the greatest general self-realization. The fulfillment of any drive or urge of human nature is pro tanto good; it is to be repressed only when its fulfillment, by inhibiting other fulfillments, would mean less fulfillment on the whole. The conflicts between the goods of different persons are dealt with in the same way. Thus Hobhouse brought into ethics a principle that corresponded to Bradley's principle in knowledge—what I have called the principle of sanity. The aim of thought was at breadth and harmony of judgment; the aim of practice was at breadth and harmony in the realization of impulse. Fanaticism, arbitrariness, self-will, asceticism, the repression of any impulse or any man except in the interest of fuller expression on the whole, was ruled out as unreasonable. *Mens sana in corpore sano* was the ideal for both the individual and the body politic.

Hobhouse, like Rashdall, was a mind of remarkable range, but neither of them, so far as I know, ever wrote on aesthetics. A widespread interest in the theory of criticism, however, was an inheritance from Victorian days. When I made my first comment on the world, "with no language but a cry," the author of that phrase, Tennyson, was the most admired of poets, and Matthew Arnold, then only four years dead, was the most influential critic. Arnold detested wilfulness and triviality in literature, and was sure there was an objective better and worse, whether he found it or not. The anthropologists were reminding men, with Kipling, that

> There are nine and fifty ways of constructing tribal lays,
> And every single one of them is right.

The Victorians and Edwardians of course did not believe that morals were merely a matter of taste, and they did not want to believe that matters of taste were either, if that meant *de gustibus non disputandum*, and that one lay or lyric or landscape was as good as another.

But if there really was an objective better and worse in art, what was the standard to be? A weighty and timely answer came from that cradle of artists, Italy, and from Italy's great philosopher, Croce. Croce answered that the standard was expressiveness. Anything was a work of art so far as it succeeded in expressing what it sought to express, and a painting or a sonnet or a single cry that expressed the artist's intuition perfectly must be conceded to be a perfect work of art. When this doctrine reached Oxford, it caused excitement and also murmurs. It was strange doctrine to come from an idealist brought up on Hegel, for it implied that the content of a work of art was of no artistic importance; all that mattered was whether the content, such as it was, was well expressed. Bosanquet, who had written a history of aesthetics, presented an indignant refutation to the British Academy. Andrew Bradley, the philosopher's brother, who was professor of poetry at Oxford, raised the issue in one of his lectures by asking whether one could write as great a poem on a pinhead as on the fall of man, and concluded that one could not. Here he had all the idealists behind him and probably most of the critics. The Anglo-Saxon tradition has never run to the narrower forms of art for art's sake. Ruskin, who could not endure Whistler, thought that art should reflect all man's aspirations; Arnold felt as strongly as Eliot did that a poet should write with the whole Western tradition in his blood. The poets of the Victorian era were spokesmen of their age; Tennyson, for example, in *In Memoriam* voiced the misgivings of faith about science; Browning was presented at book length by Sir Henry Jones, the Glasgow philosopher, as a philosophical and religious teacher. When Bosanquet gave his Gifford Lectures shortly before the First World War, he urged that the principle of individuality, which was just Bradley's principle of breadth and harmony again, was a measure of goodness and beauty as well as truth. "We adhere," he wrote, "to Plato's conclusion that objects of our likings possess as much satisfactoriness—which we identify with value—as they possess of reality and trueness." Art itself is subject to the principle of sanity.

This was the sort of doctrine we were brought up on in those antediluvian days. Perhaps we were a little intoxicated by it, for it inclined us to think of history as a triumphant advance of reason in which freedom broadened "slowly down from precedent to precedent," and would go on doing so. We were brutally awakened from our dream. Suddenly all the dams of civilization seemed to break at once. I was a bit of flotsam caught by the flood in Germany and washed up a few weeks later on British shores. Britain of course was tragically unprepared, and I remember wondering how those ragged squads drilling in London squares could meet the massed professionals across the Channel. The universities sent their young men in shoals into French trenches, from which the best of them did not return. There was a moratorium on speculative philosophy. It seemed remote now, and people did not fail to remark that it had been made in Germany. Royce in America died denouncing the Germany at whose feet he had sat so long. In England Hobhouse dedicated a book to his lost son in which he bitterly attacked Bosanquet's theory of the state. The distinguished idealist, Haldane, who had reorganized Britain's army for her, was excluded from the cabinet by the pressure of public opinion. When the universities reconvened after the war, the old philosophy was on the wane, and new voices began to be heard. A queer gospel, entitled *Tractatus Logico-Philosophicus*, arranged in numbered verses and prophesying the end of philosophy as heretofore conceived, appeared in Cambridge in 1922. The same gospel translated now into intelligible English by a youth in his twenties named Ayer, appeared some years later in Oxford under the title of *Language, Truth, and Logic.* As the chairs in philosophy fell vacant, they were filled by a new breed of men. There is not, I think, one chair in England, Scotland, or Wales, and there are very few in America, still occupied by men of the older persuasion. One wonders if there has ever been so swift a revolution in philosophy. On the continent also something like a revolution has occurred, though here the Jacobins were not analysts but existentialists.

I began by saying that I had seen both sides of a divide in the history of philosophy. I now want to look at the hither side through glasses I brought with me from the farther side and could never

231

quite get myself to discard. There is no time at the moment to test these glasses for their amount of distortion; but I must remind you that I *am* wearing glasses, that they certainly do distort in some measure, and that you would do well to check what I say with your younger and unspectacled eyes.

The philosophy that has now dispossessed that of Green and Bradley, Ward and McTaggart, even in their old haunts, is linguistic analysis. It came into general notice when it was attacked in the columns of the London *Times* by Lord Russell, and vigorously defended by its Oxford supporters. That it is of interest also to Americans is shown by the fact that *The New Yorker* allowed an article on it by a young Indian, Ved Mehta, to trickle along through a hundred pages of advertisements; any philosophy to which *The New Yorker* will devote a hundred pages has arrived. What has this new philosophy been trying to tell us?

Unfortunately, that is very hard to say, since its advocates are averse to stating in general terms what they are doing; others have to do this for them. If I had to put the new philosophy briefly, I should say that it is an attempt to read G. E. Moore in terms of the later Wittgenstein. Let me try to explain. In 1926 Moore, in a state of reaction against metaphysics, wrote a famous essay called "A Defence of Common Sense." In that essay he took the view that common sense was the test of philosophy rather than the other way round. Philosophers have often titillated their hearers by denying the existence of space, time, matter, other selves, and their own past, and while doing so have covered much paper spread out before them, have taken many hours by the clock to do it, have written with solidly material pens, have kept in mind throughout the prejudices of their readers, and have relied on their memory as to what these prejudices were. Moore thought there was something queer about this. He was far more certain, he said, that the things the philosophers were denying were true than that any of the arguments they offered against these things were sound. Does not that clearly show that common sense and not philosophy is the court of last appeal? He thought it did.

The linguistic philosophers accepted this argument of Moore's, but considered that he had not quite understood what made it so strong. It was hardly plausible to say that the plain man was somehow a philosopher who could outthink the professionals at their own game. The strength of common sense lay rather in its language. Language has so developed as to fit like a glove the vast variety of our feelings, desires, commands, intentions, and perceptions; in its ordinary uses it expresses or reports experiences we have all had at firsthand; and such reports it is idle to deny. To tell the plain man that there are no material things is to tell him that the phrase "material thing" has no correct application and this is absurd, for all he needs to do to refute it is what Moore did before an amused, if also bemused British Academy, namely to raise his two hands and say, "Here, these are examples of what I mean by material things, so of course they exist." Can the philosopher really mean to deny this? If he does, we can only tell him to his moonlike face that he is talking nonsense. It is more charitable to surmise that he is really proposing to use old words in a new way, which, having no authority in accepted usage, is just a queer way. When Berkeley denied the existence of matter, he was not trying to banish what you and I mean by tables and chairs; he was proposing to use the word for something invisible and intangible—which was permissible but somewhat silly. When Bradley denied the reality of space and time, he could hardly deny that it had taken him a minute or two to spread his last sentence across the page; he was merely using the words "space" and "time" of certain ethereal webs woven by himself. Surely it is much safer to stick to the common usage of common sense.

Once we see the strength of ordinary usage, we can also see the weakness of philosophy. Philosophic problems arise just because we have been tempted into misusing words, and we should deal with them not by trying to solve them, which would be taking them too seriously, but by a sort of Freudian therapy—by seeing how they arose and thus dissolving them. Philosophers when they have left the straight road of common usage, have proved amazingly gullible. The whole Platonic philosophy, for example, is based on a verbal confusion. Plato saw that the members of a class were alike; this suggested that they had something in common, as a class of students have when they have the same teacher; this common something was named by a noun, and since nouns usually name things, it was taken as a thing. Thus universals came to be regarded as existents. But there are no such existents; there are only things resembling each other. With this simple insight the Platonic world of ideas comes falling down like London Bridge. Again people have seen other people laughing, crying, and talking. What makes them do these things is hidden from sight, but is called "he" or "she," or a "mind," and again it is assumed that these are names for an invisible and intangible substance, a "ghost in the machine," whereas all that is really there is a set of capacities or dispositions for behaving in certain ways. And once the ghost is established there, the question arises how it can act on the machine or be acted on by it, and we have the old problem of the relation of mind and body. But the problem is wholly unreal, for there is no ghost in the machine; all that has been there from the beginning is a set of capacities or dispositions for behaving in certain ways. All these metaphysical puzzles are needless because they arise from avoidable misuses of words. We should cease to be troubled by them if we were willing to do two things: first, use words with their standard meanings; second, reflect, when such a puzzle does arise, that it must have sprung from some category mistake, that is from the application in one field of a use appropriate only in another.

There is much more, of course, in linguistic philosophy than this thesis about ordinary use, but this remains its most distinctive thesis. What is one to say about it who has been brought up in the older tradition of philosophy? It is sometimes thought to be a return to common sense. I must confess that the only common sense that seems to me authoritative in philosophy is that massive common sense which consists in the attempt to see things steadily and whole, and which I have described as philosophic sanity. Judged by this sort of common sense, that of the linguistic philosophers is a wraith that melts away when looked at. There are several reasons for saying so. For one thing, the notion that ordinary usage is infallible is nothing but a tiresome myth. Anyone who believes it must, as Russell points out, abandon his belief in physics. The plain man gazes up at the night sky and says "Look, there is an exploding star." What he means by this impeccable English is that what he sees is happening out there now. This cannot be right if the physicist says it is not happening, that the event he thinks he is seeing was over, perhaps, years ago. Again, it is perfectly good usage to say that in the next room there is a table not now observed by anyone, that is brown, smooth, and hard. Berkeley would say that this is not so; and whether one agrees with him or not (I do in fact), he is surely not to be refuted by saying that he is confused about words. He knew what the plain man meant and he declined to accept it, saying he was quite ready to speak with the vulgar if he was allowed to think with the learned.

Secondly, to confine philosophy to the sort of question to which ordinary meanings supply the answer is to impose a crippling censorship on our thought. I have heard an eminent linguistic philosopher settle the problem of free will by saying that the state-ment "I can push this inkstand" is good usage; it therefore has a clear application; I therefore *can* push the inkstand, which means that I am *free* to do it. Now, if "can" means here, as he took it to mean, merely that I am not prevented from doing it by any external restraint, the statement is true enough. But then it has nothing whatever to do with the real issue of free will, which the plain man has probably never thought of. That issue is not whether his choice would produce its normal effect, but whether there is any cause constraining his choice, and to rule this problem out because it does not use "free" in the ordinary sense is obscurantism.

Thirdly, is it true that philosophical problems arise out of verbal confusions? Some of them no doubt do. But some that are alleged to have done so have surely not done so in fact. It is hard to believe that Plato or any other self-critical mind has been so hyp-notized by nouns as to think that they had to stand for substantives. And whoever says that men owe to verbal confusions their long wrestling with the problems whether God exists and is good, whether thought and feeling survive death, whether there is a trustworthy test for right conduct, whether beliefs are made true by good consequences, seems to me not to have entered into these problems at all. Philosophy springs straight out of human life, out of such longings as Descartes's for certainty, or Spinoza's for a better way to live, or even Bradley's for a way of experiencing Dei-ty. As the great philosophers have conceived it, even as it has been conceived by those few, such as Hume and Moore, whom the linguistic sect admires, it called for breadth of understanding and imagination. One can extract from metaphysics or theology a set of verbal puzzles if one wants to. But it is a new kind of philistinism to insist that this is all there is to them—a philistinism of which minds governed by the principle of sanity would have been incapable.

We have already suggested that philosophy after the war came to a fork in the road. British philosophy, followed largely by American, took the road of analysis; European philosophy took that of existentialism. What is existentialism? It is a reaction against what it conceives as an excessive reliance on reason, but apart from this and such minor statements as that all existentialists tend to be gloomy and to write badly, it is hard to say anything that holds of all of them alike. Some of them are atheists like Sartre, some of them theists like Marcel; some of them, like Heidegger, have offered heils to Hitler; others like Sartre, three cheers for Stalin; for some of them, the dominant mood seems to be anxiety, for others nausea. It is unsafe to talk in general terms about a movement as amorphous as this, so let us focus our brief comment on the father Abraham of the tribe, that great Dane, Søren Kierkegaard.

Regarding reason, Kierkegaard held that it breaks down at two vital points. It cannot deal with existence and it cannot deal with God. It cannot deal with existence because it is at home only among essences, and existence is prior to essence. This sounds mysterious, but it is perhaps less so than it seems. If you look at an apple, you perceive something round, red, and smooth. These are qualities, characters, or essences, that is, contents that can be perceived or thought about. Does the apple reduce without remainder to a set of essences of this kind, or is there something about it that is over and above these? You can easily test that, existentialists would say. All these characters might appear in imagination, but that would not give you a real apple; for that, the characters must *exist* in space. Now existence is not just another character; it is that which when added to characters makes them real, while *not* being a character itself. And since it is not a character—not a quality or relation or any set of these—it cannot be perceived or thought. The same holds of a self. Like an apple it too has a content, a set of conscious percepts, concepts, and so on; but the content of its consciousness does not exhaust the self, for that content happens to exist in time, which is surely the most important thing about it. And this existence is something that thought can never seize. It is real, but inexplicable and unintelligible.

This is perhaps the most important single point in existentialism. Is it valid? The rationalist finds it unconvincing for two reasons. First, an entity that is neither a character nor a relation nor a set of these, an "it" to which the question "*What* is it?" must forever be irrelevant, a something that is nothing in particular, sounds uncommonly like nothing at all. Secondly, the existentialist forgets that there is an alternative view. One may say, as Montague did, that what distinguishes the imaginary from the real apple is its appearance in time and space. But since spatial and temporal relations are themselves characters, we seem not to need existence in any other sense. It may be objected that real apples and their relations are vivid and distinct in a way that ideal ones are not; but this is irrelevant, for vividness and distinctness are themselves characters again. To be sure Bradley himself wavered on this point; in the famous passage of almost Kierkegaardian revolt against Hegel in which he attacked "the unearthly ballet of bloodless categories"—the only passage from a work on logic to reach the *Oxford Book of English Prose*—Bradley confessed that a world of universals seemed to him very dreary and ghostly. But Bosanquet asked him what precisely he wanted beyond these universals, and since he was unable to answer, he withdrew from his brief incursion into existentialism. They both ended by saying that you will never reach the unique in an individual by peeling off its attributes and relations, since it will turn out, for all your troubles, as coreless as an onion; what you must do is just the opposite, namely include more and more of those relations that alone can specify it into uniqueness. Pure being, as Hegel contended, is hardly distinguishable from nothing, and in pure existence, if you ever reached it, you would have left even that wisp of content behind.

Suppose you were to admit that existence somehow exists; even so you have to deal with it in terms of content. Heidegger, to be sure, gave his profound inaugural address at Freiburg on Nothing, and he has even held that this Nothing goes nothinging about in alarming fashion. But when existentialists condescend to cases, it always seems to be some humble concrete thing, myself or this apple, that is doing the acting, and doing what it does because of what it is. And we may as well let them worship at their strangely empty shrine so long as, when they emerge from it, they talk and act like the rest of us.

I said, however, that Kierkegaard's existentialism had another side. It is this side that is most familiar, for it has been appropriated with showers of blessing by theologians in need of a philosophical *imprimatur*. Kierkegaard was brought up in a household where theological discussion was the order of the day, and by a father to whom revealed religion was the most tremendous of realities. After living for long in a hothouse, young Kierkegaard went to Berlin and studied Hegel. He became a skeptic, but soon returned to his father and the sunless religion of the big dark house in Copenhagen. But no one comes back from Hegel quite the same. Kierkegaard saw that if the men of faith were to save their faith from Hegel, if they were to stay his "new conquering empire of light and reason," they must make a clean break with reason; otherwise the rationalists would use the paradoxes of religion as a Trojan horse to invade and destroy it. There is no use in fighting fire with fire; better fight it with water; quench reason with faith. Admit frankly that faith is as full of paradoxes as the critics say it is, and then answer that it does not in the least matter, that on the level where faith moves, the laws of logic and ethics are transcended so that to demand intelligibility in religion is impious, an attempt to imprison Deity in the little cage of our own understanding.

This doctrine has become epidemic in our theological schools, which shows that there is something in it answering to a need. Faith *is* threatened again by reason, this time by the rising tide of scientific knowledge which is secularizing the world. But do we have here a satisfactory defense of faith? I cannot think so, for it carries too much that is inimical to both faith and knowledge. It undermines knowledge, because if the contradictions in which Kierkegaard revels can really be true, then logic itself is no safe guide; and if logic goes, then nothing can be depended on in the whole range of our "knowledge." If what reason warrants as true is invalid in theology, then reason *as such* is a false guide. The doctrine is likely also to be fatal to faith. For if faith can tell us, as it did to Abraham, in that legend so beloved of Kierkegaard for its rebuke to our moral certainties, that what conscience and reason condemn may nevertheless be our duty, then how are we to distinguish the inspiration of the prophet from that of the fanatic or the charlatan? Reason may be a poor thing, but it is the best we have, and the theology that discards it may live to rue its recklessness. If it succeeds in persuading men that their reason and their religion are really in conflict with each other, there can be little doubt which in the long run will come out second best. It will not be reason.

We have been remarking on new developments in speculative philosophy and religion; has anything important been happening meanwhile in the field of ethics? Fifty years ago moralists seemed to be converging toward a rough consensus. There was an objective and universal standard of conduct. Actions were to be appraised through their consequences, and what was important among these consequences was the fulfilment of human faculty. At any rate, Paulsen in Germany, Hobhouse and Bradley in Britain, and Dewey in America were so far in tune, though each with grace notes of his own. Hobhouse's panorama of "morals in evolution" showed the advance of morals as a steady increase in the control and ordering of impulse by reason, and he thought that the advance showed an accelerating spread. But storms were brewing as he wrote. Since then there have been at least four major waves of calamity for this old position, which have all but overwhelmed it and its high hopes.

The first of these, like logical positivism, was stirred up in Vienna. A courageous student of the oddities of human behavior, named Freud, trying to explain such things as slips of the tongue, dreams, and sudden rages, concluded that to explain them plausibly we must push the boundaries of mind far down into the unconscious. The more he probed into this subcellar of the mind, the more convinced he became that this was the essential part of it, that it was filled with unruly denizens, and that the respectable dwellers upstairs were scarcely more than puppets of the unruly mob below. Our attempts to justify our conduct are less reasons than rationalizations, that is, self-deceptions designed to make what this submerged crew wants us to do look like what we ought to do. Just below the polished floor on which the chairman of the board of deacons walks about in such seemly fashion lies a set of cavemen, held in precarious check.

To many this theory itself seemed to be a product of irrational misanthropy. But then came the second and most terrible of the waves, a double and tidal wave of two world wars, and they invested the caveman theory with a horrible plausibility. We had

239

read of Attila and Genghis Khan, but these monsters seemed buried safely in the dark ages. We never anticipated their resurrection in the Himmlers and Eichmanns of the most scholarly nation in Europe. Nor was the moral breakdown confined to these men and their henchmen. In talking recently with a woman who had escaped a concentration camp, I learned what I had not quite realized before, that for much of their worst work the jailors could rely upon volunteers among the prisoners themselves, who for a bit of extra food or more tolerable quarters were ready to sell out their comrades. Some of these were apparently kindly people who broke sickeningly under the strain. Many of us must have asked ourselves whether we or any of our respectable kind were quite safe against the atavism of the Neanderthal "id" within us.

A third though milder wave of dismay was stirred up by the anthropologists. Boas, Malinowski, and Westermarck collected an immense mass of facts appearing to show that in no major relation between human beings, between parent and child, for example, or man and woman, was there any stable or common pattern of conduct. Popular books by Ruth Benedict and Margaret Mead were soon disseminating the notions that right and wrong were relative to cultures, and that talk of objective standards in ethics was naive and provincial. Many youths who had served in France or Japan or the South Seas were able to verify this variability for themselves. In our sociology departments the relativity of morals became almost a truism.

Few of these anthropologists were trained philosophers, and for a time it was easy to answer that they were going beyond their brief, that no description of what *is* can settle the question what *ought* to be. But here came the fourth wave, which supplied the anthropologists with support from an unexpected quarter. It was the rise of a subtle philosophical school which undertook to offer proof that objective standards were meaningless. According to this new school, the statement that something was good, or some action right, was not strictly a statement at all; it was an exclamation, an expression of feeling, a cry of attraction or repulsion like "Cheers!" or "Shame!" If anyone did so exclaim, you could hardly say "Yes, quite so," for in what he said there was nothing true or false; furthermore an exclamation can be neither argued for nor refuted. All value judgments were thus removed at one stroke from the

240

sphere of the rational. The old idea that the good life was the rational life, or indeed that any conduct was more rational than any other, was a pleasing but rather self-righteous illusion. Lord Russell, who was converted to this way of thinking in middle life, confessed that he did not like it, but added that he liked alternative theories still less.

What are we to say of this massive drift toward ethical skepticism? One cannot dismiss these theories as merely false, for there is truth in each of them. Nevertheless, they do seem to me, one and all, to be at odds with what I have called the principle of sanity in thought. They are all generalizations from too narrow a base, which when worked out into their implications collapse into incoherence.

Many people think of Freud as the great anti-Aristotle who has shown that man is an irrational animal, and some of them are carrying over into philosophy Freud's method in religion. Just as the plain man's belief in God is a father-substitute, Bradley's belief in an Absolute is a passionate reaching out for security; even the idealism of the happy and healthy Berkeley arose out of infantile abnormalities connected with sex and excretion; and indeed it would appear that all theorizing is governed by nonrational pulls and pushes. Now no one can really hold to this consistently. No one supposes that beliefs in mathematics and physics are the puppets of passion; we know that even in psychology some men can stick to the evidence better than others; we know that unless they could, Freud, who was clearly one of them, would have no claim to be heard. It has often been pointed out that if all theory is the product of nonrational desires, then so is the Freudian theory, and in that case why should we believe it? The Freudian who believes his belief that men are irrational to have been arrived at rationally, is rejecting his own theory, for he believes that we *can* so far be rational after all. And then have we not returned to Plato and Bosanquet with their heartening insistence that men *are* rational, though imperfectly and brokenly so?

Is not this the answer also to talk about war revealing the caveman in us all? Many men did break with their ideals and principles under the terrible strain of war, but some did not; one thinks, for example, of the heroic German pastor, Dietrich Bonhoeffer. But what if it were proved that under physical duress we all have our breaking point, what would that prove? Not surely that we are cavemen in disguise, but rather that our powers of normal thought and feeling are conditioned by our frail bodies, and we knew that tragic fact before. To say that a man is really or essentially what he is under extremes of misery or pain is to write him down unfairly.

May I confess that I remain skeptical, too, not of the facts that the anthropologists have supplied us, but of the conclusion commonly drawn from these facts? What they show is that men differ widely—if you will, wildly—in their moral practices. They do not show, I suggest, that men are fundamentally different in their moral standards, because that would mean a fundamental difference in their scale of intrinsic values, and this seems not to have been made out. To show that the Aztecs resorted to human sacrifices is not to show that they approved of murder, or that their ends in life were basically different from ours; it may only show that they lived under religious delusions. If we held the unhappy belief that only by placating an angry deity with an annual sacrifice could the crops be raised on which the lives of all depended, is it so certain that we should act differently ourselves? When one comes to ends instead of means, the great intrinsic goods to which life is directed, do we not find that men agree fairly closely the world over? We have yet to come on any corner of the Sahara or Antarctica where men prefer pain to pleasure, ignorance of the world to knowledge of it, fear to security, filth and ugliness to beauty, hatred to friendship, privation to food and drink and comfort. So far as one can see, the Russians and the Chinese want very much what we do; we differ from them not fundamentally, about ends, but practically, about the most effective means of reaching them. Indeed behind the bitterest debates in the United Nations about colonialism and injustice you find this very assumption that the needs and goods of human nature are everywhere the same; that is what makes the debate possible; the have-nots of the world are saying in chorus, "what we want is what you want, and largely have; now help us to get it too."

But according to our emotivist colleagues, it makes no sense to talk about what is objectively good, or good for all men. To say that anything is good is to express how I feel about it. When a Russian and an American both say that oppression in Angola is bad, they are expressing no common belief, and when the Russian says that Soviet control in Hungary is good and the American that it is bad, they are not differing in belief. Such "judgments" are ex-clamations. Now this is the sort of theory that would have occurred only to a philosopher, and can be retained, I suspect, only by the philosophers described by Broad as "clever-sillies." I do not think it can be consistently believed or lived by. It implies, for example, not only that we never agree or differ in opinion on a moral issue but also that we never make a mistake on any such issue, that nothing in the past was either good or bad when it occurred, that objective progress is meaningless, that no one can show by evidence that any moral position is sound, that approval is never more appropriate than the opposite, since there is nothing good or bad in the object at all, that personal or national differences over moral issues are in-capable, even in theory, of rational solution. I cannot stay to argue these points, much as I should like to. I can only say that I do not think that Russell or Ayer or Carnap has dealt with them convin-cingly, and that until someone does, I shall continue to believe that there are objective moral standards binding all men, and open to study by a common reason.

May I turn now to the last field mentioned at the outset, that of criticism? Those of us who began our work before the flood had hopes that even in such treacherous fields as music and painting and poetry some sort of standard of judgment was emerging. Not that we wanted all artists to be alike, which would be a bleak con-summation, even east of the Berlin wall; but that there might be some consensus as to what made a work of art worthwhile. Need I say that in this field the confusion is worse confounded, if that is possible, than in the field of ethics? What has happened?

What has happened is the gradual extrusion of meaning from art as something aesthetically irrelevant. Until far on in the Vic-torian period, painters were still working under the influence of a theory as old as Aristotle and sturdily defended by Sir Joshua Reynolds, that a painter should concern himself not with anything his eye happened to light on, but only with things that had some meaning beyond themselves. By preference this meaning would be universal, that is, would interpret some central human experience and have something to say to all men. Thus Reynolds in his own *Age of Innocence* was trying to catch the spirit of childhood; just as Raphael in the *Sistine Madonna* was trying to record for us the rapt joy of motherhood. Now this, said the later painters of the nineteenth century, may be philosophy or psychology, but it is not art, and they set about to recapture what the eye actually saw, as distinct from what the mind imported into it. This was the period of the impressionists, of Pissarro, Monet, and Renoir. The next step was an insistence that within the crude mass of what the eye sees, there must be a singling out of satisfying form; so postimpressionists like Cezanne arranged their lines and planes into pleasing overall designs. Hard on their heels, however, came the cubists, who pointed out to them that they were still painting figures of clowns and ballet girls; but if it was really form that counted, were not these clowns and ballet girls expendable? Roger Fry thought they were. He records how he once saw a signboard done by Chardin for a druggist's shop, representing a set of glass bottles and retorts; and he says, "just the shapes of those bottles and their mutual relations gave me the feeling of something immensely grand and impressive, and the phrase that came into my mind was, 'This is just how I felt when I first saw Michelangelo's frescoes in the Sistine Chapel.'" But if it was the shapes and their relations that did this for him, why were even bottles necessary? So he and many others moved on into abstract art, the art of Kandinsky and Mondrian. Was this the end of the line? No. Both these latter artists conceived themselves as realists; they were students of nature, who sought to find there forms they could use. "But why should we follow nature at all?" was the inevitable next question, to which came the inevitable answer, "There is no reason whatever." So we come to the age of nonobjective painting in which we live. In this painting not only things and persons have vanished but also every recognizable form, and what remains is an outgushing of the painter's mood.

Is this a consummation to be wished? It certainly has its advantages. It confers the title of artist on a great many people whose claims might otherwise have passed unnoticed. This impression gains color from the ease with which the public and even the critics can be hoodwinked. Dr. Alva Heinrich of the Psychological Institute of Vienna University arranged an exhibition of thirty pictures, half of which were by artists of acknowledged distinction and the other half by schizophrenic patients in a mental hospital; she then gave to 158 persons the task of saying which were which. They were wrong in just about half of their identifications, meaning that they found no grounds for distinction at all. In Paris, on a bet, a landscape by Modigliani valued at $15,000 or more was hung in an exhibition and sale of amateur art, and tagged at $25. Though many of the other pictures were quickly sold, the one picture that was the work of a supposed master had no takers to the end. The American National Academy of Design awarded a prize to a picture which, it was afterward found, had been hanging on its side. When some mirth broke out about this, an indignant connoisseur wrote a letter which I have in my files insisting that what it showed was not the obtuseness of the selecting committee but the real distinction of the picture; only a philistine would suppose that the sort of meaning which could be affected by a picture's being on its side or upside down had the slightest importance; the aesthetic value would be precisely the same.

I think I see his point. But if we take to be purest and best the art that has left meaning behind and reduced itself to an arabesque or an exclamation, how much, I wonder, will this purified art still have to say to us? The art that flamed from the walls of Renaissance Florence and Venice was, I suppose, impure and philistine art, but it did speak with power to the people who gazed on it. Perhaps the new fashions do too, but if so, they speak to the specialists, not to the many. We have just seen that professional philosophers can be turned aside from what to me at least seems the path of sanity, and I am not sure that artists are less moved by winds of fashion.

A critic could raise parallel questions about much current poetry. There stands out in my memory a remark made to me by the head of a large publishing firm in London: "My firm will look at any sort of manuscript except a book of poetry." In *that* he thought the public no longer had any interest. A century ago, fifty years ago, poets believed that their verse should sing, and that it should communicate. Many poets of recent decades appear to have abandoned the effort after these ends. The result is that they stammer to each other in corners, out of earshot of the world. I think that here again we find a failure in sanity.

But what has poetry to do with the intellect, it may be asked. A. E. Housman said that poetry need have no meaning at all, and that his own test of it was whether, if he repeated it while shaving, he tended to cut himself. His examples of meaningless verse are not very convincing. But in any case, intelligence in art may show itself in more than one way. It may show itself, for example, in the grasp of what is essential to a given art as distinct from what is eccentric in it. Now music lies so near the heart of poetry that its loss is crippling and its deliberate forfeiture stupid. A well-wrought rhythm has an almost physical appeal to us, whether it is the rhythm of a marching band, which, an eminent Yale professor admitted, made him drop everything and go off in pursuit, or the somewhat similar drumbeat of Macaulay's *Lays*, or the more delicate measure of one of Housman's own lyrics; the appeal of this recurrent beat is connected in some obscure way with the very throbbing of our pulse. Having something organic about it, the perfect marriage of sound and sense is usually conceived not by contrivance, but by a welling up from unconscious deeps; Housman has reported of one of his poems that the first two stanzas came to him on a walk on Hampstead Heath; the third came with "a little coaxing after tea"; the fourth required a year, and thirteen deliberate rewritings. The conscious superego in these matters cannot replace the dynamic id, but it can supply the blue pencil; it can cultivate the sort of consciousness that makes for craftsmanship.

Now the trouble with contemporary poetry is that its superego has gone AWOL. This has left too many of its practitioners without an ear, and therefore without much music in their souls. Many present-day poems, if printed continuously rather than in lines, would give the impression of being peculiarly cacophonous prose. The last poet I can think of whose work was uniformly the product of a fastidious ear was Housman himself, who died in 1936.

> With rue my heart is laden
> For golden friends I had,
> For many a rose-lipped maiden
> And many a light-foot lad.
>
> By brooks too broad for leaping
> The light-foot boys are laid;
> The rose-lipped girls are sleeping
> In fields where roses fade.

Could anything be simpler than that? It is so simple that only a master craftsman could have done it. Just where are the craftsmen who could do it today?

Another thing about it: it is intelligible; though it is pure poetry, no one could fail to catch its meaning at the first exposure. The reader of contemporary verse feels rather like Carlyle who, when listening to the talk of Coleridge, thanked heaven for occasional "sunny islets of the blest and the intelligible." Having heard a bit of Housman, would you now please listen to this, a contribution to one of our most reputable monthlies.

> I said to my witball
> eye, he lid-wise, half hoodwinked, jell
> shuttered low,
> keep out, keep out what rainfalls
> of hindsights or foresights would
> rankleroot
> house, guts, goods, me
> but my eye was a sot
> in a bowl of acids, must lidlift to know:
> and hailrips had entry, enworlded us,
> inlet a sea at our cellars, wracks,
> the drag and tow.

My impulse to mutter at this as neither very moving nor very luminous is checked by my memory of having heard a distinguished critic assert that there is an advantage in leaving it uncertain what a poem is about, since it gives the reader his freedom; he can take it as Romeo to Juliet on the balcony, or a portrait of the artist as a young man.

Now when I hear this sort of thing, a still small voice inside me murmurs "balderdash." There is more in poetry than a gnarled vocabulary plus Freudian free association; at that rate anyone can write poetry, which means that poetry has lost its standards and lost its way. It seems to be about as easy to hoax the critics in verse as it is in painting; indeed it has been done over and over again. The Wesleyan University Press has recently published a most amusing account of how Witter Bynner and Arthur Davison Ficke invented a new school of poetry. They wrote a set of forty-four nonsense poems and had them printed in a book, called *Spectra*, by two new poets named Anne Knish and Emanuel Morgan. Edgar Lee Masters wrote that Spectrism was "at the core of things"; John Gould Fletcher praised the Spectrists' "vividly memorable lines"; Eunice Tietjens wrote of the book, "It is a real delight"; Harriet Monroe accepted some of Emanuel Morgan's poems for publication in her magazine *Poetry;* Alfred Kreymborg devoted an issue of his critical magazine, *Others*, to the new spectral school. Bynner and Ficke had some eighteen months of laughter before they revealed that the book and the school were one great spoof. In 1940 James Norman Hall, the novelist, thought he too would go into the poetry business, and published in Muscatine, Iowa, a book called *Oh Millersville*, by a certain Fern Gravel. Shortly afterward the grave *Boston Transcript* intoned, "The book is amazing, amusing, full of the human scene, and not to be missed, because there can't be another like it in the world." After six years, Hall told the whole story in the *Atlantic* in an article, "Fern Gravel: a Hoax and a Confession."

Poetry, no more than art or theology, can surrender itself to meaninglessness without capitulating at the same time to charlatans. Perhaps Arnold asked too much of it when he said that it should be a criticism of life, for poetry is not philosophy. But after all it can hold ideas—even great ideas—in solution. Most enduring poetry *has* been an implicit criticism of life, and most men can absorb such criticism more easily from the poets than from the bleak prose of the philosophers. It was Sophocles, not Socrates, of whom the memorable remark was made that he "saw life steadily and saw it whole." Though the *Canterbury Tales* are really tales, and *Macbeth* and *Lear* are only plays, and Gray's "Elegy" only a lament in a country churchyard, it is hard to see how anyone could read them responsively and not be wiser and better for it. They talk of ageless things, love and ambition and joy and death, which are central in every life; and they do so in a way that makes us accept these things with more understanding and reconciliation. Sanity is not the special preserve of eggheads; indeed it is apt to elude them and to grant itself to those who engage the world more generously. There is a sanity among values, just as there is a sanity among beliefs, and it lies in the power of bringing a broad experience to bear on each particular point as it arises. It is not cleverness but wisdom, and the wisdom not of the serpent but of Solomon. It does not run to verbal conceits, or adventures in punctuation, or poems that are acrostics. As John Morley said, you cannot make a platitude into a profundity by dressing it up as a conundrum.

What a tirade this has been! It has sounded, I am afraid, like the Jeremiad of an irredeemable old fogey. It is not quite that, though things are now changing at such a pace that we are all likely to be outstripped if we are granted a normal span of life. These recent decades have been impetuously hurrying years, in which we have come a tremendous distance. When I look back to the other side of the divide and recall that in those days a touch of pneumonia or tuberculosis or erysipelas might be a death warrant, that the men who worked in mines or on the railroads did ten or twelve hours a day, that there were few automobiles and no planes, that in the lonely farmhouse there were no radios or television sets to keep them in touch with the world, and that the housewife's necessities of today—electric refrigerators and washers and vacuum cleaners—were all but unknown, I recognize that our advance in many ways has been enormous.

What then am I saying? I am saying that while this technological giant we have fashioned has been striding forward with seven-league boots, the human spirit has been trotting along behind it, breathless and rather bewildered. It has lost its sense of direction and of relative importance; it has lost confidence in reason, it has lost those standards of sanity that keep the rational mind on course, and enable it to tell excellence from eccentricity, and distinction from caprice. A hundred years from now men will look back with wonder at eminent philosophers insisting that the business of philosophy is with linguistic usage, at eminent theologians pronouncing reliance on reason to be sin, at eminent moralists reducing moral judgments to boos and hurrahs, at eminent psychologists refusing to call Greek culture better than Polynesian, at eminent artists straining after the meaningless, at eminent poets flocking to the cult of unintelligibility.

But the human mind after all, is a gyroscope that tends in time to right itself, and its past gives us some idea of what righting itself would mean. The main tradition in philosophy is one that runs down from Plato through Hegel to Whitehead, a tradition that has stood for system and sweep of vision—and it will come back. The main tradition in ethics is one that has run from Aristotle through Spinoza to Butler and Green and Bradley; it too will come back. There is a great tradition in criticism that has run from Longinus through Goethe to Arnold and, at his best, Eliot; surely that will revive. These traditions are not really dead; they are only sleeping. This shrill shout of mine is an attempt to wake them up.

# 14

# *The Idea of the Gentleman*

The gentleman is an Anglo-Saxon institution. There seems to be no word for him in any language other than English. The French word *gentilhomme* is no equivalent: its overtones of social and economic class are too strong; the German *Herr* is too general in scope. When the Frenchman or German wants to speak of a gentleman, he must use a paraphrase—*honnête homme, homme bien élevé, feiner Mensch*—or else do what Frenchmen and Germans commonly do in fact, appropriate the English word for what they take as an English notion.

Where did the English and Americans themselves get the idea? The word they got from the Latin, from *gentilis*, which connoted membership in a *gens*, that is a class or clan. But where did the notion come from? There are two main sources for our Western culture, Greece and Judaea. Whitehead suggest that the idea comes from the Greeks and says that "the Iliad is probably the origin of our idea of the gentleman." But a better Greek scholar, H. W. Garrod, says that "there were no Greek gentlemen in our sense." The nearest approach to a portrait of a gentleman in Greek literature, he thinks, is Aristotle's picture of "the great-souled man." And he reminds us that this great-souled man was a coxcomb, resembling no gentleman one has ever heard of except the sort that appears in the novels of Disraeli. But then neither does the gentleman come from Judaea. Mr. Garrod reminds us that David was a hero to his people and was described as after the Lord's heart. But on one occasion David coveted the wife of his neighbor Uriah, and took a short road to his end. He pretended to honor Uriah by placing him in the forefront of battle, from which Uriah never returned. From that point on we find David rather hard to bear. Why? Is it because he was an adulterer and because he held human life cheap? Yes, but not chiefly that, says Garrod. "David is not after the hearts of most of us because, to employ a familiar phrase, he was not a gentleman. That is the sin which hath no forgiveness. . . . By not being a gentleman I understand failing in two ideals—the ideal of chivalry and the ideal of honour."

Now chivalry and honor are neither distinctively Greek nor distinctively Judaeo-Christian. Nor can we say that they are distinctively Gothic; the Teutons who threw back the Roman legions were coarse, cruel, and too often treacherous. The gentleman seems to have arisen, like a chemical compound, from a fusion of elements from each of which he was absent. The Teutons were fighting men, and when a fighting man becomes a Christian, he must do some rapid adjusting or rationalizing. The Teutons were called upon to do this when they were baptized, battalions at a time, by Charlemagne. One of the results of this conversion was chivalry. Pugnacity for its own sweet sake was now frowned upon; but fighting in the interest of either sacred or profane love was thought of as something different. St. Louis and the crusaders were great fighters, but also, they believed, true Christians. And the knights who fought for Notre Dame, "Our lady," felt it natural enough to set lance in rest for other ladies as well, above all for damsels in distress. Such Christianity as they had filtered into their none-too-luminous minds from contact with Rome or from partly Romanized neighbors. Much of the rich culture of Rome went out in the Dark Ages like a candle in the night. But the pride and stern rectitude of the Roman patrician made a lasting impression on his Teutonic conquerors, and they reappeared in altered form in the medieval sense of honor. Amid the brigandage of the time, the humbler people collected themselves around the castle or chateau; and the lord of the place, himself as a rule an unlettered barbarian, nevertheless felt pride in his position as protector of the weak and avenger of the wronged. Though he did not know it, the dwindled rivulets of three great streams of culture were flowing through him, the Christian, the Roman, and the Gothic. He was regarded by those beneath him as noble for his chivalry and honor; he was called a nobleman; and though half savage, there was stirring in his heart the spirit of *noblesse oblige.*

The notion of the modern gentleman, however, still lay far in the future. Where did it put in its appearance? Dean Church, in his beautiful book on Edmund Spenser, suggests that its first appearance was in Spenser's *Faerie Queene.* Spenser was a friend of that romantic figure, Sir Philip Sidney. Sidney is remembered chiefly for two things, first for a slender body of true poetry, second for insisting, as he lay mortally wounded at Zutphen, that a cup of water be passed to a soldier who lay near him. Spenser loved Sidney; he had an even greater gift than his friend for musical speech; and as he sat in his Irish exile, he fixed and idealized the character of Sidney in more than one fine poem. His *Faerie Queene* caught the ear of the English people; it was their greatest poem since Chaucer; and it painted in attractive colors what Chaucer would have called "a very parfit gentle knight." Here were the courage and honor of the old nobleman, but with something new added. As Dean Church says, "To birth and capacity must be added a new delicacy of conscience, a new appreciation of what is beautiful and worthy of honour, a new measure of the strength and nobleness of self control, of devotion to unselfish interests." The modern notion of the gentleman was coming to the birth.

But note this significant fact: the gentleman must belong to a special social class. Shakespeare, who was a late contemporary of both Spenser and Sidney, and may have known them both, has given us many fine ladies and fine gentlemen, but if I am not mistaken, he drew them all from the classes of privilege, the higher up the better; they come as a rule from the courts of dukes and kings. On the other hand, his tailors, farmers, nurses, plain soldiers, and merchants are a vulgar and motley crew, all thumbs.

This connection between gentlemen and the gentry persisted in English thought and fiction for centuries, producing unhappy results on both sides of the social line. In many below the line it produced a resigned conviction that they must be of coarser grain, of meaner stuff, than those who were called "the quality." On those above the line it had more than one evil effect. It tended to make them feel that people who hewed wood and drew water were made for these offices, and that if they aspired to education or letters or politics, they were getting beyond themselves. Even in Victorian times Thackeray makes one of his "gentlemen" say, when it was suggested that a tradesman might show genuine quality: "Don't come to me, Sir, with your slang about nature's gentlemen—nature's tomfools, Sir!" This is an attitude that is likely to engender revolutions, and so it did; but in England the revolution came peaceably and by degrees. This was partly because snobbery was there tempered by Puritanism, with its insistence that each man had "that of God within him," as the Quakers said, and so was of infinite worth. It was partly also because of an old tradition of political liberty, voiced in its essence by Colonel Rainboro of Cromwell's army: "I think the poorest he that is in England hath a life to live as the richest he." The snobbery was further kept in check by that sturdy English self-respect that made Samuel Johnson, when expected to dance attendance on the most famous gentleman of the day, Lord Chesterfield, tell the noble lord in immortal Johnsonese exactly what he thought of him. But in countries where this tradition of religious, political, and common sense did not prevail, the outcome of this repressive snobbery was very different. In France the long-smouldering resentment against "the proud man's contumely" at last broke out in a raging fire that did not cease till the flower of the French nobility had been consumed in it.

Another unhappy effect of this link between gentry and gentility was a widespread confusion between the accidents of social station and the essentials of personal worth. To be sure there were brave protests against this, like that of the exciseman Robert Burns, who was of course no gentleman by the standards of the day.

> What though on hamely fare we dine,
> Wear hoddin gray, and a' that;
> Gie fools their silks, and knaves their wine,
> A Man's a Man for a' that.
> For a' that and a' that,
> Their tinsel show and a' that;

The honest man, though e'er sae poor,
Is king o' men for a' that.

But this leveling philosophy was more popular in the cottage than in the castle, whose occupants and hangers-on made a singularly bad case for themselves. Lord Chesterfield would not accept Johnson as a gentleman because Johnson treated everyone, inferiors, equals, and superiors, very much alike. George IV said of his Prime Minister, Sir Robert Peel: "Peel is no gentleman. He divides his coat-tails when he sits down." It is no wonder that many who suffered under this sort of thing struck back at it bitterly. Hazlitt's essay "On the Look of a Gentleman" describes its hero as polished, heartless, and crafty. "A gentleman," said another social commentator, is "a man who is never rude except intentionally."

The fact was that the English gentleman of the eighteenth and early nineteenth century was not an edifying spectacle. He did not know how to earn a living; his vast leisure he often spent on hunting, flirting, drinking himself into the gout, and gaming; the notion of honor so degenerated that gambling debts were known as "debts of honor" and took precedence over the family grocery bills; and, as for chivalry, Burke roundly announced that "the age of chivalry is gone."

Curiously enough, what saved the gentleman was the very thing that many expected to abolish him, the democratization of England by the great reform bill. "In 1832," says the historian H. V. Routh, "when England was ripe for the Reform Bill, the gentleman of birth was ripe for effacement. Yet from that time onward, his reputation revived. . . . He saved his prestige by imparting it to his newly-established rivals. They borrowed his qualities and he had the grit to cultivate their virtues. So the Victorian gentleman came into existence." The severance of personal quality from social class had begun. Thirty years later, in 1862, John Stuart Mill wrote in his precise way:

In the present day, the word "gentleman" implies the combination of a certain degree of social rank with a certain amount of the qualities which the possession of such rank ought to imply; but there is a constantly increasing disposition to insist more upon the moral and less upon the social element of the word, and it is not impossible that in course of time its use may come to be altogether dissociated from any merely conventional distinction.

This process of severance went on through the century. Little by little it became clear that between the spirit of the gentleman on the one hand and his family, bank account, or business on the other there was no necessary connection, and that while those things might provide a good soil for a flowering of the spirit, the flower itself was the important thing, and might grow in any soil. This was a doctrine urged with eloquence by a Scottish peasant named Carlyle, an English wine merchant's son named Ruskin, and an itinerant American named Emerson. The most popular novelist of the century, Dickens, found his gentlemen in quarters where a gentleman of the previous century would hardly care to be seen. The poet laureate of the period sang that kind hearts were more than coronets, and simple faith than Norman blood.

But mention of Tennyson suggests the strain under which those were laboring who sought to keep the flower alive while its native soil was being scraped from its roots. The age was growing commercial. And since contemplation of the British businessman hardly prompted a burst of song, Tennyson had to turn to misty history, to Arthur and his Round Table, for the knightly spirit he wished to celebrate. Even Carlyle sadly contrasted past and present; Ruskin fell into depression when he found how hard it was to keep alive the pursuit of beauty as an incident in the pursuit of money; Pater retreated into aestheticism, Arnold into a culture frankly at odds with the spirit of the age. By the turn of the century people were wondering whether, with the rise of the common man, the general struggle for wealth, and the coming of applied science, an ideal so deeply rooted in class, means, and leisure had not outlived its usefulness. Such writers as Wells and Shaw clearly thought it had, and prophesied the advent of a new type of man whom we should hardly think of calling a gentleman; his qualities were irreverence, unsentimentality, intelligence, energy, iconoclasm, scientific know-how, economic expertness, and social utopianism. Routh entitles the last chapter of his book on *Money, Manners and Morals* "The Passing of the Gentleman," and says that the word "is now used only by hall-porters, shop assistants, and a few women."

Shall we let the ideal of the gentleman go? Before we do, we may well remember that it has done much to make us what we are. For the idea was essential both in the southern notion of the cavalier and in the New England notion of the "gentleman and scholar," just as it was in the more ancient tradition from which both these notions sprang. Speaking of his English compatriots, Dean Inge of St. Paul's remarked that "the character of the gentleman is universally recognized as our main contribution to social ethics." Let us ask ourselves, then, before we abandon that old ideal, what if anything remains valid in it for the circumstances of our time.

Not, certainly, the notion of an aristocracy entitled to honor by birth or means. T. S. Eliot in his later years invited us to reconsider social aristocracy as a support to culture. And it is no doubt true that the association in Britain of ancient coats of arms with a certain type of mind and manners has given this type prestige and so helped to make it general. But anyone who pleads for such an aristocracy in America is pleading to deaf ears. Rightly or wrongly, our minds are made up on that point. Experience seems to have told us that birth is not a guarantee of personal quality, and even more plainly that wealth is not; and we are unwilling to scatter our honors where honor may not be due. If the ideal of the gentleman is to survive, it must be through some grace of spirit, not through any adventitious supports. Very well, when these are dispensed with, is there anything left worthwhile?

I think there is. Indeed I think that there are priceless elements in this old ideal that not only are worthy of cherishing but are deeply and particularly needed in our day. I shall mention two of them.

First there is that ancient pair, chivalry and honor. I count them together because the ideas have now all but coalesced. Chivalry still includes helpfulness to the weak and gallantry to the other sex, but it has come to mean much more; it means that generous fairness to others which is so essential a part of honor. Honor implies that one has incorporated such fairness into one's self-respect. That is why honor is so potent a force. Convince a man that something is his duty, and he will sometimes do it and sometimes not, and often if he does do it, he drags himself like a dead weight across the line. But if he feels that his honor is involved, that doing it is the only self-respecting course, the chances that he will do it are vastly greater, for the act has enlisted the most powerful of all motives on its side. Self-respect is the one thing we can none of us bear to lose, for if that goes, everything else goes too. Whatever honor takes under its protection is underwritten with a powerful guarantee. That is why the merger of chivalry with honor is so significant. The knight who fought in the tournament for the fair lady in the stands had a very strong impulse at work in him, but when this personal interest failed, as it might toward the lady who sat next to her, or the poor varlet who served him, he might give a very different exhibition. But let considerateness without respect of persons become a point of honor with him, and he will be a different sort of man; he will have a motive that will drive him to duty in the face of love itself.

> I could not love thee, dear, so much
> Loved I not honour more.

Indeed honor may be preferred even to life. One of the prizes of the British Museum, which many thousands including myself have pored over, is the journal of Captain Scott, scrawled in pencil during the last days of his return march from the South Pole. One of the party, Captain Oates, was in very bad shape, and knew that by his limping advance he was reducing the chance of the party's reaching its base. Then appears the following entry in Scott's journal: "I want these facts recorded. . . .He was a brave soul. . . .He slept through the night before last, hoping not to wake; but he woke in the morning—yesterday. It was blowing a blizzard. He said, 'I am just going outside and may be some time.' He went out into the blizzard and we have not seen him since . . . though we tried to dissuade him, we knew it was the act of a brave man and an English gentleman. We all hope to meet the end with a similar spirit, and assuredly the end is not far." This young man Oates was a humble product of a commercial age, but for pure chivalry and honor is there anything better to show in the record of Sir Philip Sidney? In such men chivalry and honor are part of a code which is part of themselves; they have become instinctive, and "instinct is to principle as poetry is to prose." There is more than mere courage in such conduct; there is a lyric quality in it, and a quality that will wake echoes whenever and wherever men have hearts at all. While they can produce and admire such people, the age of chivalry is not gone, and Burke's great words in lamenting its passage have no doubt helped to preserve it. Chivalry he describes as "that sensibility of principle, that chastity of honour, which felt a stain like a wound, . . .which ennobled whatever it touched, and under which vice itself lost half its evil by losing all its grossness."

Such honor does not reserve itself for great occasions. It has been truly said that manners are minor morals, and if this "sensibility of principle" is really there, its pressure will be felt in countless little adjustments in every field. Consider two of these fields in which most Americans are interested, athletics and politics.

Athletics provide one of our chief schools of honor. Though recent researchers tell us that Wellington probably never made the remark about Waterloo's having been won on the playing fields of Eton, much else has certainly been won there, and on our own college fields. When we want to describe "conduct unbecoming a gentleman," a Briton says "it isn't cricket," and an American "it isn't playing the game." This notion of sportsmanship or fair play, extended to the relations of men generally, is one of the best of Anglo-Saxon exports, and the larger our supply and circulation of it, the better. The ability to take hard knocks unwhiningly, to win without preening oneself, to admire those who can beat one at the game, to go all out to win but to prefer not winning to winning dirtily, belongs to the best traditions of American sport. Is it maintaining itself? In amateur sport I think it is. There have been notable exceptions in professional sport, but the scandal raised when they come to light is itself a sign of health. One classic detail of our sports tradition is the remark of the small boy who is said to have approached his hero, Shoeless Joe Jackson, after the "Black Sox" scandal with the plea, "Say it ain't true, Joe!" Olympic competition seems to fall somewhere between amateur and professional sport. Once when casually listening to my radio I heard a famous American runner describe how he and his teammates had conspired to win for America the hundred-yard dash at the Paris Olympic games. They knew that the man they had to beat was the Cambridge sprinter, Harold Abrahams, so they arranged, according to this account, to take turns in making false starts, in order to reduce Abrahams to the jitters before the decisive heat was run. Most Americans will not be distressed to recall that Abrahams beat them, even so.

The chief danger to sportsmanship comes from the pressure to win at any cost applied by great crowds and the prospect of spoils. If basketball players start selling games, if an outstanding college football team can seek to retain its undefeated record by means of feigning injuries, it is because the players are being subjected to pressures from which college students should be exempt. Unfortunately the American national game, in professional hands, does not set the best example. I remember with amusement the exclamation of a Scottish scientist about a professional game he attended; "Why, the players reviled each other!" said he in wide-eyed astonishment. Yes, my friend, they do, and with accomplished aid from the spectators. Furthermore, it is an unwritten law that the whole season is an open season for umpires, and the baiting of this unhappy species seems to have developed with some managers into a subtle art. Some of them even defend it. "Nice guys come out last," says the redoubtable Leo Durocher. That is why, as one lowly fan, I used to hope that Mr. Durocher would come out with the "nice guys"—to his own and the general astonishment.

Some think that similar habits are invading our other national game, that of politics. If this is so, it is a pity. One of the distinguished and distinguishing marks of Anglo-Saxon political life is the ability to combine hard hitting of an opponent with respect and even friendliness toward him. If anyone doubts that we have made progress in this regard, let him recall the sort of speeches that were made by ancient statesmen about each other. It seems to have been considered fair practice in refuting an opponent's case not only to take up his distant past, to ridicule his looks, and to attack his associates, but also to make him out a monster of personal depravity. No Anglo-Saxon congress or parliament would tolerate this practice. Even the conventional forms of address make against it; members are supposed to refer to their most detested opponents as "the honorable member for Stoke Poges" or "the gentleman from Connecticut." These forms were designed to mean something about those entitled to them, as "Your Honor" does when applied to a judge; and just as a judge has outlived his usefulness if "Your Honor" is an empty term as applied to him, so a congressman is ripe for retirement when the term "honorable gentleman" has become a misnomer. Students of the mind tell us that vilification of another is often a secret outlet for the contempt one has for oneself; and, by contrast, the honorable man tends instinctively to assume honor in others. As Newman puts it in his masterly sketch of the gentleman: "He has no ears for slander or gossip, is scrupulous in imputing motives to those who interfere with him, and interprets everything for the best. He is never mean or little in his disputes, never takes unfair advantage, never mistakes personalities or sharp sayings for arguments, or insinuates evil which he dare not say out . . . . If he engages in controversy of any kind, his disciplined intellect preserves him from the blundering discourtesy of better, perhaps, but less educated minds; who, like blunt weapons, tear and hack instead of cutting clean . . . ."

While we are quoting Newman on the gentleman, let us quote another remark of his which will bring us to the second main trait of the gentleman: "It is almost the definition of a gentleman to say that he is one who never inflicts pain." He is a person of sensitive feeling, he is alive to the feelings of others, and he tempers his words and actions accordingly. This is reflected in his name; he is known for gentleness as well as for honor. There have been men of leadership and force whom one would never think of calling gentlemen. Alexander was a great force, but of his closest friends he killed one in a drunken quarrel, and when another died as a result of careless indulgence, he crucified the doctor to show his grief. Napoleon was a great force, but he was coarse of grain. Hitler was a demonic force, but a guttersnipe. Mussolini was a considerable force, but Curzon's exclamation after meeting him was, "The fellow is no gentleman." Not that the gentleman need lack force; he is notoriously exemplified by such persons as Bayard and Sidney, men whose gentleness flowered on a rock of knightly courage. That may help to explain the curious remark of Henry James about George Sand: "She was a man . . . a woman can transform herself into a man, but never into a gentleman." However that may be, the gentleman himself must be something of a hybrid; he must have in addition to his masculine qualities a dash of the feminine in his nature—of compassionateness and sensitiveness.

Now this sort of mixture is viewed with suspicion in this country. We are faced with the paradox that American men have more respect for women than any other men in the world, while at the same time their fear of effeminacy is so acute that they want to put the greatest possible distance between themselves and any trait that is recognizably feminine. Many visitors from abroad have noted this; H. G. Wells described it as the "square-jawed" attitude of American men; it is a hypertrophied masculinity, hesitant to admit or avow any delicacies of feeling because that might compromise the stern and rockbound strength of the male animal. In this matter of national ideals, we can get instructive hints from our popular journals and from Hollywood, both of which keep alert ears to the ground. To take both sources at once, consider a Hollywood actor whose popularity, long after his death, is witnessed by his continued appearances on television's late night shows. Humphrey Bogart was not quite the "hard-boiled Herman" that he looks; I was surprised to read that he had lasted three semesters at Phillips Academy, Andover, and was once headed for Yale. What he mainly stands for, nevertheless, and received $200,000 a picture for embodying, is the man of steel—hard, devil-may-care, defiant, aggressive, cool to nervelessness in all emergencies, always ready with fists or gun, flint-faced and grim-jawed, a man of few words, since these strong silent men of course prefer action to words, a man whose emotional pendulum swings monotonously from fighting to loving and back again. Mr. Bogart would not have received his $200,000 a picture unless a great many Americans admired his type; and the tragedy is that this type is a case of arrested development. All healthy boys of twelve or fourteen admire that sort of hero, and have their own secret ambitions to have jutting jaws too; but if fate is kind to them, they get over it, along with freckles and cowlicks, in their late teens. But too many Americans, I submit, never do get over it. They carry into maturity this adolescent pride in an exaggerated masculinity, which, however comfortable to have around when one is riding a range, as one does perhaps once in a lifetime, is an unmitigated bore when ideas are to be exchanged or values judged. And the widespread unconscious working of this ideal has made our American men less interesting and perceptive, more gauche and inarticulate, than they have any need of being. It has gone far toward investing the old ideal of the gentleman with the taint of effeminacy.

What is the reason for this development? There are many reasons. One is that the ideal of the gentleman was less central among the Puritans of the north than among the cavaliers of the south, and that it was the Puritans, with their middle-class heritage, that proved in the end the leading determinant of American culture. Another is the influence of the frontier, where the qualities of Henry James were conspicuously less useful than those of Jesse James. Still another is the stress that our wide open spaces and opportunities have laid on the life of action as opposed to contemplation. The American businessman is engaged in so fiercely competitive a life that he leaves the patronage of fiction, poetry, and the arts chiefly to women. For this there is a further reason. American public schools are coeducational, and it is notorious that the boys mature less rapidly than the girls, particularly in the subjects requiring responsiveness of feeling. A great many boys, being consistently beaten by the girls, come to feel that they are stupid in these subjects, try to keep up their crumbling self-respect by scoffing at them as girls' subjects, and go on to commit themselves to something accepted as manly, like science or engineering, before their budding humane interests have had a proper chance. They then carry with them through life the Philistine notion that anyone who takes seriously the impractical subjects, like poetry and music and painting and the drama and speculative thought, is something of a freak, whose triumphs are more naturally scored at afternoon tea than in the rough and tumble of the real world.

These boys do not want to be mollycoddles, and one thinks the better of them for that. But is there not something pathetic in their stunting themselves for life because of a misapprehension of both themselves and the facts? A man is not the worse engineer or doctor or lawyer—he is on the contrary much better—if he is a cultivated human being as well. The new wave of interest in the humanities in education springs partly from a new realization of where the age of technology has been taking us. It has been taking us toward a society of experts who are masters, as men never were before, of the techniques of building, communication, manufacture, destruction, and all the arts of comfortable and even luxurious living, but who, outside their offices and workshops, are pinched, meagre, and dreary. Emerson said that even in his own day society tended to make us "so many walking monsters—a finger, a neck, a stomach, an elbow, but never a man." The working week and the working day are becoming shorter, the hours men can call their own are becoming longer, but their newfound freedom will prove hollow unless they can also call their souls their own. And they cannot do this if their eyes and ears are never unsealed, if their ideas have never been taught to play about great themes with some interest and discernment, if their thought remains tethered to their newspaper, and their taste bounded by their admirable radio on one side and their superb television set on the other.

The gentleman as we have conceived him is distinguished by chivalry and honor on the one side and by perceptiveness on the other. That makes him in a sense an aristocrat. And when we say this, a doubt inevitably arises, on which we may say our final word. Is not the ideal of the gentleman an incongruous importation from an old and stratified society, an alien growth which in a democracy is bound to die from sheer maladaptation? Many discerning persons have thought so, on the ground taken by Hazlitt when he said, "The character of a gentleman . . . can hardly subsist where there is no marked distinction of persons. The diffusion of knowledge, of artificial and intellectual equality, tends to level this distinction." A recent writer on Thorstein Veblen points out that Veblen "stood deliberately for the common man," and adds: "If the chief end of mankind is to produce gentlemen . . . then Veblen was wrong. If Veblen was right, the gentleman must go." Many visitors to this country have thought they have seen the gentleman in the act of disappearing. The tendency to hit blindly at anyone who stands out from the crowd as different, to strike out at intellectuals because they make one feel stupid, and at those whose speech or manners or tastes are more exacting than one's own because they seem conceited or affected, the surrender of standards to standardization, is a special danger of the democratic way of life. It has recently invaded even our colleges. Honor societies, dean's lists, medals and prizes, even grades, are under fire as subtly undemocratic, and the new youth culture that was so bent on freedom has developed its own pressures for conformity. In view of all this, what reason has anyone to suppose that the common man if given his choice will choose the better rather than the worse?

There can be no certainty about such things. It may be that W. C. Brownell's dream of "democratic distinction in America" is an idle dream and nothing more. For myself I do not think it is, and for this I have two grounds. First, forty years of work with youth have left me with the impression that we have in our own youth a remarkable combination of fairness to what is novel with eagerness for the best. Secondly, I share a faith as old as Socrates that in truth and goodness there is a gravitational pull on the human mind, that men turn to these things, if given a free chance, as moths turn toward the light. To anyone who thinks, the ideals of the gentleman—fairness, considerateness, sensitiveness—are self-validating ideals which even the scoffer secretly admires; and the pretense of them, even without the substance, is "the tribute vice pays to virtue." If the world views Americans with some loss of sympathy, it is largely because it sees, or thinks it sees, that harder and coarser ideals and the tolerance or taste for violence are crowding the picture of the gentleman out of the American mind. I am not sure that this is true, and I hope the picture will long remain there. It is an heirloom to be prized. For in that picture are blended the best features of a long and noble ancestry that may have been forgotten but is still at work in our blood and in our ideas, an ancestry that combines the courage of the Gothic forests, the stern Roman ideal of justice, and the compassion of Judaea. Of such a lineage we may well be proud.

# 15

## Some Fringe Benefits of Education

The chief ends of a liberal education are a better understanding of the world, a mind disciplined to think accurately and fairly, and discrimination about values. I have said something about these ends in earlier talks of this series, but for the present I want to move on to less thoroughly trampled ground.

Higher education in this country is becoming so general that it is in danger of losing its distinction. We have probably all met graduates who have run the long gauntlet of college years apparently untouched by it. They have been through it all; they have sat through their hundred and twenty hours of classes; they have filled handsome loose-leaf binders with notes; in countless examinations they have readied countless blue books for recycling; they have received and filed away their diplomas. And now they have left it all behind. The notebooks and blue books, like the hours, seem to have sunk without trace. Nothing in what they do or say suggests the well-kept secret that they have had a college education. They have melted into the all-absorbent American background where they are indiscriminable from the others around them.

There is something wrong about this. Education, like murder, should come out. It is, or ought to be, a permeative process, affecting people down to their finger tips. If its powerful inoculations have taken, there should be outward and visible symptoms of something important that has gone on inside. Education should confer detectable fringe benefits that both tell a story and ease one's way. I want to single out a few of these by-products, passing from the less to the more important.

To begin with a minor one: I think education should make a difference in speech. Surely it is reasonable to expect that one who has studied literature should express himself more sensitively because of this study, and that one who has been disciplined in science or philosophy should express himself more exactly. And yet there are people who seem to think that using the language sensitively is affectation and using it exactly is pedantry. Even when they do not in their hearts believe this, they sometimes shrink from such usage because they think that other people think so. Members of Congress have been known to campaign in the language of hillbillies in order to avert the horrid suspicion that they were highbrows. I once knew a college president who had such a dread of being mistaken for an egghead that he would slouch through his speeches, apparently with an image of himself as a Lincolnian rough diamond, an image that he thought would be democratic and endearing.

Now there are probably many people who do resent signs of superiority in others, people whose smouldering sense of inferiority may be fanned into dislike by the slightest breath of implied criticism. The whispering democracy of Main Street is always lying in wait to snipe at the Carol Kennicotts of the world. But then to adopt this sort of democracy is itself a kind of upside-down snobbery, without even the excuse of the common snob that he is trying to ape distinction; it is an attempt to evade distinction and the responsibilities that go with it by compromise with herd instinct. Such conformism tends to suffocate individuality. So it is a heartening sight when someone appears like Woodrow Wilson or Churchill or Adlai Stevenson, who quietly ignores the philistines and insists on talking like an educated man. A person's speech reflects, or ought to reflect, the quality of his mind. A mind that has been tempered and whetted by a long process of education ought not to hack at its subjects verbally with a stone axe; it should cut cleanly, quickly, and easily. If it is really master of its thoughts it will not be at a loss how to express them. A student, asked by his professor to define a vacuum, answered more truly than he knew when he said, "I have it in my head, but just can't get it out." And those who affect a Lincolnian uncouthness can take small comfort from Lincoln's actual practice. Called upon to give some memorial remarks at Gettysburg, he delivered a three-minute masterpiece of relevance, conciseness, and simplicity, which has been treasured as a model ever since.

This last term, *simplicity,* is important. How often we hear complaints from those who have listened to a speech or read an article by some distinguished psychologist or sociologist that they have not understood a word of it! What has happened? Of course the issue discussed may have been so abstruse or profound that no one could have made it plain. But the probability lies elsewhere. Simplicity is not a simple thing to achieve, and the speaker may not have been willing to take the pains needed to achieve it. Or it may be that he has in the back of his head a mistaken notion of what educated speech is like. He thinks that if he weights what he writes or says with technical polysyllables, and loads his sentences with cautious qualifications within qualifications, this will show his scholarly gravity. What it more probably shows is a want of education—personal, aesthetic, and intellectual. Personal, because it is the business of a speaker to communicate, and a failure to communicate, if avoidable, is a failure in courtesy. Aesthetic, because lumbering awkwardness, however correct, is no substitute for grace. Intellectual, because economy is one of the great virtues of intelligence; in speech, as in mathematics, that achievement is most impressive which goes to its end by the shortest road.

Pedantry of speech has penetrated even into the special preserves of education. The *New York Times* editor for this field tells us that if an educational publishing house had printed Budd Schulberg's book *What Makes Sammy Run?* they would have called it "Motivational Research on Sammy's Potential." When Sammy has to be spanked by educational theorists, they administer practical negative reinforcement to him. Ivor Brown asks whether the next translation of the Bible will be allowed to heal the sick, and answers "No, it will have to rehabilitate those who are suffering from psycho-physical maladjustment." Washington has become the headquarters of a remarkable language described sometimes as Gobbledegook and sometimes as Federal Prose. In English one would say, for example, "Too many cooks spoil the broth," while in Federal Prose we would say, "Undue multiplicity of personnel assigned either concurrently or consecutively to a single function involves deterioration of quality in the resultant product as compared with the product of the labor of an exact sufficiency of personnel." Senator Simpson of Wyoming reminded us that the Lord's Prayer contains 56 words, Lincoln's Gettysburg Address 236, the Ten Commandments 297, the Declaration of Independence 300, and a government order setting the price of cabbage 26,911. After hearing that, one is the less surprised by hearing also that Einstein had to go to the local authorities for help in understanding his income tax return.

In short, what people have a right to expect is that the speech of the educated man should reflect the quality of his mind. They expect from a mind trained in distinguishing ideas that what it says will be more clear and precise; from a mind trained in thought, that it will put its case more easily and more pointedly; from a more sensitive imagination, that it will exhibit the grace, simplicity, and conciseness that are subtle forms of courtesy. Men expect, and rightly, that if one carries a light, one will not hide it under a bushel.

Another fringe benefit of education that is in danger of being lost is the power to converse. Talk with one's fellows in the form known as the "bull session" has always been a prime means of education in college, and I hope it still is; but whereas in former times conversation continued throughout life, the busyness of modern life is drying it up. "Conversation in this country," said President Griswold of Yale, "has fallen on evil days. . . . It is drowned out in singing commercials of the world's most productive economy that has so little to say for itself it has to hum it. It is hushed and shushed in dimly lighted parlors by television audiences who used to read, argue, and even play bridge, an old-fashioned game requiring speech. . . . It starves for want of reading and reflection. It languishes in a society that spends so much time passively listening . . . that it has all but lost the will and skill to speak for itself." Desmond MacCarthy reported the same thing to be happening in London. "The art of conversation has passed away. In London to tell a story well is now impossible, for it may take more than two minutes; Oscar Wilde would be voted a bore, and neighbours at dinner would begin talking to each other after his third sentence."

If this is true, it is a pity. The give and take of conversation is a civilizing force; it enriches our stock of ideas, enlarges our sympathies, rubs off parochialism, blunts the edge of prejudice, refines tact, and disciplines expression. It may become an exhibition of fine art, and there have been times when it clearly was. If Plato is to be trusted, it had a practitioner in the streets of Athens whose skill in one kind of high talk has never been equalled. The intellectual life of eighteenth-century France expressed itself in no small measure through the drawing rooms of Paris, presided over by its women intellectuals, where French wit and logic scintillated far into the night. What would we not give for a tape recording of what went on at the Mermaid Tavern when Ben Jonson rallied a young friend in the corner, or of the talk at a later club when Reynolds and Goldsmith and Garrick fell silent to listen while Edmund Burke and Dr. Johnson had it out with each other?

Why do we not hear such conversation today? We have richer materials for it than the Burkes or the Johnsons ever had. But that itself is one of the troubles. Knowledge is proliferating and industry subdividing so fast that we are becoming specialists, each farming his own little acre. When the man who knows all about fruit fly chromosomes finds himself sitting next to an authority on *Beowulf* or a vice-president for sales promotion, there may be an uneasy silence. In the humanities as in medicine, the general practitioner is suspect. A despairing college dean has recently written that "Benjamin Franklin and Michelangelo, if they were to be reincarnated today and apply for academic positions, would qualify only for the two most lowly in the hierarchy, instructor in a liberal arts college, or academic dean." Furthermore science is overtaking the humanities as a subject of specialization, and the humanities themselves are being made more scientific. The leading professor at

271

Harvard and the leading professor at Oxford who make the study of mind their specialty both deny the existence of mind as anything but bodily behavior. Now the movements of bodies, whether those of *Drosophila*, molecules, or *Homo sapiens*, are curiously undiscussable. What is discussable is human nature, its motives, ideals, and character, its foibles and enthusiasms, its taste in art and conduct, and its thousand-odd convictions about race, sex, religion, and politics. This great central area of the distinctively human and humane, in which the Johnsons and the Burkes found a fertile meeting place, seems to be withering away into a sort of dust bowl, where people look at each other forlornly for a time and then drift away to where their TV or their LP library is waiting to make them less forlorn.

This desiccation of our old common garden of humane interests presents an opportunity to our college-educated women. Women have always offered a high resistance to being dehumanized by specialization; it may be that their responsibilities for children have kept them close to what is centrally humane; perhaps that is why a woman pedant seems harder to bear than her male counterpart. A woman with intellectual interests, but with those interests mellowed and tempered by her sense of what is humanly interesting, is the natural queen of the dining room and the living room. Give her a group of not too lumpish guests, and at her best she can fan them into a harmonious glow, very much as a conductor can wave into life the wood and brass of his orchestra. She is the natural catalyst of conversation, and may perform this office superbly even when no great talker herself.

A few years ago I picked up a newspaper and read that Nancy Astor was dead. I knew that she had long been a conspicuous figure in the House of Commons and a somewhat angular agitator for suffrage and temperance. But it was something else that the headline called into mind. What came back to me was a spring afternoon some fifty years ago, when Lady Astor in her large way invited a troop of young Americans studying in England down to her place at Cliveden, I being one small item on the list. You would think that such a conglomerate would be a problem in itself to any hostess, but it was complicated by a sprinkling of gray eminences, for example, the formidably silent Field Marshal Allenby, who had lately done some unusual things like capturing Jerusalem, and a man in tweed plus fours named Bernard Shaw, who was as garrulous as Allenby was taciturn. Was Nancy Astor troubled by this motley band? Not in the least. She was in her element. Darting about with her nimble movement and nimbler wit, bringing Americans and British together with her cheerful, kindly directness, marshaling the general and the author about as willing privates of whom she was herself now the field marshal, thawing tied tongues, breaking up agglutinated groups, gently prodding her lions into roaring, she sent us all home at the end with warmer hearts and better-stocked heads.

As I watched her in operation I began to realize what an advantage a woman has in this difficult and delicate field; a crusty scholar or executive will take from her what he would not for a moment take from his own kind. I go so far as to think that our future cultural atmosphere is going to depend in no small measure on whether the educated women of the country, each mistress in her own castle, use wisely this power of theirs. It is the wife and mother who sets the tone of the household, who dampens or encourages the budding interest of her children in the world of ideas, who can best beguile her weary spouse into greener fields than his office worries. Our educated women are already the chief support of our art, fiction, drama, and music. It depends largely on them whether an atmosphere congenial to the humanities is to be maintained in this country at all.

I pass to a third fringe benefit of education, its fertilization of leisure. It looks as if the future were going to bring us far more leisure, both in the middle of our lives and at the end. It is true that the reduction of the working day from twelve hours to ten to eight to seven affects hand workers rather than brain workers; our executives and college teachers continue to be overworked. But happily not all of this work is slavery, as I can witness after forty years of it; indeed Logan Pearsall Smith tells us that "the test of a vocation is the love of the drudgery it involves." And even we ink-stained college drudges can look forward to more years of leisure at the end of our lives than our fathers and grandfathers had, and, owing to better social planning, more physical and financial security.

But what about the security of mind and spirit? Our people are supplied with all sorts of helpful devices to save their time, from electric typewriters and dictating machines to washers and dryers and precooked meals, but there is small point in this economy of time if the leisure it provides is only a vacuum. Nor can the vacuum be filled with amusement only. Dr. Hutchins says that "the deep and permanent melancholia that underlies the American temperament must be ascribed, in part at least, to the boredom that the perpetual search for amusement at length induces." I am not sure about this "deep and permanent melancholia," but there is no doubt about the boredom on the face of the amusement hunter. He will never be satisfied, because he will find, even if he gets what he wants, that men are not made for amusement.

Our age is providing more and more leisure, but it is earmarking that leisure for boredom. We are increasingly crowded into cities, where we depend for excitement not on ourselves but on stimuli from without. Our children sit passively before the synthetic entertainments of technically marvellous films, or of the always available television set, or of radio programs and long-playing records. Such experience has its value, but it is a far less lasting value than that which is gained from actively fulfilling interests of one's own, and the boy or girl who has become dependent on being galvanized from outside is headed for inevitable boredom.

The only insurance against such boredom is internal resources. And if education is successful, it provides these resources in the form of multiple enduring interests in worthwhile things. Someone has said that "the primary purpose of a liberal education is to make one's mind a pleasant place in which to spend one's leisure." What a contrast there is between the later years of people who have these interests and those who don't! Think of the blank old faces one sees on suburban porches or in rest homes, of the onetime stars of the stage or the diamond who, when their short day in the sun is over, have nothing to fall back on and become pathetic drifters. And then think of such nonagenarians as John Dewey and Dean Inge and Bernard Shaw and Bernard Berenson and Gilbert Murray and Bertrand Russell and George Santayana. They all found ninety years too short for the things they wanted to say and do. Each of them could have said with the Elizabethan poet, "My mind to me a kingdom is."

The next fringe benefit I want to name is one suggested by a remark of that delightfully unprofessional academic, Professor Walter Raleigh of Oxford. "The art of reading," he said, "is the art of judicious skipping." The educated man today must learn how to skip. We are being inundated with printed matter almost to the point of being intellectually suffocated. Our mailboxes bulge with journals, newspapers, and begging letters; our college libraries, even the largest of them, are cracking at the seams; to supply the volume of our newsprint, we are cutting down our forests at an alarming rate. One issue of the Sunday *Times* is, in reading matter, equal to about twenty-two volumes of ordinary book size. Jacques Barzun writes: "According to the latest inventory, which is already a dozen years out of date, there are in the world 50,000 scientific journals publishing some two million articles a year—forty thousand a week." On a recent visit to Ohio State University, I had pointed out to me a large building devoted exclusively to chemical abstracts, to culling out the essentials from the literature of chemistry alone; and it was soon having to move to larger quarters. What that implies is that no chemist in the world can now hope to keep up even with the literature of his own subject. Yet he is supposed not only to keep up with it as best he can, but also, as an educated man, to have views about American foreign policy, abstract art, and the Pulitzer awards.

What is one to do? People of weight have at times suggested extreme measures. Emerson counselled that whenever a new book came out, we should read an old one; Justice Holmes is alleged to have refused to read newspapers; Walter Pitkin advised that we read our first-class mail and throw the rest away; a Yale colleague of mine saves his time by electing one worthy cause to contribute to, and dropping all other solicitations in his wastebasket. These are pretty desperate measures. Should we not discriminate more nicely than that? But then discrimination implies standards, and what standards are we to use? Since we cannot stop now to philosophize about these, we can only say rather feebly, "those standards that commend themselves to the educated mind." If our "liberal" education has not supplied us with such standards, then it has not been truly liberal. And we must manage to choose in the light of them.

I was helped to see what this means by a piece of good fortune that befell me during the last war; for some months I had as a guest one of the most distinguished philosophers of our time, G. E. Moore. I was struck by the limited range of Moore's reading. He was quietly convinced that most of the matter printed even on philosophy was negligible, and he dismissed it serenely, though the few contemporary writers he did regard with genuine respect he read with extraordinary critical attention. I think he took a like attitude toward literature and music, in both of which he was deeply interested. He had been the friend and an early inspirer of the Bloomsbury group—of Lytton Strachey, Maynard Keynes, Roger Fry, Leonard and Virginia Woolf. As a result of early discussions and adventures, he had found that some writers and types of writing spoke to his condition and others not; and he would no longer waste time on those who did not, though he was willing to read and reread those who did. For example, he read to us aloud, with much pleasure and with dramatic rendering, the whole of Jane Austen's *Sense and Sensibility*. He was of course anxious to know how the war was going, but with his passion for facts exactly stated, he passed over the vast mass of reportage and editorial commentary to concentrate on the official communiqués. All this made a pretty austere intellectual diet. But in one respect at least, Moore was surely right. Though each man may choose his reading by different standards, standards of some kind he must have if he is to retain any real integrity. He cannot simply surrender himself, wide-eyed, to the flood of newsprint that swirls around him, or he will drown, and his disappearance may be no great loss. He must somehow learn to select and reject. It is a test of his education whether he can skip judiciously.

Moore's practice suggests a final fringe benefit of education which seems to me the most important of all. I do not know what to call it but intellectual Puritanism. We have become disillusioned to be sure about our grandfather's Puritan morality, which strikes us as harsh and negative. We have small use, either, for the Puritans' views on art; their suspicion of music and drama seems merely bigoted. But I submit that if, while getting rid of Puritanism in morals and art, we could become Puritans of the intellect, we should move not backward but a long stride forward. By intellectual Puritanism I mean austerity of belief, the insistence that if a belief is offered for our acceptance, it should show grounds for its acceptance, and that it has no claim on us otherwise—in short, the adjustment of thought to the evidence. On the face of it, there would seem to be nothing particularly new or exacting or exalted about such an attitude. The fact is that it is difficult in the extreme, that if adopted, it would produce a cultural revolution, and that if the revolution ever comes, educated minds must lead it. A word now on each of these points.

First as to its difficulty. Does adjusting one's thought to the evidence seem an easy matter? Then consider two facts. As things are, men's firmness of belief often varies in direct proportion to the difficulty of the problem. On a minor question—whether they should buy a new car or refrigerator—they will manage to keep an open mind, weighing the pros and cons carefully; on the question of the ultimate governance of the world, on which Buddhists differ from Catholics and Catholics from Unitarians, or on the ultimate structure of society, which is today dividing the world in two, they will have convictions that are as passionate and as confident as they are unreflective. Millions of people on each side are lined up in dogmatic hostility to each other, though it is apparent that, since their beliefs are contradictory, millions must be wrong. The Puritan principle calls for increasing inquiry and tentativeness and toleration as certainty becomes harder to achieve. This involves a reversal of ancient habits.

Again, consider this, that where one's own self-respect is involved, the tendency to repress or twist evidence unconsciously is almost irresistible. And, directly or indirectly, most important issues do involve our self-respect. How many persons, for example, white or black, can even see the facts objectively which are behind the racial crises of recent years? How many can discuss with more than outward impartiality the relations between men and women? How many can bring inward freedom to the philosophical problem of freedom, or to the probability of surviving death? We are apt to find ourselves arrayed by instinct on one side or the other before the discussion begins. Even philosophy has been described by Paul Valéry as "an attempt to transmute what we know into what we should like to know." And yet we should all agree in theory that nothing is ever true because we want it to be, or false because we detest it. There is a sort of Grand Canyon between our practice and our principles.

I suggested, secondly, that if this Puritanism of the intellect were ever adopted, it would produce a revolution. Think what would happen if our convictions normally followed not desire or feeling or authority, but the evidence open to us. It is not overstating the case to say that society would be transformed. The nationalism, bigotry, superstition, race hatred, and political fanaticism that feed our conflicts, even the egotism and suspicion that prompt so much personal unrest, would melt away like piles of dirty snow in the spring sun. Pascal thought that most of the ills of mankind were due to the fact that man could not sit in a room and think. Descartes thought that our lush crop of errors all sprang from a single root, the fact that we turned our problems over to impulse before giving our minds a chance to get clear about them. Reasonableness has always been a virtue beloved by philosophers more than by the run of men; it is an undramatic virtue, with little appeal to feeling because it makes feeling toe the line. Perhaps John Locke was merely repeating a professional prejudice when he said that the love of truth is the seed-plot of all other virtues, as I may also when I follow Locke. However that may be, I can only think a real love of truth would remake our anarchic and warring world.

Thirdly, if this evolution or revolution in reasonableness ever comes, it will be educated minds that take the lead. Of course they are taking the lead already in most fields. When it comes to formulating foreign policy, or keeping the dollar stable, or planning national defense, or designing planes or submarines, we all appeal to the expert; indeed the power of the expert in medicine to prolong our lives and in physics to destroy them has made of the man in the long white coat a sort of wizard before whom we are perhaps too ready to prostrate ourselves. "It takes a man who doesn't have one," says that stout fellow Stan Musial, "to appreciate the value of a college education." But idolatrous as our attitude has become to the expert, his specialized knowledge is not what we need most of all. What we most need from education is not the knowledge of the expert nor any kind of skill, but the reasonable temper, the habit of judging, feeling, and acting in accord with the evidence. That temper has been achieved by some with no help from formal education, but such education, after all, is the approved means of getting it, and it may be more effective than one knows while undergoing it. We may have been bored by the binomial theorem; we may never once use it when we are out in the world; but the patience and clearness exercised in seeing why it is true will be of use to us every day of our lives. The nocturnal bull sessions of college days dealt with questions we cannot even remember, but what we probably reaped from them in fairness of argument, in the control of impatience and irritation, will stand us in good stead to the end.

Education carries no guarantee of the tempered mind. As a recent writer reminded us in the official Phi Beta Kappa journal, "Wisdom has never been the sole property of Phi Beta Kappas." There are men loaded with doctorates who remain spoiled children whom we should not want to see in any responsible post. For all their brilliant work on the electrocardiograph or on Icelandic myths, we feel that they let education down. Why? Because all that research and discipline should have bred a different temper, a distinctive weather in the soul. The normal result of the search for truth is the love of truth. The constant and careful weighing of evidence should lead on to a standing fairness and honesty of mind. "Men whom reason guides," said Spinoza, "want nothing for themselves which they do not want for other men, and hence are just, faithful, and honorable." "Justice," said Leibnitz, "is nothing but goodness conformed to wisdom." "Thought," said Pascal, "makes the whole dignity of man; therefore endeavor to think well; that is the only morality." Goodness is so truly the reflection of reasonableness that I follow Pascal in doubting whether in the end there is any difference. And if reasonableness is to prevail in the counsels and practice of men, it will be through the sheer attraction of living persons who have achieved that great self-conquest.

Indeed all these fringe benefits are shadows cast by the well-shaped mind as it takes its way through the world. Of our speech and writing it has been said that "style is the man." So true it is that one's talk is self-revealing that Johnson said of his old rival Burke that one could not stand with him in a doorway for a few minutes to get out of the rain without saying, "There was an extraordinary man." Does our use of leisure tell anything about us? A great deal, answers Dean Inge; for "the soul is dyed in the color of its leisure thoughts." We could not draw our own portrait more faithfully than is done for us by what we choose and what we skip from the rich menu that modern life spreads out before us. And as for the rational temper, if you want to say that it is not a by-product at all but the very essence and end of education, I shall be content. When you look at a portrait by Rembrandt of an old face, you fairly see the soul looking out at you through its lines and furrows. If reasonableness is not the same as education, it is still the countenance, lined and sharply chiseled and finely moulded, which the formed mind turns to the world.

# 16

# The British Scholar—A Toast

*This talk was not addressed to students, but is included because it deals with relevant themes. In 1952 the British Academy celebrated its fiftieth anniversary with a banquet in the ancient Goldsmith's Hall, London. There was a series of toasts, and on behalf of the "corresponding" or foreign Fellows of the Academy, the writer responded to the toast of "The Guests."*

One who comes from overseas and from what is becoming increasingly a foreign country has a certain advantage on an occasion like this. For what we are celebrating tonight is a half-century of British scholarship; this body represents the heart and soul of that scholarship; there are many persons present whom we from abroad have come to regard as the type and embodiment of the British scholar; and such persons are cut off by instinct and custom from talking about themselves. We corresponding members, that is, we aliens, are under no such disabilities. We can look at you, if not with a knowledge, at least with a detachment, hardly possible to yourselves. And I think it would be a pity if, when we are celebrating the British scholar, we should be prevented by this modesty from hearing about the very subject of which we ought to hear most, namely himself. May I, therefore, speaking as a foreign guest, talk frankly and to their faces about our hosts, and say something of what the British scholar looks like when seen through foreign eyes?

The dominant impression is one that at first statement may be a little nettling; it is that of the splendid amateur. Let me try to explain. My own subject, and the only one of which I can speak with any knowledge, is philosophy. Think what a different sort of being the British philosopher has been from, let us say, his Teutonic counterpart. Nearly every German philosopher of consequence has been a university professor. Go down the line of them—Kant, Hegel, Schelling, Fichte, Lotze, Dilthey, Wundt, Windelband, even Nietzsche; all were holders of academic chairs. In the great tradition of British philosophy very few have been professors. Bacon, Hobbes, Locke, Berkeley, Hume, Mill, Spencer, Bradley never owned a chair among them. Nor is the story wholly different in other fields. Take history. Ranke, Mommsen, Harnack, Döllinger, Curtius, Niebuhr, Treitschke, Troeltsch—all professors again. On the other hand, Gibbon was a private gentleman of some means, Hume was a librarian and secretary to an embassy, Grote was a banker, Macaulay was a member of the Commons, Creighton and J. R. Green were clergymen, Carlyle was a free-lance journalist, Froude was, to be sure, a university professor, but only between the ages of seventy-four and seventy-six. Or take criticism. Johnson, Hazlitt, Coleridge, DeQuincey, Lamb never taught, and though Arnold held for a term a chair of poetry, who ever heard of *Professor* Arnold?

Now it is not such facts, arresting as they are, that are important; it is what they symbolize about British scholarship. The amateur spirit is subtly and significantly different from the professional or professorial spirit. For one thing, it has zest. There is a wind among its willows, a fresh wind that blows where it lists, and so has the gusto of freedom. Take a page of Kant at random, and then take a random page from either of his contemporaries across the Channel, Berkeley or Hume, and you will feel the difference I have in mind. The German was probably the greater thinker; but what a struggle he makes of it; *hic labor, hic opus est;* he is dutifully and wearily rolling his big stones uphill. Where a man's treasure is, you feel his heart should be also, while this seems like mere day labor. But you have no trouble in knowing where Hume's or Berkeley's heart is; it is there beating palpably through the words with a vitality that is infectious. They too are capable of hard work, but they remind you of one of the happiest of all facts, that work may be play, that work is what you do because you have to and play the same thing done because you want to.

There is one of the prime marks of the amateur spirit: it has the gusto of delight in activity freely chosen. Havelock Ellis, himself a remarkable example of the independent British scholar, said he didn't know whether he was a hard worker or not; he seemed to himself scarcely ever to work, and what most people called play he avoided because of its boredom. The writing of such men can hold in solution a larger volume of scholarship without dullness because of its zest. "The histories of Macaulay and his nephew," says H. A. L. Fisher, "could not have been produced from university chairs. There is something unacademic in their impetuous flood of entertaining detail. We miss the deadly relevance and cold impartiality of the seminar." British lay scholarship has even achieved the ultimate feat of producing a readable dictionary. I do not mean Dr. Johnson's. Even about his great work one must sympathize with the good lady who was presented with a copy of it and, on being asked how she found it, answered, "Oh, most instructive, though I did seem to notice a trifling want of connection." No, I am thinking of H. W. Fowler. His unfailing gusto and humor will carry you through *The Dictionary of Modern English Usage* from "absolute" to "zeugma" without letting you down for a single page.

This spirit of the amateur scholar has stolen over into the ranks of the professionals. To take living examples would bring me too near home, but can one imagine scholars more unweighted with pedantic trapping than the Cambridge man who started the school of English literature at Oxford, or the Oxford man who started the school of English literature at Cambridge? For the scholar, said Walter Raleigh, "among dead authors there is no dead man"; "The first and last secret of a good style," said Quiller-Couch, "consists in thinking with the heart as well as with the head." These scholars practiced what they preached. It is one of the distinctions of British scholarship that even the professionals have caught the amateur spirit. Who carried a greater weight of learning than that unregenerate old Tory Victorian, Professor Saintsbury? Who ever carried such a weight with more of the temper of a schoolboy on holiday?

But besides this zest in his work, I seem to see in the British scholar another distinctive quality, namely a certain breadth of humanity and common sense. This is a quality which it is increasingly hard for the scholar to retain. Knowledge is expanding so much faster than our power to keep up with it that we are beginning to feel like charlatans if we lay claim to competence outside our own square foot of ground. The vaster human knowledge becomes, the more we incline to retreat into our own little specialty. "I have wasted my energies," said the Greek professor; "I have devoted my life to the study of the ablative and the dative. Why didn't I specialize? I should have concentrated on the ablative and let the dative alone." "The broad field of human wisdom," Stephen Leacock tells us, "has been cut into a multitude of little professorial rabbit warrens. In each of these a specialist burrows deep, scratching out a shower of terminology, head down in an unlovely attitude which places an interlocutor at a grotesque conversational disadvantage." And of course the deeper down he gets the harder it is to see his subject in the light of common day. He magnifies trifles, and it has been said that "seriousness about trifles is the soul of three quarters of the dullness in the world." The public questions of the day he is disposed to evade because they are not in his line and do not admit of the precise judgments that he is alone willing to commit himself to. During the war I heard one of the most eminent of German scientists, then an emigré in America, complain bitterly of the political immaturity and indifference of his specialist colleagues at home. American scholarship has been profoundly influenced by German, both for good and for ill, and we are pressing specialization, particularly in science and technology, beyond what many would consider the danger line. Such specialization, of course, has much to do with the sudden leap of America to the first place in the world in technological inventiveness and industrial production. But too often, as Dr. Hutchins has been reminding us, when the American who knows all about Diesel engines meets his colleague who knows all about the geology of oil, they have nothing to talk about but the weather.

Now the British scholar may not always have been free from insularity, but from this insulation against all researches but his own he does seem to have been exceptionally free. He has been charged, indeed, with being too free from it; there are ancient gibes about his utilitarianism and about a nation of shopkeepers. These taunts do seem unfair against a nation that is admittedly supreme in pure poetry, and during at least the early part of the century was supreme in pure philosophy. But they are surely true to this extent, that when the Briton feels moved to let himself go without regard to practicality or common sense, he is likely to hear what W. K. Clifford called "a still small voice that murmurs 'Fiddlesticks.' " He knows that ingenuity and novelty and theoretical brilliance are good things, but he is kept by a sanity that has become almost conscience from crossing the thin line that divides specialism from fanaticism. A lamented member of this Academy, A. E. Taylor, used to say that no one had ever done first-rate work in philosophy who was not gifted with massive common sense; and however that may be, I suppose that if the Academy were to select a typical British thinker, the brilliant Coleridge, for example, would not get a vote and that fine old sobersides, Bishop Butler, would get many. If scholarship loses something in concentration by keeping fresh its contacts with the world, it gains still more in sobriety and judgment. Is there anyone who thinks that Clarendon and Gibbon and Macaulay and Fisher and Churchill were less valuable as historians for their immersion, long or short, in public life?

In rereading lately Arnold's *Literature and Dogma*, I have been struck by the strength of his case for the humanities, that is, for humanity, in religion. A man of one book, he says, even if that book is the Bible, does not know that book. A man who approaches it as an antiquarian merely, or as a linguist merely, or as a theologian merely, does not know it. No one does or can know it who does not bring to it a wide acquaintance gained through life and literature with how men's feelings mould their ideas, and their ideas their feelings. We from countries where scholarship has become fragmented into a dangerous atomism are grateful for the stubborn sane humanity of the British scholar. It was an Englishman, not a foreigner, who exclaimed, "How can they know their England who only England know?"

Some of this liberality of outlook you surely owe to the unique structure of your older universities. An American, French, or German scholar often lives in isolation from colleagues in his own or other fields. In the give and take of an English senior common room any mole that put in his appearance would be subjected to an operation guaranteed to kill or cure, to exclude him as insufferable or once for all to give him his sight. The physicist and the classicist can hardly exchange ideas over their claret year in and year out without coming to write physics more urbanely and criticism more exactly. And am I wrong in thinking that the attrition of these universities upon each other has had on British scholarship something of the same effect as the attrition that goes on within them? The specialism of Cambridge, the catholicity of Oxford—the contribution of each has been great, but has it not been greater because each has critically watched and corrected the other? You will know better than I.

In addition to its zest and its humanity, may I mention one more characteristic of British scholarship that impresses the observer from abroad, though it is hard to put this into words? An honored member of this Academy, Dean Inge, remarked that "the character of the gentleman is the finest ideal that our nation has offered to the world." By the gentleman, the Dean obviously did not mean the economic gentleman, the "man without visible means of support," whose road to extinction has been so thoughtfully smoothed by British politics since the war. He was referring to a spirit compounded of many things, of which modesty, the sportsman's interest in fair play, and what Newman chiefly stressed, the reluctance to give pain, are only a few. Some have felt that these qualities have in the past been so closely linked to social class that with the coming of the new social democracy they would be obliterated. The prediction, so far as a visitor can see, is not being fulfilled; the ideal of the gentleman appears to be not a class but a national ideal. And I think it has subtly but powerfully penetrated British scholarship.

The Briton likes modesty of claim and moderation of statement; as some observer has noted, in British journals the intemperate orgy of moderation is renewed every morning. British scholarship on the whole takes the same line. It is hard to conceive of the intellectuals in this country being swept off their feet by the histrionics and balderdash that appeared in high places in some

286

other countries during the war; they would suffocate it in laughter. Generations of young Oxonians have found something peculiarly British as well as Greek in Aristotle's teaching of "nothing in excess." Here morals and scholarship meet in the feeling that if one goes beyond what the facts warrant, one is making oneself absurd. To the Frenchman and the American, British moderation and understatement seem often tame; in the long run they are a fertile source of scholarly fidelity and general confidence.

Some of us feel the same way about sportsmanship. Many things have been won on British playing fields, even if Waterloo was not among them. Scholarship is itself a kind of great game which must be played by rules if it is to be played well; it involves personal rivalries and hard knocks, and more failures than successes in scoring goals. There are countries where to criticize a distinguished scholar is to give a personal affront and is met by the sullenness or the savage retort of outraged dignity. Am I wrong in thinking that the frequency with which a young Briton is sent sprawling on the playing field, and gets up with increased respect for the rival who could do that to him, has some connection with his later deportment on the battleground of ideas? One likes to think of the way Wallace instantly stood aside and placed the honor where it was due when Darwin and he published their theories at the same moment. One recalls that it was in Britain that the nearest approach, perhaps, in the annals of human thought to absolute fairness of mind appeared in one of the founders of this Academy, the philosopher Henry Sidgwick.

If I am right, the features that most impress the foreigner about British scholarship are drawn pretty directly from British character. The defects of that character I leave to the critics, of whom we have an ample supply on both sides of the water. I am the less concerned by our mutual criticisms because the roots of American language and literature, politics and scholarship, run so deep into British soil that it is past the power of petty malignance on either side to uproot them. In the last half-century my country and yours have come to see eye to eye and to march together as they never have before. Could this fiftieth anniversary do better than to close on the hope that these bonds of mind and policy may be drawn still closer in the half-century we are now entering?

# III
*Homilies*

# 17

## *Conformity*

Many books have been published in this country suggesting that we are ridden by an anxiety to conform. David Riesman thinks we are in transition from being an inner-directed to an other-directed people. Vance Packard thinks we are a nation of status seekers, ordered about by hidden persuaders, a set of hypnotic and ventriloqual voices projected from Madison Avenue. Sloan Wilson has aroused our sympathy for dumb driven commuters in gray flannel suits. William Lederer calls us a nation of sheep.

These are disquieting charges. They are made against the nation that has taken itself as the home and capital of individualism, which used to call itself the land of the free and the home of the brave. Are the charges true? I may as well say at once what my conclusions are in this matter. They are two: first, that we *are* in this country being subjected to a set of pressures toward conformity that are massive and powerful; secondly, that they can be escaped, and must be escaped, if we are to be ourselves.

John Stuart Mill pointed out a century ago that the danger to freedom in a democracy comes less from government than from public opinion. Our government of late has had an admirable record in its protection of individual liberties. The great decision of the Supreme Court on desegregation is being pushed slowly home. A little atheist magistrate in Maryland has been permitted to keep his job though he refuses to take an oath; it has been conceded that religious freedom includes the right to be irreligious. Jehovah's Witnesses have not been compelled to salute the flag, or the Amish to send their children to high school, however silly they may be to refuse. Important decisions in the cases of Joyce's *Ulysses* and the book described by wags as "Lady Loverley's Chatter" have let down the bars for authors almost to the ground. Legally we can say and do pretty much what we want.

Mill's point was, however, that it is possible for the government of a country to be extremely tolerant, as in general ours is, and at the same time for public opinion to exert a soft, all-enveloping pressure toward conformity and uniformity, the more powerful because hardly realized. This pressure has achieved an exceptional strength in America. I should like to suggest three reasons for this.

The first is our lack of any fixed social strata. It may seem odd to say that the *lack* of such strata produces pressure; is it not precisely their *presence* that produces such pressures? In a sense it is. In England, for example, this has been notably true till recently, though England has undergone a social revolution in the last few decades. When I went to England first as a student in 1913, I was embarrassed to find myself waited upon by a college servant old enough to be my grandfather, a man who would never dream of trying to send his own children to a university. These children did not aspire to be "gentlemen." They would continue to work on his menial level, would drop their *h*'s as he did, would dress and drink as he did, would bow to their betters, and snub their inferiors, and know their place, as he did. That kept them in a cage. But if they accepted the cage, as most of them did, it made things easier for them; it set the style of their work, thought, and speech.

Suppose now that millions of people come to America from comparatively stratified societies. They want to adjust to the new order, and their children want to do so even more impatiently. But in the new environment they are no longer flies in amber; they have room to spread their wings, and a chance, if they show ambition and energy, to make a place for themselves. But they cannot do this as mavericks. They are Americans now; their future lies in thinking and doing as Americans do; they must take on the coloring of the people about them; they must show that they belong and are at home here. They are anxious to throw off the old singularities of accent, belief, and manner, and be American through and through.

Thus the forces of hope and ambition are lined up behind conformity, and these people are anxious, as tenth-generation Americans are not, to avoid anything that would fix them in an inferior group or lift eyebrows at their expense. No doubt the only strictly native Americans are the Indians; all the rest of us are more or less recent immigrants. But in the great melting pot that is America most newcomers feel the need of being melted, and do not want to stand out as unassimilated lumps.

The second factor making for conformity is the size of the American market. The producers of books, magazines, phonograph records, movies, television sets, automobiles, clothes, and packaged foods have the largest number of potential buyers in the world. In such a market there is bound to be the keenest competition. The publishers are all looking for best sellers, for if a book like *Gone with the Wind* catches the public eye, its sale may make the fortunes of both author and publisher. Such journals as *Time* are read everywhere from Seattle to Miami, and in virtue of their immense circulation and the attendant advertising revenues, they are able to reach a size, attractiveness, and technical perfection that make competition all but impossible. Canada has been unable to put anything in the field that will compete with them, and Canadian feeling and opinion have been falling more and more under American domination.

Communications in this country are now so efficient that the President can sit down in the White House of an evening and talk face-to-face with the American people as a whole. In a similar fashion the larger organs of news and opinion penetrate, with the Sears Roebuck catalogue, into every neck of the American woods. Local newspapers and magazines are fast disappearing; local stores cannot compete with the nationwide chain stores; more and more in this country there is no east and there is no west, hillbilly or cowboy, New England Brahman or western frontiersman, but only Americans, starting their day with the standard orange juice and Battle Creek cereal, holding pretty much the same views about communism and taxes, all mildly concerned about crime, pollution, and the threat of a world war, and not knowing what to do about them, all anxious not to seem ignoramuses but anxious also not to be too highbrow. We are becoming culturally as well as politically centralized; the Luce journals, the theater chains emanating from Hollywood, and the great radio and television networks are exerting a steady, universal pressure toward a common pattern. There has, to be sure, been a rash of protest recently, set off by the most unpopular of our wars; and it seems at times as if the present generation had broken all moulds and were making themselves over on a new design. But when one finds not one or two students with long hair, patched blue jeans, and grievances against the establishment, but whole regiments of them marching together, one wonders whether the new nonconformity is not another example of the old conformity. Surrender to a wave of fashion is not the mark of individualism.

The third source of pressure is advertising. It has been estimated that we spend ten billion dollars a year on it, which would exceed the total budget of any government in the world except ourselves and Russia. Our newspapers are largely given over to advertisements; that is why they are the bulkiest ever known. Our journeys by car sometimes seem like progressions from one enormous sign blotting out the landscape with its message that some cigarette satisfies to another with a smiling damsel announcing her devotion to beer. Every few minutes our radio and television programs are halted to advise us that science is enthusiastic about some sleeping pill, toothpaste, or deodorant. The colored advertisements of clothes and foods in our glossy magazines make anything else of the kind in the world seem like the work of amateurs.

And Madison Avenue seems to be just getting into its stride. It is now using depth psychology to explore the crevices in our armor and to learn how our defences can be lowered against its products. Arnold Toynbee has made the startling statement: "I would suggest that the destiny of our Western civilization turns on the issue of our struggle with all that Madison Avenue stands for more than it turns on the issue of our struggle with Communism." He thinks that the impact of this concerted attack is moulding us into something both un-American and un-Christian. "A considerable part of our ability, energy, time and material resources," he maintains, "is being spent today on inducing us to . . . find the money for buying material goods that we should never have dreamed of wanting had we been left to ourselves." "The strategy is to try to captivate us without allowing us to become aware of what is being done to us."

What concerns us even more than the fact of these pressures is their quality. They clearly tend to level us off, but do they level us up or level us down? They do neither exclusively. Irving Babbitt used to say that standardization is being substituted for standards; but then standardization is not an unmitigated evil. There are millions of people in this country who have been living in poverty, anxiety, and disease, and if the high-powered salesmanship of our magazines and radios can suggest to them that their house and their self-respect require a bathtub, a refrigerator, and a washing machine, that may be the first step in their escape. The desire for these things is not materialism. They are, or may be, the means to a cleaner, healthier, happier life. The complaint is often made in these days that the world is being Americanized. This means in part that an ideal of health and cleanliness surrounded by labor-saving machines is radiating out from this country to the world. That is a kind of export to be proud of, not ashamed of.

It may be said that what is vicious is not the pressure toward making our lives materially better but the pressure to make them morally worse. The pull of the mass media—of radio, story magazines, movies, television, theater—so it is often said, is steadily downwards. Concern about the influence of television became so strong that a few years ago a committee of the Senate held an inquiry into it. Some interesting facts came to light. In twelve years the number of stations had increased from about a hundred to more than five hundred, and the amount spent on advertising on television from less than ten million to more than a hundred times that amount. Figures submitted to the committee indicated that in the course of less than ten years the percentage of programs containing violence during the chief showing hours, 4:00 to 10:00 P.M., had risen from 16 percent to 50 percent.

Among the witnesses was the Director of the United States Bureau of Prisons, Mr. J. V. Bennett, who told the committee that the television exploitation of "crime, mayhem, and conflict" did clearly contribute to juvenile delinquency, that in two federal detention homes for young offenders 23 percent in one and 26 percent in the other reported their own belief that television had influenced them toward crime. Mr. Bennett had heard a grim little poem which he recited to the committee as an appropriate theme song for these programs:

> Sing a song of TV
> For the little ones,
> Four and twenty jailbirds
> Packing tommy-guns..
> When the scene is finished
> The blood is ankle deep.
> Wasn't that a pretty dish
> To send the kids to sleep?

Mr. Carl Perian, the committee's staff director, estimated that some 2.5 million children had watched an episode called "The Grudge" on a leading network. The committee dimmed their lights and looked at this picture for themselves. According to the *New York Times* report the next day, "It has a theme of bloody revenge, and featured a fistfight, a gunfight, a mother horsewhipping her son, the same mother shooting her daughter, a description of how one man laughed while shooting another in the stomach six times, and a faked assignation in a hotel room."

The producers of these programs defend them by pointing out that "the good guy wins in the end" and suggesting that this makes up for the violence he has regretfully to use in making the right prevail. The defense is relevant, but inadequate. For revenge and violence are deeply evil in themselves, and continually to invest them with the glamor that belongs to courage and goodness is itself a perversion of values. One hesitates to ask for censorship in these matters. But three things are possible. One is the course taken by the Commission on Mass Media of the National Council of Churches, namely a direct appeal to the producers to live up more responsibly to their own codes of production. A second is for these producers to take the control of their programs out of the hands of advertisers, who have a large voice in them, and to sell these gentlemen space on the air, just as do the newspapers, which would not dream of letting advertisers control the content of their columns. A third is the more radical move of establishing government-supported radio and television networks with no

296

advertising at all and controlled by a commission of experts in public education and entertainment. This is the system in Britain. After observing the way it works there, I confess that I have largely lost my fear of such government control.

Perhaps the most general danger from our mass media, however, is not violence but vulgarity. That fine critic and scholar Gilbert Murray, in a lecture at Oxford in the thirties, said some things about moving pictures that he would probably repeat today of their successor, the television screen. "The greatest disseminator of ideas today is the cinema. It alone overleaps boundaries of nationality, language and colour. It is expensive to produce; and the film that will appeal to the minimum human intellect will drive out of the market the film that needs some thought or culture for its appreciation." Norman Angell noted "the operation of a psychological Gresham's Law; just as in commerce debased coin, if there be enough of it, must drive out the sterling, so in the contest of motives, action which corresponds to the more primitive feelings and impulses, to first thoughts and established prejudices, can be stimulated far more easily than that prompted by rationalized second thought."

Thus the prescription for success is to produce what can be responded to without effort by everyone. This was interestingly confirmed by Edgar Rice Burroughs of Tarzan fame. He wrote: "It has been discovered through repeated experiments that pictures that require thought for appreciation have invariably been box office failures. The general public does not wish to think. This fact, probably more than any other," he went on with charming frankness, "accounts for the success of my stories. . . . I have evolved a type of fiction that may be read with the minimum of mental effort"; and he added that his books sold over a million copies a year.

If we ask what kind of scenes everyone can respond to without effort, the answer is: actions that embody feeling and impulse directly, without being sicklied over by any self-criticism or reflection. Everybody knows what anger is, and has had dreams of doing someone down with Jack Dempsey decisiveness; everyone's blood can be more or less congealed by skilfully contrived horrors, or his sex imaginings set in motion by artfully evocative scenes.

But civilized living consists not in giving these raw impulses

297

rein but in restraining and moulding them to meet the shifting ex-
actions of life. Stories that do this need not be in the least highbrow,
but because they involve a degree more of sophistication than "The
Lone Ranger," they are passed over for some escape from actuality
into the primitive West or the South Seas, where the lowest common denominator of mankind can have uninhibited sway. The
values that emerge are not necessarily vicious or criminal; they are
just twisted and vulgarized in the direction of moronia. Their major
premises are of the sort that appeal to the junior filling station
attendant and the girl behind the counter in the chain store—this
sort of principle for example: that a proper he-man will always be
ready to deal with slights by an expert and soporific left to the chin;
that romantic love, particularly if at first sight, has the right of way
over everything else, including common sense; that the American
wherever he goes will show a natural superiority to "lesser breeds
without the law"; that money is good in itself; that excitement is
good in itself; that the only really interesting time of life is youth.
These ideas are not wicked; they are merely adolescent; and their
continual reiteration tends to prevent us from growing up. "The
chief rival of goodness," Dr. Fosdick said, "is not badness in itself,
but the attractive spectacle of lives powerfully organized on low
levels."

Here I come to my second thesis, that if we are to be ourselves,
we must escape these levels and escape them we can. How are we
to do it? Young people are trying out many routes of escape.
College chaplains have noted an increased interest in religion,
though when they see how readily it can be channeled into Zen
Buddhism, the strange behavior of the "Jesus Freaks," the
"transcendental meditation" of visiting Indian gurus, or even into
hashish dreams, their rejoicing is somewhat tempered. In the
theological schools, the ghost of that melancholy Dane, Søren
Kierkegaard, walks again; and existentialism, with its suspicion of
reason and its stress on commitment of the will, is having a heyday.
It is of course no new thing to be irrational; what is relatively new is
to be irrational and proud of it.

J. D. Salinger is sometimes pointed to as the literary pioneer of
disillusioned youth, who caught their temper as well as their idiom
in *The Catcher in the Rye*. The hero is a not unattractive

seventeen-year-old boy who has a favorite word for nearly everything and everybody, namely, "phony." All the plays and movies he sees are phony; his school and its teachers are phony; sports are phony; businessmen are phony; he wanders about, lost in a phony civilization. Many readers find acute discernment here. But if you are to call things phony, you must have some ground of your own to stand on, and this young man has nothing to stand on except a few vague likes and a vast repertory of detestations. He cannot think, and would probably regard one who organized his life by thought as another phony; he is headed nowhere; he drifts about on capricious currents of impulse. This is his way of escaping the universal phoniness without and the boredom within. But, of course, he does not escape. Sir Herbert Read has remarked that "nothing in the end is so wearisome as idiosyncrasy and waywardness." We do not escape by retreating into our own impulses. We must be able to look up and see the stars occasionally, with the hope that we can some day find one to which we can hitch our little wagon.

Here we come to the major paradox about conformity. None of us wants to be a mere stereotype; we want to be ourselves. But there is a kind of conformity that is the very condition of being ourselves. The achievement of admiration for someone else is the first step in self-discovery. "Genius," said the philosopher A. E. Taylor, "is rare and unique receptiveness." It is well, perhaps, to forget about being original. "Originality," said Fitzjames Stephen, "consists in thinking for ourselves, not in thinking differently from other people." And "to think for yourself," said the anthropologist Marrett, "does not mean that in the long run you will be likely to think differently from those who have taken most trouble to seek the truth." "It is better," said Francis James Child, the Harvard English professor, "to show a student the old ideas than to send him hunting for some miserable little idea of his own. I might say to my students, 'Shakespeare is a good writer; but then a little play of your own, you know!' "

One of the most original of British thinkers, F. H. Bradley, said near the close of his life, "If I had been able to learn more from others, I should have had more of a claim to being called original." I like to think of the essay by Pater on one of the greatest of artists,

Raphael. Raphael achieved his mastery, says Pater, by going about from one studio to another of the leading artists of his time, and with his humble and admiring openness of mind assimilating the best that each could give him, so that by the time he was thirty he was standing on their shoulders and outpainting them all.

Of course, this is an unusual kind of conformity. It is conformity to an ideal community as a means of escaping conformity to an actual one. We forget sometimes how large the spiritual community is that we can live in if we choose. It includes not only the best minds of the present but the best minds of the past. We can actually have them as counsellors and companions for the asking. "The true university," said Carlyle, "is a collection of books," and that is a university in which the poorest of us can enroll.

Why enroll in this or in any university? One reason is that unless we do, we may never find out who we really are. "Most people," said Oscar Wilde, "are other people. Their thoughts are someone else's opinions, their lives a mimicry, their passions a quotation." Now if there is nothing distinctive in you, perhaps the best thing *is* to resign yourself to being a shadow or echo. But this is almost certainly untrue. There is nobody in the world with exactly your combination of impulses, interests, and powers. Each of us is unique. I am myself a twin; for twenty years my brother and I were inseparable, and our exposures to life almost identical, but we have taken very different roads and have always been in some ways inscrutable to each other. The richest life for each person lies in the development of the unique union of faculties that is his; "Our aims," said Emerson, "should be mathematically adjusted to our powers." Each one of us has duties and possibilities that differ from those of every other living person, or indeed of anyone who has ever lived. As F. L. Lucas says, "Every person one passes in the street is a universe walking on two feet."

Now an essential point in the strategy of the good life is how to use the capital made available to us by others in a manner truly our own. The tragedy for most of us is that pressures brought to bear on us by the necessities of earning a living, or by parental insistence, or by the conventions of our community, or by our own apathy turn us into stereotypes. By becoming such, we forfeit the larger selves we might have been, the happiness we might have achieved, and the gift to the world we might have made.

One of the main purposes of a college education is to extend the time and widen the field for self-discovery. It enables us to try ourselves out. Does our written work show a native turn for style? When we do equations, or study a new language, is there an out-of-the-way facility? In public or private debate, is there something in our statement of the case that makes others want to listen? Is it in talk with our fellows, or strumming the piano, or reading Shelley, or kneeling in church, or studying government, that we seem to be most ourselves? If we can answer such questions confidently, we should follow the light they afford us.

Too often the course of our lives is determined not by authentic light but by outward accidents. I recall vividly how as an entering freshman at the University of Michigan some fifty years ago, I was uncertain whether to register in Greek or mathematics. In a big room with advisers at scattered tables, I sought out my assigned adviser and put the problem to him. He happened to be the chairman of the department of Greek. He no doubt tried to be judicial, but I ended by taking Greek. Two or three years later a scholarship to Oxford was advertised, open only to those who knew Greek, and as this requirement at once eliminated all the stronger competitors, the opportunity came my way. The decision made under that accidental advice on that remote autumn afternoon turned the current of a life. I cite it as an example of the way *not* to make such decisions.

It was shrewdly observed by Walter Rathenau that "a man must be strong enough to mould the peculiarity of his imperfections into the perfection of his peculiarities." He may have to make the niche into which he will fit. To many a young man and woman the possibilities seem to be few and fixed—he can be a doctor, a lawyer, a nurse, a minister, a teacher; he has himself all but pigeonholed already. The chances are that he should not be any of these, or that if he should, he should with a difference. The perception of this difference may give direction to his life.

I do not want to suggest that this process of self-discovery is always easy or pleasant. The youth, having read something about geniuses and their meteoric ways, may suppose that if he has a real gift it will show itself effortlessly and of its own accord; he will dash off something some day that will open people's eyes, including his own. Things seldom happen in that way. His real gift may show

301

itself only through a sustained process of trial and error. Even Bernard Shaw had a long list of rejection slips from publishers before he found his true vein.

Gwen Reverat, in her delightful book of memories called *Period Piece*, recalls overhearing in her youth scraps of conversation about "that foolish young man, Ralph Vaughan Williams," who *would* go on working at music when he was "so hopelessly bad at it." From a letter of her aunt she quotes: "He has been playing all his life, and for six months hard, and yet he can't play the simplest thing decently. They say it will simply break his heart if he is told that he is too bad to hope to make anything of it." Well, Vaughan Williams did make something of it. One hopes that aunt was still about when he was awarded the Order of Merit as Britain's greatest living composer.

To be sure, it is hardly fair to take as examples undiscourageable and authentic geniuses who must have known that they were not as other people. The real difficulty comes when you are good, but perhaps not good enough. The best course then is to take counsel with someone whose judgment you respect and insist that he be honest with you. Teachers have a special responsibility here, and one that they have often betrayed—as I am sure I have—by well-meant encouragement that led to false hopes. Our graduate schools, said William James, are filled with the bald-headed and bald-hearted who are the ruins of excellent farmers.

And the courage to accept defeat may be as important as the courage to go on. I know a young man who is convinced that he has the makings of a philosopher and has spent many years and nearly all his limited means in trying to make himself one. I feel virtually certain that even if he gained a teaching post he could not hold it, and I have spent hours in the attempt to dissuade him without disheartening him. He will not be dissuaded, and he is headed, I fear, for stubborn and needless ruin. My young friend's problem is going to crop up again in thousands of cases in the near future. Going to college and looking for a white-collar job afterward have themselves become matters of conformity. What used to be an expression of exceptional ability and ambition is now done because everybody does it. The danger of this policy, as Douglas Bush has pointed out, is that education for everyone may prove to be education for no one. If the colleges lower their standards to a point where they can take in the general population, they will no longer be institutions of higher learning. Furthermore, they will litter the landscape with unemployed and disgruntled B.A.'s. In 1900 only about 4 percent of the people of college age went to college. It is reported that four-fifths of our young people now aspire to high-level jobs, though there are not nearly enough of these jobs to go round. That means that a very large number of young men and women must find their work, and find themselves, in new ways.

We have been considering the need of escape from conformity into what may be called authenticity in the choosing of one's work. But there is another kind of conformity that is apt to settle down on us after our work is chosen. There is a great deal in anyone's work, if faithfully done, that seems utterly unexpressive of his special powers; and conformity to the routine of his task may be felt as far more galling than any pressure on his thought or taste. Sometimes indeed it seems soul-destroying. How often I have sat at night with my red ink and pile of papers, and wondered whether my eyes and soul could take this punishment indefinitely. The housewife, after doing her hundred thousandth dish, goes wearily to sleep and dreams of leaping from dish to dish down an interminable river of dishes. The postman and the milkman on their weary rounds, the accountant with his endless figures, find themselves straitjacketed; is there any sense in talking to these persons of individuality when to keep themselves and their families afloat they must take jobs whose dull routine shrivels their souls?

About this there are several things to say. For one thing, if conformity means coercion by the conditions of our task, we shall never escape it, and it is idle to try. There is an enormous amount of drudgery in any life that really counts. Carlyle thought the best chance of happiness lay in forgetting about it and making work the substance of one's life; happiness might then come as an uncovenanted blessing. Work in college should be hard enough to prepare us for the inevitable later yoke; as Mr. Eliot says, "No one can become really educated without having pursued some study in which he took no interest." "Power to drudge at distasteful tasks," said James Martineau, "is the test of faculty, the price of knowledge, and the mother of duty." "Blessed be drudgery" has been suggested by an eminent divine as a new beatitude. Perhaps that goes too far. But it is safe to say that the young man or woman who is too soft to accept a full quota of drudgery will not leave much of a mark anywhere.

Secondly, there is no sharp line between art and play on the one hand, which are supposed to be self-expressive, and work on the other. The difference lies in the inner stance. Games, if one hates them, as some who play professionally do, are work; work, if one can come to like it, may be play. Art has been defined as anything done with a passion for perfection in its execution, and on these terms there is no work that cannot be converted in some measure into art; indeed the field of the housewife seems to give an exceptional latitude for it.

Thirdly, the compulsions of our work are being progressively lightened by leisure. The worker of earlier times, who had to do his twelve hours a day, might well complain that his task was soul-destroying. Few have to live so now. The eight-hour day and the five-day week promise to be whittled still further, and the problem of how to get work is often replaced by the strange new problem of how to use the leisure our work affords. Even if one is cramped and confined for eight hours of one's day, the other sixteen may be so used as to be emancipating. My old tutor, Harold Joachim, was an excellent scholar and thinker, with high academic ambitions; he was also a nephew of Joseph Joachim, the violinist, and had musical goals of his own; he ended, with good sense, by being a professor of logic in the daytime and an admirable violinist in the evening. Grote's great history of Greece was planned and largely executed in the off-hours of a banker. For most of the day, Charles Dodgson did mathematics, but in his free times he turned into Lewis Carroll and went off through the looking glass with Alice. Charles Lamb wrote *Elia* in his spare hours from the India House; Wallace Stevens wrote his poems after leaving his desk as an insurance executive in Hartford; Mrs. Trollope, Anthony's mother, wrote many books in the hours of the early morning before her day as wife and mother began. We do not need to be figures of this heroic mould to use leisure to our enrichment. A hobby may be a safety valve or a balance wheel that keeps the engine running smoothly.

And so to my fourth and last consideration. There is a kind of conformity which is in one sense slavery and in another the highest freedom, the kind that St. Paul was thinking of when he said that he was most free when he was most a slave. The mathematician who is at his clearest and best is not free; his impulses are kept in abeyance, his thoughts channeled along the groove of necessity by the logic of his problem; but since to think straight is what he wants above all to do, he does not feel harried and confined by the laws of logic.

It is not only in thought but in action also that conformity to reason is a paramount obligation. Duty is not an alien taskmaster, but, as Kant said, the prescription of one's self at its reasonable best. An action done because one sees one ought to do it is free in a sense in which no action done from impulse is free. And the humblest sort of service may rank high on this scale; "Who sweeps a room as to thy laws," says George Herbert, "makes that and the action fine." Of this kind of conformity we can never have too much. If I do not say that it is the great need of our time, it is only because it is also the great need of every time. Conformity to reason is the only conformity of which one need never be ashamed, the only conformity that will not at some point lead one wrong. We need more individuality, to be sure, thought not of the kind that consists in indulging vagrant impulse, of which there is always more than enough. What is needed is that rarer kind which achieves meaning and richness and order by surrendering itself to the guidance of that inward light which is at its best the voice of reason speaking through us. We come round here to an ancient truth about conformity which, A. E. Housman remarked, was the profoundest discovery yet made about the spiritual life, that he who loses his life shall find it.

# 18

## *Serenity*

Serenity is not a typical American state of mind, and it is one that we are finding it harder and harder to achieve. A visiting British psychiatrist has described us as "the most worried people in the world." Many of the reasons for this unease of mind are obvious enough: the increasing complexity of American life, its strenuous competitiveness, the congestion and noise of our cities, the unrest of youth and its revolt against established ways of living, the ferment among the underprivileged, the fading of the utopian dream that has sustained so much of our history. However we came by our restlessness and lack of serenity, it remains a notorious fact. The Chesebrough-Pond's Company, which developed the first eight-hour aspirin tablet, has reported that Americans consume about thirty-seven tons of aspirin a day.

Complaints of the over-tension of American life may be growing louder, but they are so far from new as to suggest that this state belongs to our way of life. Visitors from abroad have been pointing it out for many decades. The Scottish alienist Dr. Clouston told us bluntly a century ago: "You Americans wear too much expression on your faces. You are living like an army with all its reserves engaged in action. The duller countenances of the British population betoken a better scheme of life. . . . This inexcitability, this presence at all times of a power not used, I regard as the great safeguard of our British people. The other thing in you gives me a sense of insecurity, and you ought somehow to tone yourselves down." Herbert Spencer's farewell address after an American tour was on "the gospel of relaxation" as a kind of evangel of which we stood in special need. William James, after spending much time abroad, supported Dr. Clouston and scolded his countrymen for the rate of their breakdowns, saying that in his view the cause lay "in those absurd feelings of hurry and having no time, in that breathlessness and tension, that anxiety of feature and that solicitude for results, that lack of inner harmony and ease, in short, by which with us the work is apt to be accompanied, and from which a European who should do the same work would nine times out of ten be free."

It is to be feared that figures would bear out these criticisms. In the last world war a draft board psychiatrist studied a large sample of men who were called but rejected for army service. He found that although rejections for mental instability were not alarmingly high for boys of eighteen and nineteen—about one in twenty—they amounted to nearly half the rejections of men over forty. Dr. George D. Stoddard has reported that "in the United States there are as many hospital beds assigned to mental patients as to all others put together," and that "for every hospital case there are ten others whose retreat from reality, while not dangerous or occupationally disabling, is nevertheless a liability." Charles E. Jefferson remarked: "If licentiousness is the sin of France, and drunkenness is the sin of England, surely anxiety is the sin of America."

Because tension and anxiety are epidemic in America, a spate of recipes has been offered us over the years for equanimity of mind. Joshua Liebman's *Peace of Mind,* with its appeal to depth psychology, sold over 650,000 copies; Fulton Sheen's *Peace of Soul* and Norman Vincent Peale's *Power of Positive Thinking,* with their appeals to religious faith, must have been not far behind. The New Thought told us that we should fix our attention on the blessings and beauties of existence. Christian Science tells us that the evils that alarm us, even pain, disease, and death, are mere seemings which will change their character if only we change our views about them. Dr. Jacobson tells us in his useful books on relaxation that the way to get rid of mental tensions is to get rid of muscular tensions, and prescribes useful exercises to that end. Aldous Huxley suggested that we learn the secret of serenity from the mystics of the East, and help ourselves out by judicious doses of the potent drug mescalin. Many found aid in the autosuggestion preached by M. Emil Coué on his memorable visit to this country, assuring themselves each morning that every day and in every way they were getting better and better. Many others have appealed with profit to a mixture in various proportions of Freud and faith, for example, Dr. Worcester and his Emmanuel movement and Dr. Leslie Weatherhead of London, who successfully made his ministry a ministry of healing.

Every one of these prescriptions has had its successes, and like the church of St. Anne de Beaupré, which I visited not long ago, can display its piles of discarded crutches in imposing array. Yet no one of them seems to be quite what we want. The trouble is partly that of the ancient sailor who, visiting the temple of Neptune, was shown the walls covered with the votive tablets of those who in storms at sea had invoked Neptune's aid and been saved. "Where are the tablets," asked the sailor, "of those who, after pleading for aid, were lost?" and of the answer there is no record. If these methods have their successes, they also have too many failures. Nor is there much use in telling us that the secret of a serene spirit is to embrace a set of ideas that to us seems impossible. In such a case the cure may be worse than the disease. Even peace of mind comes too high if bought at the price of intellectual integrity. Dean Inge put the case with characteristic force: "For my own part, I will have nothing to do with this world of make-believe . . . I believe that my reason was given to me that I may know things as they are . . . I will not tell myself that in all respects I am getting better and younger and handsomer every day. If I can help it, I will play no tricks with my soul, in the faith that though bluff may sometimes pay very well in this world, it will cut a very poor figure in the next."

It may be said that the causes that destroy our serenity are of a thousand and one kinds, and that each of these kinds may have its own remedy. It is no doubt true that the special circumstances that destroy your peace of mind are never the same as mine. Still, the ways in which these circumstances break us, and the ways in which they are successfully resisted seem to have certain standard patterns which study in recent decades has brought to light and on which there would now be fairly general agreement among psychologists. Lack of serenity has many occasions, but the causal patterns that it shows are comparatively few. Let us see what are its principal roots, then pass on to the practical question how to eradicate them.

Students of mind since the turn of the century have been moving toward a view of human nature that some of them think new but that in principle is as old as Aristotle. According to this view, a mind is a set of drives or impulses such that the nature of man can be understood only in the light of their ends; a man *is* a partial embodiment of what he is trying to become. This was the view of Aristotle; the modern advance consists of a better classification of the drives and a minuter knowledge of their working. Three types of instinctive drives are now commonly recognized—the drive toward self-preservation with such subordinate impulses as hunger, thirst, and the avoidance of danger; the drive toward continuance of the race, with its subordinate instincts of sex and parental care; and the drive toward unity with one's group, with its tendencies toward sympathy, suggestibility, and imitation. These drives would seem to be inborn; they are all fundamental in the sense that a person who lacked any of them would be a monster; and in the normal man they are powerful moving forces. Indeed his life consists of a continuing effort to satisfy them. So long as they are satisfied harmoniously, his life will flow along peaceably like a deep, full river. If any of them is denied fulfilment, the dammed-up waters will begin to chafe at their banks. If their demands conflict with each other, the current may be broken up into a set of impotent trickling streams. In either case the energy of one's mind will be blocked, and one will fail of one's ends, so that there will be a painful sense of frustration. Now it is this sense of frustration that for the seeker of serenity is the root of all evil. Let us see more particularly how it arises.

When we lose our peace of mind, the immediate cause is usually an emotion, and an emotion that is some variety of fear or anger. Both these emotions are symptoms of frustration. Fear is specially connected with the first of our great drives, the impulse to preserve ourselves, and may be aroused by any threat to our life, health, or possessions. Anger has a still broader base; it may be produced by the flouting of any of our instincts; the man is rare who can keep his equanimity when his egoistic interests are thwarted, as by a direct insult, or when his sex instincts are blocked, as by a rival who cuts him out in courtship, or when his gregarious impulses are spurned, as by the blackball of a group he wants to join. To be sure, we must not suppose that feeling as such is the foe of serenity; in positive emotions like the delight in knowledge, the joy in beauty, or the love of our fellows, there is clearly nothing at odds with our peace of mind. It is this pair of negative emotions that breeds the poison. There can be no serenity in the mind that is quivering with fear or constantly exploding in anger. Let us turn our thought, then, to the nature of fear and anger, and the means of dealing with them.

As for fear, which we shall be concerned with chiefly, it is the deepest of all emotions, if we measure depth by length of lineage. It is the obverse side of the will to live itself; the psychologist Stanley Hall remarked that "consciousness itself is incipient anxiety." Although the animal mind grows more and more remote from us as we go down the animal scale, we seem to know something of how the fawn feels as it runs from the dogs, how the fish feels as it struggles wildly on the hook, how the hen feels as it takes cover from the circling hawk, perhaps even dimly how the fly feels as the spider bears down on it in the web. Such comparatively superficial things as the sense of humor we inherit from some thousands of generations; fear we inherit from millions. Fear, therefore, is rooted not only in human nature but in that animal nature in which human nature itself is now known to be rooted. We may be sure that there is no such thing as a "fearless" person, though people vary greatly in the things they are afraid of and in the degree of their fear of them. Dr. Johnson, brave man as he was, admitted that he was terribly afraid of death, and I suppose nearly every honest person would say the same. Perhaps not quite all. There seem to be a few who have mastered their fear even of this last enemy. When Gilbert Chesterton was in this country, he told a story about Frederick Faber, the Victorian author of those fine old hymns "Faith of Our Fathers, Living Faith" and "There's a Wideness in God's Mercy Like the Wideness of the Sea." Faber was seriously ill, but able to listen to a friend sitting at his bedside reading Dickens. His doctor came in, made a quick examination, and looked grave. "Tell me, doctor," said Faber, "how long do you give me?" The doctor hesitated, but seeing whom he had to deal with, said, "I should guess, Dr. Faber, about an hour." "Then," said Faber to his friend, "you can read me another chapter of Dickens."

But most of us are not built on these almost incredible lines. The discovery that our heart is weak, that our bank has failed, that we are to lose our job, even the knowledge that we must make a speech tomorrow, may throw us into a panic of palpitating agitation. And naturally, too. If we are beings with normal feelings, we cling to our life and our means and our work and our good name, and we should be hardly human if we could look on indifferently while they were threatened or destroyed. Here comes my second point about fear: we cannot sensibly deal with it by trying to root out feeling altogether. There lay the weakness of that great philosophy of serenity called Stoicism. This philosophy produced two of the most impressive examples in history of an unshakable serenity, one of them the slave Epictetus, whom even the abuse of a cruel master could never perturb, the other the emperor Marcus Aurelius, who carried with equal calm the headship of the civilized world. It was the teaching of the Stoics that since the universe is governed by reason, we should acquiesce in that reason; as Aurelius put it, "Everything is fruit to me which thy seasons bring, O Nature." But what if our feeling rebels against what nature brings? What if it cries out in fear in the face of danger, and gives way to its grief at the loss of those it loves? Then, said the Stoics, feeling must be dealt with firmly. Fear and sorrow come because we have formed emotional attachments that we do not want to have broken. The cure is to get rid of the attachments, for then we can lose their objects and not care. These things cannot be of importance anyhow, or nature would not so readily take them away. The true sage, therefore, will be passionless, accepting with equal readiness the sunshine and the storm. No one can study the great Aurelius without seeing that this doctrine did actually work, and that it could produce minds of extraordinary self-mastery and poise.

But gradually it became clear that the Stoic sage had achieved his serenity at too high a cost. Because negative feelings were so perturbing, he tried to banish feeling altogether, failing to see that in doing so he was throwing out the goods of life along with its evils. "If you kiss your little child or your wife," says Epictetus, "say that it is a human being whom you are kissing, for when either of them dies, you will not be disturbed." That is not true serenity, but a desperate artificial apathy, which would sacrifice love itself in order to procure freedom from pain. To be happy and serene is not to be horny-hearted. The path to serenity lies not, as the Stoics thought, through the death of feeling, which would be death to all good too, but through the control of our negative feelings while the positive are kept, if possible, in warmth and freshness.

But thirdly, even the negative feelings should not be simply driven out. Nature would not have made fear as strong and universal as it is if it served no useful purpose. Most animals seem to spend their lives largely in fear; think of the squirrel that comes timidly down for a nut, keeps a nervous lookout, and dashes madly for the tree again if anyone comes near. Think of the cat looking warily for the dog, and the mouse creeping about in fear of the cat. And think how long the life of mouse or cat or squirrel would be without its fear. Think how long the life of a man would be—or rather a boy, since he would never become a man—who had no fear of high places, speeding cars, fires, or firearms. A perfectly fearless person, if one ever existed, would have been eliminated so quickly as to leave none of his queer descendants behind; his strain would die out because it would be hopelessly maladjusted to the world it had to live in. Fear is the insurance we pay for safety. There are some things we ought to be afraid of. The problem, then, is to dispense not with all fears, but with the needless and crippling fears.

Very well; how are we to do that? There is one answer that a great many people would put first, and which I, too, may be expected to put first because it is a remedy, proved and powerful, for every kind of fear. This is religious faith. The man who not merely repeats, but believes in the marrow of his bones, as Jesus did and as St. Francis did, that God is "nearer to us than breathing, closer than hands and feet," that he is hovering over us, noting every sparrow's fall, yearning over the least of us with a father's forgiving love, able as lord of the universe to see that all things work together for our good—the man who accepts that with heart as well as mind has in his hands the most effective of all remedies against fear. It would be stupid and silly of him to be afraid; what is there to be afraid of? If

313

he knows that he is living in the anteroom to heaven, he need no more be afraid than a boy in his father's house. This childlike trust was the open secret of men like Frederick Faber; they lived in the quiet conviction that "God's completeness flows round our incompleteness, round our restlessness his rest," and their prescription for all human disquiet would be the simple one implied in that line of Augustine: "Our hearts are restless till they rest in thee." I repeat that there is no remedy for fear as efficient as this. And yet I am not going to stress it because there are many of us for whom it is not available, and I should like to say something helpful even for them. Indeed one of the causes for our disquiet is that this faith has become for so many impossible. For them, science and philosophy have so changed the character of their world as well as the position of their church and the authority of their scriptures that to prescribe such faith as if it were something they could have for the asking is to be unimaginative or even cynical. Granting the advantages of an unquestioning faith that "God's in his heaven, all's right with the world," one can hardly offer these advantages to an intellectually honest man as a ground for believing such things. A large majority of our fellow men and a large minority of our fellow Americans stand outside the Christian faith, so that if this faith were the only source of true serenity, their position would be hopeless. I do not think it is, because there are other ways of conquering fears. I want now to suggest four of these.

First, there is the method of thought, the method of facing reflectively what we are afraid of and thereby putting it in perspective. Many fears are rooted in a childish egotism. A palpitation in the chest, a speech that fails to come off, the absence of a hoped-for letter, may loom so large as to blot out the sun. This is a failure in one's sense of humor, which is in essence a sense of propriety and proportion. Bertrand Russell says that he used to be in terror at having to give a speech, but that a very simple device went far to remove his fear. He asked himself what difference it would make a hundred years hence even if the speech were a complete failure, and at the obvious answer, "None," he found his lightness of heart returning. Emerson speaks of attending a meeting where tempers were ruffled and hot words flew, and then going out and looking up at the quiet stars. They seemed to look at him reprovingly as if to say, "Why so hot, little man?" Wordsworth, the most serene of

314

poets, reminds us that our noisy years are only moments in the eternal silence. It takes us long to learn that lesson. What makes the trials of childhood so severe is that the child cannot see them for what they are. His toy is broken; for the time being that toy was his whole world, and with its breaking his world is in ruins. Some of us live thus in the passing moment all our lives. We need the long range of reflective maturity; we need to take our eyes off the moment's worries, to lift them up to the hills, to dwell on the great things in order that the little things may be seen in scale. Some rare spirits seem to do this effortlessly. Emerson says that the great man is one who in the midst of society is able to keep the sweetness of solitude. The Quakers have known better than most people this secret of lonely visits for refreshment to high altitudes. But if the ascent is too much for us by ourselves, there are many who can help us. A little time repeatedly spent with one of those ample and serene minds whose writings can now be had by anyone, preferably a writer we have found to speak to our condition, would bring rich dividends for a small investment.

Sometimes when a reflective regard is turned on the objects of our fears, they simply dissolve. Bunyan describes in *Pilgrim's Progress* how Christian's path was beset by grotesque and alarming shapes that scuttled threateningly about in the shifting mists. When the sun came out, the sinister monsters proved to be tiny, pitiful, squeaking creatures, too feeble to hurt a child. So it often is. Lord Beaconsfield said that the worst things that had ever happened to him were things that had never happened. The person who is terrified of ghosts is likely enough to be visited by them, while the ghosts have a way of avoiding those who are sturdily skeptical of them. The man who has to face a new job, or to live on a reduced income, or to go unwillingly into retirement often proceeds on the principle of the ancient mapmakers: where a region is uncharted, there place terrors. If before peopling the unfamiliar places with spectres, he could get himself to look at them quietly and adjust himself to them in thought, he might well find that the spectres were of his own devising. He need only stare them down.

This method of meeting the enemy boldly in thought seems to be effective even with the great and final enemy. Much fear of death in the past has been due to apprehension of what might follow; Dr. Johnson's fear of death seems to have been due in large

315

part to his conviction of sin and of the dreadful possibility that he might be damned. It is a curious fact that while religion has been the chief source of serenity for many, there are types of religion that have invested death with such terror as to make peace of mind impossible; Epicurus tried to weaken religious belief in the very interest of serenity. Looked at in itself, he said, there was nothing to fear in death; indeed it was an event that no one ever experienced; as long as we are here, death is not, and when death is here, we are not; why then be afraid? That his philosophy took effect in his own life is suggested by a letter of his that has come down to us. "On this truly happy day of my life," he wrote, "as I am at the point of death, I write this to you. The disease in my bladder and stomach is pursuing its course, lacking nothing of its natural severity; but against all this is the joy in my heart at the recollection of my conversation with you." Epicurus' insistence that in death itself there is little to fear found support from the great physician Sir William Osler. "Most human beings," he said, "not only die like heroes, but in my wide clinical experience, die really without pain or fear. There is as much oblivion about the last hours as about the first, and therefore men fill their minds with spectres that have no reality." The attitude alike of the ancient philosopher and the modern physician was finely expressed by Walter Savage Landor:

> Death stands above me, whispering low
> I know not what into my ear:
> Of his strange language all I know
> Is, there is not a word of fear.

Now for a second method. Just as there are evils that we can dispel by thinking about them till we see them in their true dimensions, so there are others that are best dealt with by refusing to think about them at all. The world, to be sure, is full of misery. There are millions of animals suffering dumbly, countless children who are being maltreated, men raging their hearts out in prisons, men wasting away in slave labor camps. If we can do anything about these ills, there is a point in dwelling on them till we do it. If we can do nothing about them, we are not called upon to wring our hands impotently and add these persons' miseries to our own. So of the people around us. There may be enough meanness, stupidity, and callousness in them to furnish food for the most malicious appetite. "If you believe the doctors," said Lord Salisbury,

316

"nothing is wholesome; if you believe the theologians, nothing is innocent; if you believe the soldiers, nothing is safe"; and some people manage to combine the apprehensions of all these classes; negative thinking, negative speech has become a habit with them. This habit may itself be the product of fear, the fear of being thought naive and a Pollyanna; it seems somehow more "realistic" to see through people and perceive what selfish, shallow puppets they all are than to find them sensible, sane, and lovable. Some of the American writers who in recent years have caught the ear of the world delight in drawing characters that are twisted, sodden, or sadistic. The poet Heine once said that modern literature is one vast hospital; he could have said it with more truth if he were writing now. With the efficient help of our movie industry America seems to be moving toward an ideal of character in which a hard-jawed, grim-faced, two-fisted, suspicious, quick-on-the-trigger Bogart or Cagney or Brando gives the type. No doubt these hard-boiled fighting types are more dramatic than the quiet and kindly people, but the truth about them is that they are adolescent nuisances, unhappy and maladjusted themselves, and with a genius for making others unhappy. We need less drama and more sense in our popular ideal of character. The man who is merely thoughtful, just, and kind is worth a dozen of these pistol-packing misfits.

And my present point is that he is far happier and more content. That shrewd observer Arnold Bennett wrote that "the secret of calm cheerfulness is kindliness; no person can be consistently cheerful and calm who does not consistently think kind thoughts." Such a person is like a magnet that draws the precious metals from the things and people around him, letting the dross go. He knows that there is ugliness in plenty, but since his mind is more in tune with beauty, it beats in harmony with that. He would not dream of denying that there is evil in the world, but he sees no reason why a man, like a dog that has smelt carrion, should hunt it out and roll in it; he prefers to think no evil, and therefore not to talk about it either. We have probably all met persons whose presence leaves us feeling shrunken, mean, and out of sorts with ourselves, yet not knowing quite why; it is as if the person had an eye for our worst side and a gift for making us expose it. We have met other persons who have left us in a glow because they found so quickly and eagerly our little points of interest or distinction. A. C. Benson, in a memoir of his uncle Henry Sidgwick, the great Cambridge philosopher and scholar, cites a pretty case of this in two or three sentences:"I remember a party at Cambridge," he writes, "at which a lady was present whom it was thought desirable to ask, but who was little used to social functions. She suffered at first from obvious nervousness; but it fell to Henry Sidgwick to take her in to dinner, and he began to talk to her at once about the education of her children. The bait proved incredibly successful: it was probably the only subject in the world on which she had both views and experience; and she left the house with the manifest consciousness of having had an agreeable evening, having held her own with an eminent man, and having appeared in the light of a brilliant educational theorist, with the additional advantage of having been enabled to put her theories to a practical test." That habit of Sidgwick's, which was also a habit of William James, of seeking and seeing the best in others is not only a source of light but also a source of inward and outward peace.

I just mentioned William James, and will go on to borrow my third suggestion from him. You may recall that James held an interesting and novel theory about emotions. He held that in the presence of certain objects, we instinctively reacted in certain ways. If a man saw a grizzly bear in his path, his limbs would probably tremble, his hair stand up, his eyes dilate, his forehead break out in sweat, and he would make a wild break for safety. Now the emotion of fear, said James, *is* simply the feeling of these bodily reactions. Hence if the reaction can be controlled, the fear can be controlled. The truth, he said, is not so much that we run because we are afraid, as that we are afraid because we run. It follows that if we were to act in all details *as if* we had no fear, we should in fact *have* no fear. Most psychologists do not go all the way with James. Still, there is instructive truth in his theory. If our bodily behavior reflects our state of mind, our state of mind tends also to reflect our bodily behavior. The person who is shy in company to the point of misery should try James's prescription of resolutely acting as if he did not know what self-consciousness meant; he may be surprised at the way it defrosts his heart and tongue. James was an old-fashioned believer in the power of a disciplined will and would have been shocked at the extent to which recent teaching has demanded that feeling and impulse should be indulged; indeed he thought we should do something we didn't like every day to keep our moral muscles from getting flabby. One has been postponing a letter because one hates and dreads having to write it; a little firmness with oneself may turn a haunting reluctance into a minor triumph. One has a disagreeable interview ahead, the very thought of which makes one shrink. One may let oneself brood on the pain and embarrassment of it and crawl up to it in a state of funk that has one half-beaten already. Or one may take the line, Whether I am courageous or not, I am going to approach this thing as if I were. We shall find that the inward man has a surprising way of redeeming the pledges of the outward man.

I turn to a fourth suggestion, as obvious as it is difficult: in the face of the inevitable, we should resign ourselves to it and not go on protesting or fighting against it. Someone speaking of Irishmen has deprecated "the Celtic luxury of scheming against the inevitable." That is a luxury none can afford. Worry is not helpful even when an evil can be averted, and when it can't be averted, it is an especially corrosive kind of futility. There are men who rage and storm when they miss a train, or the car breaks down, or they catch cold and can't go to the office. Such feeling is just what makes clear thought about what to do impossible and so imprisons them more firmly in their helplessness.

It is the men of action who give our most striking examples of the serenity needed here, since they have shown how it can be preserved in the swirl of momentous events. Marshal Joffre of France carried the fate of the West on his shoulders during the First World War; and when it was triumphantly over, some reporters asked him how he had managed to win it. "How . . . did I win the war?" the old soldier mused; "I did it by smoking my pipe. I mean to say, in not getting excited, in reducing everything to its essentials, in avoiding useless emotions, in concentrating all my strength on my job." A perhaps equally impressive example is Mr. Asquith, later Earl of Oxford, the British Prime Minister. Asquith had a precious gift of throwing himself with unstinting effort into a course of action and then accepting with equanimity whatever the result might be. A little incident comes to mind as typical of Asquith's temper. He once had to leave for an important speaking engagement in the north of Britain, and the person who was to drive him to the train failed to arrive. Another car was requisitioned with some difficulty and a frantic race made across country to overtake the train at another station. The only person involved who remained cheerfully serene throughout was Asquith himself. If anxiety would serve no purpose, he would have none of it.

His daughter tells us of being with him on his last political campaign when after an exhausting program of many speeches daily in the depth of a Scottish winter, he had to sit in a dreary room and watch the figures slowly mount which meant his ejection from political life after thirty-eight years in Parliament. When it was all over, he had the agonizing task late at night of addressing his supporters who had planned a victory celebration. "Father spoke to them," writes his daughter, "with perfect fortitude and serenity, and without one touch of bitterness, sentiment, or self-pity. I have never marvelled at him more. His courage is no teeth-set, tight-lipped stoicism, but something much bigger and more natural—a power of seeing events immediately in scale and eliminating his own personal position completely from his perspective. . . . My wounds were healed—for I knew that he was invulnerable."

No doubt this absolute self-command is easier for some temperaments than for others, and as Desmond MacCarthy said of him, Asquith was a man of "Roman *aequanimitas.*" But statesmen with far more heat in their temperament have shown it too—Gladstone for example. He was a restless, pugnacious whirlwind of a man, but like other whirlwinds, he had a point of dead calm at the center, wherever the swirling exterior of his life might take him. The secret in his case was religious. He lived in the spirit of that old prayer whose author is unknown: "God grant me the serenity to accept things I cannot change, the courage to change things I can, and the wisdom to know the difference."

We have now suggested four ways of dealing practically with our fears: thinking them down to scale, keeping our attention off them when we can do nothing useful about them, acting the part of courage, and resigning ourselves to the inevitable. We now have to note that sometimes none of these methods will avail. For what destroys our serenity may have roots that run far down beneath the surface of consciousness where these methods can hardly get at them. There are two principles that will help us understand such cases. One we have already mentioned: that fear is virtually the other side of the instinct of self-preservation, and so is present far down in our own infancy as well as in that of the race. The other is the point made familiar by Freud, that we tend to avoid in memory and conscious thought what is painful and repellent to us. Now suppose that in early life we had an experience of intense fear or shock. Since it is horrible even in retrospect, we do not like to dwell on it. Without consciously trying to put it out of mind, we do so nevertheless. It becomes a "complex," an experience or set of ideas that is heavily charged with emotion, in this case negative emotion, and therefore is involuntarily repressed. We never think of it; we cannot recall it if we try. And yet in some strange sense it is still there, lurking like a poisonous squid in the deep waters of the mind and throwing off an inky cloud that discolors the medium above it. Many persons carry about with them an atmosphere of perpetual apprehension, a chronic state of worry, that has no visible cause whatever. They are physically well; they are successful in their work; they have friends; they seem to have everything they need; and yet they are depressed and irritable. To tell such a person that he is feeling and acting unreasonably may only make him worse; he knows this perfectly well; he tells himself that his fears are groundless and tries to defy them, and still they haunt him like vengeful furies. He cannot get at them, for they are operating from a source unknown and inaccessible to him.

A specific case may help. Dr. W. H. R. Rivers, in his excellent book on *Instinct and the Unconscious*, describes the case of a medical man, aged thirty-one, who came under his care in military service. He was very nervous, slept very badly, had frequent and terrifying dreams, had developed a stammer, and suffered from peculiar fears. For example, he was so uneasy and apprehensive when riding in the subway that he had now refused to use it; when he went to a theater, he was always anxious unless he could sit near the door; when he was riding in a train and passed through a tunnel, he was always frightened unreasonably; when he had to sleep in dugouts during the war, he would get out and walk miserably about in the trenches at considerable risk rather than stay under cover with the others. Strangely enough, he did not know that these fears were exceptional. But he knew that he was most unhappy, and went to a psychoanalyst for help. After two months of treatment he was worse than before. The psychoanalyst told him that the trouble was pretty certainly a repressed sexual experience,

321

so he faithfully hunted for such an experience in his past, though without result.

Dr. Rivers suspected that a repressed memory of some other kind was at the root of his trouble. He told him when next he had a frightening dream to hold on to it on waking and try to recover any memories that might be attached to it. He did so, and little by little, incidents of his childhood that were charged with emotion came back to him. Up to that time the earliest memory of his special kind of dread went back to the age of six when, sleeping next to the wall in a tiny room, with an older brother on the other side of the bed, he had spent many nights of terror. But why should a child be terrified at that? There must have been something further back. He kept searching. Then one morning as he lay musing on a dream from which he had just awakened, a much earlier experience came back to him. At the age of three or four he had paid a visit by himself to an old rag-and-bone merchant of the neighborhood, who had to be reached by opening a door and going down a long dark passage. When the child came out, he found the door at the end of the passage closed, and a growling dog approaching him from behind. Though he was apparently not attacked, an unspeakable, helpless, childish terror had overwhelmed him. Because he had been so frightened, he repressed the experience out of conscious memory, but it had gone on operating from his unconscious mind to invest with its own fearfulness subways, theaters, tunnels, dugouts—anything that even vaguely resembled this primitive situation. With the recovery of the memory, he felt at once that he had reached the root of his anxieties. The fears that haunted him were not genuine fears of anything that now faced him; they were unlaid ghosts of a fear that should have been dead for twenty-seven years. When he was able to enter their den, turn on them the full light of consciousness, and see the incident as the trivial thing it was, the whole range of terrors connected with it vanished.

Of course there are many other types of fears and anxieties. Freud is right that some of these go back to early shocks connected with sex. We know now how powerful this instinct is, and how, if a child is greeted only with a horrified "Hush, hush!" when he talks about it, the whole subject comes to be invested with fascination, furtiveness, and apprehension, and indeed may carry this atmosphere permanently. At other times the trouble is that one has

322

done something that one knows is very wrong, and the hateful memory of it, even though deeply buried, casts a shadow of self-distrust over one's life. The two world wars have produced plenty of cases in which soldiers, after an act of brutality such as the killing of wounded enemies, have lived haunted lives because of it. Sometimes again, the buried complex is the more familiar one of inferiority, growing out of some lack of stature, perhaps, or a defect of looks, with its well-known overcompensation of touchiness and aggressiveness. Sometimes a child that has been unwanted, or that has been orphaned and lacked parental love, will have his sleep disturbed, his mood permanently colored, indeed his whole life pervaded by the resulting sense of insecurity.

Any of these complexes may destroy one's peace of mind. How is one to deal with them? In principle, the answer is simple, even if in carrying it out, expert aid may be necessary. The principle is the old principle of Socrates, "Know thyself." The reason why some minds are not serene is that they are flying from themselves, unconsciously trying to escape by absorption in work or by fast living from the one thing that could bring them peace, namely confronting the source of disturbance squarely and coming to some sort of terms with it. That is what Dr. Rivers's unhappy man did; that is the essential step in the therapy of Freud; its efficacy has now been proved in countless cases. This does not mean that understanding our fears and guilts will dissipate them all; that neither will nor should happen. It does mean that the great dark cloud of morbid and irrational anxiety, which for many persons forms the larger part of their worry, will be dissolved by mere daylight. It means that the energy that has been devoted to keeping a part of ourselves down, to fighting ourselves, refusing to forgive ourselves, unconsciously overasserting ourselves, can be turned into more useful channels. It may well mean the recapture of a lost serenity.

I have been speaking almost entirely of our fears. I cannot close without saying something however briefly of the other great enemy of our peace of mind, namely anger. The two emotions are closely connected; the psychologist George M. Stratton, who wrote a valuable book on this emotion, says that "anger is perhaps never without a tinge of fear; the two are cousins and companions." Both are produced by actual or threatened frustration. If fear therefore is sometimes justified, one would expect anger to be. And surely so it is. The kind of pacifism that would prohibit not only violence but anger is hardly Christian; Jesus himself seems at times to have spoken, as when he denounced certain persons as "whited sepulchers" and "a generation of vipers," in the white heat of indignation. A distinguished expositor of Christian ethics, Canon Rashdall, has said, "To hate the right things, to hate that in persons which is worthy of hatred, is as essential an object of all moral education as to love the right things . . . ," and Carlyle in a letter to Emerson praised what he called "the divine rage against iniquity, falseness and baseness that Ruskin has and that every man ought to have." Nor is there much sense in the doctrine we hear so often that we should hate the sin and not the sinner. Professor Stratton points out that we should see the error of that at once if anyone suggested it about love. "Is one careful to explain to his wife daily," he asks, "that there is nothing personal in his affection for her; that his love is not for her, but for certain qualities in her?" No, anger against persons, like love for persons, seems to be a legitimate and necessary part of the good life.

Yet must we not add at once that it should be a very small part? Anger destroys peace of mind and, four times out of five, perhaps nine out of ten, it is a pointless, profligate waste of energy and happiness. For one thing, it is very commonly a sign of weakness, sheer weakness of the flesh. An eminent psychologist has found a clear connection between anger and the previous incidence of disease, which he summarizes by saying "the more diseases, the more intense the emotion." It is easy enough to have self-control when one is in perfect health, but one tends to fly off the handle after a sleepless night or a missed meal; and if one allows oneself to live in perpetual fatigue, one is probably neither a hero nor a martyr but a domestic and social wet blanket, who needs a sharp reminder that among one's moral duties, because it aids in the doing of all other duties, is the duty of keeping physically fit.

Again, anger is commonly a sign not only of physical but of moral weakness. "Hatred," says Arthur Clutton-Brock, "is fear taking the offensive." Oddly enough, it is not false accusations that anger us most, but those we are afraid are true; and the depth of the irritation marks the extent to which the criticism has gone home.

The man with a Congressional medal who is called a coward can afford to smile. The man who suspects he is a coward will probably be furious; and anger is the desperate offensive he mounts because he feels on the defensive.

Again, just as love breeds love, so anger and hatred breed their kind. Friendliness is always surrounded by friends. There have been people indeed, like Nietzsche, who tried to drum up their hatred of Jesus himself, but even Nietzsche could not quite succeed. Men everywhere loved Albert Schweitzer because all the world loves a lover of his kind. Unhappily there are other men, even great men, who have lived in a perpetual stew of hatreds, jealousies, bitterness, and lost friendships, and have disseminated their own spirit. I am afraid Karl Marx was one. He seems to have hated the bourgeois whom he wanted to destroy more than he loved the proletariat whom he wanted to redeem, and many of his followers have inherited that hatred. And of course this hate is answered by hate. In other parts of the world it is felt that Americans have allowed the red menace to become a bogeyman that haunts and hunts us to the verge of irrationality. There are some countrysides in which the galloping ghost of McCarthy can still be heard of nights.

How is one to get rid of the corroding vice of irritation, anger, and hatred? In principle the answer is clear: as with fear, one must pass the impulse through the alembic of thought. An animal cannot control fear and anger because it cannot think; we can, because we *can* think. But whereas in dealing with fear what we need is self-understanding, in dealing with anger what we need is rather the understanding of others, the perception of how little in their conduct springs from gratuitous malice. Plutarch says that while we become angry for different reasons, the idea of our being neglected or despised is present in nearly all of them. Now we often assume that when people neglect or despise us, they do it of free choice and are being deliberately mean. That is seldom true. William James said it was good practice to assume that one was free oneself and everyone else determined. Illogical as that is, it will remind us that people do not wound us without cause.

There always is a cause. Take the last perpetrator of some savage and brutal assault, look into his desperation about his job, into his distorted ideas, his meagre education, his depressing home, his irregular habits, his shabby companions, and little by little, as understanding comes, we find our anger at what we took to be wanton wrong evaporating; given the man and these conditions, he could hardly have done otherwise; and we begin to see that the old French proverb, "To understand all is to pardon all," is very nearly true. The charitable Charles Lamb was once discussing with a company of friends another person not present when Lamb startled his friends by saying, in his stammering way, "I h-h-hate that fellow." "Why Charles," said one of his friends, "I didn't know that you knew him." "Oh," he said, "I d-d-don't; I c-c-can't hate a man I know." Socrates, the last chapter of whose life is perhaps the greatest of all the epics of serenity, held no animus even against those who had condemned him; he expected their verdict, he understood it, and he bowed to it. All this suggests that anger and hatred usually come from myopia and may be prevented by resolute largeness of view. "It is now long ago," said Booker T. Washington, "that I . . . resolved that I would permit no man, no matter what his color might be, to narrow and degrade my soul by making me hate him."

One last suggestion: understanding, though essential, is not enough. It is natural for me to emphasize thought because my subject is philosophy, that great gray subject. But many philosophers have admitted that thought by itself never moves us to do anything at all. Thought can expose the pettiness of our fears and hates; it can set before us principles and ends; it cannot make us follow them. For that, our hearts must be engaged as well as our heads. One of the most memorable sermons of modern times was that of Dr. Chalmers on the expulsive power of a new affection, his theme being that if such distorting emotions as fear and hatred are to be driven out, the expelling power must be itself an emotion strong enough to master them. The therapy of thought can remove the cancerous growth, but it cannot by itself restore the glow and health of the spirit. For that, enthusiasm is needed for generous and far-reaching ends. Where one's treasure is, there one's heart is; and the man who has laid up his treasures where the moths and rust that are to corrupt his own little lot cannot get at them, and where the thieves are baffled that so easily rob us of our strength and our years, has the only firm basis for serenity. A few more years, and our place will know us not. But is that so great a tragedy if the children we leave behind us, the students into whose lives we have wrought something of ourselves, the business we have built up, the college we have worked for, the country we have served with love and pride, are moving from strength to strength? This is what really matters, though the preoccupations with our own little clot of ambitions and worries may drive it at times from mind. To hold it there till it becomes pervasive of thought and feeling is to drop a massive anchor in the harbor of serenity.

# 19

# Machines

When I was a boy, I lived for some years in a country town in Ohio. It was a sleepy little place, consisting chiefly of a crossroads store with a post office in it, a blacksmith shop, a pair of white-painted churches, of one of which my father was the minister, a little wooden schoolhouse of which I was a janitor, and some scattered farmhouses. There were no movie theaters, no supermarkets, no radios blaring, and only rarely a horseless carriage—as it was then called—to strike terror into the gentle Dobbins that pulled us about. But on all sides there were green spaces to play in; there were maple woods where we gathered sap for syrup in the spring, and where violets and jack-in-the-pulpits were plentiful. In the long winter evenings we piled wood into the potbellied stove, lit the oil lamps and studied our lessons. On summer evenings we played baseball in the road to a serenade of tree toads and cicadas till it was time to light the lamps again and read G. A. Henty.

I went back to that little town recently. I had not seen it in sixty years, and after some months of work in a big city, I wanted to soak up a little peace from that quiet countryside. But the village seemed to have vanished. Instead there was a highway intersection with a red light to keep the rivers of cars from piling up. The house where I lived, which stood in a great green lawn, had been torn down to make way for a garage with old tires and battered cars around it. There was a gaudy gas station or two and a quick-lunch where truck drivers could get fast service. The little Congregational church where my father preached was still there, looking tired and forlorn (its Methodist rival had long since been torn down), and its graceful old parsonage had been redone with cheap fabric shingles. The village of which I had harbored such idyllic memories had become a backwash of the machine age—sordid, littered, and tinny.

I came away meditating on the distance the world can travel in sixty years. We live today in a different epoch. Would I go back, if I could, to that earlier world? No, I think not. I should not want to live in a world without cars or radios or refrigerators or oil furnaces or penicillin or planes. We have left that world once for all behind, and I suspect, for a better one.

But that is not my point at the moment. What I want to say is that it is a different world, different in the extreme, that this difference is due largely to the triumph of the machine, that the machine has affected every aspect of our life, and that if we are to be happy or at home in this new world we must learn how to adjust ourselves to it.

Consider what has happened in a few important areas of life. First, transportation. My father's horse moved at eight or nine miles an hour, and to own a horse at all, with quarters for stables and buggy, was something of a luxury. Now the average family owns a car, in which father, driving at sixty, and junior at seventy, can shop, visit, or commute at what used to be impossible distances. Forty years ago in a house in Ann Arbor I saw two old men talking with each other earnestly in a corner. One of them was Robert Bridges, the British poet laureate; the delicate-featured man he was talking to looked like a poet too; he was seeing visions of an America on rubber wheels; it was the first Henry Ford. His dream has come true. Our railroads are dying. New Yorkers who want to go to Seattle find it less convenient to spend four or five days in a train than to leave at six o'clock, have a leisurely dinner on a plane and descend on Seattle before bed time. This will soon seem a bit slow. A new supersonic plane is under discussion that will reduce the time from New York to London to about two hours. Even now a statesman who needs to confer in Algiers or India can be there next day; indeed an Australian friend of mine, flying to America, reported to me that like "the young lady named Bright, whose speed was faster than light," he had arrived on the preceding day. Buckminster Fuller, the engineer, envisions "the day when any man anywhere can get to work half-way around the world and be home for supper."

The communications story is similar. I remember hearing the first Roosevelt in the campaign of 1912 shouting and pounding with his fist from the back of a Pullman car as his train receded into the distance; that exhausting method was his best means of communicating with the people. Now if a President wants to speak to the American people as a whole, he can sit down and talk in his office, and we can see and hear him thousands of miles away more clearly than I did the older Roosevelt in the flesh. One can now talk by telephone from the east coast to the west without calling an operator. One can sit in one's living room and see the Mets or the Orioles play, and with Tel-Star one can now see people smile or frown at that very instant on the streets of Paris.

Or consider the invasion by the machine of our more intimate life. As a boy I chopped wood for the stove; as a young instructor, I shovelled coal in the cellar while my wife shivered upstairs; as a retired philosopher, I sit in my study and meditate while a complicated thing in the cellar feeds itself oil and water, and, considerate of the economy of a pensioner, lowers the temperature at night without being told. In the kitchen there is no longer an icebox, stored with blocks of deliquescing ice from Lake Michigan, but a handsome white cabinet that purrs its contentment about the store of almost incredible edibles inside; owing to canning and freezing machinery, Americans are the best-fed people in the world. Laundry is no longer a matter of skinned knuckles and steaming tubs, but of touching a button first in a washer and then in a dryer; and that ancient problem of dishes which has made serfs of so many housewives seems to be almost solved. Americans are alleged to be the cleanest people in the world; if this is true, it is largely the work of our water engineers, with their provision of a constant supply of hot and cold water, and their unsung but momentous mastery of the problems of plumbing and drainage. I have a yard to take care of that has an ill-repressed yen for reincarnation as a hay field; but I keep it in its place, not by pushing a mower and swinging a scythe, as I once did, but by a machine that actually pulls me along as I strut exulting behind it.

And now machines have begun to do even our intellectual work for us. They keep our accounts at the bank. They bill us for our water, light, and power. Not only have they reduced many of our factories to a skeleton crew; they handle much of the registrars' work in our universities and the immense administrative labors of the Pentagon and the Veterans' Administration. I have seen a machine which can instantly convert simple spoken sentences into type on paper. Libraries are condensing books and pages to postage stamp size, though with reading aids they remain perfectly legible. The Hartford Hospital in Connecticut has an arrangement with the Public Health Service in Washington whereby in emergency cases of heart disease an electrocardiogram can be sent to a central computer and an analysis of the symptoms be reported in fifteen seconds. Machines will teach us languages at home with just the right refined accent. Examinations of certain types are graded by machines. When sociologists or insurance men must interpret statistically great ranges of data, they often find it faster and more accurate to do so by machines. And when elaborate computations are necessary in astronomy, physics or mathematics, the machine may be the only resort. Some mathematicians at the University of Illinois recently wanted to find out, for reasons I do not know, whether a certain number was a prime, i.e., divisible only by itself. Most of us can answer this question readily enough if the number is a low one; we can see that 11 or 23 or 37 is prime, but what about 379 or 12,021? That takes thought. The number the Illinois people wanted to know about was 2,917 digits long, and it was estimated that it would take a man about 80,000 years to make the necessary calculations. The machine proved the number to be really prime by completing some 750 million additions and multiplications in 85 minutes. Of course all we have is the machine's word for it that this is right; no human being will ever check it. But even if someone did live eight thousand lives and claimed in his seven thousandth life that he had run across an error, I suspect the Illini would still prefer to believe their machine.

These are a few examples from thousands of how the machine is infiltrating modern life. We are going to consider what is implied in this infiltration, and let us look first at an inference that many have drawn from this last kind of illustration. Is it not clearer than ever that man himself is a machine, differing only in degree from these marvelous machines he has made, some of which can out-think him already? After all, a human body is a material thing, an aggregate of billions of cells made themselves of countless billions more of protons, electrons, and the thirty-two other kinds of particle; and no physicist seems to doubt that these ultimates, or at least aggregates of them, obey the laws of physics. We may protest that a machine could not guide itself intelligently, as a man can. But guiding oneself seems to mean ordering one's behavior toward a result and reordering it suitably if obstacles arise. And a machine can be made to do that; for example, it can be made to play a respectable game of chess. The secret of construction here is the feedback principle, by which contingencies are provided for in advance, so that when they arise the machine will deal with them in the most effective way. I gather that no match for the championship has yet been arranged between Bobby Fischer and the IBM Company, but it is possible in theory that there should be such a match and in consequence a new champion crowned. Now the human body is a mechanism compared to which the most complex computer is a child's toy. Is there anything to prevent our saying that this body is itself just a feedback machine? Of course no engineer is now in a position to duplicate it. But does that show anything more than a lack of present knowledge? If knowledge continues to accelerate at its current rate, are we not bound to discover in a century or two that human beings too are just machines, and life itself a story written in the alphabet of physics?

The answer to that is No, it is not even a theoretical possibility. The reason why is suggested by a drawing that appeared in *The New Yorker*. A towering computer covered with rows of bulbs and buttons is issuing from its depths a slip of paper, and a pair of engineers are examining it with fascinated amazement; for what the slip is saying is, "I think, therefore I am." The picture gave me pause—could any machine say that in Descartes's famous sense? What Descartes said was that his consciousness certainly existed; he could not doubt that he was doubting, since in doubting it, he was doing the doubting he was doubting about. But then no machine doubts or is conscious. We talk, to be sure, about its calculating and remembering and making mistakes and correcting them. But it never does these things in the sense in which we do them, for we do them consciously and it does not.

I have heard engineers say that they do not know what this consciousness means, that if a machine *did* everything a human being did, it too would be human, for you couldn't tell the difference. That is a fallacy. There would still be a difference, whether you could discover it or not. Indeed there is no greater difference anywhere than the difference between a change in a dental nerve and the pain you feel as the dentist's buzzer strikes the pulp, between a feeling of anger and the blow that expresses it, between a thought and a thing. Furthermore, in this fragile flower of consciousness, which seems so expendable to our behaviorists, lies all the value in the world. I do not deny that mind has its roots in the body; I do not deny the instrumental value of the matchless machines and medicines that help us to keep those roots alive. What I am saying is that consciousness, which is not a physical thing, not a motion of particles or something that can be bounded in space, is the only thing worth having in itself, that if its flickering light were to be snuffed out tonight by the tail of some truant meteor, then so far as we know nothing good or evil would be left in the wide universe. It is in those things, and those things only, in which man is *not* a machine that his importance lies.

If this is true, the question becomes a meaningful one whether the machine age marks a real advance or not. If anyone were to ask us whether man had truly progressed in the last two thousand years, many of us would think first of airplanes, telephones, steamships, and refrigerators as evidence that he has. But once we have clearly seen that these are instruments rather than values in themselves, and that the test of advance lies in the quality of man's consciousness or spirit, their abundance is not conclusive. The Greeks had none of these things. But even without them, certain flowers of the spirit managed to grow in the Greek garden—Pericles, for example, and Phidias and Demosthenes and Sophocles and Plato. The food these men ate, their cleanliness, their medicine and surgery, their clothes, streets, and houses, were probably wretched by our standards. And such things are of course important; life itself often depends on them; and it is better to be George F. Babbitt alive than Plato dead. But granting this, the question is still arguable whether life was more worth living for the average citizen of Attica than it is for the average citizen of America.

What is not arguable, I suppose, is that the means are in our hands for a life better by far than men ever lived before. Better food, health, comfort, longevity, income, means of knowledge—these are prodigious advantages; and if you were to consider the matter fairly, comparing the quality of life, not of a constellation of Greek geniuses, nor even of the free citizens of Athens, but of the Greeks generally, including women and slaves, with that of Detroit or Chicago, the result is by no means a foregone conclusion. Still, it is disquieting to think that there could be a real question about it. A recent book by Chad Walsh, *From Utopia to Nightmare*, points out the curious fact that the old delight in Utopia-making has turned sour, that the castles men are now building in the clouds are dystopias, places of boredom or terror like Aldous Huxley's *Brave New World* or George Orwell's *1984*. One reason for this is the disillusionment about what can be done by external reforms. The reforms urged by socialist dreamers have largely come true; we have enough food for all, cars and television sets and gangploughs on the farms; most people have incomes that would have spelled luxury not long ago. Yet few of them feel as if they were living in Utopia. A land may flow with milk and honey and not, after all, be the promised land. It may be purgatory.

The fact is that the machine age generates currents that tend to paralyze its natural beneficence. If we are to avoid such paralysis, we must take thought of these currents and how to neutralize them. Let me mention a few of them. I will not talk about nuclear explosions or the population explosion, vastly important as these are; I am more interested at the moment in what the new age is doing to us immediately and personally.

One thing you will have noted is that we are changing rapidly from a country people to a city people. Farming machinery has been so successful as to have destroyed much of our farming community. Our granaries are full to overflowing; the farms of Vermont and New Hampshire are being sold for summer places because they cannot compete against the giant mechanized acreages of the Middle West. Happily there are still open spaces where men can farm and fish and live like Thoreau if they care to, but these are not the places where people go to live. They are going to the cities.

During the first century of our national life, from 1790 to 1890, our total population increased sixteen times, our urban population a hundred and thirty-nine times, and urbanization is accelerating. At the last census the vast majority of us lived in cities or their suburbs. The time is not far off when our eastern seaboard from Boston to Baltimore will be virtually one continuous city.

This urbanization is changing our character as a people. It is changing us physically. The boys of my distant childhood thought nothing of walking miles to school, and mowing the yard and currying the horses when they got back; they went to bed at night, as Stevenson said sensible people should, "tired and content and undishonored." The boys in our city apartment anthills do not know what to do with their physical energy, and they reach bedtime untired and discontented and quite possibly dishonored because their overflowing youthful energy has exploded in petty delinquency. They and their fathers go wistfully to look at professionals playing ball under the arc lights, but that is a very different thing from playing themselves. The popularity of westerns in our movies is largely due, I suppose, to the imaginative escape they provide to boys and men whose life no longer provides for physical exploit and adventure.

Fitness is important, because our minds have their roots in our bodies and cannot flourish if those roots are untended. The American tradition in this matter is curious. Our Puritan ancestors had a dash of asceticism which made them regard flesh and spirit as somehow enemies of each other, but for all that, the exacting outward conditions of their life made bodily vigor indispensable. Their descendants have broken free from this inward asceticism only to find themselves in outward conditions that require almost nothing from them; they get out the car to go a block or two. If we are to prevent a flabby degeneracy from setting in, we must take matters in our own hands, with the clear realization that healthy minds cannot flourish in overfed and undermuscled bodies. There are few things that would pay off so well in the life of the mind as a sensible program of physical fitness.

If I insist on this, it is because physical vitality is probably the most important condition of happiness, and with such vitality modern life is at war. With the honk and roar of mechanized traffic invading sleep, with the nervous weariness of commuting to and from business in a river of cars, with theaters beginning at about what used to be bedtime, countless men in gray flannel suits are also turning gray inside. The grayness may be due to nothing more sinister than a continually low barometer of energy. "If I sought a symbol for happiness," writes F. L. Lucas, "it would perhaps be a mountain spring gently, but unfailingly, overflowing its basin with living water. There seems to be nothing in life more vital than to keep always this slight surplus of energy. One should always overflow." Modern life, if we let it, can swiftly drain that fountain dry.

A man's worth depends on how he orders such energy as he has. And here we come to another point of tension between modern man and his age. The satisfaction and distinctiveness of his life lies in fulfilling his own powers. On the other hand, the machine age will iron him out flat if it can. May I develop these two theses a little further?

As for the first, a line of thinkers reaching from antiquity to Freud has taught us that the good life lies in being ourselves, in finding and fulfilling our powers. Our chief duty, said the poet Pindar, is becoming who we are. Plato distinguished between a free man and a slave by saying that the free man accepts his purposes from his own nature, while a slave accepts them from someone else. For the sober Aristotle and the sober Butler, the richest life consisted in the harmonious free play of the nature with which a man was endowed. "Every man truly lives," said Sir Thomas Browne, "so long as he acts his nature, or some way makes good the faculties of himself." A porpoise cuts a beautiful figure in the sea, but would hardly do so in the treetops; a monkey is a genius in the treetops, but a pitiful sight in the sea. So it is with men. For the sake of both joy and effectiveness, they must find what they are made for if they can. The miseries of Macaulay doing mathematics, of Clarence Day trying to play the violin without an ear, of Phillips Brooks trying to teach when he was made to preach, are witnesses to the unhappiness and impotence of people who have not discovered themselves. It may be objected that the full life lies, not in being oneself, but in the service of others. That is an important comment, but I will stay on it only long enough to quote the advice of Ibsen, who was not lacking in social conscience, to the young Georg Brandes: "There is no way in which you can benefit society more than by coining the metal you have in yourself."

Now no two of us are quite alike, not even twins. "Ah, sir," said Thackeray, "a distinct universe walks about under your hat and under mine—all things in nature are different to each. . . ." "A man," says Emerson, "is like a piece of Labrador spar, which has no lustre as you turn it in your hand, until you come to a particular angle: then it shows deep and beautiful colors. There is no adaptation or universal applicability in men, but each has his special talent, and the mastery of successful men consists in adroitly keeping themselves where and when that turn shall be oftenest to be practised." It is a tragedy for some of us that our lot never provides for that particular turn which would reveal the light that is in us; one wonders what Emerson would have been if he had spent his youth in the General Motors factory at Flint. Education is a sort of spit for turning us artificially and exposing every side to the light.

Now, for the second point: the danger of the machine age is that it will mass-produce not only things but minds. As Prime Minister Asquith said, "The modern world with its steam-roller methods, its levelling of inequalities, its lopping of excrescences, its rounding of angles and blunting of edges . . . tends inevitably and increasingly towards uniformity, sameness, monotony." Two hundred million people, speaking the same language, and so near together that in the age of planes they almost make one great city, invite centralization, and we have it. Just as we are governed not from Hartford or Boston, but from Washington, so in entertainment, literature, and religion, we are increasingly moulded by certain great centers of influence. We look at the same movies, whose capital is Hollywood; we read the same technically superb magazines, supplied by the Luce or McCall empires; we tend to read the same books, helped out by book-of-the-month clubs; more of us, both absolutely and relatively, are coming under the sway of the most powerful of the Christian churches, though not the one most disposed to encourage individual thought.

Even going to college, the traditional means to individuality, has now become something to do because everyone else is doing it; and when a youth does enter college, he often finds himself submerged in a mass of students so great that little special attention can be paid to him. He responds to mass methods by conforming to the mass mind. In my forty years of teaching I have read thousands of papers by young Americans, and I look back at them, not as over a desert—they were too intelligent for that—but as over a vast plateau. The average ability was high, but the flatness of that great plain! How the truly individual essay stood out, the essay with distinctiveness of thought or distinction of style!

I recall an article about Americans and their ways by that keen and critical visitor from abroad, Lowes Dickinson, in which he wrote: "I have visited many of their colleges and universities, and everywhere . . . I have found the same atmosphere. It is the atmosphere known as the 'Yale spirit,' and it is very like that of an English Public School. It is virile, athletic, gregarious, all-penetrating, all-embracing. It turns out the whole university to sing rhythmic songs and shout rhythmic cries at football matches. It praises action and sniffs at speculation. It exalts morals and depresses intellect. It suspects the solitary person, the dreamer, the loafer, the poet, the prig. . . . I know Americans of culture, know and love them; but I feel them to be lost in a sea of philistinism." That was written many years ago; was it the sour estimate of a carping alien? Not wholly, I am afraid; it has been repeated too often by reflective Americans themselves. Professor Douglas Bush of Harvard said at a recent conference on education: "The only kind of individuality that is generally admired is skill in sport or smartness in business; the individuality of the cultivated mind and taste meets only indifference or antagonism in school, in college, and in society."

Here, then, are two facts: If we lived fully and freely, each of us would differ from all others; the pressures of our age are toward making us the same. What is to be done about this tension? If it were a problem that could be settled by organization and expenditure, you could trust Americans to deal with it effectively. They have done some notable things in educational organization, for example President Aydelotte's reconstruction of Swarthmore to break the educational lockstep. But in the realm of the spirit, no organization can guarantee results. The required changes must be inside. Let me suggest a few that might help.

One is a larger tolerance of people who do not toe our line. "I do not know of any salvation for society," says Justice Douglas, "except through eccentrics, misfits, dissenters, people who protest" (and Mr. Douglas has not been afraid to practice what he preaches). McCarthyism is always smouldering below the surface, ready to erupt at weaker spots. Our most pressing national problem is that of race; it has not been solved even by the great civil rights movement. There is only one thing that can possibly solve it, namely a regeneration of inward attitude that would seem now to be a miracle, but is not beyond hoping and working for. And full tolerance means more than toleration; it means looking at the person who differs, not with automatic suspicion or aversion but with interest, as one who may have something to give us. This does not require us to entertain fools gladly and beam on all Communists, Birchers and beatniks alike. Tolerance based on the principle that everything is as good as everything else is not real tolerance, for then there is nothing left to tolerate. Real tolerance does not deny us our disapprovals, but only the right to disapprove someone merely because he is different. And just as true tolerance will not condemn someone because he is different, it will not praise him either for that reason. There is no merit in difference as such. Originality springs from thinking for oneself, not from trying to think differently from others. Minds of real power have sometimes yielded to this temptation. Mencken, Chesterton, and Shaw seem at times to have used a formula: find out what most people regard as self-evidently true and announce that of course this is nonsense. The pattern grew tiresome after a time.

But difference from the run of people, when expressive of conviction or character, needs encouragement, both in others and in ourselves. There is so strong a pressure in a business family to become a businessman, in a medical or academic family to become a medic or an academic, that it may need no little courage to follow one's own gift for repairing machines or writing verse or planning houses. Such courage may make all the difference between a drab life and a life with heart in it. James Truslow Adams, having gone abroad to take stock of his countrymen in perspective, spoke strongly on this matter: "If our lives are to be based on any art of living, if our souls are not to be suppressed and submerged under a vast heap of standardized plumbing, motor cars, crack schools for the children, suburban social standards and customs, fear of group opinion, and all the rest of our *mores* and taboos, then the first and most essential factor is courage, the simple courage to do what you really want to do with your own life." On all this our classic document is Emerson's *Self-Reliance;* I hope that mighty sermon is still read.

No doubt the comment of many would be: "My trouble is not that I have convictions without courage; I'm sure I'd have courage enough if I had any special convictions to express; unfortunately I haven't any." And all too possibly that is correct. Convictions, if they are worth having, require thought; thought is an activity and a hard one; and the machine age breeds passivity by doing *for* us much that was once done *by* us. Children no longer need ingenuity to entertain themselves; they can sit before the TV set and be entertained without effort by the hour. Looking requires less effort than reading, and even in the rising tide of paperbacks, the art of reflective reading seems to be falling off. F. R. Leavis remarks: "There seems every reason to believe that the average cultivated person of a century ago was a very much more competent reader than his modern representative. Not only does the modern dissipate himself upon so much more reading of all kinds: the task of acquiring discrimination is much more difficult."

Have you not often reflected, as I have, that one could spend one's life in reading the journals that the postman deposits at the door, that one is expected somehow to keep up not only with the books and journals of one's profession but also with the political explosions around the world, with what Saul Bellow and Iris Murdoch may have written recently, and what the Death-of-God theologians have been arguing, and what astronauts and artists and doctors and dictators have been doing. We have courses in speed-up reading; no matter; we shall never catch up. And as T. S. Eliot reminded us, "Where there is so much to be known, when there are so many fields of knowledge in which the same words are used with different meanings, when everyone knows a little about a great many things, it becomes increasingly difficult for anyone to know whether he knows what he is talking about or not."

Yet I suggest that it is rather important to know just that. And in order to know it, one must go beyond passive reception to active reflection. There is a vast difference between being well informed and being educated, between being learned and being thoughtful, and anyone who has tried to write a book or even an article will know how wide apart are the inward attitudes of the absorbent reader and the active thinker. I am sure that many students go through high school and college without ever learning this difference; sometimes it takes the struggle for a Ph.D. to bring it home to them. One needs to have done a good deal of thinking even to learn what sort of evidence to be satisfied with, for as Aristotle pointed out, the kind of evidence with which a thinker should rest content in natural science is very different from that in morals or mathematics.

I have often thought with pleasure of an incident that comes, with what truth I do not know, from the early days of our history. An assorted group of travelers who had taken lodgings for the night was sitting before the fire at a wayside inn. Conversation fell on religion, and a couple of young men who had been reading the latest tracts threw their weight around with a cleverness and conceit that had the rest of the company reduced to exasperated silence. An old man had been sitting a little apart and listening without joining in the discussion. Noticing him at last, the pair condescended to say that it was time they heard from him. And they did hear from him. Quietly the old man proceeded to restate their conclusions for them, expose their assumptions, and dissect their arguments, with a logic and lucidity that was not merely damaging; it was annihilating. At the end the abashed pair were not unnaturally curious. "May we ask your name, sir?" "My name is Marshall," he said. They knew what that meant; the old man could only be John Marshall, Chief Justice of the United States. What an exhilarating thing it is anywhere to stumble upon this power to think, to state a case, to move to a conclusion in a straight line!

Surrounded on all sides by mountains of miscellaneous fact that the vast presses of the machine age are piling around us, we could all profit by more of that power. Some of the mountainous stuff is important; much of it is not; and only a mind disciplined in interpreting fact can tell which is which. There are plenty of agencies ready to do our thinking for us, from *The New Republic* to *The*

*National Review*, and if they did not contradict each other so flatly, it would save us a great deal of trouble to let them do it. But that would be unfair to oneself. Do you remember the chapter on Individuality in Mill's fine old essay on *Liberty?* "The human faculties of perception, judgment, discriminative feeling, mental activity, and even moral preference," says Mill, "are exercised only in making a choice. He who does anything because it is the custom makes no choice. He gains no practice in discerning or in desiring what is best. . . . He who chooses his plan for himself employs all his faculties. He must use observation to see, reasoning and judgment to foresee, activity to gather materials for decision, and when he has decided, firmness and self-control to hold to his deliberate decision. . . . It really is of importance not only what men do, but also what manner of men they are that do it." And Mill practised what he preached. He can still warm young minds to a rosy glow, for there is a fire burning in him, the fire of a genuine passion to see things for himself and see them as they are.

We need this power of authentic judgment for a further reason: our age is bombarding us with specious values, and many people, having lost the power to judge between them, become the prey of propaganda. "Madison Avenue," says Vance Packard, "is fascinated with the possibility of making us more hedonistic. America is going through a revolution in self-indulgence. . . . Living on credit is both moral and fun, they tell us. American people are told the way to live is to be happy all the time. We are subject to constant titillation of the senses. We spend nine times as much for liquor as we do for books." There is the same confusion of voices in the realm of art. "We once had an art," said Gilbert Murray, "which was enjoyed and admired by ordinary intelligent people; now we have school upon school, system upon system, of art—all transient, and each in its time enthusiastically admired by cliques of artists and up-to-date reviewers, while the ordinary intelligent man remains skeptical or repelled."

Now the ground on which we should appraise values is one of the hardest questions in contemporary philosophy, and to ask that plain men should think these matters through for themselves does seem unreasonable. Is the achievement of an authentic discrimination in values therefore impracticable? I do not think so. There is no need to carry the world on our own shoulders. We have had millions of ancestors on the planet who have had experience in these matters and have left registers of what they found. And judging by these registers, they achieved pretty general agreement that some ventures into poetry, to take but one art, have been supremely successful and others not. The vote is not quite unanimous; it never is. Tolstoy railed against Shakespeare, and Goethe against Dante, and Herbert Spencer against Homer, but do we not feel that they wrote themselves down in doing so? On some candidates for our suffrage, the polls are all but closed. We know well enough where to find the best that has been thought and said in the world; and the proved prescription for a discriminating taste is to live with this best until it has entered into our bloodstream and affected our heart and brain. There is no need to drown in the tides of formless art and meaningless verse and hedonistic morals that swirl about us. After all, there are firm islands in the flood.

Let us turn briefly to a final problem of adjustment. Perhaps the most striking thing about the recent past is the accelerated pace of change. For many thousands of years, and until the middle of the nineteenth century, the horse remained our fastest means of conveyance. But in the last fifty years we have moved from the Wright brothers' little flying machine to propeller planes moving at 300 miles an hour to jets at 700 miles an hour, and to astronauts at 17,000 miles an hour. Even in little things our way of life has been changing at a fantastic speed. When I was a student in England, there were laid out for us on our examination tables quill pens of the type used by John Locke and, I suppose, by Duns Scotus. Since then I have lived through the age of steel pens, fountain pens, ballpoint pens, manual typewriters, electric typewriters, space-adjusting electrics, and portable recorders; by the time I typed this paper I had reached the electric eraser.

Such accelerated change, occurring in every department of life, calls for continual readjustment. Many people are not equal to it and break down in the attempt. The strain is greatest in our cities. Sociologists working on the topography of insanity have found not only that the rate is higher in the city than in the country but that within the cities themselves there are well-defined insanity zones, so that the rate of lunacy rises as you travel towards the heart of the city. Life in this roaring traffic, where there are no neighbors, no morning dews or evening quiet, and no green things growing, may be dreadfully dehumanized.

Faced with this dehumanization, people have tried two extreme kinds of response. One is the line of Thoreau, Tolstoy, and Gandhi, the line of revolt and withdrawal from the machine age and of return to the simple life. Thoreau lived alone in the woods, never married, never voted, and refused to pay taxes. Tolstoy wanted to get rid of electricity and railways and to go back to tilling the ground with sticks pulled by horses. Gandhi, one reads, wanted people to spin their own clothes, objected to being fanned by electric fans, questioned irrigation projects, and, like Tolstoy, disliked railroads. Samuel Butler said that "every machine of every sort should be destroyed by the well-wisher of his species." These were in some ways great men. But their way of meeting the machine age is surely self-defeating. To abolish railways in Russia or India would mean starvation for great numbers of people. Tolstoy depended on the machines he detested even for disseminating his detestation of them. When Louis Fischer went to see Gandhi, he found that while Gandhi would not allow an electric fan in his hot room, he allowed his wife to sit stolidly and fan him by the hour. To retire from the machine age is too likely either to make others pay the price of one's large-mindedness or, if carried consistently through, to decimate and decivilize the race.

The other extreme is that of surrender to the machine age. One may let the gadgetry of modern life prescribe its means and ends. Why call one's legs into needless play if one has a car to transport one into the next block? While there is TV to look at, why converse? While there are instalment plans open to us, why be content with the old car, or with one car, or, for that matter, with anything but the latest in what all salesmen now describe as "homes"? The glossy magazines tell us, with their incomparable colored plates, that we can achieve what is called "glamour," not by doing or being anything, but by wearing something, and they suggest powerfully that if we do not wear it, if we are content with what is merely comfortable and becomes us, if we venture on a plane with that shabby luggage of ours, if we go on with our black telephones and our white bathrooms when in both cases we might have lavender, we are falling behind the times. Now the trouble with this train of thought is that there is no end to it. The appetite for these appurtenances grows by what it feeds on, till one becomes like Sisyphus, rolling his great stone endlessly up hill. One works harder and harder to get more things and then more, only to have to replace them faster and faster by working harder and harder. That is what the East means when it charges Americans with materialism. It is a way of life in which things are in the saddle and ride mankind.

Now surely the way to deal with machines is neither to flee from them nor to surrender to them, but to use them, to use them as means to ends appointed not by them, but by ourselves. The great Greek achievement was based on freedom, but that freedom was based in turn on the slavery of human beings. Our freedom rests not on slaves or even servants, for they have vanished, but on an army of sleek new retainers who are always on call, who are never sick or tired, and who never go on strike if decently treated. I submit that the so-called machine-age provides, on the whole, the best conditions in history for a widely lived life of the spirit. The new world of automation promises us a leisure owned in other days only by aristocrats. Machines are not hateful monsters; they make us possible. Lord Snow is surely right that we should have more understanding of the science and technology that have produced them. Still, the real danger in America is less that we should ignore technology than that we should miss the point of it, which is, quite simply, that it should further the life of the spirit. Apart from that, it has no point, and is only too likely to turn life into the rat race that for some of us it has already become.

But "the life of the spirit"; what in the world does that mean? The phrase has a religious ring, and I may be asked if I am urging the kind of otherworldliness that might come out of a seminary and end in a monastery. Religion is, of course, one of the great traditional forms of the life of the spirit. But that life has many forms—how many may be suggested by naming a few people who in my judgment have lived it. I should say that Socrates lived it, and Leonardo, and Spinoza, and Mozart, and John Keats, and Charles Darwin, and Albert Einstein, and Albert Schweitzer. Different as these men were, they had something in common: they ordered their life from within; things were their servants, not their masters. They lived among intrinsic values, and great ones; even when they were lords of gadgetry, like Leonardo, they never sold their souls to it. Some were men of means; most were not; but their treasure in all cases was laid up where moth and rust could not corrupt. They were lovers of beauty in sounds or words, or lovers of truth as it presented itself to quiet reflection or to the watchful eye; they were lovers of life and full of zest in it. Inwardly they were rich, for they had found themselves; their wants were matched with great goods; their grasp of these goods was strong and authentic, and it carried them beyond the petty embroilments in which most of us live. This firm distinction between means and ends, this insight at firsthand into what counts, this habitual living among things that are good in themselves, is what I mean by the life of the spirit.

Many people think that our machine age is at hopeless odds with such a life. David Riesman argues that it is making us an other-directed people, following public pressures rather than our own lights. Mary McCarthy is vehement about it: "People's lives are becoming more and more thin and impoverished and ugly. It's part of the development of industrialism, and now it's absolutely unchained. Atoms for peace will be the final blow." Well, I have admitted that the life of the spirit is encompassed and endangered by pressures. I repeat, nevertheless, that it has today an unprecedented opportunity. To say that with the amplest means in history for education, health, and leisure, we must live more impoverished and ugly lives is sheer defeatism. The remedy is in our own hands. We need to lift up our eyes to the hills, above our hundred-page newspapers, above the traffic snarls and the smokestacks. We shall get more from the world if the world is not too much with us and we can reap the harvest of a quiet eye. In their last Yearly Message, the Philadelphia Quakers proposed this question to their members: "Have I allowed my life to become so filled with activities, even with good works, that I am always under pressure, lacking in serenity and peace, and having neither time nor strength for renewal?" It is a good question for all Americans.

Count Keyserling said that Americans were people without inner lives. It is not true. But it is true that the machine age will turn us, if it can, into bustling, overgregarious extroverts while some of the best things in life are labeled "for introverts only." Philosophers on the whole have been an odd lot, but their art of contemplation, discovered by the Greeks, is one of the most precious achievements of men; to stand off from things and see them in perspective, to be, in Plato's large words, "a spectator of all time and all existence"—that protects any mind that attains it from engulfment in the immediate. True poetry—not the conundrums and acrostics that are sometimes served to us as such; true art—not Rorschach tests on canvas; great fiction as opposed to newsstand whodunits—these are an inexhaustible refreshment. These deep wells of the humanities are open to all of us as never before. And we need them as never before. In the babble and roar of our society we must keep some corner apart where we can drink from them, think our own thoughts, perhaps even see visions and dream dreams. To live aright *in* the machine age, one cannot be wholly *of* it.

# 20

## *Art*

One of the satisfactions of growing older is the discovery that the interest in knowing seems to become stronger rather than weaker. I find myself more than ever able to stand, like some Dobbin in a fence corner, gazing at the world by the hour with a pleased curiosity. I cannot keep my eyes in my own pasture, but am constantly gaping across the fences of my ignorance at the rich fields beyond. One of these fields that I have been looking into of late is art. I have never known much about it, so that many things that would be familiar to a better-educated person have struck me with the force of novelty. I have been reading things and looking at things—fearful and wonderful things—which I should never have dreamed to exist.

For example, I find myself puzzling out poems, firmly labeled as such, that seem to be the inventions of a tipsy typesetter. I find myself peering doubtfully at the products of Lawrence Woodman, the "pre-visualist," who painted with his thumb, and whose great achievement was a four-way picture. At the starting position, it is entitled "Bottom of the Sea Romantic"; turned ninety degrees, it is entitled "A Missionary Lady's Peace Offering to a Stone Goddess";

upside down it is "The Primordial Desert"; and three-fourths round it is named, more or less appropriately, "The Idiot Boy." Even classics leave me puzzled at times. I am not clear, for example why Marcel Duchamp's "Nude Descending a Staircase" was given that title rather than one proposed by a critic, "Explosion in a Shingle Factory." I turn to sculpture and find myself gazing at a boulder that seems to have been smoothed by the sea; but no, I am wrong; there is a label on it; it is an idyll and a tender one, called "Mother and Child." Or I contemplate somewhat helplessly the gigantic designs of Claes Oldenburg for sculptures in New York City—a baked potato for the Grand Army Plaza, a peeled banana for Times Square, and a hot dog with a toothpick for Ellis Island. I look and listen while a gentleman on a podium, gifted as a conductor and also, I note, as a contortionist, beguiles out of his orchestra a storm of wind and brass which—I am relieved to be assured—is an outpouring of genius and much, much better than it sounds.

But after a while I begin to wonder. Art is evidently long and life is fleeting; perhaps one should not have blundered into this bewildering field. It is clear that I am far stupider than I knew. And yet this is a sort of morsel that no one likes to swallow. I look around to see if I am alone. I find that I am not, and that the same nettled frustration appears in the eyes of other people. Indeed I see them turning their backs on art. If poetry is to be a set of acrostics, if smudges without form and void are to be solemnly pronounced great painting, they can only say forlornly: This may very well be true; you the critic know, and I too plainly do not. But then art is not for me. It is something esoteric, like Sanskrit, a field for researchers and specialists; it is not the sort of thing that plain people, with an intelligence that is only average and a somewhat bourgeois hunger for light, can hope to make much of.

That is a perfectly natural conclusion. But I think it is a tragic conclusion, and I want to protest against it on two grounds. In the first place, the notion, suggested by so much contemporary work, that art is a remote and eccentric specialty belies the history of art. The great artists of the past have spoken to the people and for the people. Sometimes indeed they have *been* the people; the Parthenon and the great cathedrals were communal enterprises. Sophocles, Shakespeare, Molière were not remote eccentrics but the heroes and spokesmen of their day. Titian, Michelangelo, Raphael, Rubens, Leonardo did much of their finest work on the walls of churches, where it served to express the common devotion. Homer, Virgil, Chaucer, Wordsworth wrote what wayfaring men could understand and say over again with delight. It is true that great artists have at times produced work that was crabbed and only half intelligible; there is, of course, Browning's frank confession, "When I wrote that poem, only God and Robert Browning knew what it meant, and now God only knows." But then if his name had to stand on Childe Roland and Sordello, it would be little noted nor long remembered. We may listen to the critics respectfully while still having counsels of our own. Let us recall John Morley's remark that you do not turn a platitude into a profundity by dressing it up as a conundrum. When we are offered as a shining masterpiece the latest essay in darkness, and after due exposure we find our minds and hearts without response, we are within our rights in reminding the critics that the burden of proof is theirs, not ours. Here history is on our side.

Secondly, we Americans of all people cannot afford to revolt against art; we need it too badly. Our past and our present have conspired to starve us of it. Our Puritan tradition instilled into us a lasting suspicion of it. We lack the magnificent reminders of it in ancient churches, cathedrals, and collections with which the Italian or Frenchman is surrounded. What has provided the American with excitement is not contemplation or creation, but action, the conquest of "success," the reclaiming of a continent, the execution of his business in a manner highly competent, but also competitive, engrossing, and exhausting. The sense of beauty does not flourish in such an atmosphere. It is an arbutuslike sort of thing; it prefers quiet and shady places, and like the girl of the Grecian urn it is the "foster-child of silence and slow time." When so fragile a plant crops up by the side of our American roads, filled with their roaring traffic, it is likely to get silted over with dust and to wilt away unnoticed.

But when the sense of beauty dies, the result cannot pass unnoticed. In a thousand ways we are paying the price of this atrophy of taste. Think what we must put up with daily. We turn the dial on our radio and after three minutes of exquisite music comes a blurb about somebody's soap. We turn to a picture magazine and find reproduced with equal technical perfection, and side by side, an actress' swimming pool with contents, starving children in Bangladesh, and on the cover an American teenager slowly ingesting, like a boa constrictor, a soda that costs a dollar. We go to the movies to witness an iron-jawed hero and a doll-faced heroine disporting themselves in a moral vacuum produced with vast virtuosity at an expense that would almost endow a college. We get into our car and try to escape to where there are green things growing, but find our vision arrested at every turn by an announcement, perhaps twenty feet by forty, that some cigarette will be found to satisfy. If we do arrive at our woodland nook, we find it littered with the remains of those who in this way alone can leave footprints on the sands of time. If our escape is by train or bus, we look out from the windows on miles of houses with their fences awry, with ancient motorcars rusting in the yards, with yellowing newspapers flying in the wind. These people presumably love their homes. But their love of beauty has not risen to the level of investing these homes with the bare essentials of cleanliness and order.

You may say, What has all this to do with art? Nothing, if art is the recherché activity of specialists and eccentrics. But everything, if it means, as I think it ought to mean, one of the elemental concerns of all men. Art is not primarily an affair of galleries and exhibits. We do it an injustice and we rob ourselves if we take it so. Art is the conscious attempt to see that what we do or make expresses well the mind within. Far from being exclusive of ordinary life, it may and ought to embrace it, pervade it, and transform it. There are some men who have the gift of expressing themselves through the common media of fine art—paint, stone, and sound. But it is a mistake to suppose that art *consists* in using these tools and is exhausted by it. Everything we do or say may be an instrument of taste. Every word and act has its artistic aspect, in which as a bit of creation it succeeds or fails, just as it has its moral aspect, in which it is right or wrong. Carlyle used to say that a carpenter could break the whole Decalogue with every stroke of his hammer. In the same way every stroke may show that he is, or is not, an artist. Molière's M. Jourdain was pleased and surprised to find that he had been speaking prose all his life; but the fact is that he was doing more; he was speaking poetry. All speech is art. Anything is art that is an attempt at effective expression of what we think and feel. We little suppose when we write letters, or talk over the telephone, or converse at table, or dress ourselves, or make pies in the kitchen, or repair cars in the garage, that we are artists. But we are. In a sense all our conscious life is expression and therefore art, good or bad. We cannot even berate this conclusion without berating it more or less artistically.

It is the same with art as with philosophy—a very difficult subject which in a fumbling way I try to teach. I am brought up sharp occasionally by learning what my friends take philosophy to be. A book will come out on some new development in semantics, written in a jargon of its own, and impenetrable as an iron curtain to all who are not of its party line. Its murkiness and uncouth polysyllables are supposed to attest its depth and mark its author a philosopher. And so, perhaps, he is. But philosophy is not to be *identified* with this sort of thing. It is less a specialty than a spirit, a spirit of determined reasonableness which, if present as it ought to be, pervades and permeates life, affecting the manner of every decision and belief, directing impulse, restraining bias, stabilizing judgment, moulding the mind from within into conformity with the ideal of the life of reason. Art in our sense is like that. It may never take form in anything we could hang on a wall or set on a pedestal, and yet may so diffuse itself through all the capillaries of our being as to touch with life every word we say and every act we do.

What are its marks? How are we to know it when we see it in operation? Three things, I think, are present whenever it is present. There may be more, but there are at least these three, and I want to stress them because they are qualities that run far beyond the making of pictures or carvings or music; they are qualities that, if given their chance, will make life itself a thing of beauty. These three are spontaneity, craftsmanship, and the economy of means to ends.

First, spontaneity. No artist can do without it. Poe claimed that he could, and wrote an essay to show that his poem "The Raven" was a mechanism produced by pure calculation. The response of the critics was cold. Some said that since it was no poem anyhow, they could well believe the repulsive tale; others said that since it clearly *was* a poem, Poe was spoofing his public. What nobody was willing to admit was that fine art could ever be ground out by machinery, physical or mental. And surely here they were right. A work of art is individual; you cannot build it out of clichés, plastic, musical, or verbal; it must be freshly thought and felt; it must spring from your own authentic seeing; it may be a poor thing, but if it is art, it must be your own. The work of every true artist is saturated with idiosyncrasy; "Art," said Zola, "is nature seen through a temperament." Who could confuse an El Greco with a Rubens, a Holbein, or a Whistler?

Now think what our lives would be like if this spontaneity of the artist, this authenticity of vision and sincerity of utterance, instead of keeping itself for special moments, could invade the rest of our days. Life for us now is largely habit and automatism. "Already at twenty-five," says William James, "you see the professional mannerism settling down . . . on the young doctor, on the young minister, on the young counsellor-at-law . . . by the age of thirty, the character has set like plaster, and will never soften again." Habit is of course necessary, and the more of the recurrent detail of life we can hand over to it, the better. But that is because in the rest of life we want to escape the chains of habit and be more freely ourselves. And how seldom people are themselves! Henry Sidgwick, the philosopher, once woke with a dream running through his head, which he found, when he had jotted it down, to be as follows:

We think so because other people all think so,
Or because—or because—after all we do think so,
Or because we were told so and think we must think so,
Or because we once thought so and think we still think so,
Or because, having thought so, we think we will think so.

Perhaps Sidgwick had had a bout the night before with students' papers. After reading many thousands of these myself, I can report that the ones that really depress me are not the products of good healthy moronia which I can brand with a thumping D or F and forget, but the unflunkably respectable, studiously second-hand, soullessly perfunctory recitatives in middle C which are droned out frankly for credit. It is a delight that ought to come oftener than it does to find, while roaming this broad acreage, a little sunburst of real literature, a page that comes straight and clean from the student's own heart and mind. That is the best compensation for what to some of us are the dreariest hours of a teacher's work. I have sometimes imagined myself a teacher in Stratford about the year 1580, ploughing through piles of youthful script—whose spelling would no doubt be more wildly anarchic even than now. I can imagine myself sitting in the candlelight, quill pen at ear, following the halting flow of adolescent prose—and then the sudden thrill of the authentic new note, heard first in a magic phrase or two, then in one of those haunting lines the like of which had never been heard in the world before.

It would be as idle to ask or expect notes of this quality as to expect selves of this quality. What one would like is a firmer loyalty to such selves as we are. There is that in everyone's life that would, for example, make his talk a thing of interest. Most talk we are willing enough to let die. When Dr. Johnson talked, those who heard it were *not* willing to let it die, because everything he said carried so unmistakably the marks of the mint that coined it. How many of the letters we write are, in substance if not in form, "Yours duly to hand and contents noted." But when William Cowper or Bernard Shaw takes pen in hand on the grayest of gray days, the spirit of the man seems to flow out on the page and hold its phosphorescence there.

The spontaneity I am praising, however, is not a matter of mere literature; it may express itself in keeping house or in selling socks. A teacher whom many generations of Yale men think of affectionately because his whole life was a case in point, "Professor Billy Phelps," tells of going into a shop in New York one day to buy a pair of socks.

> A boy clerk who could not have been more than seventeen years old came forward. "What can I do for you sir?" "I wish to buy a pair of socks." His eyes glowed. There was a note of passion in his voice. "Did you know that you had come into the finest place in the world to buy socks?" I had not been aware of that, as my entrance had been accidental. "Come with me," said the boy ecstatically. I followed him to the rear to the shop, and he began to haul down from the shelves box after box, displaying their contents for my delectation. "Hold on, Lad, I am going to buy only one pair!" "I know that," said he, "but I want you to see how marvellous these are. Aren't they wonderful!" There was on his face an expression of solemn rapture . . . I became far more interested in him than in the socks. "My friend," said I, "if you can keep this up . . . in ten years you will own every sock in the United States."

Whatever became of the young sock seller I don't know. But it is clear that he had already taken the first step in giving work the delight of art.

Have you noticed how often the heroes of stage and screen are artists of one stripe or another, young painters, playwrights, or composers? They are not, to be sure, mere artists, for our tradition has made us suspect the pure artist as a little unmanly; so provision is carefully made for his knocking somebody down, after which precaution he may be an artist to his heart's content. But it is worth asking, Why is it that the artist is so popular a figure in these places? Is it not because people feel that, so far as he is really an artist, he has escaped from the treadmill where most men live into spontaneity, freshness, and freedom? The artist cannot be a drudge, because only as he is not a drudge, only as the spirit genuinely moves, can he create at all. Art is work, but it is also play, since it has to be done from the heart. Dorothy Sayers, the novelist and playwright, put the point well:

> The great primary contrast between the artist and the ordinary worker is this: the worker works to make money, so that he can enjoy those things in life which are not his work and which his work can purchase for him; but the artist makes money by his work in order that he may go on working. The artist does not say: "I must work in order to live," but "I must contrive to make money so that I may live to work." For the artist there is no distinction between work and living; his work is his life and the whole of his life.

Havelock Ellis, a writer who transmuted even science into art, writes in his autobiography: "I never knew what was play and what was work. . . . Throughout life people have told me how they marvelled at the amount of work I accomplished. I have been tempted to reply: But I never work at all." The difference between him and other scientists was not in the amount or kind of their work, but in the temper in which it was done, for the distinction between work and play is an inward one. Work is what we do because, for some ulterior end, we have to do it. Play is what we do for the love of the doing. The moment one sees work as the artist sees it, as a chance to let oneself go in something done from the heart and as best one knows how, the grayness begins to lift from the workaday world.

"As best one knows how." There comes in the second tool in the artist's kit, craftsmanship. He must be a technician, and take pride in his craft. Spontaneity is not enough. The idea of the artist as a man who always carries about his divine afflatus and has only to turn the tap, who just sits down before his palette or piano and lets go, does not suit with what artists tell us. Work that is play may be hard work nonetheless. There are no greater names in music than Bach and Beethoven. Bach wrote of himself, "Analysis, reflection, much writing, ceaseless correction—there is all my secret." Of Beethoven, Sir George Grove wrote: "There is hardly a bar in his music of which it may not be said with confidence that it has been rewritten a dozen times." "Mendelssohn used to show a correction of a passage by Beethoven in which the latter had pasted alteration after alteration up to 13 in number. Mendelssohn had separated them, and in the thirteenth Beethoven had returned to the original version." Genius is not, as Carlyle suggested, *merely* an infinite capacity for taking pains, but the genius who is incapable of taking pains must be content to be considered, as he not improbably is, a spoiled child.

Here again I think that most lives would be transformed if there could be imported into them this solicitude of the artist for the quality of his work. The woods are full of boys who would like to hear the grandstands applauding but would never pay the price that the trained athlete must pay, full of girls who would like to be Eleanora Duses, but have no idea of how completely a priestess of her work that great artist was. Every employer of labor, whether manual or white-collar, knows how hard it is to find persons to whom he may give a job and then go away, confident that their pride in thorough work will do the rest. One would not suppose that housework was the most exacting of occupations, but when one hears present-day grandmothers talking of some of the housekeepers they used to employ when housekeepers were extant, one knows that such work may be an art.

It may be said, housework is hardly the sort of thing on which one can found one's self-respect. I venture to answer that this view is mistaken in theory and tragic in practice. Not that whatever is worth doing is worth doing well; I do not believe that; I do not want to be denied my miserable game of chess because I shall never in the world play it well. What I am saying is that life everywhere, and not on levels of worldly dignity alone, offers the stuff of art and therefore of joy. Self-respect is a major key to happiness, and the consciousness of work well done, whatever it may be, is a major key to self-respect. And there is more ground for such respect in cooking or car repairing superbly done than in half-baked verses or canvases. Pop Anson, the baseball player who captained the Chicago Cubs in long-gone days, once said that he wished engraved on his tombstone the inscription, "Here lies a man who batted .300." I must confess that to bat .300 is not one of my major ideals, though I should be inordinately proud if I could do it. What one is sure of is that there must have been a great deal of satisfaction in Pop Anson's life if he felt that way about his job. The parable of the talents does not give highest praise to the man who had most to begin with, or most to end with, but to the man who made most of what he had. Out of the sands of Egypt there was once dug an astrolabe, which, when it was cleaned off, was found to bear an inscription. The inscription ran: "This astrolabe is the work of Hussein Ali, mechanic and mathematician, and servant of the most high God." That is the sum of what we know of Hussein Ali. Yet how much it tells us about him! Far back down the centuries we can see him, sitting cross-legged in his shop with that astrolabe before him, fashioning it cunningly, precisely, proudly, as his special gift to the world, the outward and visible symbol of Hussein Ali. Can we doubt that while he shaped and polished it he was a happy man?

The world is looking for Hussein Alis, looking for them in every field of endeavor. Field Marshal Wavell once made a detailed comparison of the great commanders of history. Many of the colorful so-called geniuses, Napoleon for example, he dismissed as falling short in this part or that of their formidable craft, and ended, if I remember rightly, by saying that there were only two all-around masters of the art of war, Belisarius and Marlborough. If there is any soldier that emerged from World War II with universal acclaim, I suppose it is General Montgomery. Montgomery had in abundance the first quality I mentioned in the artistic temperament, a quality too often taken as the whole of it, spontaneity; and one would be reluctant to part with that beret, worn at its jauntiest angle when things were thickest. But what carried Montgomery from El Alamein to the Baltic was not so much the beret and what it stood for as a tremendous seriousness about his craft, an enormous pride in it, and an extraordinary mastery of its technique. He might, as Churchill said, be as insufferable in victory as he was indomitable in defeat, but when the empire itself depended on someone's doing the most perfect possible job with the materials at hand, Churchill sent Montgomery to Egypt.

"The most perfect job with the materials at hand." Here appears the third component of the artist's equipment. First he must have the spontaneous impulse to create; secondly, this must be embodied in a product by craftsmanship; but what sort of product is it to be? These factors are of small avail unless they are presided over and guided by the sense of beauty, or if you prefer, of artistic perfection. Now I do not propose to go into the tortured question what this means. But I am going to name one thing which lies, I think, near the heart of it, the economy of means to ends. If art is to be perfect, it must be without excess or defect. It must go to its goal without getting lost, and without waste of matter or motion.

We may illustrate from an art we all practice, the art of writing. Take the Gettysburg address. One would find it hard either to add to that address or to subtract from it without altering the total effect; that is what I mean by economy of means to end. What is excess in this art? It is the use of syllables, words, or sentences that are not called for by the end. George Henry Lewes quotes the great line from Genesis: "God said: Let there be light! and there was light," and asks whether this would be strengthened by writing: "God, in the magnificent fullness of creative energy, exclaimed: Let there be light! and lo! the agitating fiat immediately went forth, and thus in one indivisible moment the whole universe was illumined." The effect of course is ruined, and ruined by excess. Sometimes, on the other hand, the expression is too bald and meagre to do justice to the meaning. Captain Walton, reporting to his superiors from the battleship *Canterbury* in the Mediterranean, August 16, 1718, wrote: "Sir,—We have taken and destroyed all the Spanish ships which were upon the coast, the number as per margin. I am, etc., G. Walton." Am I wrong in suspecting that even the Admiralty would not have objected to a little more local color? As a naval officer—and no doubt this was all he cared about—Captain Walton did not err by defect. As an artist he did.

This principle of economy holds throughout the arts. It holds in the most complex, the most challenging of all arts, that art of arts which is the art of life. It holds in every particular activity of that life. In the intellectual sphere it appears as the principle of Occam's razor, the principle that one must not multiply one's points beyond need. Suppose that a mathematician has two proofs of the same theorem, one simple and one complex; he always prefers the simpler. Suppose that a scientist has two hypotheses, one simple and one complex, both of which cover the facts; again it is always the simpler that he selects. Why? Why should the scientist assume that nature itself prefers the short cut? I once asked this question of an eminent mathematician, Bertrand Russell. He said he thought it impossible to justify the principle, even though our intellectual life is built on it; we accept it because our nature demands it. Indeed in the highest regions of known thought, the sense of beauty and the sense of truth are curiously fused, so that the mathematician is at times uncertain whether it is his sense for elegance or for logic that vouches for his result. "Beauty," said Remy de Gourmont, "is a logic which is perceived as a pleasure."

What holds of art and intellect holds of practice. Aristotle made our principle his main rule for conduct: *meden agan*, nothing in excess. The educated man will go to his end with a minimum of fuss and feathers, with no bravado, no circumlocution, no awkwardness. There will be grace in his life, in the little and in the large, because the outward man will express with fidelity a mind that is itself disciplined and balanced. This view that the good life is the beautiful life is of course not peculiar to Aristotle. "He who would train the limbs of the body," said Plato, "should impart to them the motions of the soul, and should practice music and all philosophy if he would be called truly fair and truly good. "Beauty," says Emerson, "is the mark God sets upon virtue." "He who would not be frustrate in his hope to write well in laudable things," said John Milton, "ought himself to be a true poem; that is, a composition and pattern of the best and honorablest things." "Style," said Whitehead, "is the ultimate morality of mind."

How our lives would be transformed if we took these high words seriously! We should begin by making clear to ourselves what we wanted to be and do, and we should then proceed to simplify our lives accordingly—to get rid, for example, of the hundred assorted pieces of impedimenta that clog our movement—the papers we take and never read, the make-work societies, the reunions that do not cheer but do inebriate, the grim and galvanized adventures in nightlife, the joyless attempts of the introvert to be one of the crowd, of those with subpar I.Q. to be intellectuals, of those without ears to rejoice in Shostakovitch. Sometimes prudence calls for resolute amputation. Do you remember Clarence Day's account in *Life with Father* of his adventures with a violin? He sawed away heroically in the cellar for months to the excruciation of his family and the neighbors before it was discovered that his heroics had been wasted; he had no ear. What was wanted was not grim persistence in a hopeless task, but the prudence to trim one's sails to one's capacity.

It is astonishing how far some men have gone, even some very limited men, through ordering their lives by this principle of economy. One thinks of that odd, unprepossessing, awkward, fat, silent, little eighteenth-century figure, Edward Gibbon. His father had left him a moderate competence, and he could do with his life pretty much what he would. He could spend it, if he wanted, the way others of his class spent it, in taking snuff, following the hounds, and making the rounds of London. He hesitated. After a time he decided to write history, but did not know whether to do King Alfred and early England or Rome. Deciding in the end on the declining days of Rome, he quietly laid out his life with reference to his design. When he completed that design shortly before his death, the unlikely little man had produced the most magnificent monument of literary history that the hand of man had ever raised. To be sure, he paid a price, as all men must who do great things. He identified himself with the empire so completely that in the end, it is said, there was an amiable confusion in his mind as to where one left off and the other began. But after all, what he bought with the price was fulfillment and immortality.

I may be reminded that I am speaking in Quaker surroundings° and that in all this discussion of life as art, there is something very un-Quakerly. It must be admitted that the sober garb, the plain speech, and the austere life of the traditional Quaker do not at once suggest a consuming interest in beauty. Indeed his apparent indifference to beauty has often brought him castigation. There is a

---

° This was a baccalaureate address at Swarthmore College.

361

remarkable letter of Ruskin, for example, to a Swarthmore teacher of my time, John William Graham, in which he says: "Your early Friends would have carried all before them if they had not been false to that which is obeyed by the whole of the animal creation, the love of color." Now so far as the Quaker really has been hostile to art or indifferent to it, I have no defense to offer of him; he has been the loser by it and deserves to be. But this criticism of Ruskin's seems to me rather petulant. Indeed much of the criticism that has been made of the Friends on this matter is external and wanting in understanding. Whatever their attitude may have been to art in the formal and technical sense, the fact is that the principles they stood for were singularly close to those we have been developing.

They believed in sincerity and spontaneity of spirit. They believed in it so thoroughly that they banished the written liturgy and the prepared sermon from their meetinghouses, insisting that any sermon they had to listen to should come straight and fresh from the heart, or else that they be allowed to dwell in silence on what welled up from within. They disliked rules that made life mechanical, and preferred, as John Woolman did, to follow the guidance received from moment to moment. Their tradition has been that the letter killeth but the spirit giveth life. Again, while inclined to regard the craftsmanship of the avowed artist as a little frivolous, they took the principle of workmanship seriously. Their merchants were famous for the quality of the goods they sold and the accuracy of their claims about them. And while Quakeresses, young and old, were required to wear dresses severely plain in design and color, there was nothing to prohibit the wearers from compensating for this by the very finest quality and workmanship, and this privilege was joyfully exercised.

More to my purpose is the way the Quakers have accepted and exemplified the third of our principles. In a world increasingly complex and distraught, they have given their testimony, age after age, for simplicity in all things. They have eschewed lavish and unmeaning expenditure. They have sought in the architecture of their lives as in the architecture of their meetinghouses to avoid gewgaws, irrelevancies, vanities, surplusage, whatever did not conform to the austere ideal within. They have taken seriously the biblical injunction to let their conversation be Yea, Yea, and Nay, Nay, and insisted that speech should be direct and simple and sincere. It is therefore no accident that when the Quaker spirit has, as it has at too rare intervals, broken out in verse, it has produced some of the most exquisite hymns in the language. You will remember some of them:

> Immortal love, forever full,
> Forever flowing free . . .

and

> The healing of the seamless dress
> Is by our beds of pain;
> We feel him in life's throng and press
> And we are whole again.

More important still is the depth of the Friendly insight into what is essential in life and what is artificial and dispensable. Titles, money, social rank, the color of one's skin, the royal state or the state of servitude—all these to the Quaker are adventitious. To him the central fact about man is that he has that of God within him, and his high calling is to conform his life to that, regardless of his station, and to treat others in the light of it, regardless of theirs. Thus for the Quaker, the art of life is an infinitely exacting art. He has received a command: Be ye therefore perfect. He accepts the command. He knows that complacency is a sin, that a man's reach should exceed his grasp, that his possibilities in the way of justice, knowledge, and love are without limit.

Hence he knows too, if he is wise, that the architecture of his life must be Gothic, not Greek. There are two supreme architectural types. One is the Greek temple. It is Aristotle in stone. The proportions and the balance are perfect; there is no waste or tawdriness or irrelevance; it is serene, unalterable, and final. But as a symbol of the human spirit, that is just where it fails. Man is not like that, for he is still in the making; we know not yet what we shall be. It is rather in the Gothic cathedral, with its wings and buttresses slowly added over the years, its spires of uneven height, its confused and crowded pinnacles aspiring upward but always falling short, that we find the true symbol of the spirit. Art is long and life is brief, and the house of the spirit that we plan in youth will never be complete. But that is "the glory of the imperfect." The Greek temple, perfect already, does not admit of growth or of improvement. The cathedral is never done. It is the perfect expression of imperfection, of that divine discontent that keeps throwing out new buttresses in order that it may throw up new arches and new pinnacles into the sky. What measures us in the final reckoning is not so much the imposingness of the house we build as what we do with the material that has been given us. And we are told that in this test the first may be last and the last first.

# 21

## *Courage*

What virtue would you guess to be the one most universally admired? Compassion? Hardly. If the world is full of suffering, it is also full of indifference to it, and persons who are actively compassionate are sometimes sneered at as do-gooders. Justice? Hardly, again. There is too little agreement as to what, in the concrete, justice means. Does it lie with the Arabs or the Jews, with the government that taxes us for war or the Quaker who refuses to pay those taxes, with the Communist who says that justice means first economic security or the democrat who says that it means first individual freedom? No, the best loved virtue, the virtue that is most continually celebrated on stage and screen, the virtue that our heroes of fiction must possess, that collects at football stadium and ringside the most enormous if not the most intelligent crowds, that makes national idols of the Lindberghs and T. E. Lawrences and Churchills, what is it but the virtue that takes its very name from the heart of man, the virtue of courage? It is this virtue, the most praised in all times, and one greatly needed in our own, that I want to talk about. And first, why do we all admire it so?

We admire it because it is the antidote to the emotion that is at once the deepest, the most universal, and the most disagreeable known to man, the emotion of fear. We all know what fear is, and what a deadly palsy it may cast over the joy and zest of life. And we admire courage because we know that it alone can stay that hateful hand. But even so, we can see its full power only when we see how closely entwined fear is with the very roots of our being.

It is older than our race, old almost as life itself. Some of our feelings are recent acquisitions; they have cropped out late in the history of our kind; hope, for example, reverence, remorse, the sense of humor. It is doubtful if any of these have a history that would carry it back in the scale of life beyond the appearance of man himself. Your dog does not properly laugh, or your cat grow despondent through remorse. But in point of fear we are all kin, for fear is the obverse side of the impulse to life itself, and we inherit it from an overwhelming animal lineage. Mr. W. E. Green, on his return some time ago from the Brazil jungles, reported that when the cry of a tiger was heard in the offing, the party's oxen always became unmanageable, and that he has seen an ox fall down and die of fright as that freezing cry drew nearer.

There is much in the animal mind that will remain forever sealed to us, but when we see a rabbit running breathlessly from hounds, or a chicken dashing for cover as a hawk circles above it, or even a fly buzzing in a web as the spider moves out from his lair, there is something in us that leaps the bounds of genus and species, and reveals by a primal sympathy what is going on in those strange little alien minds. If we measure the depth of an instinct in ourselves by the length of its inheritance, fear belongs to the heart of our being. Even the behaviorist Dr. Watson, who carried his war on instinct to extreme lengths, admitted there are fears which we are born with, the fear of loud noises, for example, and of falling. And my first point is that the depth of our admiration for courage is due to the depth in our nature of this dread instinct for which it is the cure.

The second point is this, that the varieties of courage correspond to the varieties of fear which courage may overcome. Of these we may note three great classes. There are first the fears of bodily harm. Then there are fears of the opinions and attitudes of others. Then there is a third and strangest class, the fears of oneself. Let us look at each of these.

We hear it said sometimes that a certain man is afraid of nothing. But it is safe to say that this is true of no man alive, except perhaps a few who are not right in their minds. Miles Standish could face cannon without a tremor, but he could not face Priscilla. Samuel Johnson was a brave man if ever there was one, but there were two things of which Johnson was hauntingly afraid. One was loneliness; he used to follow his friends to their very doorsteps in the hope that they might come back and not leave him alone. The other was death. "Oh! my friend," he wrote in a letter, "the approach of death is very dreadful. I am afraid to think on that which I know I cannot avoid. . . . In the meantime, let us be kind to one another. . . . Do not neglect, sir, Yours affectionately, Sam. Johnson." Even from our first class of merely physical fears, none of us is wholly free. It may be snakes; it may be darkness, or the dentist, or ghosts; but undoubtedly if we look, we shall find crevices in our armor.

Now the courage that conquers these physical fears is itself of various grades. Sometimes it is little more than stupidity. Many a criminal has shown reckless courage in defying apprehension and a probable death penalty, and then when the law has caught up with him, and he is facing the final chapter, has shown an abject and hysterical terror that has revealed his earlier courage for what it was—the soddenness of mind that could not think ahead or imagine the result. At a higher level is the man who can imagine the results but who faces them with spirit because he likes to live dangerously. The celebrated Irishman who, seeing a brawl in the street, inquired whether this was a private fight or anyone could get in; the knights of the Middle Ages, who tried to fuse their Teutonic pugnacity with Christian charity in a new chivalry that sent them scouting for maidens tied to trees, not so much to rescue the maidens as to chastise the culprits; the frogmen and parachuters and racing drivers and test pilots of today—all are examples in point.

It is easy for the philosopher in his study to deprecate this sort of impulse as a mere recrudescence of primitive pugnacity, of the sort of courage shown by cats when they wander out at night to fight and caterwaul. But we take this attitude at our peril. Those of us who detest pugnacity as a danger and a bore will go farther in dealing with it if we recognize frankly the appeal that mere physical courage has to ourselves as well as to everyone else. That appeal is deep, it is all but universal, and it is here to stay. The fact that its most favorable theater is war, and that war is becoming more hateful rather than less, should not blind us to its appeal, for otherwise we shall not understand why so many people find war tolerable and even inviting.

Literature, particularly ballad literature, is full of the sagas of such exuberant courage. One thinks of Tennyson's Sir Richard Grenville, the man with the quaint habit of chewing up wine glasses, of Drake calmly finishing his game of bowls when news came that the Armada had been sighted, of Nelson turning his blind eye to the signal for retreat and insisting he saw no signal, of the apparently disastrous beginning of Caesar's landing in Africa. Caesar knew that his men were extremely superstitious, and ready to be discouraged by any unfavorable omen. Unfortunately, when he was landing at their head, he stumbled and fell flat on his face. What did he do? He did just the incalculable thing that made Caesar Caesar. "Africa, I embrace thee," he cried out with apparent delight, and a sinister omen turned into a happy augury. Or one thinks of Andrew Barton in the old Scots ballad:

> Fight on, my men, said Sir Andrew Barton;
> I am hurt, but I am not slain;
> I'll lie me down and bleed a while
> And then I'll rise and fight again.

The gay bravado of this kind of courage appeals less to age than to youth. But it does set young blood a-tingling, and unless we can sympathize with it, we shall hardly understand the delight of the boyish mind in Superman and Dick Tracy and the Lone Ranger. Every normal boy yearns to be some sort of iron man, who can disdain danger and hardship and pain. He may have had so little of these things in his protected young life as hardly to know what they mean, and yet this yearning of his is not to be laughed at; it is a thing to be prized and given some sort of outlet.

We read constantly in the newspapers of young thugs who carry on gang warfare, or lead the police wild chases in stolen cars. It is sad to think that not only these boys, but the very impulses in them that are so roundly condemned, would under happier circumstances gain general admiration. They are misguided hero worshippers, idolaters of raw courage, with a store of it clamoring for use, only the drab streets where they live and the dullness of their ghetto lives give them no obvious chance to use it except by baiting the law. They are in need of what William James called in a famous essay "the moral equivalent for war," some activity in which this admirable quality could find a useful or at least innocent way of working itself out of their system—hard games, for example, under wise direction. I remember being heartened some years ago by seeing on television the story of how an imaginative coach got hold of an unmanageable brat named Jackie Jensen in a reform school and turned him into a solid citizen and a star outfielder on the Boston Red Sox. Indeed, the Boston outfield was littered for a time with juvenile delinquents who were the cynosure of young eyes in that city.

Everyone knows that the youthful crime rate in this country is appalling. And America is not alone in this respect; the most orderly and civilized countries in the world are worried about the increase in the lawlessness of youth. And well they may be. For what they are all facing is a widening gap between the order demanded by instinct and the order supplied by civilization. In the average civilized man there is a large residue of the caveman, as two world wars have made painfully apparent—a heritage of restless, predatory, competitive, antinomian, adventurous instinct. In time it may die away. But it is still there and still clamorously alive. Like the sexual instinct, it is likely, if repressed, to break out in unexpected and disagreeable forms. And the orderly peaceable routine of civilized society does tend to repress it. We expect our young men to keep loyally to their routine of books or selling or factory work; at the same time we hang before them on theater and television screen the images of violence and wild adventure. This speaks to something deep and primitive in them; and we expect that when the match is thus put to the tinder, nothing will happen. Something is bound to happen; indeed, the tinder is always smouldering. What we must manage to do is to turn the energy of heat into kinetic energy as constructively as we can, through camp and gymnasium and outing club and athletic meets and scouting and work camp and sandlot game and whatever else will offer a safe outlet to the boy's love of giving hard knocks and taking them unwhimperingly. The boy who is to be father to a courageous man should not be a mollycoddle, nor is there any necessity that he should be a brute.

We have been speaking of physical courage, the type exhibited by the Old Testament warhorse that sayeth among the spears "Ha Ha!" The philosopher Kant thought that such instinctive courage deserved no moral credit at all; given its peculiar mettle, it was following the line of least resistance. Without wholly accepting this, I think we can see that even of physical courage, there is a higher type. The man who, lacking the adventurous impulse, sees that something dangerous and costly should be done, and does it simply for that reason, is both a rare spirit and a more trustworthy one. He may cut a less dashing figure; he may lack the precious gift of high spirit; but then he is not dependent on it either, and may be counted on in all weathers.

A former Harvard student has remarked that merely to see the erect figure of President Eliot striding to his office of an autumn morning was a tonic to less firm minds. There were many who disagreed with Eliot, and some who disliked him; but all knew that they had in him a man who would hew to the line of principle as he saw it and would do the disagreeable as a matter of course if that lay in his path. Francis Peabody, in writing of him says, "Moral timidity is as a rule a sign of self-consideration; one is thinking of how the act or word may affect his own security or influence. President Eliot's courage was not self-display, but self-effacement; not the audacity of vanity, but the fearlessness of faith." There is something rocklike about these people, and the rest of us, beset by our doubts and our timorousness, feel a little safer in the shadow of such rocks. They change our ideas of what men can do in the face of fate, and so change what we expect from ourselves, and so change what we get from ourselves. We are a little firmer of purpose when we read of Bruno's remark to his judges who had been trying vainly for months to make him retract his beliefs: "Perchance your fear in passing judgment on me is greater than mine in receiving it." We are one degree less likely to wilt before evil when we read how it was faced by Sir Thomas More. When his opposition to wickedness in high places had brought on him the literally deadly hatred of the king, the Duke of Norfolk expostulated with him: "By the mass, Master More, it is perilous striving with princes; the anger of a

370

prince brings death." "Is that all, my lord?" answered More; "then the difference between you and me is this—that I shall die today and you tomorrow."

But more moving to my mind even than any of these great sayings is the remark of a young man aged twenty-one, of the Yale class of 1773. His remark is now engraved on the base of a statue of him that stands outside his college dormitory. When Nathan Hale was caught and about to be hanged, he did not know that he was to become a subject for statues and legends; all he knew was that an unheard-of young life was about to be snuffed out in the line of duty. But when he was asked if he had anything to say, an enemy officer happened to take down his remark, and that remark, quiet as it was, has gone on reverberating in men's hearts ever since: "My only regret is that I have but one life to lose for my country."

Here is a different and higher courage than that of the temperamental adventurer. It is the courage that calmly looks in the face the worst that can happen and walks to meet it unflinchingly. But the fears of pain and death are of course not the only kind of fears for which courage is needed as an antidote. There is also the fear of what others will think and feel and say about us. We are members one of another. Each of us is a climbing vine whose root indeed is in himself, but whose tendrils are wrapped around others on all sides; and if they are cut off from their supports, we fall in a sorrowful limp mass. The reflection of us that exists in other people's minds is so like a part of our real self that a hurt to it may cause all the suffering of a serious physical wound. "No more fiendish punishment could be devised," said William James, "were such a thing physically possible, than that one should be turned loose in society and remain absolutely unnoticed by all the members thereof. If no one turned round when we entered, answered when we spoke, minded what we did, but if every person we met 'cut us dead' and acted as if we were non-existent things, a kind of rage and impotent despair would ere long well up in us, from which the cruelest bodily tortures would be a relief." We are gregarious animals; we want to be noticed; we want to be liked; we want, if may be, to be admired.

And yet if our selves are to be more than adjectives to the selves of others, there comes a time when to believe and say and do what we think is right requires us to give up deliberately the liking

and admiration that the best of us hunger for. It is no use saying
that by tact and compromise differences with others can be avoided. They may be blunted, but they cannot by these means be
removed. Sometimes, much as we dislike it, we must stand up and
be counted, since remaining silent would in substance be a vote for
the wrong side. It may be said that reasonable people will respect us
all the more for having the courage of our convictions, and that, no
doubt, is true. But the trouble is that the world is filled with unreasonable people who will assume without question that if you
criticize their religious beliefs, you are a bigot, that if you are
politically left of center, you are a fellow traveler, that if you aspire
to think and talk like a person of cultivation, it is a sign of affectation and conceit, in short that if you do not fit yourself firmly into
the great honeycomb of commonplaceness in which they con-
tentedly live, there is something perverse about you. Now sensitive
persons as a rule dislike intensely to be thought religious or political
bigots, or snobbish, or perverse. And so there is a conflict between
duty and our pathetic liking to be liked.

It is to be noted that this conflict is very much more distressing
in some minds than in others. There are persons with so powerful a
passion to figure in the public eye that they would rather be known
and detested than not be known at all. Alexander Woolcott was a
case in point. Woolcott was on occasion a most sensible and
generous man. Yet according to his biographer, Samuel Hopkins
Adams, he had such a passion for publicity that he actually courted
detestation if it was the means to more publicity: he would publicly
greet distinguished ladies as "Mrs. Emptyhead" or "Lady
Brainless"; in his capacity as critic, he would attend first nights in
huge galoshes in which he would flip-flop down the aisle; he would
contrive conspicuous scenes in which he would scatter insults. "You
know," he once wrote, "I was born in Macy's show window"; "I
love to be libeled"; and when a reporter took him at his word and
wrote a brutally coarse description of him, he sent the reporter a
note of congratulation. To those of us who are constructed on
different lines, it may be hardly credible that there are such people.
But they do exist, and sometimes in unlikely places. A few days ago,
two Yale students were apprehended by the campus police in the
unprovoked but systematic endeavor to smash up a college
quadrangle. They were haled before the dean and invited to ex-

plain. Their explanation was that they had never been recognized at Yale, and they were going to be recognized now. They gained their wishes, though not quite in the way they hoped.

Now it is clear that if one is built on the Woolcott model, it will take very little courage indeed to incur public dislike. But most of us are so made that it takes a great deal of courage to do so, and the more in proportion as those whose moral support we are dispensing with are near and dear to us.

It takes no courage for you or me to invite a black friend to dinner. But it has not always been so. In large sections of this country until quite recently, anyone who treated blacks as social equals would do so at the cost of his own equality within the social circle he lived in; and if that day has passed, it is not only because of Mr. Warren's court, but because of the courage of individual men and women who, through their minute but millionfold violation of old unreasonable taboos, have worn them away by attrition.

Of course this minor pioneering, while it draws jibes from one quarter, does draw cheers from another. And therefore a still finer quality of courage is called for when one gets no applause even from those for whom one acts. Are there such cases? Yes, there are. There are sufferers who will never speak their gratitude because they cannot. I suppose the thing I admired most about John Galsworthy was not his writing, fine as that often was, but something else that is less widely known. Galsworthy was very sensitive to suffering, animal as well as human, and because of that he used to make lonely and shuddering trips to the slaughterhouses of London to see for himself how long it took for a butchered cow or sheep to die, and then write to the newspapers urging methods that might reduce their agony by that minute or so which in the aggregate would mean so much. Galsworthy knew that most of the people who enjoy lamb chops do not think, and do not want to think, about the cutting of lambs' throats. He did think about it, and tried to do something about it. He was the attorney without fee to a great army of tongueless and defenseless clients, and I hope that when John Galsworthy's case comes up in the great assize, he may find himself surrounded by a cloud of eloquent dumb witnesses.

Such courage demands nonconformity, and it may be said that nonconformity is so far from being a rare virtue in this country that it has become the order of the day. But when Emerson said that whoever would be a man must be a nonconformist, he did not have in mind the current type of nonconformity. There is nothing very reflective or independent or courageous in the surrender in droves to "drug culture," or "youth culture," or "black culture," or "the Jesus cult," or Zen Buddhism, or Yoga. What Emerson meant by nonconformity was self-reliance, the following not of the crowd or one's whim of the moment, but one's best and clearest inner light, arrived at reflectively and responsibly. That sort of individual commitment is always difficult and rare.

One who has courage of this kind has more than courage; he has a whole sheaf of virtues. Phillips Brooks was inclined to regard courage as the root virtue of all others. He pointed out that the classic name for courage is *virtus*, which means the practice of being a man, of playing a man's part. "Courage lies behind every other quality and is rather the soil in which all the qualities grow, than a separate, distinguishable quality itself. The heart is the man, and so courage is the man. Give a man courage, and you have given the groundwork on which every good quality may spring. Take away courage and you have taken away the base on which every virtue rests . . . a man who will stand any other taunt is furious if you call him a coward. It seems as if you charged him with every vice at once!"

What makes courage so essential a virtue is that it shows in large measure both of the components that are most important for the good life. On the one side the man of courage must show largeness of view; he cannot be self-centered; he must look to ends beyond himself and beyond the immediate; he shows that power which marks man off from every other creature in the universe and makes morality possible—the power of living in the light of the absent, the remote, and the ideal. He has escaped the prison of pettiness and self-preoccupation, and has begun to live in the upper air where there is sweep of vision. Courage has been defined as the power of being mastered and possessed with an idea. To have moral courage is to have hitched one's wagon to a star. And to let oneself be pulled by stars is the essence of morality.

But courage implies not only vision; it implies on the other side will. We can all dream dreams and see visions; the courageous man embodies them in act. He is ready to commit himself, to pay the price in practice, to take risks, to burn his bridges. He not merely owns an idea; he is possessed by it.

The debt we owe to such courage is beyond all calculation. If people in this country can worship in their own way, I suppose it is because four centuries ago in a Catholic diet at Worms, an obscure monk lifted up his voice against corruption in the face of the greatest powers of the world, temporal and spiritual. If the black has gained some measure of freedom in this country, his debt is owed in some part to a persistent voice that emerged long ago from a Boston attic, a voice crying out in the wilderness, but saying over and over again: "I am in earnest—I will not equivocate—I will not excuse—I will not retreat a single inch—and I will be heard." And William Lloyd Garrison *was* heard. If at the conclusion of the last world war, one man was by general consent the world's leading citizen, it was not primarily because he was an eminent historian or had held many public offices; it was because of the unconquerable courage that led him, when his country stood alone against a mounting wave of nazism and fascism that threatened to submerge the world, to stand up in Parliament and offer his countrymen his un-yielding program of "blood, sweat and tears." The memory of such great-heartedness neither they nor we can willingly let die.

But all this, it may be said, is hardly fair. It is easy enough to be courageous, and even to be a bit dramatic about it, when the eyes of the world are on you and you are sure you are right and confident that right in the end must prevail. What is hard is to be courageous when giving your little all may mean going down obscurely along with the cause you are fighting for. There are two answers to this: first, that when Luther spoke out as a reformer, he was an obscure priest whose chances to prevail against the world empire he was op-posing would hardly have induced a gambler in the Derby sweepstakes to place a penny on him; that when Garrison threw down his gauntlet to slavery the obloquy of a jail sentence was hanging over him and he was sleeping on the floor of a bare room, too poor to buy a bed; that Mr. Churchill's voice was never more uncompromising and more eloquent than when the outlook for his country was most unqualifiedly black. These men did not speak out because they had caught the ear of the world; they captured the ear and the heart of the world because they spoke out.

But the second answer is this, that the objection is largely valid. It *is* vastly harder to be courageous when you are fighting in an obscure corner and nobody much cares whether you win or lose. I dare say it has cost many a man as much strain to break with a local political ring, or make a little private stand against race prejudice, as it cost Churchill to defy the Nazi world. And if, in addition to obscurity, you have to face the doubt whether, as against so many, you *are* right, the business is harder still.

Thus we come to our final form of courage, the courage that overcomes distrust of self. Many of us are not conspicuously lacking in physical courage, and would not lack in courage to face hostile opinion if only we were sure of our own opinion. But lacking confidence in our own judgment, feeling that our own poor thought or taste hardly counts, we insure that they won't count by becoming contented echoes. To be anything but an echo is getting harder and harder; modern civilization is against it. It leaves us as little time to think as possible. With its deluge of books, magazines, newspapers, movies, radios, television, it puts a premium on passivity; with its crowded schools given over to mass production, one can say of its education what Tennyson said of nature, "So careful of the type she seems, so careless of the single life."

How are we to keep a voice that is audible or worth hearing if it is inaudible amid this rising and roaring sea of voices which threatens us with drowning? We must manage to find and be ourselves, to speak with an accent a little queer and provincial perhaps, but still our own. How are we to do that? It is idle to do it by trying to rid oneself of repressions and falling back on impulse, as if one became a free untrammeled spirit by doing whatever at the moment one wanted to do. Instincts and impulses are the lowest common denominator of the race; they are very much alike in everybody; and the man who surrenders to them, instead of becoming an individual, makes himself indistinguishable from the mob.

But no two men are quite alike in their capacities, and the road to individuality lies through self-knowledge. Some time ago I had a miserable dream; I dreamed that I was about to go on the stage and play Hamlet, and I was in a state of paralyzed terror, for I knew I couldn't play Hamlet. Some people live in perpetual internal division because with no ear they are trying to sing and play; with no powers of statement they are trying to teach; with no tact or natural sympathy they are trying to make themselves nurses.

They need the courage to win their freedom by facing the truth about themselves. To quote Emerson's *Self-Reliance,* that charter of American individualism, "There is a time in every man's education when he arrives at the conviction that envy is ignorance, that imitation is suicide, that he must take himself for better or worse as his portion." "A man should learn to detect and watch that gleam of light which flashes across his mind from within, more than the lustre of the firmament of bards and sages." "Trust thyself"; "God will not have his work made manifest by cowards." "It is easy in the world to live after the world's opinion; it is easy in solitude to live after our own; but the great man is he who in the midst of the crowd keeps with perfect sweetness the independence of solitude."

One last word. What if you do stay loyal to the light that is in you, and find that you haven't much to say, that you are not Emerson, but only John Smith or Mary Jones? Many of us in this country have been urged to think of ourselves as potential Lincolns or Einsteins, and we are bound to be disillusioned. Ten years, fifteen, twenty years go by after we have got our diplomas, and we come back to our class reunions, stoutish and a little slow, hair shot with gray, looking back from days that were to have been masterly and triumphant a little wistfully to the unreturning days when all was yet before us. If youth has a way of hitching its wagon to a star, middle age has a way of finding the wagon detached and in imminent danger of landing on the woodshed.

What can we do about it? We can do what that indomitable little mass of courage, St. Paul, did. We can keep our hearts unbeaten. We can run our race fairly, we can fight the good fight cleanly, we can keep faith with ourselves. We may not be masters of circumstance, but we can be captains of our own souls. And to remain generous and unembittered when the colors in our dreams have begun to run, to see one after another of our classmates pass us in the race and know we shall finish not among the first but among the undistinguished many, to see all this quite clearly and yet to offer no alibis, to say and think no evil of those who have succeeded where we have failed, that will perhaps be the supreme test of our courage. "Our business in this world," said Robert Louis Stevenson, "is not to succeed, but to continue to fail in good spirits." But of course that kind of failure is a high kind of success. Stevenson achieved it in his own short and heroic life. Browning put the spirit of it in that epilogue to *Asolando* which was in a way his own epitaph, since it was given to the world on the day he triumphantly left it. This is his little portrait of the man of courage:

> One who never turned his back but marched breast forward,
> Never doubted clouds would break,
> Never dreamed, though right were worsted, wrong would triumph,
> Held we fall to rise, are baffled to fight better,
> Sleep to wake.

# 22

## *Books*

The library should be the center of a liberal arts college. To know that five minutes away from one's room there is a vast magazine of fact and thought, in which may be found the answer to virtually every question now answerable by man, adds something to the student's stature and to his assurance in facing the future.

To a bookworm, however, whether insect or human, a library presents a problem. Everyone would like to keep up, more or less, with the treasures of literature and science that the human mind is producing, but suppose we know that every year a row of books two hundred yards long is being added to the library shelves. No bookworm, however dashing, will ever burrow his way through that row. If he tries, he will only find himself falling farther and farther behind; the fraction of what we *can* read over what is there to read gets smaller every day. If it is true that of the making of books there is no end, the modern reader is in a dilemma. If he reads merely at random, he is likely to waste much time and to get nowhere for his pains. If he is to pick and choose in his reading, he needs reliable rules of choice, and where are they to be found?

Many lovers of books have proposed such rules, the precipitate of their own experience. Probably there are no maxims that would give safe guidance for all readers alike. But there is one set of rules, suggested long ago by an exceptionally seasoned and thoughtful reader, that seems to me well worth our attention. The reader was Emerson. The rules he proposed for himself and others were surprisingly simple and few. They were as follows: (1) Never read any book that is not a year old. (2) Never read any but famed books. (3) Never read any but what you like. These rules, like so much of Emerson, will never do as they stand, but I think we shall find them suggestive.

First, never read a book that is less than a year old. That has a churlish sound. It sounds unfair to the authors, who are standing there in the wings, like candidates on election night, biting their nails till they know what the public thinks. It sounds unsporting also to other readers, who are to be pushed forward as guinea pigs and exposed to the unknown for our advantage.

But Emerson would have his reply. "There are plenty of people who are interested passionately in serving as scouts of what is novel. They are the intellectual first-nighters, for whom the excitement of drama or art or literature lies in being in the avant garde, and for whom the last thing is the last word. Between these people on the one hand and the reviews, advertisements and blurbs on the other, we need not worry greatly that what is new will go unnoticed. If it is worth reading, it will still be around at the end of a year; if it is not, you will have saved time through bypassing it."

There is force in this. Best sellers are often birds of passage, here today and tomorrow gone forever. The names of the books that have had the largest contemporary sales in our history would make a curious list. According to the *Literary History of the United States*, the book that "is said to be the most popular of all modern novels," which sold some twenty million copies and was translated into more than twenty languages, was *In His Steps* by Charles M. Sheldon. How many of us have read it or recognize the author's name?

Do you know who is the most successful writer of our day in terms of copies sold and dollars received? I did not until I read an enlightening article on him in *Life* magazine. His name is Harold Robbins. "As of last spring," the article reports, more than forty million copies of his books had been sold. "If I never write another word," Mr. Robbins says, "I have a guaranteed income of from $400,000 to $500,000 a year until 1981." "Someone recently asked him how he ranked himself as a novelist. 'There's no question about it,' he said . . . 'I am the best there is.' " What makes him the best is partly that "his characters seldom think; they act," and partly that "he spills sex in such abundance, and so imaginatively. . . . " For just one recent book, and the film rights connected with it, "by his own estimate, he had been paid about what it cost to build the New York Public Library—or, to put it in another way, more than Shakespeare, Dickens, Thoreau, Whitman and probably the Brontë sisters made all together in their lifetimes." He "may be," the writer tells us, "the best-selling author of all time," and when he is in form he can dictate his stuff at 5,000 words a day. And shall I read this genius? I shall not.

Indeed Emerson's advice to wait a while seems to apply specially to our time. I am lamentably ill read in contemporary literature, but when I do dip into it, I wonder whether it is it or I that is seeing American life with a squint. I was speaking recently at a Catholic woman's college in the West, and as I was leaving, one of the kindly nuns who taught there pressed into my hands a paperback of a current play which she said she wanted me to read and comment on for her. It seemed to me pretty strong meat for nuns; it was Albee's *Who's Afraid of Virginia Woolf?* I think she wanted to know from someone coming from the outside world whether the world, and particularly perhaps the non-Catholic college world with which the drama dealt, was like that. I confess that in writing to her about it I felt a bit cloistered too. I had taught at only one small college, Swarthmore, and Swarthmore, as I remembered it, was not at all like that.

In fact, in my recent academic rambles about the country, I have been struck by two things regarding our young people. One is their astonishing appearance, which suggests that a world congress of hippiedom is convening on each campus, and the other is the sense and intelligence that emerge when you start talking with these apparent emigrants from Skid Row. The heart of America, at all ages, seems to be beating healthily. It is the more to be regretted, therefore, that American writers of drama and fiction are not doing more to exhibit this health and to maintain it. Let me quote the substance of a paragraph from my friend Douglas Bush, who knows much more about current writing than I do, though as a Harvard emeritus and therefore over thirty, he may be suspect.

The Harvard catalogue used to list a course called "Deviant Behavior and Social Control"; the student's name for it was "Nuts and Sluts." This label might cover a fair amount of current writing. Not to mention the conspicuous preoccupation with various kinds of abnormality and subnormality, it may be supposed that even run-of-the-mill fiction has put the sex manuals pretty well out of business, and it is on much the same artistic level. The Victorian novelists have often been accused of hypocrisy because of their reticence—although they knew, like all great writers, that human emotions are more important than the technology of sex, that crude scenes and language are not proofs of bold insight, and that people have more than one interest in life. But our age of honesty seems to have its share of hypocrisy. As artists, our novelists take a high line in regard to the sanctity of freedom—and that, having now been fully attained, has left crusaders without a cause. At the same time they exploit sex with the automatic monotony of slot-machines, in ways and degrees not practised by the far greater writers of the past but strongly advisable in terms of popular demand, prestige and profits. . . . Sex is, of course, the easiest thing in the world to write about, and love is very difficult, although it is still one of the major facts of life. [*Harvard Today*, Autumn, 1966.]

Another critic whose knowledge and judgment I respect, Joseph Wood Krutch, wrote an article in the *Saturday Review* of May 6, 1967, entitled "Must Writers Hate the Universe?" He pointed out that this preoccupation with what squirms on the underside of logs was an international and not merely a local fashion. He reminds us that, in the year before, Cyril Connolly was asked by the *London Sunday Times* to make a list of "the hundred literary works which best presented various aspects of modernism in intellectual literature." Of this set of books Mr. Krutch remarks: "At least a half—and perhaps two-thirds—of them might, I think, be classified as guideposts to perdition." He asks whether there is any characteristic that marks this kind of modernism, and answers that there are several.

Thus one distinguishing characteristic is the tendency to elevate raw sexual experience to a position of supreme importance. . . . Other characteristics are homosexuality, nihilism, and that impulse to self-destruction typified in the cult of drugs. Still another is that taste for violence which, as in the case of Baldwin, becomes unmistakably sadistic. If I had to answer the question, "What is most fundamental?" I should be inclined to say "the taste for violence." The belief that violence is the only appropriate response to an absurd world is the one element most often present in any individual's special version of the moment's avant-gardism.

My own impressions would have little weight without support from critics who are better read. So let me quote another, Archibald MacLeish, who quotes still another, Susan Sontag, as a point of departure. Miss Sontag says:

> One of the primary features of literature, as of much activity in all the arts of our time, is a chronic attachment to materials belonging to the realms of extreme situations—madness, crime, tabus, sexual longings, drug addiction, emotional degradation, violent death. . . . It is felt that such situations are somehow "more true" than others, that an art immersed in such situations is "more serious" than other art, and finally, that only art that embraces the irrational and repellent, the violent and the outrageous can make a valuable impact on the sluggish consciousness of the audience. [From *Yale Reports,* Jan. 1, 1967, as is the quotation that follows.]

With this estimate Mr. MacLeish agrees. He says: " . . . the new experience of Miss Sontag's writers is a new experience of man . , . a vision of man to which madness and emotional degradation and illicit love and drug addiction are more true than sanity and emotional harmony and health and love itself." And he goes on: "Any civilization rests on a single cornerstone: its belief about man. And if the new literature challenges, as it clearly does, the classic confidence in man on which Europe rested and on which this Republic was founded, then it raises a question which not even the most brilliant of literary critics can dispose of with a literary judgment. For the real issue then is the issue of truth. Is it true?"

If Mr. MacLeish is addressing that question to the people who deal in fact, not fiction, the answer must be No. You do not see man in true perspective, or what he is essentially, by taking him in extreme cases. Granting (what is probably untrue) that if we were all to be put in concentration camps and starved and abused, we should all have our moral breaking points, that does not prove that men are essentially rats. Granting that with a little sleuthing or slumming you can find characters in any large town or army unit that are slimy, what ground does that give for inferring that in these people we are seeing the real human nature, that man as such is slimy and smelly?

Incidentally, I think that many contemporary theologians, with their talk of original sin, are similarly falsifying human nature; it is a myth that we have been a mass of corruption since the fall of man, which is of course itself a myth. Granting again that when Romeo is drawn to Juliet, his love has roots in biology, it is false to say that romance is reducible to biology, and for a writer to take that line is like peeling an onion; when he has removed all the implications that lift man to a human and civilized level, there is little left worth writing about. It would be wrong undoubtedly to say of present-day writers generally that they are engaged in peeling the human onion down to its vanishing core, but if Mr. Bush and Mr. Krutch and Miss Sontag and Mr. MacLeish are right, there is point in Emerson's first rule not to seize things as they fall hot from the press, but to let the sieve of time do a little sifting for us.

Emerson's second piece of advice is to read only famous books. From him this is curious counsel. Many books, as we have seen, have achieved fame that are hardly worth reading. He must have had his own meaning for "famous." We may be helped to see what it was if we recall a distinction of Carl Van Doren's between greatness and popularity. "A book is great," he says, "when it speaks to the best minds. It is popular when it speaks to the most minds." It may be great without being popular; he mentions Doughty's *Arabia Deserta* as an example—a strange, powerful, individual book, but so alien in style and subject to most people's taste that few even attempt it. As an example of a work that is—or was—famous without being great, he mentions *The Americanization of Edward Bok*. This book, today little read, I suspect, even in Philadelphia, is a thoroughly American success story which had a vast vogue in the 1920s. Then there are books, Van Doren goes on, that are both great and popular. His instance is *Gulliver's Travels*, which is really two books in one—a book that can be read in the nursery, and another that is a profound and bitter commentary on human life, to be read between the lines by philosophers and

384

statesmen. When Emerson recommended famous books, he must have meant something like Van Doren's third class, those comparatively rare books that combine fame with greatness, the books that Robert Hutchins had in mind when he defined a classic as a book contemporary with every age.

What books would be included in a shelf of real classics? There is an almost pathetically general desire to know what they are, and a great many attempts have been made, by persons qualified and unqualified, to satisfy that desire. In my youth we had a list of "the hundred best books" drawn up by John Lubbock (Lord Avebury), and President Eliot's "five-foot shelf"; today there is Hutchins's own list of the "great books," which has become the main fare of some college curricula. A college could do worse; you will recall Carlyle's remark that "the true university is a collection of books." These lists are certainly helpful. Many a person browsing in a library or eyeing the paperbacks in a railway bookstall, will see a title of which he knows nothing except that it has appeared in some great-book list—perhaps Marcus Aurelius's *Meditations* or Mill's *Autobiography*. He may pick it up, sample it, and begin a friendship that will last through life.

But any shelf of alleged great books needs to be approached cautiously. If there is anyone who has ever succeeded in reading such a shelf through, I have not met him. He would be like the friend of mine who set out to read all the historical articles in the *Encyclopaedia Britannica*. John Bunyan and Benedict Spinoza were contemporaries, and would appear in any chronological shelf of classics back to back, but there are a thousand persons who can read Bunyan to one who can read Spinoza.

A great book does not necessarily wear its meaning on its face. If you were to ask what is the greatest single book in the history of modern thought, the answer would not improbably be Kant's *Critique*. Let me quote the comment made on that masterpiece by no less a mind than Macaulay. "I received today a translation of Kant. . . . I tried to read it, but found it utterly unintelligible, just as if it had been written in Sanscrit. Not one word of it gave me anything like an idea except a Latin quotation from Persius. It seems to me that it ought to be possible to explain a true theory of metaphysics in words that I can understand." What this shows is not that Kant's book is not a great one, nor that Macaulay's mind was not a rich and clear one, but that Kant and Macaulay were out of tune; they were not on the same wavelength; Kant was not the sort of person, as Friends would say, who spoke to Macaulay's condition. Macaulay had intense interests in persons and in style; Kant had little of either.

The meeting of a man and a book must be a meeting of hearts as well as minds if the friendship is to take. The setting should be propitious. A classic may fail to speak to a youth because the circumstances are not right, or because the will is not there, or because the youth has not yet grown ears to hear.

Think of the circumstances under which many of us begin the reading of the great novels and dramas. Such books should carry us along by their own delight and fascination; that is part of their nature and purpose. Well-meaning high school teachers set novels and dramas as texts, with the hope that exposure to great literature will awake that delight and fascination in the vagrant minds of John and Jane. These young heroes of the resistance movement are assigned two chapters of *Silas Marner* or Act I of *Hamlet* to read, and are invited to get up the facts about the date of composition, the steps of the plot, the psychology of the leading characters, and the unusual words employed. This is a natural pedagogical ploy, but for John and Jane, reading under these circumstances is a sentence to compulsory labor, and from that time on, so far as concerns George Eliot or Shakespeare, they have had it, as they say; they want no more of either. The vitality, the mastery, the moving power of these classics is barnacled over with footnotes, glossaries and appendices, and buried in boredom.

When John and Jane reach college, the chances of their gaining the freedom of great literature by the academic route may be no better. The tradition of Teutonic erudition in Germany, of Anglo-Saxon scholarship in England, and of both in this country has made many teachers of literature into neo-scholastics rather than humanists. I still remember the sense of incongruity I felt as I listened long ago at a dinner party to a distinguished professor of English from a large university. Someone mentioned Keats. "Yes," he said, "there is a lot of work to be done on Keats," and he proceeded to outline for us some areas in which the factual rooting about that he called literary research might be carried on. What would that bright spirit have thought of becoming a mummy for autopsy at a kind of "grammarian's funeral"? "The heart-breaking thing," says F. L. Lucas, "about the academic teaching of literature which now rages all over the world is that it so often consists of trying to teach the unteachable to the unteachable. For the love and knowledge of literature are things far more often self-taught than taught." And when it is taught, it is not by logical or factual analysis. The teaching of literature would seem an impossible task if it were not that on rare occasions and by rare persons, it is done. Dean Briggs of Harvard, who was one of them, perhaps yielded the secret when he said that "the highest teaching is less pedagogy than contagion."

I suggested that in approaching the great books, not only should the circumstances be right, but the will should be there. At the best, this is a will touched with humility, even perhaps with reverence and wistfulness. One cannot accost a classic with a demand to stand and deliver. You will remember Keats's own approach to even a second-rate translation of Homer, and how the young apothecary's apprentice stood before it with a wild surmise, silent upon his peak in Darien. It has been my lot in recent years to visit a number of small middle western colleges, where the boys and girls come in straight from the farms, look with awe at the college library, and think it a wonderful thing that they—they with their cowlicks and heavy boots and calloused hands—should have the run of all these riches. And I suspect that it is from people of this kind that will largely come our future men of letters and lights of humanist scholarship—people who do not approach higher education with the assumption that it is what society owes them, but rather that it is a shining city set on a hill, which perhaps they may one day reach if they are stout of heart and prove worthy of it.

There is another condition of getting the most from the great books. They should be read at the right time. What is the right time? That depends on the subject. Sir Richard Livingstone, a classical scholar, startled his public some years ago by quoting and embroidering Aristotle on the issue. "One may enquire," said Aristotle, "why a boy, though he may be a mathematician, cannot be a philosopher. Perhaps the answer is that mathematics deals with abstractions whereas the first principles of philosophy are derived from experience. . . ." Mathematics is notoriously difficult, but the difficulty does not arise from the need of a mature experience; mathematicians do their best work young. Livingstone thinks the same applies to music so far as it is a grasp of the abstract relations of sounds; he points out that Mozart wrote a concerto at five and that Schubert in his eighteenth year wrote two symphonies, five operas, and 137 songs. "But how few," he exclaims, "have ever written anything worth reading on history or politics or ethics or even on literature before the age of twenty-five! What great tragedy was ever written by a young man?" "Ask anyone what is the right age for education, and the reply will probably be from 6 to 15 or 16, with an extension to 18 for more intelligent children, and to 21 or 22 for a picked few. . . . But, after 50 years spent in receiving or giving education, I am convinced that for the studies in question (the cultural studies) the years after 18 are a better age, and those after 30 better still." That is one reason why Livingstone was so enthusiastic about adult education, and also a reason why, if he is right, we should be enthusiastic about libraries. They supply the continuing means of education to those who missed college, or missed it in college. It is not, of course, that Livingstone or any sensible man would discourage youth from reading the classics, but merely that if they do read them, they will not fully understand them till years have brought the experience of life.

Emerson's first two rules, read seasoned books and read famous books, we may accept with some qualifications. What about his third rule, "Never read any but what you like." Our first response is that it will not do at all. No college student equally likes the reading he has to do in history, comedy, economics, and religion, and if he is to be educated he must plainly read much that is boring or even repellent. An education at any level is preparation for life in the world; life in the world is full of drudgery; and education must prepare him to face it. Furthermore, he may have to serve an apprenticeship in a subject before he knows whether he likes it or not; he may have to acquire a feeling for the subject, that is, a set of ideas in the field and a certain facility in handling them, before he knows where he stands about it. You will recall the famous judgment of the Tübingen professors on Hegel at his graduation, that he was proficient in classics and theology but deficient in philosophy. Sometimes when a student complains that he has no interest in a subject, the proper comment is: Read on till you have.

I cannot think Emerson meant to deny these things, even if they were inconsistent with what he also said—which indeed would not have troubled him unduly; a foolish consistency, he said, is the hobgoblin of little minds. But we, as little minds who are troubled by such hobgoblins, can hardly take so high a line. Emerson's rule, accepted literally, would make a rounded education impossible. What he meant, I suspect, was not what he said but what Goethe said: "We learn from what we love." If we are bored with a book, our attention wanders, and if we do not give it our attention, we shall not hear what it says. If we hate it, we shall see its warts and squints and wrinkles, but not the face as a whole that it turns to us. It is the same with a book as with a friend; only if we delight in it can we know it well.

That is one among many reasons why it is best to give rein to one's enthusiasms while they are hot. They may not be the enthusiasms of twenty years hence, but that does not matter now. I knew a student who lost his heart to Thomas Wolfe and read everything Wolfe wrote, till at last he wearied of egocentricity; he later hitched his wagon to Bernard Shaw and inched his way along that portentous row of volumes till their clever, brassy omniscience began to pall on him. Learning from his loves and disillusionments, he went on to become wiser, sadder, and a professor of English literature. He learned in the hard and the best way what an authentic interest in literature means.

I recall a tiny but significant anecdote told by Helen Darbishire, the distinguished Wordsworth scholar. She said that she was once sitting on a committee whose subject at the time was how to interest children in good books. One of the members was that formidable critic and historian of literature, George Saintsbury. Everyone wanted to hear what the old man had to say, but he was bored by the whole problem, which had been no problem to him. Finally, cupping his hand in mock secrecy, he said in a loud whisper: "Leave books around." He was confident that any intelligent child, seeing his parents reading with evident enjoyment, and having the run of their shelves, would sample them for himself and find by trial and error what he liked. His choosing a book for himself was an important act; here he was staking out for himself a little acre of his own in the kingdom of ideas, feeling himself at last a person, a mind to be reckoned with who could reach out for sympathy and leading to other minds across the years. I dare say we could all give testimony here in Saintsbury's favor. I certainly could. At some point in my early youth someone left around in the house a copy of the *Cosmopolitan* magazine that had an article in it entitled "The Breadth of Herbert Spencer's Teaching." I picked it up, started reading it, and found to my astonishment that I could understand it. It was such a shock of delight that the very look of that old magazine is before my mind's eye still.

These discoveries may of course come later too. My former teacher William Ernest Hocking tells of how one rainy Sunday afternoon, while an impecunious student at the State Agricultural College in Ames, Iowa, he dropped in at the college library and asked the kindly lady who was on duty whether she had anything new to recommend. Well, she answered, a big book had just come in called *Psychology* by a man named William James; would he care to look at that? Hocking thought he might as well. He sat down to it. He began reading, and he read on and on and on. A resolution slowly formed itself in his mind. He was going to find this man; he was going to save up, and find him wherever he was, and study human nature with him. He dropped out of the agricultural college, taught for several years in a secondary school to earn money, and finally, at the age of twenty-six, still an undergraduate, appeared in Cambridge to sit at James's feet. One wishes that all rainy afternoons turned out as well. Fifteen years of ripening followed and then Hocking was called back to Harvard to become one of James's most distinguished successors.

Books, then, are a means of self-discovery. And owing to the mushroom growth of the paperback industry, they are available as never before; everyone who really wants to can have a library of his own. I wish that every college student could be to that extent a bibliophile, and feel the truth of the old Persian saying that a book is like a garden in the pocket. We cannot, or at least should not, express ourselves on the margins of borrowed books, and we cannot copy out from them all the passages we should like to keep, but we can do that with books of our own, and as our little collection grows with the years, we find we have not only a private treasury of memorable ideas, but also a logbook of our changing inward weather. There is room for a fascinating book on the marginal comments of readers on writers. There are three battered works in my own library that I prize above all the others. One is a four-volume set of Hume which I picked up for ten shillings in an English bookshop and which turned out to be the personal copy of the great philosopher and editor of Hume, T. H. Green, and to have some of his comments on the text. Another is Henry Sidgwick's *Elements of Politics*, which not only was his autographed copy but contained, folded inside, an extended set of notes for a second edition and two letters from Lowes Dickinson to Mrs. Sidgwick counseling her on their use. The third is G. E. Moore's copy of Wittgenstein's *Philosophical Investigations*, containing more than five hundred marginal question marks at points where Moore had found himself baffled or disagreeing.

It seems to be a sad fact that as the ease of accumulating a library goes up, the chances of using it go down. Books call for leisure and a quiet corner, and though any well-conceived library will provide that, the cluttered apartment of your future may not. The clanging telephone, the clamorous children, the hundred-page newspapers, the tonnage of junk mail, the laborsaving devices that need laborsaving devices to save the labor of their repair, the competition of the radio, of television, of the movies, all of which demand less of us than books, make old-style leisurely reading almost impracticable. How recently have you got through a Waverley novel? I did hold on to the end of Thackeray's *Pendennis*, but then concluded that I could not attempt another such because it occupied too much of my limited sojourn in this world. The great French scholar Renan said that he would have liked to read novels if they carried marginal summaries or something like newspaper headlines to give him the gist of the appalling flood of words.

If I may pass on to you the preference of a slow reader, I would suggest that for those whose interest in persons is great, it may be well to shift from fiction to fact, in the form of the lives of great men and women. The truth is, as Mr. Lucas says (to quote him once more):

> . . . the novelist competes with life at a disadvantage. Fiction, if it grows fantastic, often ceases to fascinate: but with a true story, the more fantastic it grows, the greater, very often, its fascination. And in fact Time has produced tragedies, comedies, and romances more dramatic than Shakespeare's. The supreme storyteller is Life. Ivan the Terrible and Peter the Great outdo the most bizarre characters of Dostoevski; indeed Dostoevski and Tolstoy themselves had lives and characters stranger than anything imagined in their novels. Gulliver is a figure far less enthralling than Swift; Rasselas than Johnson.

Being one of those persons who are reluctant to admit that the day is over and it is time to turn in, I keep in my bedroom, by way of stimuli to climbing into bed, some shelves of books any one of which I know will give me a self-indulgent spell of gloating; and I find myself turning increasingly, not to novels, but either to delectable froth like P. G. Wodehouse (who is said to have been for a time the favorite reading of the British Cabinet) or else to biography. There is no short novel in the language that competes, for me, with Lytton Strachey's sketches in *Eminent Victorians*, biased as they are; and there is no long one that competes with Trevelyan's *Macaulay* or with Froude's *Carlyle*, where you are confronted by one master of English prose telling the story of another.

In sum, Emerson's third rule, read only what you like, is no advice to hang on the wall of an office or a study. It is, rather, a sage counsel for one's hours of freedom. It reminds us that food is most nourishing when consumed with relish.

These suggestions of Emerson that we have been considering go back a hundred years, and some would say that they are out-of-date because reading itself is going out-of-date. Marshall McLuhan thinks that we have depended too much on the written word, and that moving pictures, sound tracks, and the multiple other gadgets of our computerized world are superseding it. And remembering that there was a time, only a few centuries ago, when printed books were themselves new gadgets, we should certainly welcome anything that enlarges and enriches the human spirit. But for those who have felt the delight and exhilaration of great books, it is hard to believe that anything else can take their place. Plato and Bacon, Browning and Tennyson, Goethe and Emerson, chose the way of words for communicating with us, and whatever other ways experiment may discover, these minds are accessible only through what they wrote. And what they wrote will remain. It may be pushed aside for a time by some new cult or fashion. But as long as our libraries offer for the asking so much refreshment, so rich and inviting a life for the inward man, they will remain as orchards of the human spirit.

# 23

## Admiration

In a well-known poem of St. Paul's, the chief Christian virtues are listed as faith, hope, and love. In a poem by Wordsworth, there occurs a striking emendation of this list: "We live by admiration, hope and love." What is surprising is to find the great traditional virtue of faith replaced, not by honor, not by justice, not by truthfulness or purity or courage, but by admiration. What an odd new version that is of the things we really live by! But the more I have thought about it, the more significance I have seemed to find in Wordsworth's suggestion. It is true that the very compass of our lives is supplied by the things we admire. Do you want to know the quality, the direction, the force, of a young man's or woman's mind? Then look to its admirations. That is the burden of what follows.

It may be thought that there is nothing especially admirable about admiring; anyone can do it. But that is not quite true. Sometimes when you look for a person's admirations, you find nothing but a blank. To admire calls for a capacity to go beyond oneself in sympathy and imagination. We say that a cat may look at a king, but can he really? The cat never does see the king as a king; it would have to be more than a cat to do that. William James says somewhere that if a dog were shut up in the Vatican gallery, where it was completely surrounded by masterpieces, the best it could do would be to go to sleep. Some people seem to have no chords in their nature that can be set in vibration by greatness of any kind, and some people who once had them seem to have lost them. The power to admire, like other powers, may die through disuse.

Sometimes it is not so much disuse as discouragement that destroys the power to admire. I once knew a young woman of good mind whose parents had done an effective job of killing this capacity in her, for without knowing it they were cynics. The scholars who came to their house they set down as freakish; the men of affairs who visited them they dismissed as shrewd driving people of coarse grain; whoever came was taken apart and catalogued as twisted, mean, or naive. The parents had so deflated everyone that the daughter was left with no ambition to be like anyone. That was a grave disservice to her. Youth is the seeding-time for enthusiasms, and if they do not take root then, they probably never will.

Why is it that these enthusiasms and admirations are so important? They are important, for one thing, because they are means of self-discovery. Genuinely to admire a hero, as Carlyle pointed out, is to have something of that hero in one's self. The girl who turns on Pablo Casals on her phonograph because she likes his playing is revealing to others and to herself something significant about her mind, for she would hardly feel as she does about that master musician unless there were music in her own soul. The boy who, though outwardly a wayward nuisance, secretly admires his father's orderliness, energy, and decision, is already a bent twig that may reveal the inclination of the coming tree. In late years prospectors have been going over many possible uranium sites with Geiger counters, which detect with an uncanny accuracy the presence of the precious metal below the earth's surface. Our admirations are the Geiger counters of the spirit. They locate for us our real sympathies; they disclose to us our affinities and powers. I like to think of that dinner long ago in Copenhagen when there appeared at the table some butter, not lying dead in its dish, but carved with delicate skill into little statues. The master of the house looked at it wonderingly, asked how in the world the butter had got that way, and was told that there was a boy working in the kitchen who liked to carve things. He saw at once that behind this odd enthusiasm there was power; he called the boy in, questioned him and offered him help with his education. The little statuettes provided a correct prognosis. The boy's name was Thorwaldsen, now the most distinguished name in the history of Danish sculpture.

An admiration is a type of enthusiasm, and our enthusiasms disclose our identities. Charles Darwin (as well as Shakespeare) was curiously lacking in one kind of responsiveness. In fact, he was lacking in many kinds. He tried in his youth to be a scholar, but he made small headway in that line, and when he went to Cambridge, attempted only a pass degree. He was frail of health, backward in the humanities, and so entirely lacking an ear that his fellow students used to tempt him to try "God Save the King" or other such simple tunes to see how far he would go off-key. But young Darwin was not dull in all directions. He had enthusiasms of his own, which were regarded as rather queer. He loved to watch beetles and their strange ways; it is alleged that he scandalized his Latin teacher by coming to class with beetles in his mouth. Fortunately he inherited a small competence that enabled him to watch and think about beetles and butterflies and earthworms as much as he wanted. His interest grew into a consuming passion to observe, record, and interpret the facts about living things; and we can now see, as we look back, that this boy's strange enthusiasm was not only the key to his own life, it began a new era of modern thought about man's place in nature. On walks across the downs his little son used to trudge admiringly at his side, seeing through his father's sharp eyes the wonders to which alone he would have been blind. Once he found a grass that even those eyes had not noticed, and his idol praised him for his keenness. The little lad fairly burst with pride; "I are a wonderful grass-finder," he announced to all within earshot. His boyish enthusiasm too paid off, and he went on to a national name in science.

The value of school and college is largely that they are adventures in self-discovery. It is by making contacts with other persons, directly or through their work, by noting what they do or say, and by finding ourselves admiring them for saying this or doing that, that we bring our own powers to light. "Other men," said Emerson, "are lenses through which we read our own minds." No doubt the minds of many go undiscovered to the end, both by themselves and others, because there are no personal radio stations about, that can put their own receiving sets in vibration. Suppose that the young John Keats had been placed in a factory where he never had a chance to read, or therefore to admire the poets; would he ever have found himself by his own efforts alone? Probably not. We know what did in fact happen. One day he picked up by chance a copy of Chapman's translation of Homer, and before the revelation that opened up to him he stood

> like stout Cortez when with eagle eyes
> He stared at the Pacific—and all his men
> Looked at each other with a wild surmise—
> Silent, upon a peak in Darien.

He had been moving about in worlds not realized, and all of a sudden he came to see that they were there, and were his native country. School and college expose us to poets and painters, philosophers and scientists, orators and statesmen, most of whom may not "speak to our condition" at all; but if just one of them does draw echoes from the caverns of our mind, it may disclose a new self there, feeling toward the light. Van Wyck Brooks, speaking of the lives of older Russian writers, says: "It was not for nothing that Turgenev bore in his memory, as a talisman, the image of Pushkin; that Gorky, having seen Tolstoy once, sitting among the boulders on the seashore, felt everything in him blending in one happy thought, 'I am not an orphan on the earth as long as this man lives on it.'" Admiration is the path along which greatness is transmitted.

Our admirations, then, are diagnostic of what we are. Now for their second service: they help us translate our newfound powers into action; they supply interest and zest in trying out a new line. If anyone, hearing another speak or sing, says, "Wouldn't it be really something to speak like that? What wouldn't I give to sing like that?" he has taken the small but necessary first step toward doing just this. Seeing another do it may make the critical difference.

In that delightful book, *Elephant Bill*, written by the chief elephant keeper for the British army in Burma during the last world war, the writer tells us how he managed his formidable charges, whom he came to know and like as he did his human friends. Elephants, he found, are sensitive, timid, and suggestible. One time in getting a refugee train over the mountains into India, he had to take a long procession of them, with invaluable human and other cargo on their backs, along a narrow, winding, mountain path with a sheer cliff above and a sheer precipice below. A misstep, a stumble, a single beast trumpeting in fear, might set off panic and catastrophe. But Elephant Bill knew his elephants. Among his charges was one magnificent fellow who was every inch a leader and was plainly recognized as such by the others. This animal was proud of himself and sure of himself, and Bill was confident that if he put him in the van of the procession he would carry his part to perfection, and that if the others saw him do it, they could do it too. He was right. With big Jumbo at the head giving them confidence, the great beasts edged along the wall above the precipice, with inches to spare, like so many surefooted antelopes, and the whole convoy came safely through.

After reading the book, one feels it a good deal to ask of human beings to be like elephants, but still at our best there is some resemblance. We too take heart in the presence of natural leaders. If they can be stout in crises, then so can we. Like Popeye the Sailor Man, we draw new strength from the spinach of admiration. It is said that when Cromwell appeared on the field of battle, his presence was worth a regiment; each man was more of a man with that solid unflustered captain about, "what every man in arms would wish to be." Nor is it merely courage that is contagious; any virtue is apt to be catching, once admiration has reduced our resistance to it. To my mind the most attractive figure that ever occupied an American pulpit was Phillips Brooks, and it is said that wherever he went, little Phillips Brookses kept bobbing up in his wake. They couldn't be like him exactly; he was six feet five, weighed three hundred pounds, and spoke about three hundred words a minute. For all that, they said to themselves:"What would it be I wonder to talk like that, to have a mind and temper like that? Is there a chance that I could be that way too?" And before they knew it, the contagion of that large spirit was doing its work.

This suggests that admiration may not work through conscious will, but silently and effortlessly like a force of nature. Some forces of nature do work, to be sure, with noise and strain, as when rocks are riven in two, or mountains spew out their lava. But the greatest forces work in silence. The ocean rises soundlessly to the suasion of the moon. The sun holds the planets in their courses without so much as a whisper anywhere. So it may be with the tides and forces of the spirit. A great personality may silently magnetize the minds of his people. It was more than a hundred years ago that Lincoln left the White House; Hayes and Garfield and Arthur are all nearer to us in time. But how much nearer to us he seems! He was president in a more crucial period, no doubt; but is that the real difference between them in their hold on the American mind? Surely not. The difference between them lies in the fact that this strange, gawky, humble, magnanimous man caught the imagination of a people; he has been carried into a unique primacy on a wave of admiration. Americans love Lincoln for what he was, even more than for what he did; and because they do, a million youths who read about him in New York and Omaha and Seattle find it, they don't know why, a little more possible to feel malice toward none and charity for all.

How does admiration act when it works in this effortless way? Of course it keeps our attention fixed on something we admire, but is not thinking about it one thing and acting it out another? Yes, but the connection between them is closer˙than one would expect. Merely thinking about doing something may give one a set toward doing it, may innervate the body for doing it. "As a man thinketh in his heart, so is he." The psychologists have illustrated that principle for us in many ways. William James said that if you hold your finger up before you and think intently and exclusively of crooking it, it will soon fairly ache with the impulse to crook. Have you ever stood on a high place, begun to think of going over, felt your legs turning to water as the horrid suggestion persisted, and sat down in order to feel right again? I have, and I do not think there is anything unusual or morbid about it. When Dr. Coué was in this country many years ago, he used to blindfold people and ask them to think intently of falling backwards; he held that if they really played the game with him, they always did fall backwards, and of course he was always ready for it.

These experiments were carried further by a British neurologist. He tested three soldiers with a device that measured the strength of their grip. He found their average normal grip to be 101 on his scale. He then hypnotized them and told them that they were very weak and feeble; their strength of grip went down to 29. He then substituted for the suggestion of weakness the suggestion that they were very strong; their grip went up to 142. A mere conviction, if sufficiently unqualified, could depress their strength 70 percent or raise it 40 percent. We have no doubt all tested this for ourselves in less dramatic ways. The boy who is learning to ride a bicycle and thinks of hitting the tree ahead finds that his cycle has acquired a diabolical tendency to do just that. The man who is making a speech and allows himself to think how terrible it would be if he forgot what is coming next is only too likely to find the action following the thought. Not long ago I saw a picture taken at a track meet, in which a pole-vaulter was going over the bar. What was interesting was how many of the spectators were unconsciously lifting one leg off the ground in sympathy with the man in the air.

The inference from all this is that our admirations can do things to us merely by fixing our thoughts on objects. The hero-worshiper tends, whether he knows it or not, to be what his hero is, and to do what his hero does. Of course this holds for the worse traits as well as the better. For some years in the 1930s Ludwig Wittgenstein was the most influential philosopher in England. He was a remarkable mind, but a very eccentric person, who, when he lectured, knit his brows, wrung his hands, stared at the ceiling, and fell at times into dead silence with his head in his hands. Some of his disciples appropriated not only the master's teaching, but unfortunately also much of his manner, so that even now after many years one sometimes goes to hear a former student of his only to murmur shortly, "Aha, Wittgenstein again." But the very fact that admiration for a man may make one take over his trivial or tiresome mannerisms is itself a witness of what a force it may be. And there is no need, when we borrow the gold of a man's character, to borrow also the lead.

I am not suggesting that we forget the leaden alloy and the clay feet of our heroes; Lincoln was sometimes gross; John Stuart Mill was sometimes unreasonable; Schweitzer was not wholly free from fanaticism. It is a good thing that the Victorian biographical habit of putting one's subject on a pedestal as high as a pillar has been abandoned. Sometimes it does one good to know that a great man forgot an engagement or lost his temper; it puts his greatness more nearly within our range; he was tempted, even as we are, and, on the whole, got the better of it. Still, what makes him worth our admiration is not his peccadilloes, which others have too, but his greatness, which is his alone. For all the common clay in his composition, Lincoln remains a model of simplicity and magnanimity, Mill a model of the reasonable mind, Schweitzer a model of the merciful concern for all beings who know pain. To be of their company, even in thought, is good for us. Thackeray once said in a lecture: "Might I give counsel to any young hearer, I would say to him, 'Try to frequent the company of your betters.' In books and life, that is the most wholesome society; learn to admire rightly; the great pleasure of life is that."

Thackeray's surprising remark that the great pleasure of life lies in admiration suggests the third value of this attitude. If meant as a statement of fact, the remark is hardly true. There are many people whose chief pleasure seems to lie in eating, drinking, and generally indulging their appetites. There are even people who seem to get genuine pleasure from their detestations—Hazlitt, for example, who wrote a famous essay on "The Pleasures of Hating." But in general I think we can distinguish positive or expansive emotions, such as the love of persons or knowledge or beauty, from the negative or contractive emotions, such as fear, jealousy, and hate; and we can say that while the first take us out of ourselves, enlarge our horizons, and give us joy, the second force us back on ourselves, divide us from others, and bring us bitterness. Now admiration belongs in the first group. Genuinely to admire a fine actor, a fine executive, a fine character, is to go through a self-enlargement; and self-enlargement, Spinoza thought, was a very synonym for happiness. The negative emotions are often a sign of low vitality; have we not all noticed how much more likely we are to be apprehensive and irritable when we are tired, or when we find ourselves lying awake at 3:00 A.M.? But if admiration strikes the chord of self, that self tends to "pass in music out of sight"; one feels oneself taken up in the larger self of another, thinking with some of his wisdom, acting with some of his force. Admiration is spiritual experiment, adventure, and growth, and these are sources of delight. It is not the only key, but it is an important key, to the happy life.

We have been considering ways in which admiration does things for us without effort on our part. But its fourth and perhaps plainest value is just that of galvanizing us into effort that we should otherwise make less effectively, or not make at all. Take an example. For many years I have been trying to get students to write essays in acceptable English. I have penned endless red-ink critiques, and finding the same defects appearing ad infinitum, I have wondered how much good it all did. Surely no first-rate writers ever learned to write by fixing attention on their defects, even by way of eliminating them. They wrote as they did because somewhere along the line they had a love affair with great writing. Often you can see the prose of one man showing through the prose of another, as on some old parchments you can see the letters of an earlier script showing beneath the text. As you read Bernard Shaw you can often hear the accents of his model, Samuel Butler; in Ruskin it is sometimes the King James version you are hearing, sometimes plainly Carlyle. Now Shaw and Ruskin are two great original masters of prose, and no one could accuse them of being echoes merely. Nevertheless, they found their own style, as Robert Louis Stevenson did, by studying styles they admired.

I don't mean that one should "play the sedulous ape" to another's way of saying things, though that is a useful exercise. I mean that, taking some writer that one finds admirable, one should surrender to him in delight, note his mixture of big words with little, mark his easy transitions, listen to his rhythms, catch his feeling for clearness and force, and then, with his sentences and periods working, so to speak, in one's blood, use him as the silent partner in one's own writing. Let a student catch from a master the idea of good prose, and he will do for himself what a hundred corrected themes will not do for him. Sometimes a carrot at one end of a donkey will accomplish more than a rain of blows at the other end. We teachers go on grimly pouring water into these young sieves. Most of it runs right out again, and no amount of patching the holes will make them retentive of our precious wisdom. But sometimes a happy lecture brings a gleam in a young eye; sometimes a student comes to you, as I recall one of my Yale boys doing, to share a discovery of his: "That essay on *Liberty* is great stuff." For the teacher, these are reassuring moments, for such admirations are the growing points of a life.

Some people would question what we are saying as putting too little stress on originality. About this I can only differ. Original creation, I agree, is the proper end of any young thinker or writer. But nothing is more boring than attempts to "create" by thinkers with no idea of a good argument, or by writers with no craft. Many of our young writers never do anything of which they can be proud because, with all their gifts, they lack that gift of humility which is so necessary to make the most of the others. The path to genuine creation lies through enthusiastic apprenticeship. This holds, I think, of every kind of creative work. It certainly holds in philosophy. Edward Caird, Master of Balliol, wrote about the richest mind in modern philosophy: "The basis of sound education was, for Hegel, obedience and self-surrender—the submission of the mind to an eternal lesson, which must be learnt by everyone . . . with utter disregard of individual tastes and desires; only out of this self-abnegation, and submission to be guided and taught, could any originality spring that was worth preserving."

Original minds in literature have taken the same line. Goethe said to Eckermann: "If I could give an account of what I owe to great predecessors and contemporaries, there would be but a small remainder." Even in art, where it is popular nowadays to think of genius as a sort of wayward geyser, the same holds. Mr. Eliot remarks that "the progress of an artist is a continual self-sacrifice, a continual extinction of personality." But it is of course the sort of extinction in which one loses a lesser self to gain a larger one.

Here we come to the important truth about our admirations that they ought to change; they ought to grow with our widening interests and powers. There are some achievements of mind and spirit that cannot be properly admired unless one has gone a long way already, so that, as Hegel said, if a hero is not a hero to his own valet, that is because the valet is a valet, not because the hero is not a hero. It is told that some American Indians were once brought from their reservation to New York, and, to the surprise and disappointment of their hosts, looked at the tall buildings, the elevated railway, and the flow of traffic, with dull unresponsive eyes. Then one of them by chance saw a telephone repair man going up a pole with the little spurs on his feet that such men wear. At once the group was filled with admiring delight. Here was a man doing easily something that they had tried and knew was hard. You need to have gone some distance in art or engineering to be able to appreciate what distinction in these fields means. A little girl in Princeton, hearing that a nice fuzzy-haired old man who lived nearby knew something about figures, took her arithmetic lessons around to him for help, and when she found that he was really able to do her hardest sums, she of course admired him. If she had known ten times as much, would she have admired Einstein less or more?

When one is a child, one understands and admires as a child; when one becomes a man, one should put away childish things. I suppose that there are many boys of ten or twelve who, if they were to name their hero honestly, would nominate the current Mickey Mantle. Whom girls of the same age admire I cannot guess. I do remember, however, that when I was walking down Whitehall in London a few years ago, I saw a crowd assembled in a side street, blocking the traffic; and, wondering what was happening, I inquired of someone on the outskirts what was behind all this. "Oh," came the reply, "Marilyn Monroe is in that building, and they are waiting for her to come out." Perhaps in view of her sad later story, they would be less envious now. Let us admit between ourselves that the person who could find nothing to admire in Mickey Mantle or Marilyn Monroe would be something of a stick. But may I add that the person who still puts them at the top of the list when he is fully grown up has probably failed to grow up and is suffering from arrested development? One of the things that seem to me worrying in our American scene is the persisting adolescence of its enthusiasms, the genuine admiration, as measured at least in the box office, of young men whose prowess is chiefly with guns or muscles, and of young women whose only endowments are those that meet the eye. We ought to have graduated from such admirations before we are out of our teens, and if they remain to crowd out more mature satisfactions, we are destined for a rather dreary middle age. In the diary of our enthusiasms the earlier ones should transcend themselves in the course of fulfilling themselves.

It is plain from all this how potent a part our admirations play in education. During our formal schooling, we may be kept at our task by no better motive than to avoid reproof or a bad grade card. But that is of no use when we pass through college gates for the last time. Then we shall be out on the sea alone in our own little boat, and whether we shall arrive anywhere depends on whether there is a motor in the boat and something to steer it by. A person with authentic admirations has both. *What* he admires will serve to give him direction. On his degree of devotion will depend his motor power.

We began, you will remember, with Wordsworth's introduction of admiration among the Christian virtues. He is right, I think, that it has a place even in that high company. On its moral side at least, the Christian life is a struggle after perfection, and, as Whitehead says, "Moral education is impossible without the habitual vision of greatness." That vision is possible, of course, in other faiths, as it was possible to pagans before the Christian era began. "I would have you day by day fix your eyes upon the greatness of Athens," said Pericles in his best-known speech, "until you have become filled with the love of her." But admiration, as it appears in the Christian life, is distinctive in two respects. First, it is directed not upon a city or a tradition or an abstract ideal, but upon a person, of whom it was said that if he were lifted up, he would draw all men unto him. But he will not draw unless he *is* lifted up to be seen and known, and though we do much lip service to him, he is so remote from our bustling and mechanical age that our admiration is often perfunctory. We should not let it remain so, for here we have the noblest of objects with which to rekindle it.

But secondly and lastly, the Christian sort of admiration differs from others, and notably the Greek, which I have just mentioned, in something that George Herbert Palmer used to call "the glory of the imperfect." It is always unsatisfied with what is, always reaching out for what is beyond, committed to a quest that is endless. "Be ye therefore perfect"—but we know that we shall never reach perfection. "Does the road wind uphill all the way? Yes, to the very end." There is no Shangri-La that we can take as the journey's end, where we can live like lotus-eaters. The successive plateaus we reach in our ascent are only resting places, not levels that we can live on. Sir Edmund Hilary, asked why he climbed Mount Everest, answered, "Because it was there." Man is a climber because he is made that way, and becomes unhappy unless he is climbing. Admiration dispels complacency, and is always raising its eyes to a summit higher up. Does it see *the* summit, the snowy peak where the flag can at last be planted and the ascent declared at an end? No; for that highest summit is always veiled in mist. And if men can learn, with Stevenson, that it is a better thing to travel than to arrive, they will be prepared to face the secret hidden behind that mist. The secret is that there is no summit there at all. There is only an infinite slope that goes up and up till it is lost among the stars.

# Index

# Index

# Index

411

# Index

# Index

# Index

415